THE KŌAN

The Kōan

Texts and Contexts in Zen Buddhism

Edited by

Steven Heine
Dale S. Wright

OXFORD

UNIVERSITY PRESS

2000

OXFORD
UNIVERSITY PRESS

Oxford   New York
Athens   Auckland   Bangkok   Bogotá   Buenos Aires   Calcutta
Cape Town   Chennai   Dar es Salaam   Delhi   Florence   Hong Kong   Istanbul
Karachi   Kuala Lumpur   Madrid   Melbourne   Mexico City   Mumbai
Nairobi   Paris   São Paulo   Singapore   Taipei   Tokyo   Toronto   Warsaw

and associated companies in
Berlin   Ibadan

Published by Oxford University Press, Inc.
198 Madison Avenue, New York, New York 10016

Oxford is a registered trademark of Oxford University Press

Library of Congress Cataloging-in-Publication Data

The Kōan : texts and contexts in Zen Buddhism /
edited by Steven Heine, Dale S. Wright.
p.   cm.
ISBN 0-19-511748-4; ISBN 0-19-511749-2 (pbk.)
1. Koan.   I. Heine, Steven, 1950–   .   II. Wright, Dale S.
BQ9289.5.K625   2000
294.3'927—dc21   99-23112

1 3 5 7 9 8 6 4 2

Printed in the United States of America
on acid-free paper

Acknowledgments

The editors thank Cynthia Read for her support and guidance in developing this project. All of the chapters in this volume have been presented at panels of the national meetings of the American Academy of Religion and the Association for Asian Studies, among other conferences, and we appreciate the opportunity these forums provided for stimulating discussion and reflection. Steven Heine also thanks Professor Sueki Fumihiko of the University of Tokyo for inviting him to present an overview of the book at a Buddhist studies seminar in June 1998, and thereby to benefit from the constructive feedback of Sueki and Professor Matsumoto Shirō of Komazawa University. Finally, we appreciate Morten Schlütter's insightful comments that were helpful in writing the introduction. The editors thank Dr. Louise Yuhas for assistance with the cover art and Glenda Epps for help with the index.

98883

Contents

Abbreviations

BOOKS

HTC   *Hsü tsang ching* (rpt. J. *Dai Nihon zoku zōkyō*), 150 vols. (Taipei: Shin wen fang, n.d.).

T   *Taishō shinshū daizōkyō,* 100 vols., eds. Takakusu Junjirō and Watanabe Kaigyoku (Tokyo: Taishō issaikyō kankōkai, 1924–32).

ZZ   *Dai Nihon zoku zōkyō,* 150 vols, ed. Nakano Tatsue (Kyoto: Zōkyō shoin, 1905–1912).

TERMS

C.   Chinese

J.   Japanese

K.   Korean

S.   Sanskrit

List of Contributors

T. Griffith Foulk is Associate Professor of Religion, Sarah Lawrence College, and co-editor-in-chief of the Sōtō Zen Translation Project. His publications include the forthcoming *Ch'an Myths and Realities in Medieval Chinese Buddhism* (Stanford) and numerous chapters and articles on Ch'an history.

Steven Heine is Professor of Religious Studies and director of the Asian Studies Program at Florida International University. His publications include *Dōgen and the Kōan Tradition* (SUNY, 1994), *Japan in Traditional and Postmodern Perspectives* (SUNY, 1995), *The Zen Poetry of Dōgen* (Tuttle, 1997), and *Shifting Shape, Shaping Text* (Hawaii, 1999), as well as numerous articles on Japanese Buddhism and intellectual history.

G. Victor Sogen Hori is Associate Professor of Religion, McGill University. He has nearly twenty years' experience as a monk in a Japanese Rinzai monastery and is currently completing a translation of the classic kōan text, the *Zenrin kūshū*.

Ishii Shūdō is Professor of Buddhist Studies, Komazawa University, Japan. His publications include *Sōdai Zenshūshi no kenkyū* (Daitō, 1987) and *Chūgoku Zenshū shi hanashi* (Zen bunka kenkyūjō, 1988), as well as dozens of articles on the historical development of Ch'an/Zen literature.

Ishikawa Rikizan, who passed away in the summer of 1997, was Professor of Buddhist Studies at Komazawa University, Japan. A specialist in the history of the Sōtō sect and the relation between Zen and popular religiosity, he published several books and dozens of articles, particularly an extended series of critical editions of *kirigami* texts.

Alexander Kabanoff is Senior Researcher at St. Petersburg University, Russia, and head of the Japanese section of the Institute of Oriental Studies. His publications include over seventy chapters, articles, and reviews in Russian, English, and German.

John R. McRae is Associate Professor of Religious Studies, Indiana University. His publications include *The Northern School and the Formation of Early Ch'an Buddhism* (Hawaii, 1986) and the forthcoming companion volume, *Evangelical Zen: Shen-hui, the Sudden Teaching, and the Southern School of Chinese Ch'an Buddhism.*

Michel Mohr is Professor at Hanazono University in Kyoto, Japan, and director of the International Research Institute for Zen Buddhism. His publications include *Treatise of the Inexhaustible Lamp of Zen: Tōrei (1721–92) and his Vision of Awakening* in the series "Mélanges Chinois et Bouddhiques" (Institut Belge des Hautes Etudes Chinoises, 1997), in addition to numerous articles in English, Japanese, and French.

Morten Schlütter, formerly on the faculty of Victoria University of Wellington, New Zealand, has completed a dissertation on the Ts'ao-tung sect during the Sung period at Yale University, and has published several articles on the institutional and textual history of Ch'an.

Albert Welter is Associate Professor of Religion, University of Winnipeg. His publications include a book on Chinese Ch'an, *The Meaning of Myriad Good Deeds: A Study of Yung-ming Yen-shou and the Wan-shan t'ung-kuei chi* (Peter Lang, 1993), and several articles and reviews on East Asian Buddhism.

Dale S. Wright is Professor of Religious Studies and Chair of the Program in Asian Studies, Occidental College. His publications include *Philosophical Meditations on Zen Buddhism* (Cambridge, 1998) and numerous articles on Hua-yen, Ch'an/Zen Buddhism, and theoretical issues in cross-cultural understanding.

THE KŌAN

Introduction

Kōan Tradition: Self-Narrative and Contemporary Perspectives

STEVEN HEINE AND DALE S. WRIGHT

Aims

The term kōan (C. *kung-an,* literally "public cases") refers to enigmatic and often shocking spiritual expressions based on dialogical encounters between masters and disciples that were used as pedagogical tools for religious training in the Zen (C. Ch'an) Buddhist tradition. This innovative practice is one of the best-known and most distinctive elements of Zen Buddhism. Originating in T'ang/Sung China, the use of kōans spread to Vietnam, Korea, and Japan and now attracts international attention. What is unique about the kōan is the way in which it is thought to embody the enlightenment experience of the Buddha and Zen masters through an unbroken line of succession. The kōan was conceived as both the tool by which enlightenment is brought about and an expression of the enlightened mind itself. Kōans are generally appreciated today as pithy, epigrammatic, elusive utterances that seem to have a psychotherapeutic effect in liberating practitioners from bondage to ignorance, as well as for the way they are contained in the complex, multileveled literary form of kōan collection commentaries. Perhaps no dimension of Asian religions has attracted so much interest and attention in the West, from psychological interpretations and comparative mystical theology to appropriations in beat poetry and deconstructive literary criticism.

There have been numerous excellent studies in English of the role of kōans in the history of Zen thought, as well as several important translations of kōan collection literature. In addition to the works of D. T. Suzuki, especially the three-volume *Essays in Zen Buddhism,* which covers the history of kōan writings, a major early study was *Zen Dust* by Isshū Miura and Ruth Fuller Sasaki, which is particularly known for its comprehensive annotated bibliography of original sources.[1] A number of more recent works specialize in particular

3

thinkers, schools, or approaches to the use of kōans, including Robert Buswell's examination of the "short-cut" approach of Sung-era Lin-chi master Ta-hui, "The 'Short-cut' Approach of K'an-hua Meditation," Kenneth Kraft's book *Eloquent Zen* on Japanese Rinzai master Daitō's capping phrase commentaries on the *Pi-yen lu* (J. *Hekiganroku*), Steven Heine's *Dōgen and the Kōan Tradition* on the role of kōan discourse in the *Shōbōgenzō*, and a chapter on the role of kōans in the post-Dōgen Sōtō sect in William Bodiford's *Sōtō Zen in Medieval Japan*.[2]

Translations of the three major kōan collection commentaries compiled in the twelfth and thirteenth centuries include a half dozen versions of the *Wu-men kuan* (J. *Mumonkan*), one complete and one partial version of the *Pi-yen lu,* and one complete version of the *Ts'ung-jung lu* (J. *Shōyōroku*).[3] In addition, there are numerous translations of other genres of Zen texts from which some kōans have been extracted, especially the recorded sayings of individual masters.[4] But there remains a great need for renderings of the voluminous "transmission of the lamp" histories, especially the seminal work of this genre, the *Ching-te ch'uan-teng lu* (J. *Keitoku dentōroku*) of 1004, since these texts transcribe and are the storehouse for the original Zen encounters from which the more famous kōan collection texts have been derived.[5] The role of the transmission of the lamp texts, along with the genre of monk biographies, which contain passages on a wide variety of Buddhist practitioners in addition to Zen masters, is one of the central topics dealt with in chapters 1–6, 8, and 10.

Despite great strides made in some areas of kōan studies, the underlying thesis here is that our understanding of the diverse factors leading to the formation and development of the Zen kōan tradition has been severely limited by a number of historical and interpretive factors. It is our hope that this volume will contribute to a deeper and more thoroughly historical understanding of the kōan tradition by opening for analysis the complexity of this tradition, including a rich variety of social, political, and popular cultural elements that framed the unfolding of various usages of kōan literature.

There are several factors that have inhibited the development of a critical understanding of the kōan tradition in Zen Buddhism. Most obvious, and important, is that kōans as religious symbols are purposefully elusive and enigmatic, often defying logical analysis by creating a linguistic double bind or culminating in absurdity or non sequitur. For example, in *Wu-men kuan* case 43 the master holds up a stick and dares his disciples, "If you call this a stick you will be clinging; if you do not call this a stick you are ignoring [the obvious]. So, now, tell me, what do you call it?" Also, in three consecutive cases of the *Pi-yen lu* (nos. 70, 71, and 72), Pai-chang taunts, "Keeping your tongues still and lips closed, how will you speak?"

Since this double bind, "thirty blows whether you do or don't" pattern is emulated in dozens of examples, interpreters have typically devoted themselves more to the assertion that kōans cannot or should not be subject to examination than they have to an attempt to understand and explicate them. Some commentators, such as Suzuki and Akizuki Ryūmin, tend to insist that interpretation must be limited to practitioners or initiates into the tradition, because kōans elude objective, rational analysis. While that posture may be appropriate from the subjective, experiential standpoint of practice, it should by no means be taken to exclude historical criticism or to rationalize conflating critical hermeneutics with traditional religious function.

Another factor contributing to misimpressions is that the modern understanding of the character of kōan practice has been shaped almost entirely by the tradition's own self-narrative, constructed in texts that were largely hagiographical or pseudohistorical rather than fully historiographical. This self-narrative depicts the Zen lineage as an unmediated, unbroken line of transmission passed from master to disciple through the use of kōans. At the same time, the results of sectarian debates and partisan polemic that took place subsequent to the formative period of kōan literature in T'ang and Sung China are frequently applied to this epoch retrospectively. Many of the assumptions about the early period in China are actually based on controversies between the Rinzai (C. Lin-chi) and Sōtō (C. Ts'ao-tung) sects that took place nearly a millennium later in late Tokugawa Japan, when mutual sectarian opposition became stiffened in part as a result of the political pressures of the period. This misleading orientation has led to inappropriate generalizations, such as that one sect throughout its entire history has endorsed kōan training while another sect has not, or that kōans have a single, uniform function such as defeating logic that may have been appropriate in one historical context but not in others. Challenging this stereotype, several chapters, especially 6 and 9, show that at crucial junctures of history it was actually the Ts'ao-tung/Sōtō sect that kept the tradition vital. Another problematic assumption based on the tradition's self-narrative is the focus on a small handful of collections that have been passed down with their standpoints repeated uncritically. Chapters 1–4 show that in early stages of the formation of the tradition from the pre-T'ang through southern Sung periods there was a remarkable variety of texts and perspectives.

Moreover, because the current Western understanding of kōans largely derives from twentieth-century Japanese Rinzai Zen as depicted by Suzuki, it has focused almost exclusively on the psychological or mystical aspects of kōans. A comment by Ruth Fuller Sasaki typifies the view that kōans necessarily culminate in a nonconceptual, ineffable awareness: "Kōan study is a unique method of religious practice which has as its aim the bringing of the student to direct, intuitive realization of Reality without recourse to the mediation of words or concepts."[6] Chapters 10 and 11 dispute this contention by looking carefully at the issue of nonduality in the epitome of the very tradition—Tokugawa and post-Tokugawa Rinzai training—from which the argument derives. Furthermore, the presumption that kōans function in one way to the exclusion of others overlooks the diversity of kōan practice and literature, which includes ritual, institutional, social, literary, and popular religious dimensions in a variety of contexts. This volume seeks to uncover and clarify hidden layers of the kōan tradition and muted relationships between the Zen school and the structures of government and popular culture, challenging traditional representations by showing the richness that alternative approaches can reveal. For example, chapter 5 examines the context of folk religions and visionary experience, chapter 7 explores the impact of non-Buddhist ideologies, and chapter 8 discusses the relation between the allusive, indirect quality of expression of kōans and *kanbun* poetry (composed in Chinese script) in Japan.

Thus, this volume is a collection of essays by leading scholars in Zen studies that attempts to correct problematic understandings by undermining inappropriate stereotypes and pointing out the variability of interpretations and applications of kōan practice. It reflects the most current, innovative, and exciting perspectives on the Zen kōan tradition. While the chapters treat elements that are obscure or heretofore unknown or unrecognized, including ritual and sociopolitical factors, the contributions also highlight, explain, and critically probe the real significance underlying many of the better-known aspects of the tradition. These include the meaning of silence in relation to the motto of a "special transmission outside the teaching"; the implications and techniques associated with the "Wu/Mu" kōan; the teachings of leading figures portrayed in kōans such as Yün-men, as well as thinkers who forged new methods of using kōans in religious training such as Ta-hui; the relation between kōan practice and related notions such as *kenshō* and *satori;* and differences between the way kōans functioned in the classical period and their appropriation by modern, including Western, forms of Zen Buddhism. The scholars represented here are international in scope, including five working in North America who travel extensively to East Asia, two Japanese, a Japanese-American, a Russian, and two Europeans doing research in Japan and New Zealand. We are especially pleased to be represented by two of the leading Japanese scholars of Zen Buddhism, Ishii Shūdō and the late Ishikawa Rikizan.

The essays employ a variety of methodological perspectives, such as textual analysis and literary criticism, philosophical hermeneutics and phenomenology, and social historical and history of religions approaches. The volume examines previously unrecognized factors in the formation of the tradition, such as the impact of other types of Zen records as well as non-Zen Buddhist and secular materials. It also highlights the rich complexity and diversity of the tradition's maturation process, including the intricate conceptual context of particular kōans or the philosophical settings within which kōans have been utilized.

The first seven chapters deal with kōans in China. Several focus on the origins of kōan literature in the late T'ang and Sung era, which derives from oral dialogues and colloquial anecdotes (chapter 2), depends on pre-Zen Buddhist formulations of religious language (7), intersects with other Zen literary genres including discourse records or recorded sayings as well as transmission of the lamp histories (4), and culminates in nearly two dozen collections rather than the two or three usually discussed (1). Other chapters deal with the diverse developments of the tradition by examining specific examples of case records or of theorists of kōan practice in their appropriate context. These include the kōan of "Śākyamuni passing the flower to Mahākāśyapa" (3) and kōans dealing with pilgrimages to the cultic site of Mount Wu-t'ai (5), as well as the leading twelfth-century Lin-chi sect thinker Ta-hui and the Ts'ao-tung rivals such as Hung-chih, with whom he engaged in debate (6).

The final four chapters explain the significance of kōans in the Japanese setting from medieval times through the Tokugawa era until the modern period. Chapter 8 focuses on the influence of kōans on Ikkyū's poetry in the Muromachi era, and chapter 9 deals with the esoteric style of *kirigami* interpretations in late medieval and early modern Sōtō Zen. The book concludes with a discussion of the Tokugawa era systematization of kōan training by Hakuin (10) and an examination of the role this system plays in the current Rinzai monastic curriculum (11).

Overview

Focusing first on the origins of the tradition, the volume opens with T. Griffith Foulk's analysis of various conceptions and misconceptions of kōan practice. "The Form and Function of Koan Literature: A Historical Overview" surveys the evolution and the roles played in modern sectarian perspectives by the genre of medieval Chinese Ch'an kōan collections, of which more than twenty examples survive in East Asian Buddhist literature. As Foulk shows, these collections generally adhere to a complex pattern of multilayered, interlinear prose and verse commentaries on the records of paradigmatic cases which were formed according to models based on cases judged by precedent as used in the legal system of the time. Foulk uses methods of form (literary) criticism to analyze the complex structure of the literature, to describe the social and institutional contexts in which it was compiled and used, and to show how its ritual function followed its literary form (and vice versa).

"The Antecedents of Encounter Dialogue in Chinese Ch'an Buddhism" by John R. McRae shows that the kōan approach to spiritual self-cultivation evolved from a long tradition of using oral repartee and anecdote as devices for teaching and for practicing meditation. This chapter reconsiders how oral dialogue, colloquial anecdote, and unspoken rules of rhetoric and narrative were used in the early periods of Chinese Ch'an, especially the Northern school as well as the records of first patriarch Bodhidharma and his epoch. These developments eventually led to the emergence of the Sung texts, such as the *Tsu-tang chi* of 952, which was the first transcription/compilation of encounter dialogues along with other stories of the Buddhas and patriarchs down to that time. In particular, McRae suggests that it is possible to trace the increasing importance of orality as the Ch'an tradition develops and gain new insights regarding the image of spontaneity depicted in the kōan texts by examining the manner in which colloquial language was being transcribed in medieval China.

Chapter 3, by Albert Welter, "Mahākāśyapa's Smile: Silent Transmission and the Kung-an Tradition," treats one of the most famous kōans in the Zen tradition, *Wu-men-kuan* case 6, relating the story of how the Buddha's disciple, Mahākāśyapa, broke into a smile when the Buddha held up a flower to the assembly. Mahākāśyapa receives the transmission when the Buddha acknowledges his intuitive understanding. The episode displays one of the cardinal features of Chinese Ch'an: the silent transmission of Buddhist truth between master and disciple as a "special transmission outside the scriptures." This chapter examines the origins and development of the story in Ch'an transmission of the lamp histories, especially the *T'ien-sheng kuang-teng lu* and apocryphal scriptures before it became enshrined in kōan collection texts, and it shows how this development parallels the growth of Ch'an identity as a silent transmission during the Sung dynasty.

Chapter 4, by Japanese scholar Ishii Shūdō, "Kung-an Ch'an and the *Tsung-men t'ung-yao chi*," beautifully translated by Albert Welter, continues an exploration of the impact of transmission of the lamp histories on the formation of kōan literature. Ishii, a professor at Komazawa University in Tokyo, is one of the leading authorities on historical criticism of Zen texts, following the two towering figures in the field, Yanagida Seizan and Iriya Yoshitaka, both based in universities in Kyoto, with whom Ishii has worked closely on several projects. This chapter argues that the transmission text, the *Tsung-men t'ung-yao chi* (J. *Shūmon tōyōshū*), first issued in 1093, is an essential source for determining the distinctive character of Sung-era Ch'an since it served as the basis for many of the cases used in kōan collections, including the *Wu-men kuan* and the *Pi-yen lu*. However, most scholars, even in Japan, continue to overlook the importance of this text while focusing on other works of the period. Ishii traces the development of scholarship in the field of Ch'an literature and demonstrates with numerous examples just how influential the *Tsung-men t'ung-yao chi* proved to be in the tradition.

The next several chapters continue a focus on the development of the tradition during the Sung dynasty. In chapter 5, "Visions, Divisions, Revisions: The Encounter Between Iconoclasm and Supernaturalism in Kōan Cases About Mount Wu-t'ai," Steven Heine examines the role of popular religiosity expressed in several kōans dealing with the sacred mountain, Wu-t'ai-shan, especially case 35 in the *Pi-yen lu* collection (along with cases 31 in the *Wu-men-kuan* and 10 in the *Ts'ung-jung lu*). Mount Wu-t'ai, believed to be the earthly abode of Mañjuśrī, was a primary pilgrimage spot (generally considered off limits for antiritualistic Zen monastics) for seekers who traveled to attain visions of the bodhisattva riding a flying lion amid multicolored clouds. The *Pi-yen lu* kōan seems like a typical "encounter dialogue" between Mañjuśrī and an itinerant Zen monk, but the chapter argues that what is really being expressed is a sense of ambiguity and irony in the ideological encounter between two levels of Zen discourse: the theory of iconoclastic antiritualism, and the appeal of supernatural visions and practices.

In chapter 6 Morten Schlütter, in " 'Before the Empty Eon' Versus 'A Dog Has No Buddha-Nature': Kung-an Use in the Ts'ao-tung Tradition and Ta-hui's Kung-an Introspection Ch'an," deals with the Sung debates between Lin-chi and Ts'ao-tung (which Michel Mohr shows were continually reconstructed through the Tokugawa era in Japan). This chapter analyzes the way in which certain key phrases such as "before the empty eon" were used frequently in the revived Ts'ao-tung tradition of the twelfth century. Several of the masters were said to have been enlightened upon hearing this catchphrase kōan which emphasized the doctrine of original enlightenment, and Lin-chi master Ta-hui often attacked its usage. Schlütter argues that there was little difference in how kōans were used in the two schools until this controversy developed, and that the differences were played out amid the political and intellectual landscape of China dominated by scholar-officials in the period following the 845 suppression of Buddhism.

The final chapter dealing with China, "Kōan History: Transformative Language in Chinese Buddhist Thought" by Dale S. Wright (chapter 7), offers a philosophical reflection on the origins and consequences, or the roots and branches, of the kōan tradition. This article traces the concept of religious, transformative language presupposed in kōan practice to earlier sources in the history of Buddhism, such as sacred formulas (*dhāranī*), devotional recitation (*nien-fo*), and forms of meditation (*vipaśyanā*) employing visualization and concept contemplation. The article's thesis is that kōan language is best interpreted in relation to the larger narratives of the Buddhist tradition, and that this interpretation requires a reconsideration of the nonconceptual dimension of the religious practice. Wright also comments on the reasons for the decline of the tradition in post-Sung China as well as for the current fascination with kōans in the West.

The first chapter in the Japan section, Alexander Kabanoff's "Ikkyū and Kōans," (chapter 8), focuses on the influence of kōans on Ikkyū's poetry. Ikkyū Sōjun (1394–1481), an eccentric Zen monk, became a legend during his lifetime and turned into a shibboleth for those who were not familiar with Zen. Because his behavioral antics have frequently been the focus of attention in popular stories since the Edo period, there has been a tendency to overlook his profound knowledge of the written Buddhist tradition. This chapter provides an attentive reading of his *kanbun* poems written in Chinese and collected in the "Crazy Cloud Anthology" (*Kyōunshū*), which abound in allusions and quotations from classical Chinese works and poems as well as from Zen records including the major kōan collections.

Chapter 9 is Ishikawa Rikizan's "Transmission of *Kirigami* (Secret Initiation Documents): A Sōtō Practice in Medieval Japan" (originally published as "Chūsei Sōtōshū ni okeru kirigami sōjō ni tsuite," *Indogaku Bukkyōgaku kenkyū,* no. 30/2 [1982]: 742–46). It paints a very different picture of the role of kōan literature in medieval Japan by covering an esoteric approach to kōans extending from late Muromachi through much of the Tokugawa era. The chapter was translated with introductory comments, emendations, and annotations by Kawahashi Seishū, who holds an M. A. degree in Chinese intellectual history from Arizona State University and is abbot of Reiganji temple in Toyota City, Aichi Prefecture, Japan. Kawahashi was assisted by Sugawara Shōei, professor at the University of Tokyo. Ishikawa, who died an untimely death in 1997 at age 55, was a professor of Buddhist studies at Komazawa University particularly renowned for his pioneering work on the impact of popular religions on the development of the medieval Sōtō sect, as well as for his efforts on behalf of recent sectarian reform movements. The translator notes that according to Kumamoto Einin, one of Ishikawa's Dharma pupils, this was the first of Ishikawa's publications to focus precisely on *kirigami* documents.

In this chapter Ishikawa situates the genre of *kirigami,* which literally refers to "paper strips" on which masters transmitted esoteric interpretations of kōans with cryptic sayings, formulas, and diagrams, in the context of a larger body of material known as *shōmono.* The *shōmono* documents are a complex body of commentaries on traditional kōan collections and recorded sayings texts by late medieval and early modern Sōtō priests. As Ishikawa shows, the *kirigami,* a term that also refers to similar forms of communication in other medieval aesthetic traditions such as the tea ceremony, were based on an intense apprenticing, master–disciple relationship. Despite being rejected by some factions in Zen as a compromise with popular religiosity, they reflect an individual, spontaneous expression of a particular case's applicability to a disciple's level of understanding. The *kirigami* are crucial for an understanding of how kōans were kept alive in Japanese Zen between the Kamakura era and the time of Hakuin's systematization of kōan study. However, it is especially difficult to analyze *kirigami* because they were originally fragile strips of paper that either were never collated or were grouped into collections only at a much later date.

The last two chapters trace the role of kōans in modern Rinzai Zen and question conventional interpretations of nonduality in relation to assertions of nonconceptuality and silence. While Ishikawa's chapter overcomes the stereotype of Sōtō versus Rinzai schools, Michel Mohr in chapter 10 shows the historical circumstances in the Tokugawa era that actually did give rise to this opposition. In "Emerging from Nonduality: Kōan Practice in the Rinzai Tradition Since Hakuin," Mohr challenges the simple claim that kōan practice is a means of reaching "nonduality." He explains that kōan practice, which had changed significantly since the period of Sung China, underwent additional transformations in Tokugawa Japan, taking a form at that time that is still used in Japanese monasteries and is frequently communicated to the world at large. Although this type of practice is not limited to Rinzai adherents, its systematization has been largely attributed to Hakuin and his followers. The chapter examines the ingenuity of the reforms implemented during the eighteenth century.

Finally, in chapter 11, "Kōan and *Kenshō* in the Rinzai Zen Curriculum," G. Victor Sōgen Hori, a Rinzai priest and professor of Buddhist studies, argues against a widely accepted account that a Zen kōan is a clever psychological device designed to induce *satori* or *kenshō* by breaking through the rational, intellectualizing mind to a realm of preconceptual, prelinguistic consciousness called no-mind or without-thinking. His chapter demonstrates that the non-rational, instrumental account of kōan practice is misleading with regard to the Rinzai monastic curriculum, in which (1) there is a rational content; and (2) *kenshō* is not a realm of no-mind but the engagement of emptiness through the conventional realm of thought and language. Despite the rhetoric which suggests that Zen insight lies totally outside of language and thinking, actual practice in the Rinzai school suggests that awakening cannot be adequately described in terms of a dichotomy as a domain that is either rational or irrational, cognitive or noncognitive.

Unfolding of the Kōan Tradition

Another way to survey the contributions in this volume is Table I.1, which diagrams the relation between different historical and practical developments in the kōan tradition and the respective chapters' topics. The origins of the tradition lie in the encounter dialogues, which were oral, spontaneous repartees attributed to T'ang masters and inscribed in a variety of Sung texts. These include, as Foulk shows, the transmission of the lamp hagiographies and the recorded sayings of individual masters that began to be collected in the eleventh century as well as the kōan collection commentaries that were collected beginning in the twelfth century. As several authors point out, this attribution of the dialogues to pre-Sung figures may or may not be valid, for they exist only in recorded, textual forms stemming from the Sung period. The source dialogues are of varying lengths but are generally brief, allusive, elusive, and enigmatic, as is shown by McRae.

Eleventh-century Zen texts tended to focus on the dialogues as a means of highlighting the life and teachings of particular masters. However, the transition, as discussed by Ishii, to the kōan collections of the twelfth century stressed the importance of the dialogue itself as a device of edification, stripping away or recontextualizing much of the hagiographical material. This ten-

Table I.1 Unfolding of the Kōan Tradition

Era	Kōan tradition developments				Contributor
T'ang	Oral encounter dialogues				McRae
11th c.	Transmission of the lamp hagiographies	Recorded sayings of individual masters			Foulk Ishii
12th c.	Kōan collections' multilevelled prose and verse commentaries				Welter Heine Wright
13th–17th c. (China)	Short-cut method	Lin-chi style			
		Ts'ao-tung style			Schlütter
(Japan)	(Dōgen's wraparound commentary)	(Daitō's capping phrases)	Ikkyū's poetry	Sōtō sect's *Kirigami*	Kabanoff Ishikawa
18th c.	Hakuin's systematization				Mohr
Modern	Current Rinzai curriculum				Hori

dency, Welter explains, gave rise to the Zen characterization of itself as a "silent transmission" in spite of the proliferation of texts containing kōans. The main collections built up a complex, multilayered commentarial structure, examined by Heine, encompassing an introductory pointer, the case (or dialogue), prose and verse commentary, plus additional capping phrase comments on the first layer of prose/verse expressions. After this style was perfected, a reaction set in that emphasized, not elaborate commentaries, but the reduction of the kōan's dialogue to its essential point or punch line. This developed not only in the Lin-chi school, led by Ta-hui, but also, as Schlütter argues, in the Ts'ao-tung school, especially for Ta-hui's apparent rival, Hung-chih. However, a consequence of this tendency in China, according to Wright, may have been a debilitating effect on the intellectual fiber of Zen, leaving it vulnerable in the face of stiff competition with sophisticated and highly critical Neo-Confucian rivals and leading to the decline of the sect after the Sung.

In Kamakura Japan, on the other hand, Dōgen's wraparound style of commentary and Daitō's capping phrases kept the extended commentarial tradition alive (although these topics are not discussed extensively in this volume). But the trend toward abbreviation was carried on effectively in the medieval period through the 28-kanji poetry of the Rinzai school's Ikkyū, discussed by Kabanoff, and the esoteric *kirigami* comments of the Sōtō school, examined by Ishikawa. After several centuries of disparate functions of kōans, Hakuin systematized Zen training into a coherent program in the Rinzai school, as is shown by Mohr, which, Hori explains, is still followed with variations and modifications in the curriculum at Daitokuji, Myōshinji, and other leading training temples today.

Finally, there are several important areas of kōan studies that are not covered in this volume, including the influence of esoteric/tantric practices, Taoist dialogues, the interaction of Zen and Neo-Confucianism in China, the roles played by Dōgen and Daitō in Kamakura Japan, and the development of the tradition in Korea and Vietnam. It is our hope that this volume stimulates further reflection on the Zen kōan in these and other contexts.

Remarks on Transliteration

In this volume Chinese terms appear in Wade-Giles romanization, and East Asian names are listed with family name first. Readers will find different usages of key terms, such as "kōan" and "kung-an" (in singular or plural form) or "Zen" and "Ch'an." The authors have been permitted to use terminology as they see fit. Generally, the chapters dealing with China use "kung-an" and "Ch'an," while those dealing with Japan use "kōan" and "Zen," but there are some variations, in part because of crossover sources and themes. Griffith Foulk makes an intriguing suggestion of using "koan" as a generic term and "kung-an" and "kōan" in referring to Chinese Ch'an and Japanese Zen, respectively, but this system is not followed by most of the contributors. Also note the differences in translating key terms such as *hua-t'ou* (J. *watō*) as "critical phrase" (in Foulk, McRae, and Wright), "crucial phrase" (in Ishii), and "punch line" (in Schlütter).

NOTES

1. D. T. Suzuki, *Essays in Zen Buddhism,* 3 vols. (New York: Grove Press, 1953); Isshū Miura and Ruth Fuller Sasaki, *Zen Dust: The History of the Koan and Koan Study in (Lin-chi) Zen* (New York: Harcourt, Brace and World, 1966); an abbreviated version (minus the extensive bibliography) is Miura and Sasaki, *The Zen Kōan* (New York: Harcourt, Brace & World, 1965). Another important source is Heinrich Dumoulin, *Zen Buddhism: A History,* 2 vols. (1: India and China, 2: Japan), trans. James W. Heisig and Paul Knitter (New York: Macmillan, 1988–90).

2. Robert E. Buswell, Jr., "The 'Short-cut' Approach of K'an-hua Meditation: The Evolution of a Practical Subitism in Chinese Ch'an Buddhism," *Sudden and Gradual: Approaches to Enlightenment in Chinese Thought,* ed. Peter N. Gregory (Honolulu: University of Hawaii Press, 1987), pp. 321–77; Kenneth J. Kraft, *Eloquent Zen: Daitō and Early Japanese Zen* (Honolulu: University of Hawaii Press, 1992); Steven Heine, *Dōgen and the Kōan Tradition: A Tale of Two Shōbōgenzō Texts* (Albany: SUNY Press 1994); William M. Bodiford, *Sōtō Zen in Medieval Japan* (Honolulu: University of Hawaii Press, 1993). Other important studies are John R. McRae, *The Northern School and the Formation of Early Ch'an Buddhism* (Honolulu: University of Hawaii Press, 1986), on the formation of early encounter dialogues; and Bernard Faure, *Ch'an Insights and Oversights: An Epistemological Critique of Ch'an* (Princeton, N.J.: Princeton University

Press, 1993), for a literary critical examination of the kōan tradition. Mario Poceski (also known as Cheng Chien Bhikshu) is currently writing a Ph.D. dissertation at the University of California at Los Angeles on the role of encounter dialogues in the T'ang-era Hung-chou school.

3. Translations of the *Wu-men kuan* are in Zenkei Shibayama, *Zen Comments on the Mumonkan* (New York: Mentor, 1974); Robert Aitken, *The Gateless Barrier: Wu-men kuan (Mumonkan)* (San Francisco: North Point Press, 1991); Thomas Cleary, *No Barrier: Unlocking the Zen Koan* (New York: Bantam, 1993); Paul Reps, *Zen Flesh, Zen Bones* (New York: Anchor, n.d.); and Kōun Yamada, *The Gateless Gate* (Tucson: University of Arizona Press, 1990). The *Pi-yen lu* is in Thomas Cleary and Christopher Cleary, *The Blue Cliff Record,* 3 vols. (Boulder, Col.: Shambala, 1977), and Katsuki Sekida, *Two Zen Classics* (New York: Weatherhill, 1977), which also contains the *Wu-men kuan*. The *Ts'ung-jung lu* is in Thomas Cleary, *Book of Serenity* (Hudson, N.Y.: Lindisfarne Press, 1990). There are also several versions of Dōgen's *Shōbōgenzō,* which comments on dozens of kōans, often in ways that are radically different from the commentaries of his commentaries of his contemporaries, and a rendering of the first third of Dōgen's *Mana Shōbōgenzō* (or the *Shōbōgenzō sanbyakusoku*) collection of 305 kōans.

4. Some examples are Cheng Chien Bhikshu, *Sun-Face Buddha: The Teachings of Ma-tsu and the Hung-chou School of Ch'an* (Berkeley, Cal.: Asian Humanities Press, 1992); Thomas Cleary, *Sayings and Doings of Pai-chang* (Los Angeles: Zen Center of Los Angeles, 1978); Ruth Fuller Sasaki, Iriya Yoshitaka, and Dana R. Fraser, *The Recorded Sayings of Layman P'ang* (New York: Weatherhill, 1971); Yoel Hoffman, *Radical Zen: The Sayings of Jōshū* (Brookline, Mass.: Autumn Press, 1978); Urs App, *Master Yunmen: From the Record of the Chan Teacher "Gate of the Clouds"* (New York: Kodansha, 1994); William F. Powell, *The Record of Tung-shan* (Honolulu: University of Hawaii Press, 1986); Ruth Fuller Sasaki, *The Recorded Sayings of Ch'an Master Lin-chi Hui-chao of Chen Prefecture* (Kyoto: The Institute for Zen Studies, 1975); Christopher Cleary, *Swampland Flowers: The Letters and Lectures of Zen Master Ta Hui* (New York: Grove Press, 1977); and Yūhō Yokoi, *Eihei Kōroku* (Tokyo: Sankibo Buddhist Bookstore, 1987).

5. There is a partial translation of the *Ching-te ch'uan-teng lu* by Tao-yüan in Sohaku Ogata, *The Transmission of the Lamp* (Wolfeboro, N.H.: Longwood Academic, 1990), with selections also included in Chung-yuan Chang, *Original Teachings of Ch'an Buddhism* (New York: Vintage Books, 1971), and Charles Luk, *Ch'an and Zen Teachings* (London: Rider, 1961). But there is no complete version, and none of the numerous subsequent works in this genre have been translated.

6. In Miura and Sasaki, *The Zen Kōan,* p. x.

1

The Form and Function of Koan Literature

A Historical Overview

T. GRIFFITH FOULK

Any discussion of koans in the history of East Asian Buddhism needs to start with a definition of the word "koan" itself, for although the word has entered into relatively common English usage, few people have a clear idea of what it refers to, and ambiguities remain even in scholarly studies.[1] The first part of this chapter, accordingly, is dedicated to a brief history of the koan, with particular attention to the etymology of the word and the evolution of its meaning in China and Japan. The second part delineates the range of texts that I take to be "koan literature" and explains my reasons for regarding them as such. The remaining parts of the chapter are dedicated to a form-critical analysis of the complex internal structure of the koan literature and an exploration of how that literature has both mirrored and served as a model for its social and ritual functions.

The treatment of the koan as a literary genre in this chapter may strike some readers as peculiar or even irrelevant. After all, many accounts of koans today, both popular and scholarly, describe them as devices that are meant to focus the mind in meditation, to confound the discursive intellect, freezing it into a single ball of doubt, and finally to trigger an awakening (J. *satori*) to an ineffable state beyond the reach of all "dualistic" thinking. What, a critic may ask, does any of that have to do with literature, let alone the social and ritual uses of it?

This chapter demonstrates that even the aforementioned type of koan practice, which is known in the Ch'an, Sŏn, and Zen schools as the "Zen of contemplating phrases" (C. *k'an-hua Ch'an*, K. *kanhwa Sŏn*, J. *kanna Zen*), has its roots in an older, essentially literary tradition of collecting and commenting on dialogues attributed to ancient masters. For the historian of East Asian Buddhism, a knowledge of the prior development of koan literature and its social and religious function in medieval Chinese Ch'an is crucial if one is to understand the thrust and significance of the movement to promote *k'an-hua ch'an* that arose in the eleventh century. But even if historical issues are of little concern and one simply wishes to understand contemplating phrases as a contemporary practice, an appreciation of the formal structure of koan literature is indispensable as background.

There are a number of reasons for this. First, the demand for interpretation that is implicit in every "critical phrase" (C. *hua-t'ou,* K. *hwadu,* J. *watō*) held up as an object of meditation is best explained as a function of literary framing. That is to say, it is the literary context from which the phrase is lifted—its attribution to an ostensibly awakened master who uttered it in response to a question about ultimate truth—that gives it a meaning deeper than its surface semantic value and renders it worthy of mental concentration. Many other features of *kanna zen* as it is actually practiced in Japanese Rinzai Zen monasteries today are also best interpreted as ritual reenactments of certain formal relationships that are established in the koan literature. The juxtaposition of enlightened and unenlightened voices in a koan dialogue, for example, is replicated in the rite of individual consultation (J. *dokusan*) between a Zen master and his disciple. Even the rhetoric of *kanna zen,* with its emphasis on nondiscursive modes of thought, makes more sense when interpreted in the context of the literature that it ostensibly rejects. Finally, it is a historical fact that the practice of contemplating phrases, wherever and whenever it has flourished in the Ch'an, Sŏn, and Zen traditions, has always coexisted with the older and more widely accepted practice of commenting on koan literature.

A Brief History of the Koan

As understood today in the Ch'an, Sŏn, and Zen schools of Buddhism, koans are brief sayings, dialogues, or anecdotes that have been excerpted from the biographies and discourse records of Ch'an/Sŏn/Zen patriarchs and held up for some sort of special scrutiny. That scrutiny always involves interpreting and commenting on the passage in question, which is assumed to be an especially profound expression or encapsulation of the awakened mind of the patriarch to whom the words are attributed. In the specialized practice of "contemplating phrases," the investigation of a koan also entails using the passage, or a part of it (the "critical phrase"), as an object of intense mental concentration, which is cultivated mainly in conjunction with seated meditation (C. *tso-ch'an,* J. *zazen*). In any case, the sayings, dialogues, or anecdotes that are selected for use as koans frequently comprise elements that render them difficult to understand at first glance. Many contain statements that appear to be non sequiturs or to otherwise defy logic or common sense. They also include reports of startling behaviors, or words and gestures that are apparently intended to be symbolic but are left unexplained. But even if the meaning seems clear and straightforward, there is an implicit demand for interpretation in the very selection of a passage for use as a koan. That is to say, to treat a particular passage from the patriarchal records as a koan is precisely to single it out and problematize it as something profound and difficult to penetrate.

The practice of commenting on sayings selected from the records of ancient patriarchs is first attested in Chinese Ch'an literature dating from the middle of the tenth century.[2] It may have begun somewhat earlier than that, but we have no way of knowing for sure. The use of the term *kung-an* to refer in a general way to such sayings, however, does not seem to have come into vogue until about the twelfth century. Prior to that, passages from the patriarchal records held up for commentary were known as old cases (*ku-tse,* literally "ancient precedents"), a usage that has continued to the present. Before addressing the question of the etymology of the word *kung-an* and its meanings in the context of medieval Ch'an, let us briefly consider the early history of the practice of commenting on old cases.

The primary sources for that history are the discourse records (*yü-lu*) of Ch'an masters who flourished in the tenth century and later.[3] Those texts depict their subjects commenting on old cases in a number of formal settings, including public gatherings, such as the rite of ascending the dharma hall (*shang-t'ang*), and private or semiprivate meetings with disciples who entered their rooms (*ju-shih*) for individual instruction.[4] In either situation, it was often a disciple, or some other member of the assembly in a dharma hall (a large hall used for lectures and debate), who elicited a master's comment by "raising" (*chü*) or "holding up" (*nien*) a passage from the patriarchal records. The disciple would come before the master's high seat and ask, "What about [the story (case) in which] Master So-and-so said such-and-such?" There were also instances in which a master himself raised a case, either to elicit comments from the audience which he then judged, or simply to set the stage for his own comment. The practice of commenting authoritatively on old cases, in any event, was not simply a means of elucidating the wisdom of ancient patriarchs for the sake of disciples or a larger audience. It was also a device for demonstrating the rank and spiritual authority of the master himself.

Discourse records compiled from about the latter half of the eleventh century on often contain separate sections entitled "comments on old cases" (*chü-ku* or *nien-ku*).[5] In these texts the cases that serve as topics are rarely quoted in their entirety but rather are raised in shorthand fashion, by "title," as it were. For example, a monk may ask a master, "What about 'Nan-ch'üan cutting the cat in two'?" alluding to an anecdote that appears (among other places) in the biography of Nan-ch'üan P'u-yüan in the *Ching-te Record of the Transmission of the Flame* (*Ching-te ch'uan-teng lu*).[6] A master's comment or exchange with his interlocutor that focuses on a case raised in this abbreviated fashion, however, is recorded in full. We may therefore infer that certain passages from patriarchal records had already (at least by the time the discourse records were edited for publication) become fixed as old cases that the audience (or readership) was expected to know.

In addition to comments delivered (ostensibly) orally in formal settings, many discourse records dating from the mid-eleventh century and later include sections entitled "verses on old cases" (*sung-ku*).[7] If we are to take those discourse records at face value, it would seem that it was fairly common for Ch'an masters to write verse commentaries (*sung*) on cases (*ku*) that they found particularly interesting. Unlike the records of oral comments, the excerpted topic passages of written verses were cited in their entirety. This convention may indicate that the passages were not previously well known, or it may simply have been a device that enabled the reader to compare the topic cases and commentarial verses side by side and thus better appreciate the wit and subtlety of the latter.

Whenever a number of cases with verses attached are grouped together in a discourse record, it can be said that they constitute what we today would call a koan collection, although it may not be clear who actually put the collection together—the Ch'an master who was featured or some later compiler of his writings. Nor is it clear from the discourse records just how such collections were used. They may have served as a means of instructing disciples, or they may have been written by Ch'an masters for their own edification, or for posterity.

Old cases eventually came to be known within the Ch'an tradition as kung-an, but it is not entirely clear how or when that usage developed. What is certain is that the usage was initially figurative, for the word *kung-an* did not originate as a Buddhist technical term but rather belonged to the realm of jurisprudence in medieval China. Its literal meaning is the "table" or "bench" (*an*) of a "magistrate" or "judge" (*kung*). By extension, kung-an came to signify a written brief sitting on a magistrate's table, which is to say a case before a court, or the record of a judge's decision on a case.

Another meaning of *kung* is "public," "official," or "unbiased," as opposed to "private," "partial," or "self-interested" (*ssu*). This is what modern scholars have in mind when they say that "koan" literally means "public case." By the end of the thirteenth century, we shall see, old cases were indeed being compared to legally binding official documents (*kung-fu an-tu*), the idea being that they should be regarded as authoritative standards for judging spiritual attainment. The concrete image that the expression *kung-an* originally evoked, nevertheless, was that of a magistrate, a representative of the central government who has absolute local authority, sitting in judgment behind his bench.

In fact, an examination of the earliest occurrences of the word *kung-an* in Ch'an texts shows that it was first used simply to compare the spiritual authority of a Ch'an master with the legal authority of a civil magistrate, not to refer to the old cases of the patriarchs. In the biography of Chun Tsun-su, a mid ninth-century disciple of Huang-po Hsi-yün, we find the following exchange:

Seeing a monk coming, the master said, "[Yours is] a clear-cut case (*chien-cheng kung-an*), but I release you of the thirty blows (*san-shih pang*) [you deserve]. The monk said, "This is the way I am." The master said, "Why do the guardian deities in the monastery gate raise their fists?" The monk said, "The guardian deities are also like this." The master struck him (*pien-ta*).[8]

A similar anecdote appears in the *Extensive Record of Ch'an Master Yün-men K'uang-chen* (*Yün-men k'uang-chen ch'an-shih kuang-lu*):

Master Mu-chou, seeing a monk come in through the gate, said to him: "[Yours is] a clear-cut case (*hsien-cheng kung-an*), but I release you of the thirty blows [you deserve]."[9]

In both of these dialogues, the master uses the expressions *kung-an* (legal "case") and *san-shih pang* ("thirty blows"—a typical punishment administered in medieval Chinese courts) figuratively to imply that he himself sits as judge of another's spiritual attainment and that he finds the monk who has just come into his monastery lacking in that regard. The master, in other words, likens himself to a magistrate whose word is law and who can mete out punishment, while the interlocutor is compared to the accused. To be found "guilty" in the terms of this trope is to be deemed deluded, whereas "innocence" is equated with awakening. In these examples, the term *kung-an* alludes to a case in a civil court but not to any sort of written record or old case involving earlier Ch'an patriarchs.

One of the oldest Ch'an texts in which the term *kung-an* does refer to a recorded incident that occurred in the past is *Master Hsüeh-t'ou's Verses on One Hundred Old Cases* (*Hsüeh-t'ou ho-shang pai-tse sung-ku*),[10] which presumably was compiled around the middle of the eleventh century, (Hsüeh-t'ou died in 1052). The term appears only once in the collection, in case 64, which follows immediately after the case of Nan-ch'üan and the cat (case 63):

Nan-ch'üan raised (*chü*) the preceding story again and asked Chao-chou about it. Chao-chou took off his sandals, put them on top of his head, and left. [Nan-] Chüan said, "If you had been there, you would have saved the cat."

[Hsüeh-t'ou's] verse says:
Although the case (*kung-an*) was clearly decided, he asked Chao-chou, and let him wander at his leisure within the walls of Chang-an [the capital]. If no one understands the sandals on his head, he'll return to his home in the mountains and take a rest.[11]

Here we see the compiler of a collection of old cases, Hsüeh-t'ou, comparing the actions of a protagonist (Nan-ch'üan) in two of the cases with those of a judge in a court case. What Hsüeh-t'ou's comment seems to mean is that the case of the cat, although already settled by the judge (Nan-ch'üan), was re-opened so that the judge could hear further testimony (by Chao-chou). This is not quite the same as calling the story (i.e., a discrete unit of text) about Nan-ch'üan and the cat a kung-an, but it is close.

However, when we come to the systematic commentary on *Master Hsüeh-t'ou's Verses on One Hundred Old Cases* written by Yüan-wu K'o-ch'in (1063–1135) in his *Blue Cliff Collection (Pi-yen chi)* some three generations later, the term *kung-an* is clearly used to refer to the dialogues themselves as textual entities. In his pointers (*ch'ui-shih*) and prose commentaries (*p'ing-ch'ang*), Yüan-wu repeatedly calls the root cases kung-an. In his commentary on Hsüeh-t'ou's verse in the fourth case, for example, he says "Because Hsüeh-t'ou attached verses to one hundred cases of kung-an, burning incense [in venerative offering] to each and holding it up [for comment], they became well known in the world."[12] In instances such as these, the metaphor of the case in court works by drawing an analogy between the written records of dialogues involving bygone Ch'an patriarchs and documents containing civil court deci-sions. The implication is that when Hsüeh-t'ou collected and attached evalua-tive comments to those dialogues, he was taking the position of a judge in some higher court, whose job it was to review the proceedings of a lower juris-diction. In other words, the "cases" that Hsüeh-t'ou was said to be judging were understood to be textual records rather than the words and actions of people who confronted him directly. This is clearly a different usage of the term *kung-an* than those of Chun Tsun-su or Mu-chou, who reportedly told monks coming in through the monastery gate that "[yours is] a clear-cut case."

Significantly, Yüan-wu also echoes that earlier figurative use of the term *kung-an* in some of his interlinear capping phrases (*chu-yü*) in the *Blue Cliff Collection*, where he remarks, "A clear-cut case" (*chien-cheng kung-an*).[13] Be-cause these are comments made in response to particular phrases in a root case or in a verse by Hsüeh-t'ou, *kung-an* here cannot be taken to mean an old case. Rather, this is Yüan-wu's way of saying, while alluding to Chun Tsun-su, that he is in a position to judge the quality of the phrase that has just, as it were, come through the gate of the text, and that he finds it lacking in perspicacity. Similarly, the expressions "thirty blows" (*san-shih pang*) and "I strike" (*pien-ta*), when used by Yüan-wu as capping phrases,[14] are intended to mete out punishment to the offending phrases, just as Chun Tsun-su did to the glib monk who made it past the guardian deities in the front gate.

Thus far we have seen examples of the term *kung-an* used in three different ways: (1) to imply that a master in a dialogue sits in the position of judge vis-à-vis his interlocutor, (2) to suggest that a master commenting on a written dialogue sits in the position of judge vis-à-vis that particular old case, and (3) to refer in a general way to units of text (old cases) that are collected and held up for comment. Once a certain body of old cases became more or less fixed as a repetoire by virtue of their inclusion in published collections and their frequent use in ritual settings, however, the term *kung-an* began to take on yet another meaning: that of a body of laws or set of legal standards used to regulate the Ch'an school as a whole. This last interpretation was stated explicitly during the Yüan dynasty by Chung-feng Ming-pen (1264–1325), a prominent Ch'an master whose influence was widespread in both China and Japan. In his discourse record, the *Extensive Record of Master Chung-feng* (*Chung-feng ho-shang, kuang-lu*), we find the following interpretation of *kung-an:*

Someone also asked, "Why is it that the [records] of the [teaching] devices and circumstances (*chi-yüan*) of the buddhas and patriarchs are commonly called *kung-an*?"

Huan [Chung-feng, of the Huan-chu Hermitage] replied, "The term *kung-an* is a metaphor that compares [the records of Ch'an dialogues] to government documents (*kung-fu an-tu*). The latter are what embody the law, and the suppression of disorder in the kingly way truly depends on them. Government (*kung*) is the principle (*li*) which unifies the wheel ruts of the imperial sages and standardizes the roads of the empire. Documents (*an*) are the official texts in which the sagely principle is recorded. The existence of an empire presupposes government, and the existence of government presupposes legal documents. After all, the purpose of laws is to cut off impropriety in the empire. When government documents (*kung-an*) are employed, then legal principles are in force; and when legal principles are in force, the empire is rectified. When the empire is rectified, kingly rule prevails.

Now, when the devices and circumstances of the buddhas and patriarchs are called "government documents" (*kung-an*), it is because they are also like this. After all, they are not matters for individual speculation. [They are about] the ultimate principle that corresponds with the spiritual source, tallies with the marvelous signification, destroys birth and death, transcends sensate calculation, and is proclaimed alike by all of the hundreds of thousands of bodhisattvas in the three times and ten directions. Furthermore, [this principle] cannot be comprehended through meanings, transmitted by words, discussed in texts, or passed on through consciousness. . . .

[Cases] such as "the oak tree in the courtyard," "three pounds of flax," and "a dried piece of shit," which are impenetrable to the intellect, were devised and given to people to bore into. This is like having to penetrate a silver mountain or a steel wall. Even if there are bright-eyed people who can turn the tables and usurp [some meaning from] the written expressions, their every comment in harmony, like the tracks of a bird in the sky or the traces of moon in the watery depths, if they wander self-indulgently every which way on the thousand roads and ten thousand wheel ruts, they are without attainment and their opinions are fraudulent. . . .

Those who are regarded as elders [Ch'an patriarchs] in the world today are, as it were, the "senior government officials" of the public [Ch'an] monasteries. Their published biographies and collected records are the "official documents" (*kung-an*) that record their inspiring pronouncements. Occasionally, men of old, when they had some leisure from assisting disciples or when their doors were shut, would take up (*nien*) those documents, categorize (*p'an*) them, comment on them in verse (*sung*), and supply alternate responses (*pieh*) to them. Surely they did not do so just to show off their own opinions or contradict the ancient worthies. Certainly they did it because they grieved to think that the great dharma might be misapprehended in the future. They only resorted to such expedients (*fang-pien*) to open the wisdom eye of all who followed, and because they hoped to enable them to attain awakening. [The records of the patriarchs] are called "official" (*kung*) because they prevent private interpretations, and they are called "documents" (*an*) because they require that one match tallies with the buddhas and patriarchs."[15]

It is clear from this passage that by Chung-feng Ming-pen's time, at least, the word *kung-an* had come to refer to collections of old cases with one or more layers of commentary appended. It referred, in other words, to texts such as the *Blue Cliff Collection* or the *Gateless Barrier* (*Wu-men kuan*),[16] which today are known as kōan collections. Chung-feng's main point in the passage was that such works of literature should be used as objective, universal standards to test the insight of monks who aspired to be recognized as Ch'an masters. Those texts were called *kung-an,* he argued, because they set precedents in the same manner as civil laws and were embued with an analogous level of authority. Chung-feng's interpretation became the standard one in medieval Japanese Zen and is in fact the *locus classicus* for the modern scholarly gloss of "koan" as "public case." It is well to remember, however, that as a figure of speech appearing in Ch'an texts dating from the T'ang and Sung, the expression *kung-an* has a richer range of meanings and associations than that indicated by Chung-feng.

A watershed in the history of the practice of commenting on old cases was the development during the Sung dynasty of the "Ch'an of contemplating phrases" (*k'an-hua ch'an*). This was the meditative practice of "looking at" or "observing" (*k'an*) a single "word" or "phrase" (*hua-t'ou*) with the aim of frustrating or stopping the discursive intellect and eventually, in a sudden breakthrough, attaining enlightenment. The "words" to be used in this manner usually derived from a root case (*pen-tse*) in what we now call a koan collection, that is, from one of the original dialogues that traditionally had been "held up" (*nien*) for verbal or written comment by a Ch'an master.

The practice of contemplating phrases is something that first became widespread among followers of the influential Ch'an master Ta-hui Tsung-kao (1089–1163). Ta-hui was a disciple of Yüan-wu, the compiler of the *Blue Cliff Collection,* but he decried the style of commentary embodied in that text as overly discursive. As Robert Buswell explains,

In kung-an investigation, according to Ta-hui, rather than reflect over the entire kung-an exchange, which could lead the mind to distraction, one should instead zero in on the principal topic, or most essential element, of that exchange, which he termed its "critical phrase" (*hua-t'ou*). Ta-hui called this new approach to meditation *k'an-hua Ch'an*—the Ch'an of observing the critical phrase—and alleged that it was a "short-cut" (*ching-chieh*) leading to instantaneous enlightenment.[17]

Any attempt to grasp the meaning of the old cases conceptually, Ta-hui argued, was a species of gradualism, whereas the superior "sudden enlightenment" approach entailed the frustration and final abandonment or transcendence of such merely intellectual approaches.

Buswell sees the development of contemplating phrases as the culmination of a "long process of evolution in Ch'an whereby its subitist rhetoric came to be extended to pedagogy and finally to practice."[18] In my view the development of contemplating phrases can also be interpreted as a reemergence in Ch'an of a very traditional Buddhist concern: the correlation of the practice of calm (*S. śamatha, C. chih*) with that of insight (*S. vipaśyanā, C. kuan*).[19] Despite Ta-hui's use of the rhetoric of sudden enlightenment to legitimize his approach, one of the main thrusts of his argument was that the mode of commenting on old cases current in his day was unbalanced: it allowed for the development of insight by reflecting discursively on the profound sayings of the patriarchs, but it was entirely lacking in the cultivation of the calm, concentrated state of mind that was a prerequisite for insight according to traditional Buddhist meditation manuals.[20] The practice of contemplating phrases restored that balance by using the words of the patriarchs as objects of mental concentration in addition to their function as expressions of profound insight that could be interpreted and commented on. If Ta-hui had been interested only in promoting the cultivation of trance states as a means of cutting off discursive thought, he could have avoided the words of the patriarchs altogether and recommended other, entirely non-discursive objects of mental concentration, such as the devices (*S. kasiña, C. ch'u*) of a circle of earth, bowl of water, or blue-colored object that were described in "Hinayana" meditation manuals. An important feature of Ta-hui's contemplating phrases, however, was that success in the practice was measured by the meditator's ability to grasp the meaning of the words and to comment on them spontaneously and incisively. In short, Ta-hui viewed the cultivation of calm (stopping the mind on the critical phrase) as an aid to the attainment of insight, which again manifested itself in verbal expression. Viewed in this light, contemplating phrases appears to be more a variation or refinement of the traditional practice of commenting on old cases than a rejection of it. If anything, it reinforced the notion that commenting on old cases authoritatively was the prerogative and mark of the enlightened Ch'an master.

In Japanese Rinzai Zen and Korean Sŏn monasteries today, the practice of contemplating phrases is closely linked to the practice of seated meditation (J. *zazen*) in a communal hall. Because both the Rinzai Zen and Sŏn traditions regard themselves as heirs to Ta-hui's legacy, it would seem likely that he and his followers in Sung China were the ones who first established a connection between contemplating phrases and seated meditation (C. *tso-ch'an*). In point of fact, the historical evidence that may be adduced in support of that hypothesis is not as strong as one might expect.

Prior to the development of contemplating phrases in Sung China, certainly, there is no evidence whatsover that the practices of holding up, commenting on, and collecting old cases were ever associated with the practice of seated meditation, or indeed with any sort of "meditation" in the sense of a disciplined effort to alter one's state of mind. And even in the period following Ta-hui's innovations, the discourse records of Ch'an masters continue to portray old cases almost exclusively as objects of literary appreciation and written commentary, and as topics raised for comment by a master in the ritual contexts of "ascending the hall" (*shang-t'ang*) and "entering the room" (*ju-shih*). They make no mention of seated meditation in connection with the raising of old cases, nor do they suggest that the disciples who raised particular old cases for a master to comment on were constantly "working" on them in any kind of sustained meditative effort. Sung Ch'an meditation manuals (*tso-ch'an i*), on the other hand, have much to say about the proper posture and mental attitude to be assumed in seated meditation but are utterly silent on the topic of contemplating phrases. Ch'an monastic rules (*ch'ing-kuei*) dating from the twelfth and thirteenth centuries, moreover, draw no connections between old cases and seated meditation. Nor do they give any indication that the rite of "entering the room" was associated with contemplating phrases as such, although they do make it clear that the raising of old cases for comment by a master was standard procedure in that context.

The best indication that Ta-hui or his followers did link the practices of contemplating phrases and seated meditation is found in the attack that they made on a style of seated meditation that did not make use of old cases, namely, the so-called "Ch'an of silent illumination" (*mo-chao ch'an*) that was taught by Ta-hui's contemporary and rival, Hung-chih Cheng-chüeh (1091–1157). Silent illumination, as it is usually interpreted, entails quieting (*mo*) the mind so that the innate buddha-nature shines forth or is illuminated (*chao*). Hung-chih himself, it is important to note, had nothing against commenting on old cases. Indeed, he himself engaged in the practice and left two collections that subsequently became the basis for a full-blown koan collections similar to Yüan-wu's *Blue Cliff Collection*.[21] For Hung-chih, however, commenting on old cases was one thing and seated meditation was another. In this respect, he represented a tradition older than Ta-hui's "Ch'an of contemplating phrases" and may be seen as a conservative who resisted Ta-hui's innovations. In any case, if Ta-hui and his followers had not sought to bring contemplating phrases together with seated meditation, they would have had no particular reason for castigating Hung-chih's failure to do so.

In medieval Japanese Zen monasteries associated with the Sōtō lineage, *kōan* were widely used in the contexts of public sermons and private meetings between masters and disciples,[22] but *kōan* commentary was not linked with seated meditation in the manner of the "Zen of contemplating phrases." In latter-day Sōtō Zen the tradition of *kōan* commentary has been largely suppressed and forgotten, although it does survive in a few rituals such as the "chief seat's dharma combat rite" (J. *shuso hossenshiki*).[23] One reason for the demise of *kōan* commentary in Sōtō Zen was the success of a late eighteenth- and nineteenth-century reform movement that sought, in the interests of unification, to standardize procedures of formal dharma transmission and eliminate the transmission of esoteric lore (including *kōan*) that had previously distinguished various branches of the Sōtō school. In their zeal to create a new identity for the Sōtō school as a whole, reformers began to celebrate the teachings of the "founding patriarch" Dōgen (1200–1253), which they cast in a way that emphasized the differences between Sōtō and Rinzai Zen. Perhaps because influential Rinzai reformers such as Hakuin Ekaku (1685–1768) were stressing the importance of contemplating phrases in their own tradition, the Sōtō side sought to distance itself from *kōan* as much as possible, characterizing Dōgen's approach to Zen practice as one of "just sitting" (J. *shikantaza*). The irony is that Dōgen's *Treasury of the Eye of the True Dharma* (*Shōbōgenzō*),[24] the work that modern Sōtō Zen reveres as its bible, is in good measure a collection of comments on Chinese *kung-an*, although the comments were delivered in the vernacular for the benefit of Japanese disciples. That is not to say, of course, that Dōgen advocated the use of *kōan* in the manner of Ta-hui's contemplating phrases. Rather, he followed the lead of Hung-chih and others who wanted to keep commenting on old cases and sitting in meditation distinct from one another, as they had been in the Chinese Ch'an school prior to Ta-hui.

Latter-day Japanese Rinzai Zen monastic training is, to a considerable degree, organized around the meditative practice of contemplating phrases (J. *kanna*). The practice of "entering the room" (J. *sanzen nisshitsu*), more commonly known as "individual consultation" (J. *dokusan*) with a master, is given over almost entirely to the testing and instruction of disciples who are striving to "pass" a series of *kōans* by contemplating the critical phrases and demonstrating their ability to comment on them. Monks and lay trainees are instructed to work on their *kōan* while sitting in meditation and while engaged in all other activities as well.[25] The connection between commenting on *kōans* and meditation is reinforced by the fact that individual consultation with a master almost always takes place during scheduled periods of seated meditation: disciples who wish to see the master leave their seats in the meditation hall when the bell signaling "entering the room" is rung, and they return to their seats and resume the meditation posture when their meeting with the master is over.

Nevertheless, even in contemporary Rinzai monasteries the older ritual and literary uses of *kōan* are still in evidence. For example, during the three-month-long summer and winter retreat periods (J. *kessei ango*), Zen masters usually give a series of lectures (J. *teishō*) on the *kōans* in the *Gateless Barrier* or *Blue Cliff Collection,* with no presumption that any of the monks or laypeople in attendance are necessarily working on the particular cases being treated. Preparation for such lectures is a matter of individual study in the privacy of a master's quarters, and it typically draws on earlier masters' published lectures and works of secondary scholarship on the koan collections in question. *Kōan* commentaries produced in this way are also published in book form. Sometimes distribution is limited to disciples and lay patrons, but if a master is famous enough, his *kōan* commentaries may become available to the general public in bookstores.

Modern English dictionaries sometimes define "koan" as a "riddle" or a "nonsensical question" posed to a student with a demand for an answer. That notion, confused and incomplete as it is, apparently derives from explanations of the practice of contemplating phrases that stress the use of terse, "flavorless" phrases such as the "oak tree in the courtyard" or "three pounds of flax" to cut off discursive thinking. There is also a tendency among Western students of Zen at present to call anything that becomes the sustained focus of an existential problem or life crisis a "koan," or to suggest that such things can be "used as koans" to transform them from negative experiences into opportunities for spiritual growth. Those notions, too, seem to be an extension by analogy of the practice of contemplating phrases, the underlying assumption being that koans are difficult things that one becomes fixated and stuck on, and that by confronting and "working through" them one can resolve one's problems. Modern Sōtō Zen commentaries on the chapter of Dōgen's *Treasury of the Eye of the True Dharma* entitled "Genjōkōan" have also fed into this usage, for most of them miss the point that Dōgen, like many Ch'an masters before him, was simply putting himself in the position of judge and pronouncing something "a clear-cut case" (J. *genjōkōan*). Instead, they reason that because Dōgen did not make use of contemplating phrases, the kōans, he had in mind were not old cases as such but something else, such as the "problem" of existence itself. Any and all aspects of our daily lives, according to this interpretation, can function as "koans" that lead us to enlightenment. The idea that "anything can serve as a koan," however, is a modern development; there is scarcely any precedent for it in the classical literature of Ch'an, Sŏn, and Zen.

An Overview of Koan Literature

Given the range of denotations and connotations that the word "koan" has had from ancient times down to the present in East Asia and the West, it behooves modern scholars who wish to use the word in an unambiguous fashion to stipulate their own working definitions of it. For the purposes of the remainder of this chapter I shall regard as a "koan" any text that combines, at a minimum, the following two formal features: (1) a narrative that has been excerpted from the biography or discourse record of a Ch'an, Sŏn, or Zen master, and (2) some sort of commentary on that narrative. To restate this definition using the terminology of medieval Chinese Ch'an, a koan is a "comment on an old case" (*chü-ku, nien-ku*) or a "verse on an old case" (*sung-ku*), that is, a discrete unit of text in which an old case (*ku-tse*) is cited and commented on.

It is true that, as a matter of historical fact, the word "koan" has had other meanings. It has been used, we have seen, to refer loosely to anything that serves as an object of meditation in a manner analogous to the contemplation of a critical phrase. It has also been used to refer in a general way to any intriguing dialogue (C. *wen-ta*, J. *mondō*) that appears in the biography or discourse record of a Ch'an, Sŏn, or Zen master. For scholarly purposes, however, I think it best to restrict the meaning of "koan" to dialogues and anecdotes from that literature that have in fact been singled out and commented on. Such a restricted usage has considerable precedent, for the root metaphor at play in the medieval Ch'an use of the word *kung-an* is that of a magistrate passing judgment on a legal case. Without the elements of evaluative and authoritative comment, I would argue, a dialogue or phrase should not be considered a koan in the technical sense.

Koans, thus defined, appear in a number of different contexts in the classical literature of Ch'an and Zen. They occur within the biographies of individual masters that are found in the genre known as "records of the transmission of the flame (or lamp)" (C. *ch'uan-teng lu*, J. *dentōroku*), or "flame histories" (C. *teng-lu*, J. *tōshi*) for short. Flame history biographies typically contain two kinds of material: (1) factual data concerning a master's birth, training, teaching career, and death, and (2) ostensibly verbatim records of verbal exchanges with disciples and other interlocutors. Occasionally those exchanges take the form of a question about an old case and a response in which the master comments on the case. Such exchanges constitute koans, as I have defined them. The biographies of masters that appear in individual discourse records (C. *yü-lu*, J. *goroku*) also contain, among the numerous exchanges they cite, some that are koans.

The occurrence of koans in the two aforementioned genres of Ch'an/Zen literature is a more or less random phenomenon that reflects the historical practice of raising and commenting on old cases. There is, however, another genre that focuses exclusively on koans, one that we may aptly refer to as the "koan collection." Such texts contain virtually nothing but a number of koans, given in more or less random order, and sometimes numbered for ease of reference. Some koan collections, as noted above, exist only as separate sections within the discourse records of Ch'an, Sŏn, and Zen masters, grouped under the headings of "comments on old cases" and "verses on old cases." Other koan collections, including all of the most famous ones, have circulated and been published as discrete, independent texts, which are often furnished with prefaces that explain the aims or circumstances of their compilation.

Among the independent texts, a further distinction can be drawn between koan collections that feature only one level of commentary on each old case and those that have two or even three levels of commentary. That is to say, some collections consist simply of a number of old cases that a single Ch'an or Zen master has selected and commented on; I shall refer to those as "primary collections." Examples are *Pearl String Collection of Verses on Old Cases from the Ch'an Lineage (Ch'an-tsung sung-ku lien-chu t'ung-chi)*,[26] *Verses by Patriarchs of the Ch'an School (Ch'an-men chu-tsu-shih chieh-sung)*,[27] *Grouped Sayings from the Ch'an Collections (Ch'an-lin lui-chü)*,[28] *Collection of Comments on Old Cases from the [Ch'an] Lineage (Tsung-men nien-ku hui-chi)*,[29] and the most famous of primary collections, the *Gateless Barrier (Wu-men kuan)*.[30]

Other koan collections, which I shall call "secondary," are basically primary collections that have been taken up and extensively commented on by a second master. Noteworthy examples are the *Blue Cliff Collection (Pi-yen chi)*,[31] *Fo-kuo's Commentarial Record (Fo-kuo chi-chieh lu)*,[32] the *Ts'ung-jung Record (Ts'ung-jung lu)*,[33] and the *Empty Valley Collection (K'ung-ku chi)*.[34]

There are also numerous works that we may regard as "tertiary collections." These are secondary collections that have been commented on by contemporary Zen masters or by scholars who have translated them into modern Japanese and other languages. Most primary koan collections remain embedded in discourse records, although a number have circulated as independent texts. All secondary and tertiary koan collections, on the other hand, stand alone as independent works.

The Structure of Koans

The koans found in secondary collections such as the *Blue Cliff Collection* and *Ts'ung-jung Record* are highly complex literary productions in which numerous voices speak on different levels.

Embedded in the text of the *Blue Cliff Collection* is a core collection of old cases with verses attached that is attributed to Ch'an master Hsüeh-t'ou Ch'ung-hsien (980–1052). That earlier work, which originally circulated independently, is known as *Master Hsüeh-t'ou's Verses on One Hundred Old Cases (Hsüeh-t'ou ho-shang pai-tse sung-ku)*.[35] Each of the old cases in the core collection is marked by the word "raised" (*chü*), meaning that it is raised as a topic for comment, and each of the verse comments is introduced by the words, "[Hsüeh-t'ou's] verse says:" (*sung yüeh*). In addition, within some of the old cases themselves the dialogue is interspersed with comments by Hsüeh-t'ou, which are marked by the words "the teacher's added remark says:" (*shih chu-*

yü yü). Such interlinear comments in a koan collection came to be known in the Ch'an/Zen tradition as "capping phrases" (C. *chu-yü,* J. *jakugo*).

The *Blue Cliff Collection* proper was composed by Ch'an master Yüan-wu K'o-ch'in, who added another layer of commentary to *Master Hsüeh-t'ou's Verses on One Hundred Old Cases.* Specifically, Yüan-wu added (1) an introductory pointer (*ch'ui-shih*) which precedes the citation of each old case, (2) a prose commentary (*p'ing-ch'ang*) on the case, and (3) a prose commentary on Hsüeh-t'ou's verse. Moreover, Yüan-wu broke each original case and associated verse into separate phrases that he commented on individually with brief, interlinear capping phrases (*chu-yü*).

Consider, for example, the sixty-third case of the *Blue Cliff Collection,* which takes as its root case the story of Nan-ch'üan and the cat. This story, we saw, appears in Nan-ch'üan's biography in the *Ching-te Record,* but versions are also found in a number of other Ch'an records, so there is no way of knowing for certain what Hsüeh-t'ou's source was when he selected it for inclusion in his *Verses on One Hundred Old Cases.* The root case and Hsüeh-t'ou's verse commentary read as follows:

Raised (*chü*):
At Nan-ch'üan [monastery] one day, the [monks of the] east and west halls were arguing over a cat. When Nan-ch'üan saw this, he held it up and said, "if you can speak, I will not cut it in two." The assembly had no reply. [Nan-] Ch'üan cut the cat into two pieces.

[Hsüeh-t'ou's] verse (*sung*) says:
Both halls alike are confused Ch'an monks,
kicking up all that smoke and dust for no purpose.
Fortunately, Nan-ch'üan could make a decisive judgment;
with a single slice he cut it into two pieces, however uneven they
    might be.[36]

These are the root case and verse as they must have appeared in *Hsüeh-t'ou's Verses on One Hundred Old Cases.* Now let us look at them as they appear in the context of the *Blue Cliff Collection,* together with Yüan-wu's pointer, interlinear capping phrases, and commentaries. For the sake of contrast, the root case is in upper case letters, Hsüeh-t'ou's verse is in upper case italics, and all parts of the text written by Yüan-wu are in lower case:

The pointer (*ch'ui-shih*) says: Where the path of thought does not reach, that is where your attention is best directed; where verbal commentary does not reach, that is where you should quickly fix your eyes. If lightning turns [your gaze] and [you glimpse] a shooting star, then you can overturn lakes and topple peaks. Is there no one in the assembly who can manage this? To test, I raise [the following case] to see.

RAISED: AT NAN-CH'ÜAN [MONASTERY] ONE DAY, THE, [MONKS OF THE] EAST AND WEST HALLS WERE ARGUING OVER A CAT. It is not just this day that they squabble together. The entire scene is one of deluded disturbance. WHEN NAN-CH'ÜAN SAW THIS, HE HELD IT UP AND SAID, "IF YOU CAN SPEAK, I WILL NOT CUT IT IN TWO." When a true imperative is put into effect, all the seats [for the assembly] in the ten directions are cut off. This old guy has the tricks for distinguishing dragons [truly awakened people] from snakes [pretenders]. THE ASSEMBLY HAD NO REPLY. How pathetic to forgive their transgressions. A bunch of lacquer buckets—what are they good for [besides holding food]? Phoney Ch'an monks are [coarse] like hemp and [as common as] millet. NAN-CH'ÜAN CUT THE CAT INTO TWO PIECES. So quick, so quick. If it were not like this, then all of them would be guys playing with mud balls. [But my comment is like] drawing the bow after the thief is gone. Already it is secondary. Better to strike before it [the cat/case] is even raised.

[Prose Commentary on the Root Case]
[Nan]-ch'üan was an accomplished master of our school. Observe his movement, his stillness, his leaving, and his entering. Now speak: what did he mean to indicate? This story about cutting the cat is discussed in a great many public monasteries all over the empire. There are some who say that the point consists in the holding up [of the cat]; others say that it lies in the cutting. But all [of these explanations] are utterly irrelevant. If he had not held it up, they would still go around and around making all sorts of interpretations. They really do not know that this man of old had the eye that determines [what is] heaven and [what is] earth, and he had the sword that determines heaven and earth. So now, speak up: in the final analysis, who was it that cut the cat? When Nan-ch'üan held up the cat and said, "If you can speak, then I will not cut it in two," if at that moment suddenly there had been someone able to speak, then tell me: would Nan-ch'üan have cut it or not? Thus I say, "When a true imperative is put into effect, all the seats [for the assembly] in the ten directions are cut off." Go out beyond the heavens and take a look: who is it that joins the assembly? The truth of the matter is, at that time there was fundamentally no cutting. This story does not consist in cutting or not cutting . . . [remainder elided].

[HSÜEH-T'OU'S] VERSE SAYS:
BOTH HALLS ALIKE ARE CONFUSED CH'AN MONKS, Intimate words from the mouth of an intimate. With this one phrase speech is cut off. This settles the case in accordance with the facts. KICKING UP ALL THAT SMOKE AND DUST FOR NO PURPOSE. Look: what settlement will you make? It is a clear-cut case. Still, there is something here.
FORTUNATELY, NAN-CH'ÜAN COULD MAKE A DECISIVE JUDGMENT; I raise my whisk and say: "It is just like this." Old teacher Wang [Nan-ch'üan] amounts to something. He uses the precious sword of the Vajra King to cut mud. WITH A SINGLE SLICE HE CUT IT INTO TWO PIECES, HOWEVER UNEVEN THEY MIGHT BE. Shattered into a hundred fragments. If there were someone who held his knife still, let's see what he would do then. I cannot excuse this transgression, so I strike.[37]

As was noted in the previous section, the *Blue Cliff Collection* can be classified as a secondary collection insofar as it represents a preexisting koan collection (*Hsüeh-t'ou's Verses on One Hundred Old Cases*) that was taken up and extensively commented on by a second master, in this case Yüan-wu. It should be clear from the example of this sixty-third case, however, that the secondary level of commentary provided by Yüan-wu is not simply a response to Hsüeh-t'ou verse, but that it operates on a number of different levels. In the first place, there are remarks that pertain to the root case as a whole, namely, the initial pointer and the prose commentary on the case. Yüan-wu says, as if addressing an assembly of monks in a dharma hall, that he is holding up the case of Nan-ch'üan and the cat as a "test" of his audience's understanding. He also indicates that the case is widely known and discussed in the monasteries of his day, but that in his judgment it is universally misunderstood. At this level of commentary, Yüan-wu clearly takes upon himself the mantle of authority: it is he and only he, the text implies, who is qualified to judge other people's interpretations of the case. The interlinear capping phrases that Yüan-wu attached to the root case represent commentary of a different sort. Here Yüan-wu evaluates the protagonists in the case and engages in repartee, as it were, with the various voices speaking, therein. Although he takes the position of judge at this level, too, he has nothing but praise for Nan-ch'üan, his ancestor in the lineage. Yüan-wu's remarks on Hsüeh-t'ou's verse constitute yet another style of commentary. Here he sits in judgment on Hsüeh-t'ou's previous judgments, like a magistrate in some higher court reviewing the records of an earlier decision.

Turning now to the *Ts'ung-jung Record,* we see that it is similar in arrangement to the *Blue Cliff Collection,* and that the koans it contains have basically the same internal structure. At the core of the text is a collection of verses on old cases (*sung-ku*), one hundred in all, attributed to T'ien-t'ung Chüeh, a prominent abbot of the T'ien-t'ung Monastery whose full name was Hung-chih Cheng-chüeh (1091–1157). That core collection, which may have circulated independently from Hung-chih's discourse record, is called *Hung-chih's Verses on Old Cases (Hung-chih sung-ku).* The *Ts'ung-jung Record* as we know it today took shape in 1223 under the hand of Ch'an master Wan-sung Hsing-hsiu (1166–1246), who was living in the Ts'ung-jung Hermitage (Ts'ung-jung-an) at the Pao-en Monastery in Yen-ching. To each old case and attached verse found in the core text, Wan-sung added: (1) a prose "instruction to the assembly" (*shih-chung*) which precedes the citation of the case and serves as a sort of introductory remark; (2) a prose commentary on the case, introduced by the words "the teacher said" (*shih yün*); and (3) a prose commentary on the verse, also introduced by "the teacher said." Moreover, Wan-sung added interlinear capping phrases to each case and verse.

The headings "instruction to assembly" and "the teacher said" give the impression that Wan-sung's introductory remarks and prose commentaries on each case were delivered orally in a public forum and recorded by his disciples. It is not impossible that Wan-sung actually gave a series of lectures on *Hung-*

chih's Verses on Old Cases which, when recorded and compiled by his disciples, resulted in the *Ts'ung-jung Record*. Such lectures would have been extremely difficult to follow, however, unless the members of the audience had the text of *Hung-chih's Verses on Old Cases* in hand to consult as the master spoke. Perhaps that was the case, but the complex structure of the *Ts'ung-jung Record* is such that I am inclined to view it as a purely literary production, albeit one that employs headings normally found in ostensibly verbatim records of oral performances.

Finally, consider the *Gateless Barrier,* the third of the three medieval Chinese koan collections that have been especially celebrated within the world of Japanese Zen, and hence in the West as well. It differs from the *Blue Cliff Collection* and the *Ts'ung-jung Record* in that it has but one author, the Ch'an master Wu-men Hui-k'ai (1184–1260). The text consists of 48 old cases which Wu-men himself selected, adding to each a verse (*sung*) and a prose comment under the heading "Wu-men said" (*Wu-men yüeh*). Some modern scholars believe that Wu-men first collected 48 old cases and attached verses to them, thereby creating a koan collection, and that he only later added the prose comments.[38] If that was indeed the process by which the text as we now have it came into existence, then we could perhaps view it as structurally similar to the other two works in having at its core a collection of old cases with attached verses, to which a secondary comment was subsequently added. Wu-men's prose comments, however, focus only on the root cases. They do not engage in any second-order criticism of the verses attached to each root case (which would have entailed Wu-men criticizing his own verses), so they are fundamentally different from the prose comments that Yüan-wu attached to Hsüeh-t'ou's verses in the *Blue Cliff Collection* or those that Wan-sung attached to Hung-chih's verses in the *Ts'ung-jung Record*. With its single author who comments on a number of old cases excerpted from the patriarchal records, the *Gateless Barrier* is actually closer in structure to *Master Hsüeh-t'ou's Verses on One Hundred Old Cases* and *Hung-chih's Verses on Old Cases,* the core collections found within the *Blue Cliff Collection* and *Ts'ung-jung Record,* respectively.

According to Wu-men's preface to the *Gateless Barrier,* the *kung-an* included in the text were ones that he just happened to use to instruct disciples in the course of a monastic retreat that he led at the Lung-hsiang Monastery in Tung-chia in 1228.[39] Wu-men also says that at the outset of the retreat he had no intention of compiling a formal collection, that the number 48 and the order in which the cases appear was mere chance, and that the title "Gateless Barrier" was an afterthought. It is not clear from the text exactly how Wu-men used koans to teach his disciples, but there are indications in his preface and prose comments that he expected them to focus their minds on particular old cases in some sort of protracted meditative effort. Perhaps the *Gateless Barrier,* unlike the *Blue Cliff Collection* and *Ts'ung-jung Record,* was conceived from the start as an aid to the practice of contemplating phrases that came into vogue following Ta-hui.

Voices of Authority

Studying the internal structure of individual koans and the arangement of these three famous Chinese collections in which they appear helps us reflect further on the understanding of religious authority that is evidenced in the traditional koan literature. There is, within that literature, a pattern of discourse that both replicates and informs the ritual and social functions of koans in the Ch'an, Sŏn, and Zen traditions.

At the core of complex koan collections such as the *Blue Cliff Collection* and the *Ts'ung-jung Record,* we have seen, there are root cases to which verse comments are attached. The root cases are understood to be a verbatim quotations of ancient patriarchs in the Ch'an lineage. Typically a root case takes the form of a dialogue between a patriarch and a disciple or some other interlocutor who serves as a foil for a demonstration of the patriarch's wit and insight. It is a convention of the dialogue genre in Ch'an/Zen literature that the voice of the master (the figure whose status as an heir to the lineage provides the raison d'être for "recording" the dialogue in the first place) always represents the standpoint of awakening, speaks with the greatest authority, and thus occupies the position of judge. The voice of the interlocutor, on the other hand, may represent abject delusion, striving for awakening, or awakened insight rivaling that of the master, but it is always in the inferior position of being evaluated by the voice of the master.

When a recorded dialogue such as "Nan-ch'üan halving the cat" is lifted from its context in a biography, commented on, and included in a koan collection, however, the locus of final authority shifts, for the voice of the commentator assumes the position of judge. The root case itself then serves as a foil for the commenting master's critical verse in much the same way that, within the case, the interlocutor provides a foil for the words of the ancient patriarch. In other words, at the level of commentary there is a replication of the basic relationship between master and disciple—the voice of judge and the voice of the judged—that is found in the root text. The process of replication, however, does not simply add a second awakened voice (that of the commenting master) to the voice of the ancient patriarch who is featured in the root case. Rather it creates a hierarchy of authoritative voices in which the level of commentarial discourse is privileged over that of the root case. Thus, for example, in *Master Hsüeh-t'ou's Verses on One Hundred Old Cases,* each of Hsüeh-t'ou's verse comments not only provides an interpretation of the meaning of a particular root case, it also puts Hsüeh-t'ou himself in the position of demonstrating his status and insight as a Ch'an master—an arbiter of awakening and discourse on awakening. The root case itself serves as a foil to Hsüeh-t'ou's judgmental and instructive verse in just the same way that, within the case, the interlocutor provides a foil for the words of the ancient patriarch.

This structure puts a commenting master such as Hsüeh-t'ou in an interesting position vis-à-vis the old patriarchs, one that remains fundamentally subordinate and yet manages to evince ultimate authority. On the one hand, it is clear that the patriarchs, being ancestral figures, have seniority in the Ch'an lineage. Their words, especially ones that have repeatedly been raised as koans within the tradition, are invested with great prestige. To be a living heir in the lineage—a Ch'an or Zen master—is to benefit from association with the eminent patriarchs of old. To comment on the words of the patriarchs, similarly, is to be on the receiving end of the prestige with which those words are invested. Nevertheless, when a Ch'an or Zen master remarks on an old case (whether orally or in written form), he assumes a position of spiritual authority, not only vis-à-vis a living disciple who may have solicited his comment but also in relation to the root case and the ancient patriarch whose words it contains. The mark of the master, or rather the formal position of master, is to have the last word and pronounce the ultimate judgment.

The ambiguous status of the Ch'an or Zen master—a spiritual leader whose authority is both derivative and absolute—is thus reflected in the structure of the koan literature and in the ritualized practice of commenting on koans. It is also consistent with the quasi-genealogical model of succession that is understood to be operative in the Ch'an/Zen lineage. In the traditional "Confucian" family structure, the mantle of clan leadership passes to the oldest direct male heir (usually the oldest son) upon the death of the previous patriarch. The head of the clan is thus its most senior living member, but he remains junior and beholden to all of his ancestral predecessors. It is his job as leader of the living to officiate at the regular offerings of sustenance to the ancestral spirits, to interpret their wishes, and to make sure that those wishes are obeyed. Ch'an and Zen masters, similarly, preside over their disciples and followers as the most senior members of a particular community of the living, but within the lineage of Ch'an/Zen patriarchs, most of whom are dead, they occupy the ranks of the most junior. Just like the head of a lay family, the Ch'an or Zen master has the job of leading the regular memorial services in which offerings are made to the patriarchs, of interpreting the wishes and intentions of those ancestors to the living, and of ensuring that their standards are upheld. It is thus the role of the master to comment authoritatively on the words of the patriarchs as those are contained in koans, and to pass judgment on other people who would assay interpretations of koans.

A different but equally fruitful way of interpreting the authority of the commentarial voice in koan literature is with reference to the dialectics of the perfection of wisdom (S. *prajñāpāramitā*), as represented in the genre of Mahayana sūtras known as *Prajñāparamita Sūtras*. Given the principle of the emptiness of all dharmas, those texts suggest, any positive statement about the nature of things (or, indeed, any negative statement) makes the mistake of assuming the existence of some substantial subject (dharma) about which something can be meaningfully predicated. All predications, therefore, are ultimately false and susceptible to rebuttal, including those that directly or indirectly posit the falsehood of a previous statement. Thus a peculiar dialectic of negation is set up in which each successive rebuttal of a preceding remark is both "true" in that it points to the impossibility of the attempted predication and "false" in that it unavoidably employs predication in the process. As was noted above, in the koan literature there is a hierarchy of authoritative voices in which the level of commentary is privileged over the root case or dialogue that is commented on. In part, hierarchy can be explained in purely structural terms, as a formal requirement of the Ch'an/Zen dialogue genre itself, which always juxtaposes the voices of "judge" and "judged." In part, too, it can be explained sociologically, for it is the duty and pregrogative of the Ch'an or Zen master to interpret the words of the deceased patriarchs for the community of the living. However, the authority of the commenting voice in the koan literature derives from the dialectic of negation, according to which even the words of the patriarchs are fundamentally flawed and in need of rebuttal lest someone cling to them as ultimately meaningful expressions of truth.

There are, therefore, considerable tensions and ambiguities built into the practice of commenting on old cases. On the one hand, the voice of awakening is a matter of positioning in a formal ritual or literary structure: whatever the voice of the "judge" in a dialogue says, regardless of its semantic content, represents the truth, or the standpoint of awakening.[40] In a social context, this means that whoever can work himself (by whatever means) into the position of speaking as a judge of old cases will thereafter be deemed a worthy spokesman of the awakened point of view, regardless of what he says. Such a position is enviable, indeed, for while the "judged" may or may not pass muster, the "judge" always has the last word. On the other hand, the dialectic of negation dictates on equally formal grounds that the "last word" is always false. The last word is, as it were, a sitting duck: an easy target for subsequent commentary and negative evaluation. Once the judge actually expresses an opinion, he is doomed to become the judged in some higher court. This too has an analogue on the sociological level. To be a Ch'an or Zen master is to reign within a particular community as final arbiter of the spiritual value of all words past and present. At the same time, when a master exercises his prerogative of authoritative comment, he exposes himself to the challenging, critical judgments of the upcoming generation of monks who are honing their rhetorical and literary skills in the hope of succeeding to leadership of the lineage. In the long run, too, his discourse records will become the object of critical comment.

Taken together, these rhetorical and sociological dynamics help explain how certain collections of koans with verse commentaries attached, such as

Master Hsüeh-t'ou's Verses on One Hundred Old Cases, came to attract secondary (and, especially in Japan, tertiary) levels of commentary. When Yüan-wu added his prose comments and capping phrases to Hsüeh-t'ou's koan collection, thereby producing the *Blue Cliff Collection,* he was honoring (and deriving prestige from) the ancient patriarchs whose words were recorded in the root cases. He was also paying respect to Hsüeh-t'ou's work as a compiler and connoisseur of koans. At the same time, however, he was exercising his prerogative as Ch'an master by freely passing judgment, sometimes negative, on the words of the ancients and Hsüeh-t'ou alike. Many of those words, after all, were not simply "sitting ducks" in the game of dialectic negation; they were more like stuffed ducks sitting in Hsüeh-t'ou's trophy case: glass and feathers alike presented stationary targets just begging to be riddled with clever shots. We should remember, however, that the "bullets" Yüan-wu used were themselves written words, and that the result of his persistent sniping was a literary production that was peppered with capping phrases and was altogether larger and more complicated than the one he took aim at in the first place. We might say that Yüan-wu filled his own "trophy case"—the *Blue Cliff Collection* itself—which in turn became an irresistible target for future generations of Ch'an and Zen masters eager to make their reputations.

The phenomenon of secondary commentary, in which not only an old case, but an old case coupled with a Ch'an master's verse, became the topic of a later master's comment, may have appeared first as an oral practice. All that was necessary for that practice to develop was the publication of koan collections (verses on selected old cases) in the discourse records of eminent Ch'an masters, something that became quite common in the eleventh century. It is not hard to imagine that, in the context of a public assembly or private interview, the disciples of Ch'an masters would have begun to raise for comment old cases that were already paired with verse comments in some earlier master's discourse record. Be that as it may, the oldest extant texts containing secondary commentary on koans date from the twelfth and thirteenth centuries, when full-blown commentaries on entire koan collections began to be compiled. At present the *Blue Cliff Collection* and *Ts'ung-jung Record* are the best-known examples of such commentaries, but that is so because they subsequently became the focus of numerous tertiary commentaries in the Japanese Zen tradition. Those two texts were not as uncommon in their day as modern scholarship might lead one to suppose. As was noted above, various other commentaries on koan collections, similar in structure, were also compiled in China from the twelfth century on.

The voice of the secondary commentator in all of these works, like that of Yüan-wu in the *Blue Cliff Collection,* assumes a position of authority vis-à-vis the rest of the text that replicates not only the relationship between patriarch and interlocutor that is depicted in the root cases, but also the relationship between verse comments and root cases that is embodied in the core koan collection. Once such secondary commentaries on entire koan collections began to be produced, it was perhaps inevitable that a replication of their internal structure would also occur, giving rise to tertiary commentaries. Once the precedent of commenting on some earlier master's comments on root cases was established, a model for the addition of yet another layer of "comments on comments" was in place, and works such as the *Blue Cliff Collection* themselves became the object of systematic critiques. Tertiary commentary was also encouraged by the dialectic of negation and by the simple passing of generations of Ch'an and Zen masters. It has always been the duty and prerogative of living masters in the Ch'an/Zen lineage to interpret the words of their ancestors. There is no evidence that the practice of tertiary commentary ever resulted in the compilation of full-blown works of literature (e.g. systematic commentaries on the entire *Blue Cliff Collection*) in China, but a number of such works have been produced in Japan and the West.

The Literary Context of "Contemplating Phrases"

The most famous koan to be used in the tradition of contemplating phrases is the first of the 48 cases in the *Gateless Barrier,* entitled "Chao-chou's Dog" (*Chao-chou kuo-tzu*). The root case reads:

A monk asked master Chao-chou, "Does a dog have buddha-nature or not?" The master said, "Not."[41]

Although the root case itself is relatively short, the traditional way of using it is to take the single word "not" (C. *wu,* J. *mu,* literally "there is none") as the critical phrase (C. *hua-t'ou,* J. *watō*) that the mind should be focused on in meditation. The word "not" is said to be ideal as a starting point for the practice of contemplating phrases because it quickly frustrates discursive reasoning about the meaning of the case and enables the meditator to enter into a state of intense mental concentration. When, after an extended period of effort, the mind freezes in a single, all encompassing "ball of doubt" (C. *i-t'uan,* J. *gidan*) that is focused on the word "not," conditions are ripe for a sudden flash of insight into Chao-chou's intent, which is to say, the awakened mind from which Chao-chou's reply "not" originally emerged. When that happens, as the traditional understanding would have it, the practitioner is suddenly able to comment freely and incisively on the root case. According to one prevalent view, the practitioner should also be able immediately to grasp the import of and comment spontaneously on other koans as well.

One corollary of this process is that "Chao-chou's Dog," or indeed any other koan, may be used to test a person's spiritual state. Another is that if someone fails the test (is unable to comment appropriately), the remedy is not to ponder the case intellectually, but rather to fix the mind on the critical phrase in seated meditation. The practice of contemplating phrases, it is said, may also be carried on apart from the meditation hall, throughout all of one's daily activities. Once a person can freely comment on all koans, however, they are presumed to be awakened: no further training in seated meditation or any other Buddhist practice is necessary, except perhaps to provide a model for others to follow.

This understanding of koans as devices for focusing the mind and cutting off the discursive intellect derives largely from the tradition of contemplating phrases that is championed by the Rinzai school of Zen in Japan. Many popular and scholarly books written from the standpoint of the modern Rinzai school characterize koans as (1) spontaneous expressions of the awakened minds of the patriarchs who originally uttered the words in question, (2) tests that Zen masters use to gauge the state of mind of their disciples, and (3) conundrums designed to frustrate the discursive intellect and eventually lead the meditator to "break through" with an awakening of his own.

In an article published in 1931, for example, the Rinzai Zen master Asahina Sōgen explained koans in the following way:

Koans are expressions in words or actions of the enlightened state of mind of people who have gained awakening through the intimate practice of Zen. Some of those words or actions are just spontaneous expressions arising from the enlightened state of mind, with no intention of showing anything to other people, but others are formulated with just such a purpose in mind. In either case, the words and actions express the enlightened state completely. But people who are not awakened yet cannot understand them, whereas awakened people react immediately—"Oh, I see"—and have no problem with them. Although they are simple words or actions, one of the special characteristics of koans is their function as a standard to distinguish between enlightened and unenlightened people. That special characteristic always causes unenlightened people to feel that koans are something extraordinary, and to think that they belong to some realm where commonsense understanding is impossible. As a result, people are led to question why there are such words and actions, and to wonder whether the way of life and looking at the universe that they reflect is really true. It is in the nature of human beings to feel compelled to find an appropriate explanation whenever they encounter any new and strange phenomena. When people are uneasy or dissatisfied with the realities of their lives, and when they are motivated by religious needs, yearning for a realm in which their problems are resolved and they are at peace, their minds are even more caught by this special characteristic of koans, which has for them an extraordinary appeal. In Zen it is said, "At the root of great awakening is great doubt." The more profound the unease or dissatisfaction that one feels about the realities of one's life, the greater and more thoroughgoing one's interest in a koan will be. That is so because it is precisely at the point when one's intellectual investigations of reality intensify and have clearly reached an impasse that the enlightened state of mind becomes the only thing one values, one's only aspiration. Thus, koans are not simply words or actions that express the mental state of enlightened people. They are things that inspire the minds of unenlightened people, draw them into the abyss of doubt and intellectual investigation, and lead them to practices that help reach across to the realm of enlightenment.[42]

Such accounts of the meaning and function of koans appear relatively simple on the surface and, to judge from their widespread acceptance, have proven to be very compelling. From a sociological perspective, what Asahina Sōgen says about koans is true: they are, in fact, used by Rinzai Zen masters to test the state of mind of their disciples, and they do function within the Rinzai school as a litmus test for deciding who has *satori* (understanding) and who does not. From a psychological perspective, too, Asahina's remarks are insightful: koans do appear extraordinary, mysterious, and attractive to many who first encounter them, and they do inspire Zen trainees to make great efforts to "penetrate" them and attain a point of view from which they make sense.

But such accounts entirely ignore the key fact that koans constitute a literary genre. In particular, they fail to point out that if it were not for the unspoken conventions of that genre, koans would have no power to function as they do sociologically and psychologically. That is so because what identifies words or actions as "expressions of the mental state of enlightened people" is never the semantic content of the words themselves, but only their attribution to a Ch'an patriarch in a flame history biography, a discourse record, or (subsequently) a koan collection. Without that attribution, which is after all a literary device, the words in question would no longer seem extraordinary, profound, or particularly worthy of contemplation. This is especially true of old cases like the ones that Chung-feng Ming-pen celebrated as "impenetrable to the intellect . . . like having to penetrate a silver mountain or a steel wall": Chao-chou's "Oak Tree in the Courtyard,"[43] Tung-shan's "Three Pounds of Flax,"[44] and Yün-men's "Dried Piece of Shit."[45] These sayings, if they were not attributed to famous patriarchs in the Ch'an lineage and therefore taken to be direct expressions of ultimate truth, would be entirely mundane and unremarkable. It is only their literary frame that makes them "impenetrable to the intellect" and suitable as objects for the practice of contemplating phrases.

Consider, for example, the old case known as "Chao-chou's Wash Your Bowl," which appears as case 7 in the *Gateless Barrier*.

A monk said to Chao-chou, "I have just arrived in this monastery; may the master please teach me something."
Chou asked, "Have you eaten your rice gruel yet?"
The monk said, "I have eaten my rice gruel."
Chou said, "Go wash your bowl."
The monk comprehended.[46]

An exchange such as this, if it appeared in a different context, might be read as a teacher's curt dismissal of a student's question by means of changing the subject. Perhaps the student was approaching the teacher at an inappropriate time, or perhaps the teacher was simply too tired or irate to respond. Such commonsense interpretations are not possible within the frame of koan literature, however, because the genre itself dictates that the subject is never changed: whatever a master says or does in that context is always about awakening, so the more mundane it looks, the more profound it must be. The reader is forced, by the very conventions of the genre, to interpret "go wash your bowl" as some sort of indirect speech, that is, as a figurative statement that is not about bowls at all but about the ultimate truth. At the same time, however, Wu-men's commentary on this and other koans in the *Gateless Barrier* stresses that the meaning of the patriarchs' words are "perfectly clear" and that any attempt to interpret them symbolically is a mistake and a sure sign of a delusion. It is this tension between the implicit demand for interpretation that the root case presents and the explicit rejection of interpretation by the commentary that renders the koan a conundrum and frustrates the discursive intellect.

We have seen that, in the koan genre, the authoritative "awakened" statement, as opposed to the judged or "deluded" one, is a matter of formal positioning, not semantic content. Thus the outcome of a Zen master's testing with koans is a foregone conclusion: as long as a person accepts the master's authority and thereby takes the position of disciple, whatever the person says is going to be deluded. Indeed, it is a well-established custom in Japanese Rinzai Zen for masters summarily to reject, for an extended period of time, whatever comments their disciples make on the first koan that they are given to contemplate (usually "Chao-chou's Dog"). When disciples attempt to make sense out of the case by interpreting its symbolism, moreover, they are told that such efforts at intellectual understanding, being the workings of a deluded mind, are precisely the problem, not the solution. Being continually rebuffed and frustrated in this way, if a practitioner believes that the old case he is unable to comment on acceptably is indeed a "spontaneous expression" of the awakened mind of a patriarch (and not merely words that are framed as such in a piece of literature), and if he continues to contemplate the phrase, then he he may in fact begin to experience the "ball of doubt" that the tradition speaks of. He may also, at some point, come to realize the actual nature of his problem with the old case and thereafter cease to be befuddled by it.

Such a realization is traditionally called *satori*. In some accounts it is described as a sudden flash of insight that is accompanied by a great emotional release. The claim, of course, is that it is an awakening similar to the one experienced by the Buddha himself and that it entails "seeing the [buddha] nature" (J. *kenshō*) or the innate buddha-mind. It is well to remember, however, that this kind of *satori* is characterized chiefly as a release of the tension built up in the meditative practice of contemplating phrases and that it is said to manifest itself primarily in the ability to comment freely on koans. Indeed, if we look more closely at the manner in which this *satori* is traditionally demonstrated, we can see that it entails the reversal of each of the sources of frustration that led the practitioner into the "ball of doubt" to begin with.

In the first place, the "awakened" person naturally refuses to occupy the position of disciple, whose commentary is ipso facto "deluded." He insists, rather, on seizing and holding the position of master in the dialogue, which means that he must be prepared not only to comment on the root case, but to pass critical judgment on his teacher's remarks as well when the teacher tries the usual gambit of putting him in his place. The confidence to stand one's ground in this situation comes from understanding the basic message of Chao-chou's "Not" (and many other Ch'an/Zen dialogues), which is simply that words and signs utterly fail to convey the true dharma. Viewed from that standpoint, all of the old cases and anything that anyone might say about them are so much hot air that can be instantly dismissed with any words or gestures one pleases. The position of master (awakening) is impossible to sustain, however, if one still harbors the belief that the words of the old cases actually convey some profound awakening that is beyond one's ken: any hesitation on this point results in immediate reversion to the position of disciple (delusion).

The second source of frustration that is manifestly reversed by *satori* is the prohibition against the interpretation of koans as symbol systems. All authoritative ("awakened") commentary, as modeled in the discourse records and koan collections, is grounded in the principle that the language of the old cases is figurative and the actions they report are symbolic. Clever commentary may acknowledge and play with the literal meaning of a saying, but it must never fail to interpret and respond to the figurative meaning. By the same token, the comments themselves must be couched in indirect speech. The real sin of "intellectualism" or "discursive thought" does not consist in the act of interpretation, as Ch'an/Zen masters like to pretend, but in the expression of one's interpretation in direct, expository language.

Finally, the *satori* that gives one mastery over koans is traditionally expressed in statements to the effect that one will never again be tricked or sucked in by the words of the patriarchs, which is to say, by the koan genre itself. To be sucked in is to look for the profound meaning hidden in the words, which are taken to be direct manifestations of a patriarch's awakened state of mind. Not to be sucked in is to realize that the words could not possibly embody or convey awakening, and that their imputed profundity is actually a function of the literary frame in which they appear. To fully master the koan genre, in other words, one must realize that it is in fact a literary genre with a distinct set of structures and rules, and furthermore that it is a product of the poetic and philosophical imagination, not simply a historical record of the utterances of awakened people. To say this in so many words, however, breaks the rules of the genre, not to mention the magic spell that keeps the frogs many and the princes few. Hence the preferred indirect locution, "I will never again be tricked by the words of the patriarchs."

These things—the confident seizing of the position of judge vis-à-vis an old case and the expression of one's interpretation in figurative language—are the marks of (and tests for) satori in the traditional "Ch'an/Zen of contemplating phrases." Despite the claims to the "suddenness" of this satori, and its equivalence to the awakening of the Buddha, however, it has been admitted tacitly in some branches of the tradition that it takes a lot of study and practice to master the koan genre. The basic confidence to comment on koans authoritatively may come from an initial experience in which one's "ball of doubt" is suddenly shattered, but expert commentary also requires, at a minimum, familiarity with a broad range of old cases and a thorough grasp of the rhetorical conventions of the genre. In addition, a solid grounding in Mahayana sūtra and commentarial literature and a knowledge of the Confucian classics are highly desirable qualifications. In medieval China, monks who became Ch'an masters sometimes obtained such training in the monasteries where they grew up, but many came from literati families that had provided them with an education in the classics in the hope that they would be able to pass the tests for government service. In medieval Japan, of course, the ability to comment on koans was also predicated on an education in classical Chinese, which was rendered all the more difficult by the fact that it was a foreign language. In modern Japanese Rinzai Zen, it is customary when reading to convert the Chinese of the koans into classical Japanese, but doing that too requires considerable literary expertise and tends to make the meaning of the original even more obscure.

In any case, disciples today are expected to spend a dozen or more years with a master to complete a full course of training in koan commentary. Only when a master is satisfied that a disciple can comment appropriately on a wide range of old cases will he recognize the latter as a dharma heir and give him formal "proof of transmission" (J. *inka shōmei*). Thus, in reality, a lot more than *satori* is required for one to be recognized as a master (J. *shike, rōshi*) in the Rinzai school of Zen at present. The accepted proof of *satori* is a set of literary and rhetorical skills that takes many years to acquire.

NOTES

1. In this chapter I use the English word "koan" to refer in a general way to what are called *kung-an* in Chinese, *kongan* in Korean, and *kōan* in Japanese. When discussing koans in specific geographic or linguistic contexts, however, I use the corresponding Chinese, Korean, or Japanese terms.

2. One of the oldest reliably datable texts in which the practice is evidenced is the *Patriarchs Hall Collection* (*Tsu-t'ang chi*), compiled in 952. For an edition, see Yanagida Seizan, ed., *Sodōshū, Zengaku sōsho*, no. 4 (Kyoto: Chūbun, 1984).

3. Early examples include the discourse records of Yün-men K'uang-chen (864–949) (T 47.544c–576c); Fa-yen Wen-i (885–958) (T 47.588a–594a); Fen-yang Shan-chao (947–1024) (T 47.594–629c); Yang-ch'i Fang-hui (993–1046) (T 47.640a–646a); and Huang-lung Hui-nan (1002–1069) (T 47.629c–636b).

4. For a description of these rites and the monastic setting in which they were held, see T. Griffith Foulk, "Myth, Ritual, and Monastic Practice in Sung Ch'an Buddhism," in Patricia Buckley Ebrey and Peter N. Gregory, eds., *Religion and Society in T'ang and Sung China* (Honolulu: University of Hawaii Press, 1993), pp. 147–208.

5. Among the earliest examples are the discourse records of Hsüeh-tou Chung-hsien (980–1052) (T 47.669a–713b), and Yüan-wu K'e-ch'in (1063–1135) (T 47.713b–810c), two figures best known as the compilers of the *Blue Cliff Collection* (*Pi-yen chi*).

6. T 51.258a. The use of this anecdote as a koan is discussed below.

7. Again, the discourse record of Yüan-wu K'e-ch'in (1063–1135) (T 47.713b–810c) is among the oldest to include such a section.

8. T 51.291c.

9. T 47.547a. My understanding and translation of the expression *hsien-cheng kung-an* (J. *genjōkōan*) is indebted to Urs App, *Master Yunmen: From the Record of the Chan Master "Gate of the Clouds"* (New York: Kodansha, 1994), p. 107.

10. The original text survives today only within the *Blue Cliff Collection* (*Pi-yen chi*), T 48.140a–225c. For a modern Japanese edition see Iriya Yoshitaka, Kajitani Sōnin, and Yanagida Seizan, eds., *Setchō juko. Zen no goroku* 15 (Tokyo: Chikuma, 1981).

11. T 48.195a–b.

12. T 48.144b.

13. For example, case 9 (T 47.149a) and case 21 (T 47.162b).

14. "Thirty blows" appears, for example, in capping phrases in case 1 (T 47.141a), case 4 (T 47.143b), case 25 (T 47.165c), case 26 (T 47.167a), etc. "I strike" appears in capping phrases in case 4 (T 47.144b), case 6 (T.47.146b), case 9 (T 47.149), case 12 (T 47.153a), case 16 (T 47.156c), case 17 (T 47.157b), case 22 (T 47.163c), etc.

15. *Chung-feng ho-shang kuang-lu* 11 (*Shan-fang yeh-hua*); *Shukusatsu daizōkyō* (Tokyo, 1880–85), 0193a–0194a.

16. T 48.292a–299c.

17. Robert E. Buswell, Jr., "The 'Short-cut' Approach of K'an-hua Meditation: The Evolution of a Practical Subitism in Chinese Ch'an Buddhism," in Peter N. Gregory, ed., *Sudden and Gradual: Approaches to Enlightenment in Chinese Thought* (Honolulu: University of Hawaii Press, 1987), p. 347.

18. Buswell, "The 'Short-cut' Approach of K'an-hua Meditation," p. 322.

19. For a detailed discussion of these issues, see T. Griffith Foulk, "Issues in the Field of East Asian Buddhist Studies: An Extended Review of *Sudden and Gradual: Approaches to Enlightenment in Chinese Thought*," *The Journal of the International Association of Buddhist Studies* vol. 16, no. 1 (1993): 141–155.

20. See, for example, Chih-i's *Essential Methods of Seated Dhyāna for Practicing Calm and Insight* (*Hsiu-hsi chih-kuan tso-ch'an fa-yao*), T 46.462b7–16. The text is also known as the *Smaller Calm and Insight* (*Hsiao-chih-kuan*), to distinguish it from Chih-i's massive *Great Calm and Insight* (*Mo-ho chih-kuan*). For a translation of the *Hsiu-hsi chih-kuan tso-ch'an fa-yao*, see Lu K'uan Yü (Charles Luk), *The Secrets of Chinese Meditation* (New York: Samuel Weiser, 1964), pp. 111–160.

21. Hung-chih's comments on "old cases" were the basis for the *Ch'ing-i Record* (*Ch'ing-i lu*) (ZZ 2–22–4.406a–451a), written by Wan-sung Hsing-hsiu (1164–1246), and the *Ts'ung-jung [Hermitage] Record* (*Ts'ung-jung lu*) (T 48.226a–292a, and ZZ 2–22–4.321b–391b), also by Wan-sung Hsing-hsiu.

22. See William M. Bodiford, *Sōtō Zen in Medieval Japan* (Honolulu: University of Hawaii Press, 1993), pp. 143–162.

23. *Sōtōshū gyōji kihan* (Tokyo: Sōtōshū Shūmuchō, 1988), p. 171.

24. T 82.7a–209b.

25. The former exercise is called "work in stillness" (J. *seichū kufū*); the latter is called "work in the midst of activity" (J. *dōchū kufū*).

26. ZZ 2–20–1, 2, 3.
27. ZZ 2–21–5.
28. ZZ 2–22–1.
29. ZZ 2–20–3, 4, 5.
30. T 48.292a–299c. Full title: *Gateless Barrier of the Ch'an Lineage* (*Ch'an-tsung wu-men kuan*).
31. T 48.139–225; ZZ 2–22–2. Full title: *Blue Cliff Record of Ch'an Master Fo-kuo Yüan-wu* (*Fo-kuo yüan-wu ch'an-shih pi-yen lu*).
32. ZZ 2–22–3.
33. T 48.226a–292a; ZZ 2–22–4.321b–391b. Full title: *The Ts'ung-jung [Hermitage] Record: Old Man Wan-sung's Evaluations of Master T'ien-t'ung Chüeh's Verses on Old Cases* (*Wan-sung lao-jen p'ing-ch'ang t'ien-t'ung chüeh ho-shang sung-ku ts'ung-yung lu*).
34. ZZ 2–22–3. Full title: *The Empty Valley Collection: Old Man Lin-chüan's Evaluations of Master T'ou-tzu Ch'ing's Verses on Old Cases* (*Lin-chüan lao-jen p'ing-ch'ang t'ou-tzu ch'ing ho-shang k'ung-ku-chi*).
35. For a modern edition see Iriya, Kajitani, and Yanagida, eds., *Setchō juko*.
36. T 48.194c–195b. My translation is based in part on the Japanese translation and notes found in Iriya, Kajitani, and Yanagida, *Setchō juko*, pp. 181–182.
37. T 48.194c–195b. My translation is indebted in part to the Japanese translation and notes found in Iriya, Kajitani, and Yanagida, *Setchō juko*, pp. 181–182, and to Thomas and J. C. Cleary, trans., *The Blue Cliff Record*, 3 vols. (Boulder Col.: Shambala, 1977), II:406–408.
38. See, for example, the two Japanese translations of the first preface (*piao-wen*) in. Hirata Takashi, *Mumonkan, Zen no goroku* 18 (Tokyo: Chikuma, 1969), pp. 5–6. Hirata's translations indicate that Wu-men first published and subsequently commented on the 48 cases in honor of the emperor's birthday. The original Chinese text of the preface, however, seems to state that Wu-men "published the forty-eight cases . . . that he had commented on" (T 48.292b). A second preface, written by someone other than the author, states that Wu-men had the collection of 48 old cases that he had compiled the previous summer printed a month before the emperor's birthday, which was on the fifth day of the first month of 1229 (T 48.292a–b).
39. T 48.292b.
40. This principle is illustrated, incidentally, in anecdotes where a master rejects a disciple's words or gesture as deluded but uses precisely the same words or gesture to demonstrate the awakened point of view; see, for example, case 3 of the *Gateless Barrier* (Wu-men kuan), "Chü-chih raises a finger" (T 48.293b). It is also dramatized in anecdotes in which a disciple's clever response to a master's question is to forcibly take the latter's seat or grab some other symbol of his authority, such as his staff or whisk; see, for example, the anecdote of Ma-yü in the *Discourse Record of Ch'an Master Lin-chi Hui-chao of Chen-chou* (T 47.504a); also Ruth F. Sasaki, trans., *The Recorded Sayings of Chan Master Lin-chi Hui-chao of Chen Prefecture* (Kyoto: the Institute for Zen Studies, 1975), p. 47.
41. T 48.292c.
42. Asahina Sōgen, "Zen no kōan," in Nagasaka Kaneo, ed., *Zen*, vol. 3 (Tokyo: Yūzankaku, 1931), pp. 1–2.
43. Case 37 of the *Gateless Barrier*: A monk asked Chao-chou, "What is the meaning of the patriarch [Bodhidharma] coming from the west?" Chou said, "The oak tree in the courtyard" (T 48.297c).

44. Case 12 of the *Blue Cliff Collection:* A monk asked Tung-shan, "What is buddha?" Shan said, "Three pounds of flax" (T 48.152c). It also appears as case 18 of the *Gateless Barrier* (T 48.295b).

45. Case 21 of the *Gateless Barrier:* A monk asked Yün-men, "What is buddha?" Men said, "A dried piece of shit" (T 48.295c).

46. T 48.293c.

2

The Antecedents of Encounter Dialogue in Chinese Ch'an Buddhism

JOHN R. MCRAE

The Role of Dialogue in Ch'an

Why are descriptions of Ch'an practice, both medieval and modern, so dominated by dialogues, narratives, and orality? Where other schools of Buddhism may be described in terms of relatively succinct lists of doctrines and practices—four of this, eight of that, a dash of ritual, a measure of self-cultivation—it seems that the only way to describe Ch'an is by a succession of narratives: to explain the Ch'an emphasis on understanding the mind, tell the story of Hui-k'o cutting off his hand to hear the teachings from Bodhidharma; to explain Ch'an's attitude toward seated meditation, recount how Huai-jang prodded Ma-tsu by pretending to grind a tile into a mirror; to explain how true spiritual understanding goes beyond words, describe Huang-po and Lin-chi prancing through their unique combination of fist and shout. This is not just the odd proclivity of medieval Chinese; Ikkyū's sojourn under the Nijō bridge in Kyoto is just one example from medieval Japanese Zen.[1] And one can hardly read a page of twentieth-century writings on Zen without encountering the use of story as explanatory device. The most notable practitioner of this strategy is of course D. T. Suzuki, whose standard approach is effectively to write that "Zen is such-and-such, and let me tell a few stories that exemplify what I mean," with little or no real attempt at explanation. And in virtually all of these stories the direct words are put in the mouths of enlightened Zen masters. Why, in the explanation of Zen Buddhism, is there such an emphasis on dialogues, narratives, and orality?

For many readers it might not be immediately obvious why this is a reasonable and important question, since the equation of Ch'an with stories has all the feeling of a shared cosmology, a worldview that we think of as naturally and obviously true.[2] That is, the orality of Ch'an practice is as much a given as the air we breathe, the water in which fish swim. To think of why Ch'an and the descriptions of Ch'an should emphasize orality is roughly akin to asking why there is gravity. But this is just the point: just as modern physics may thrill at the explanation of that most omnipresent of forces, so should we turn our collective gaze to perhaps the most common feature of Ch'an Buddhism, its peculiar use of language. The first step in this process is to recognize that the use of language, narration, and orality in and about Ch'an is indeed profoundly "peculiar," that we should self-consciously defamiliarize ourselves with the conventional Ch'an rhetoric that teaches us to be comfortable with paradox and absurdity, to accept too easily the bizarre as merely "the way Ch'an masters behave." I would argue there is nothing preordained or obligatory about how Ch'an masters and their students are depicted in Ch'an literature; the first step in understanding Ch'an as a cultural and religious phenomenon is to realize how deeply contingent, how specifically conditioned in historical terms, such descriptions are. To paraphrase Suzuki Rōshi, the founder of the San Francisco Zen Center and one of the most beloved icons of Zen in America, we need an attitude of "beginner's mind" toward the understanding of Ch'an itself.[3]

This chapter will specify and describe the various factors that influenced the appearance of Ch'an encounter dialogue. Given both the limitations of space and the preliminary nature of my own research on the matter, I will not attempt to analyze how all these factors may have operated with each other to yield the results apparent in the historical record; the focus here is on the apprehension of the most likely culprits, not the unraveling of the entire conspiracy.

Before this inquiry can begin, however, we must understand what "encounter dialogue" is and how its appearance may be recognized. This will draw us into two separate areas: first, issues of orality versus written transcription and, second, the historical evolution of Ch'an and the types of texts that may contain the transcriptions of encounter dialogue.

The term "encounter dialogue" renders a Chinese term used by Yanagida Seizan to refer to the questions and responses that take place between Ch'an masters and their students, *chi-yüan wen-ta* (J. *kien-mondō*).[4] As used here, encounter dialogue is a particular type of oral practice in which masters and students interact in certain definable, if unpredictable, ways. Ideally, the goal of the interactions is the enlightenment of the students, and since the teachers cannot simply command their students to achieve this, they use various verbal and physical methods to catalyze the event. Often the exchanges of encounter dialogue can be understood in terms of both the assumption of a spiritual path (*mārga, tao*) and its negation: students ask questions positing a path to liberation, and teachers undercut the implicit assumptions involved so as to indicate the immediate perfection of the here-and-now.[5] There are, of course, also negative examples, in which a student is dismissed for not being a true seeker, or a student or other questioner turns out to be beyond the need for spiritual assistance. And sometimes a student or fellow teacher will catch a master napping, so to speak, using an inadvertent dualism. Even in these cases, there is a palpable sense of lively immediacy in encounter dialogue exchanges. What is not included in the definition of encounter dialogue are questions that seek to elicit explanations about Buddhist doctrine or the spiritual path in general, as well as answers that seek to provide information. Such topics miss the mark because they are only "about" seeking and do not speak to the needs of an actual seeker in the immediate present.

The preceding definition should suffice for the moment, in spite of its incompleteness and lack of detail. More important, it is almost certainly an idealized abstraction which fails to capture the vitality, variegation, and nuance of encounter dialogue itself, and which perhaps incorporates too much of our own projections onto medieval Chinese Ch'an. We can ignore these issues for the present. A pair of significant problems occurs, however, because of the spontaneous fluidity of oral exchange and the fixity of written language. First, what we have to go on are written texts, which contain not encounter dialogue itself but the transcriptions thereof. This is a crucially important distinction. There is good evidence to suggest that something like encounter dialogue was in vogue within Ch'an practitioner communities long before it came to be written down, and that the very act of transcribing it was both difficult and significant.

Second, how do we recognize when a particular exchange is one of encounter dialogue rather than some less inspired form of communication? Are there specific characteristics of written language by which we can differentiate between knowledge- and enlightenment-oriented discussions? Although it would be a difficult, if useful, exercise to enumerate such characteristics, the task is probably easier done than said: we may not be able to explain it well, but we can recognize encounter dialogue when we see it. In addition, I will argue that the transcriptions of encounter dialogue exchanges use a set of literary techniques to generate the impression of oral spontaneity and lively immediacy, and it will be useful to observe the extent to which this literary effect has shielded us from seeing the dramatized nature of the transcriptions. That is, encounter dialogue exchanges do not necessarily record what "really happened," although they are rendered with such lively immediacy that they appear this way to the reader. It is important to recognize literary efficacy for what it is.

When did encounter dialogue emerge in the Ch'an tradition, and when did it first come to be transcribed in written form? The following is a quick summary of the historical evolution of Ch'an, organized into a convenient set of periods or phases.[6]

Proto-Ch'an

Although the historical identity of Bodhidharma is now unrecoverable, a group of meditation specialists celebrated him as their spiritual model from at least the middle of the sixth century. This group of practitioners seems to have wandered to various locations in northern China, carrying with them the *Treatise on the Two Entrances and Four Practices* (*Erh-ju ssu-hsing lun*), a text composed in Bodhidharma's name to which they appended a substantial body of material. Much of this latter material is anonymous or attributed to figures unknown. Also the provenance of this material is also in question, some of it probably deriving from the eighth century. None of the exchanges included seem to fit the definition of encounter dialogue given above, but there are several that might be considered questionable.

East Mountain Community

During the half-century from 624 to 674, Tao-hsin (580–651) and Hung-jen (601–74) stewarded a monastic community at Shuang-feng ("Twin Peaks") or Huang-mei in what is now Hupeh Province. Tao-hsin actually resided on the western peak; the name "East Mountain" is taken from the location of the community during Hung-jen's time, since he was the central figure of this phase of Ch'an. We know that this was a meditation community attended by Buddhists of various inclinations from all over China. We know a certain amount about the teachings of Hung-jen, or at least those attributed to him retrospectively, through a text known as the *Treatise on the Essentials of Cultivating the Mind* (*Hsiu-hsin yao lun*), which was compiled by his students some years or even decades after his death. There also exists a text attributed to Tao-hsin, but this was probably composed even later than the *Treatise on the Essentials of Cultivating the Mind.*[7] In any case, there is nothing resembling encounter dialogue in either of these texts, and the closest we get to any sense of dialogic immediacy are the following statements attributed to Hung-jen.

> My disciples have compiled this treatise [from my oral teachings], so that [the reader] may just use his True Mind to grasp the meaning of its words. . . . If [the teachings contained herein] contradict the Holy Truth, I repent and hope for the eradication [of that transgression]. If they correspond to the Holy Truth, I transfer [any merit that would result from this effort to all] sentient beings. I want everyone to discern their fundamental minds and achieve buddhahood at once. Those who are listening [now] should make effort, so that you can achieve bud-

dhahood in the near future. I now vow to help my followers to cross over [to the other shore of nirvana]. . . .

QUESTION: This treatise [teaches] from beginning to end that manifesting one's own mind represents enlightenment. [However, I] do not know whether this is a teaching of the fruit [of nirvana] or one of practice.

ANSWER: The basic principle of this treatise is the manifestation of the One Vehicle. . . . If I am deceiving you, I will fall into the eighteen hells in the future. I point to heaven and earth in making this vow: If [the teachings contained here] are not true, I will be eaten by tigers and wolves for lifetime after lifetime.

This material from the very end of this text clearly evokes the voice of the compilers, who identify themselves as Hung-jen's students. However, both here and in the repeated injunctions to "make effort" throughout the text, we may be hearing Hung-jen's own voice as well.

Northern School

In 701 Shen-hsiu (606?–706) arrived in Lo-yang at the invitation of Empress Wu, an event that constitutes the debut of Ch'an among China's cultured elite. For the next two or three decades Shen-hsiu and his students maintained an extremely high profile in imperial court society, where they presented themselves as transmitters of the "East Mountain Teaching" of Tao-hsin and especially Hung-jen. (Actually, the East Mountain Teaching period of Ch'an might be extended past Hung-jen's death to include Shen-hsiu's residence at Yü-ch'üan ssu during 675–700, and the Northern school phase may be said to have begun with Hung-jen's student Fa-ju's [638–89] activities on Mount Sung in the 680s.) The Northern school represented a great flourishing of Ch'an activity and writing, and the first examples of the "transmission of the lamp history" (ch'uan-teng shih; J. dentōshi) genre of Ch'an texts appear during this phase. It is in one of these texts that we find the first incontrovertible evidence that something like encounter dialogue was being practiced within the Ch'an community but was not yet being transcribed in full.[8]

Southern School

Beginning in 730 a monk named Shen-hui (684–758) sharply criticized the Northern school in public, promoting instead his own teacher, Hui-neng (638–712), as the Sixth Patriarch in succession from Bodhidharma and the exponent of the true teaching of sudden enlightenment. Shen-hui's career included activity both in the provinces and centered on Lo-yang, and he was an active missionary for the new Ch'an movement as well as a factionalist partisan and fund-raiser. Indeed, research into his life and teachings suggests that his vocation on the ordination platform helped to determine the content and style of his teachings. We have a remarkable collection of texts recording the teachings of Shen-hui, which include a considerable amount of oral exchange, and although he likely had a significant influence on the transformation of Ch'an discourse, none of this oral exchange constitutes encounter dialogue according to the definition given above.[9]

Oxhead School

Although this faction describes itself as a subsidiary lineage deriving from Tao-hsin, its real heyday was the second half of the eighth century. Two texts associated with this school will be discussed below: the *Treatise on the Transcendence of Cognition* (*Chüeh-kuan lun*), an anonymous text from sometime after 750, and the *Platform Sūtra of the Sixth Patriarch* (*Liu-tsu t'an-ching*), the first version of which dates from about 780. In addition, a few brief passages will be presented from biographical sources for members of the Oxhead school, which in spite of its shadowy historical reality had a very creative impact on the evolution of Ch'an rhetoric and doctrine.

Provincial Ch'an

During the second half of the eighth century or the beginning of the ninth, a new style of Ch'an developed in what is now Kiangsi and Hupeh. This chapter will focus on Ma-tsu Tao-i (709–88) and his Hung-chou school.[10] Ma-tsu and his disciples are depicted in Ch'an records as engaging in spontaneous repartee in what is almost a barnyard atmosphere of agricultural labor and other daily tasks, and this style of interaction seems to fit perfectly with the descriptions of Ma-tsu's teachings about the ordinary mind and the activity of the Buddhanature. If so, this would be the earliest incontrovertible appearance of encounter dialogue, and indeed the accounts of Ma-tsu and his first- and second-generation disciples form the core repertoire of encounter dialogue anecdotes in Ch'an literature. There is just one problem: the presentation of Ma-tsu and his disciples in this fashion does not occur in writing until 952, and earlier writings relating to Ma-tsu and his faction present a somewhat different image of his community.

A comment is in order on this crucial incongruity. The first text to transcribe Ch'an encounter dialogue bursts onto the scene in 952, a twenty-fascicle compilation of dialogues and stories associated with all Buddhas and patriarchs down to that time. The is the *Tsu-t'ang chi* or *Anthology of the Patriarchal Hall,* which was compiled by two third-generation students of Hsüeh-feng I-ts'un (822–908) living in Ch'üan-chou (Fukien). The compilers worked during the period of disturbances and political unrest following the collapse of the

T'ang dynasty, but in the peaceful haven of the Five Dynasties regimes of the Min-Yue region of the southeastern coast. One can only imagine that the two compilers were amazed to discover an unexpected characteristic about the Buddhist monks arriving in Ch'üan-chou during this period: so many of them told encounter dialogue anecdotes about their teachers, their teachers' teachers, and their fellow practitioners. Presumably, until this emergency gathering of the Saṃgha or Buddhist community no one had quite paid attention to the prevalence of such anecdotes, which probably circulated in the form of monastic gossip as practitioners traveled from one place to the next. Thus the two compilers must have recognized that so many were celebrating the same types of stories and realized the magnitude of a new development that the participants in this informal, "back room" enterprise had heretofore considered interesting individually.[11]

At the same time as the *Tsu-t'ang chi* compilers discovered the widespread nature of this gossip and its intrinsic religious value, they must also have become aware of its precarious existence: further civil disturbance might do irreversible damage to the Buddhist establishment, and this ephemeral oral genre would be lost. Thus, along with their surprise at recognizing this new and widespread phenomenon of encounter dialogue practice, was their horror at the prospect that, unless it were recorded, the entire body of material and indeed news of the genre itself were liable to disappear with the civil and military unrest of the times.

One of the innovations of encounter dialogue transcriptions as a genre is that they record not only the sage pronouncements of Buddhist teachers, but the sometimes foolish and often formulaic questions of their students as well. I am not certain the *Tsu-t'ang chi* compilers were aware of the significance of their decision to record the students. Perhaps they could see no other course of action, given the quality of the dialogue material they had collected, although from our vantage point this appears to be a shift of major significance in the evolution of Chinese Buddhism.[12] Whatever their reflexive awareness of the processes involved, they established a format in which written re-creations of oral dialogue could be transcribed in a standardized format (i.e., Mandarin) of colloquial speech and thus be widely understandable, without the barriers of regional dialect transcriptions that would have rendered the text inaccessible at various points to all Chinese readers. In Ch'an studies we have tended to disregard the significance of representing oral dialogue in writing, but of course this is not a trivial process. Even though many of the dialogues recorded in the *Tsu-t'ang chi* were between southerners or residents of other regions who must have been spoken in some form other than northern Mandarin, that is the form in which they are represented in the anthology. Thus one or both of two conditions apply to virtually the entire contents of the *Tsu-t'ang chi:* (1) dialogues had to be converted from some non-Mandarin dialect into Mandarin, and (2) literary techniques were used to make the written product appear as if transcribed from actual speech.[13] The first condition suggests that in the very act of transcription some "translation" took place; the second is merely our recognition of the fact that we are dealing with a genre primarily of "text" rather than "event." In other words, rather than thinking of *the Tsu-t'ang chi* anecdotes as sources of information about what happened in Ch'an history in the eighth century, we should approach them as evidence for how Ch'an figures thought and wrote in the tenth.

These speculations and inferences have played an important role in determining the course of the present research, but they will have to await another venue to be examined as they deserve. Here I will merely emphasize the extraordinary nature of the *Tsu-t'ang chi* and the great temporal disconformity between the supposed emergence of encounter dialogue as a religious practice and its transcription into written form.[14] True, this text is one in a series of "transmission of the lamp" history texts, which begins in the second decade of the eighth century, so its basic structure is not unprecedented. However, with the exception of some partial or equivocal examples introduced below, no earlier transcriptions of encounter dialogue now exist, and it is stunning for the first-known representatives of this new genre to appear for the first time in such extensive form. It is striking not only that such a substantial volume of this material appears in one text, but also that the material shows all the signs of a mature oral genre. These are not raw, disconnected stories. Often we find different versions, comments, and changes that imply both a lively discourse community and conscious editorial intervention. Obviously, the Ch'an community as a whole was engaged in a shared dialogue about the spiritual implications of a number of profound statements and telling anecdotes. And of course they were organized into the comprehensive genealogical framework of the "transmission of the lamp history" genre.

Eventually, processes such as these lead to the emergence during the Sung dynasty of the *kung-an chi* (J. *kōan shū*) or precedent anthologies, in which particular snippets of encounter dialogue were collated into series and their most crucial passages were used to form curricula of meditation subjects. This practice is referred to as "viewing the critical phrases," *k'an-hua* (J. *kanna*) and is seen in texts such as the *Blue Cliff Record* (*Pi-yen lu;* J. *Hekiganroku*) and *Gateless Barrier* (*Wu-men kuan;* J. *Mumonkan*). Although it would be convenient to think of these precedent anthologies as a later development, we will see that the tendency of teachers to put questions to their students becomes apparent well before the appearance of the *Tsu-t'ang chi.* Was it possible, in fact, that the very editorial tendencies that led to the emergence of the precedent anthologies were already apparent in the *Tsu-t'ang chi?* We will not be able to address this intriguing question in this chapter, but there is good evidence that early Ch'an teachers posed unsolvable conundrums for their students to contemplate, a practice inescapably similar to the *k'an-hua* style of meditation which came later. Therefore it makes excellent sense to couch these inquiries not only in terms of the oral practice of encounter dialogue, but also so as to include certain encounter-style interrogations by teachers. ("Encounter-style", here of course means inquiries that conform to the style of emphasis on individual spiritual endeavor described for encounter dialogue above.)

An example from the *Tsu-t'ang chi* will be introduced at the end of this chapter. On the basis of the preceding considerations, though, the following questions can be asked of the available evidence on Ch'an prior to the appearance of this important text: Does any of the dialogue material of early Ch'an bear similarities to mature encounter dialogue? Are there any partial transcriptions of encounter dialogue exchanges, especially teachers' questions that might have been used to guide students' meditative endeavors? At the most basic level, what are the criteria we should use for identifying encounter dialogue material or its prototypical variants, if any? And, at the opposite end of the scale, is there any evidence for tendencies similar to those that led to the emergence of *k'an-hua* or "viewing the critical phrase" type of Ch'an, which seems to be a natural progression from the devotion to encounter dialogue per se?

The Eightfold Path to the Emergence of Transcribed Encounter Dialogue and K'an-hua Ch'an

An admittedly sketchy review of the evidence has revealed eight separate characteristics of early Ch'an Buddhism that may have contributed to the eventual emergence of encounter dialogue and *k'an-hua Ch'an*. I have avoided previously discussed doctrinal issues, such as the concepts of *śūnyatā* (emptiness) and *prajñā* (nondiscriminating wisdom), the impact of Mādhyamika dialectic, and other issues. But this by no means limits us to linguistic issues; below I will suggest that Ch'an had to develop a rationale for socially oriented practice prior to the perfection of dialogue techniques. Obviously, none of these characteristics is shared throughout the entire early Ch'an movement, and there are almost certainly others not yet identified.

The Image of the Ch'an Master Responding
Spontaneously to His Students

There are numerous descriptions of early Ch'an teachers having special teaching abilities, which they exercised in an unstructured moment-to-moment manner. Some of the earliest known expressions of this concern Hung-jen, the central figure of the East Mountain Teaching and so-called fifth patriarch. Hung-jen forms the original nucleus of the hagiographical persona of the unlettered sage, and he is described as spending his days in meditation and his nights tending the monastery cattle. As soon as he was appointed successor to

Tao-hsin, the previously silent Hung-jen was immediately able to understand the problems of his students and teach them with a fluid, spontaneous style that combined an appreciation of the Ultimate Truth with complete expertise in the expediencies of religious practice.[15] Fa-ju, who was unique among Hung-jen's students for spending so many years with the master, is described as having unique abilities in his interactions with his students, so that he could remonstrate them strongly without incurring resentment. His anger is described as two empty boats hitting each other in the middle of a lake, which I take to mean having a hollow sound that signified an absence of attachment or resistance. Also to be considered here are Lao-an, or Hui-an (584?–708), and I-fu (661–736) of the Northern school, who were the subjects of various occultish anecdotes.[16]

The primary examples of this religious type are of course Bodhidharma and Hui-neng. The portrayal of Bodhidharma teaching Hui-k'o and others clearly developed over time and has been documented so clearly by Sekiguchi Shindai as to represent something of an index to the entire evolution of the Ch'an ideology. Based solely on date of first occurrence, though, it is significant for our purposes that the famous "pacification of the mind" exchange between Bodhidharma and Hui-k'o (cited in *Wu-men kuan* case 41) does not appear until the publication of the *Tsu-t'ang chi* in 952. In earlier texts, Bodhidharma is represented as teaching Hui-k'o by means of the transmission of the *Lankavatara Sūtra* (in the *Hsü kao-seng chuan* of 667) or *Diamond Sūtra* (the appendix to a text by Shen-hui, who died in 758); even the famous exchange between Bodhidharma and Emperor Wu of the Liang dynasty, a celebrated mismatch that neatly illustrates the difference between the conventional "Chinese mārga model" and the Ch'an "encounter model" of master–disciple exchange, is not recorded for the first time until 758 or shortly thereafter (in the same appendix to Shen-hui's text).[17]

Hui-neng is of course a different story. Here we can safely accept the date of 780 suggested by both Yampolsky and Yanagida as the date of the Tun-huang version of the text, so that later in this chapter we may consider an accretion to the text in at least its two tenth-century versions.[18] That is, we can avoid consideration of the existence of any earlier version of the text and take the *Platform Sūtra* as pertaining to a legendary creation of the late eighth century and beyond, rather than the historical figure who supposedly died in 713. Here we have a figure who responds to situations with remarkable élan and spiritual brilliance, in spite of the fact that he is supposedly quite untutored in the literary arts: he composes insightful poetry (the "mind verse" [*hsin-chieh*] offered in response to "Shen-hsiu's" verse), makes mysteriously profound pronouncements (informing two monks that their minds were in motion, not the flag and wind about which they were arguing), and poses miraculous challenges to individual seekers (showing the pursuing Hui-ming that he could not lift the robe, let alone take it back to Huang-mei).[19] In all these cases Hui-neng is represented as enlightened, not by any doctrine he pronounces or essay he produces, but rather in his interactions with the figures around him.

"Questions about Things" in the Northern School

How did early Ch'an teachers interact with their students? The hagiographical images of Hung-jen and Hui-neng are not our only clues: we do not know how the students responded, but at least we have some evidence for the types of questions early Ch'an masters placed before them. The *Leng-ch'ieh shih-tzu chi* (*Records of the Masters and Disciples of the Lankāvatāra*), a transmission of the lamp history written in the second decade of the eighth century, contains an intriguing set of rhetorical questions and short doctrinal admonitions, which it refers to as "questions about things" (literally, "pointing at things and asking the meanings," *chih-shih wen-i*).[20] Such questions and admonitions are attributed to several of the early masters, as is shown in the following examples:

(Gunabhadra)

When [Gunabhadra] was imparting wisdom to others, before he had even begun to preach the Dharma, he would assess [his listeners' understanding of physical] things by pointing at a leaf and [asking]: "What is that?"

> He would also say: "Can you enter into a [water] pitcher or enter into a pillar? Can you enter into a fiery oven? Can a stick [from up on the] mountain preach the Dharma?"
> He would also say: "Does your body enter [into the pitcher, etc.,] or does your mind enter?"
> He would also say: "There is a pitcher inside the building, but is there another pitcher outside the building? Is there water inside the pitcher, or is there a pitcher inside the water? Or is there even a pitcher within every single drop of water under heaven?"
> He would also say: "A leaf can preach the Dharma; a pitcher can preach the Dharma; a pillar can preach the Dharma; a building can preach the Dharma; and earth, water, fire, and wind can all preach the Dharma. How is it that mud, wood, tiles, and rocks can also preach the Dharma?"

(Bodhidharma)

The Great Master [Bodhidharma] also pointed at things and inquired of their meaning, simply pointing at a thing and calling out: "What is that?" He asked about a number of things, switching their names about and asking about them [again] differently.

He would also say: "Clouds and mists in the sky are never able to defile space. However, they can shade space [so that the sun] cannot become bright and pure. . . ."

(Hung-jen)

The Great Master [Hung-jen] said: "There is a single little house filled with crap and weeds and dirt—what is it? . . ."

> He also said: "If you sweep out all the crap and weeds and dirt and clean it all up so there is not a single thing left inside, then what is it?"
> Also, when he saw someone light a lamp or perform any ordinary activity, he would always say: "Is this person dreaming or under a spell?"
> Or he would say: "Not making and not doing, these things are all the great *parinirvāna*."
> He also said: "When you are actually sitting in meditation inside the monastery, is there another of you sitting in meditation in the forest? Can all the mud, wood, tiles, and rocks also sit in meditation? Can mud, wood, tiles, and rocks also see forms and hear sounds, or put on robes and carry a begging bowl?"

(Shen-hsiu)

[Shen-hsiu] also said: "Is this a mind that exists? What kind of mind is the mind?"

> He also said: "When you see form, does form exist? What kind of form is form?"
> He also said: "You hear the sound of a bell that is struck. Does [the sound] exist when [the bell] is struck? Before it is struck? What kind of sound is sound?" He also said: "Does the sound of a bell that is struck only exist within the monastery, or does the bell's sound also exist [throughout] the universe [in all the] ten directions?"
> Also, seeing a bird fly by, he asked: "What is that?"
> He also said: "Can you sit in meditation on the tip of a tree's hanging branch?"
> He also said: "The *Nirvāna Sūtra* says: 'The Bodhisattva with the Limitless Body came from the East.' If the bodhisattva's body was limitless in size, how could he have come from the East? Why did he not come from the West, South, or North? Or is this impossible?"[21]

There are a number of observations to be made about these interrogatives, even if we cannot develop them all fully here. First, to me the image of Bodhidharma asking about the things around him has the ring of believability, but only because I know what it is like to move into a new language community and struggle to communicate with those around me. By the rule of dissimilarity used in biblical interpretation,[22] I wonder if this may be a detail deriving from the shared life experiences of foreign missionaries that was so trivial as to escape polemical alteration. I can easily imagine Bodhidharma struggling with language and yet at the same time transforming some of his questions from simple linguistic issues into more profound religious and philosophical queries.

Second, although I have not made an extensive search, my readings over the past decade and occasional discussions with specialists in Indian Buddhism have not shown any specific antecedents to this type of inquiry in any earlier Buddhist context. One of course might draw comparisons with the questions found in *ch'ing-t'an* or "pure conversation" Taoist-oriented literature of the third and fourth centuries, but I have not found this line of investigation to be fruitful.[23]

Third, this style of interrogation probably had some general currency at the beginning of the eighth century among Northern school figures. In the strictest sense, of course, all we can say is that it was known to the compiler of the text, a successor to Shen-hsiu named Ching-chüeh (683–ca. 750). The attribution of "questions about things" is clearly unreliable with regard to Gunabhadra, who is included in the Ch'an lineage solely in this text and without any known basis in fact. In spite of my speculative comment just above, it is not fair to assert on the basis of this text that such questions were actually known to Bodhidharma, either.

Fourth, the terminology used here is clearly based on a Chinese dictionary usage, in which *chih-shih* or to "indicate [a] thing" refers to characters whose shape immediately invokes the abstract meaning involved, such as the numbers one and two and the directions up and down.[24]

Fifth, the logical similarity and content of several of the questions implies a consistent intellectual perspective, which seems not thoroughly undercut by their paradoxical nature. The doctrinal implications of these questions would certainly merit further investigation.

Sekiguchi has already suggested that these "questions about things" resemble the kung-ans of later Ch'an. Although his analysis was superficial and unconvincing to the extent that it inspired unusually harsh criticism from Yanagida, I believe that his observation deserves reconsideration.[25] Obviously we cannot jump immediately from these questions to the kōan anthologies of the eleventh century and beyond, but instead need to take into account the intervening efflorescence of encounter dialogue. However, it certainly is reasonable to infer that these represent something like the same sort of questions posed by masters to students in that later genre. In contrast to encounter dialogue, here we have only one side, the masters' questions; in contrast to kung-an anthologies, there is no context or literary structure to explain how such questions were intended.

The "Ch'an" Style of Explanation in Eighth-Century Sources

In addition to these "questions about things," there are various hints in texts from this period and slightly later of what seems like the idiosyncratically "Ch'an" style of discourse glorified in the later tradition. It is not always clear, to be sure, that one unified style of explanation is indicated, but the references are enough to suggest that something interesting is being reported though not yet recorded in full.

The central figure in this respect is Shen-hsiu, already introduced, who had a special role as "Ch'an commentator" on the meaning of the sūtras as translated by Sikananda during the first few years of the eighth century. One longs to know what the "Ch'an meaning" of any scriptural term might be, but no doubt Shen-hsiu's style of interpretation was largely identical to the "contemplative analysis" found in his *Treatise on the Contemplation of the Mind* (*Kuanhsin lun*) and related works. Here Shen-hsiu represents all of Buddhism as metagogy for the "contemplation of the mind" (*k'an-hsin*), declaring that the Buddha was simply not interested in the nominal subject matter of some of the sūtras but instead gave them an esoteric meaning. Thus rather than actually describing how monks should bathe themselves, the Buddha was actually building an extended metaphor for meditation, with the heat of the fire standing for the power of wisdom, the cleansing effect of the water the efficacy of mental concentration, and so on. Rather than describing actual votive lamps to be used for devotion, the Buddha described the "truly enlightened mind," in which the body was metaphorically the lamp's stand, the mind the lamp's dish, and faith its wick, and the like. Shen-hsiu writes, "If one constantly burns such a lamp of true enlightenment, its illumination will destroy all the darkness of ignorance and stupidity."[26]

Another clue for the prevalence of unconventional "Ch'an-style" dialogue occurs in the epitaph for the Northern school figure I-fu by Yen T'ing-chih, in which the author recounts that he and Tu Yü, another of I-fu's epigraphers, collected the departed master's sayings as they were remembered by his students. The two men were apparently unable to write down all of those sayings, presumably because of their great number. Even though they recognized the value of these sayings, neither of their epitaphs for I-fu contains anything that might correspond to the subject of such a search.[27] Although the format of disciples collecting a master's sayings is known from the earliest days of Ch'an (witness the material associated with Bodhidharma's *Treatise on the Two Entrances and Four Practices* and the *Treatise on the Essentials of Cultivating the Mind,* the latter of which declares explicitly that it was compiled by Hung-jen's students), the manner of the statements by Yen T'ing-chih and Tu Yü implies that a special kind of pronouncement was involved.

As time went on, the epitaphs of members of the Northern school and other figures important in the development of Ch'an began to include precisely this sort of material. For example, note the following exchange and commentary from the epitaph for P'u-chi's (651–739) student Fa-yün (d. 766):

"Has the Buddha's teaching been transmitted to you?"

"I have a sandalwood image [of the Buddha] to which I pay reverence." [This reply was] profound yet brief, and those listening felt chills of loneliness. The day after [the questioner, a prominent official] left, Fa-yün died without illness while sitting cross-legged, on his chair.[28]

After all the hyperbole about Shen-hsiu's being equivalent to a buddha and P'u-chi's being the religious teacher of the universe (themes stated in documents from the first half of the eighth century as part of the Northern school's campaign for public recognition), it is perfectly natural to find a slightly later master deflating the idea of the transmission altogether.

The epitaph for Hui-chen (673–751), who was more closely affiliated with the T'ien-t'ai and Vinaya schools than with Ch'an, includes a more explicit reference to and several examples of what seems like encounter dialogue:

When people do not understand, I use the Ch'an [style of] teaching [ch'an-shuo].

QUESTION: Are not the teachings of the Southern and Northern [schools] different?

ANSWER: Outside the gates of both houses is a road to everlasting peace.

QUESTION: Do the results of religious practice vary according to the extent [of realization]?

ANSWER: When a drop of water falls from the cliff, it knows the morning sea.

QUESTION: How can one who is without faith achieve self-motivation [in spiritual endeavor]?

ANSWER: When the baby's throat is closed [i.e., when choking], the mother yells to frighten it [loose]. Great compassion is unconditioned, but it can also cause [a student to] whimper.[29]

A confirmed skeptic might suggest that Hui-chen is merely answering in easily understood metaphors rather than in some really new "Ch'an [style of] teaching." If this is the case, then we must infer that a new type of metaphorical or metagogic usage became the vogue in Ch'an Buddhism during the second half of the eighth century, for such usage is also apparent in the biographies of Fa-ch'in (714–92) and Hsüan-lang (673–754), well-known representatives of the Oxhead and T'ien-t'ai schools, respectively.[30] The *Sung kao-seng chuan*

[*Biographies of Eminent Monks (Compiled During the) Sung*] and *Ching-te ch'uan-teng lu* [*Records of the Transmission of the Lamp (Compiled During the) Ching-te (Era, or 1004)*] contain several examples of encounter dialogue involving Northern school figures, although of course these examples may be later fabrications.[31] The practice of this prototypical encounter dialogue may have had a much wider currency than the extant body of literature suggests, and the members of the Northern school may have been only the first to legitimize its use within the Ch'an tradition.

Doctrinal Bases for the Social Orientation of Early Ch'an Practice

What were early Ch'an practitioners doing when using paradoxical interrogation, dialogue, and interactive training methods? Since they do not tell us explicitly,[32] our only recourse is to turn to the voluminous writings they did bequeath to us and explore them for clues, even though there are obvious methodological problems in this approach requiring interpretive leaps and projections.

One of the most apparent features of the *Treatise on the Two Entrances and Four Practices* attributed from quite early on is its bimodal structure, which consists of one abstract and one active "entrance" or "access" to accomplishment of the Dharma. Although there are several different ways in which one can read this text, one of the most appropriate and useful readings is to take it as both introvertive and extrovertive. That is, the "entrance of principle" refers to interior cultivation, mental practice undertaken deep within the individual's psyche, and the "entrance of practice" refers to practice undertaken actively and in interaction with the world.

Other than dialogue per se, the other important question to be considered here is the extent to which the doctrinal formulations of the Northern school's *Five Expedient Means* (*Wu fang-pien*) may have provided justification for the emergence of encounter dialogue. Here I am thinking of encounter dialogue not so much as an oral practice, but in the more general category of a social practice. That is, is there anything in the *Five Expedient Means* that provides justification for the outward, social dimension of Ch'an religious practice?

The answer to this question is of course affirmative, the key passage being the following (from section J):

Bodhisattvas know the fundamental motionlessness of the six senses, their internal illumination being distinct and external functions autonomous. This is the true and constant motionlessness of the Mahayana.

[QUESTION]: What do "internal illumination being distinct" and "external functions autonomous" mean?

ANSWER: Fundamental wisdom [*ken-pen chih*] is "internal illumination being distinct." Successive wisdom [*hou-te chih*] is "external functions autonomous."

[QUESTION]: What are fundamental wisdom and successive wisdom?

ANSWER: Because one first realizes the characteristic of the transcendence of the body and mind, this is fundamental wisdom. The autonomous [quality of] knowing and perception and the nondefilement [associated with the enlightened state] are successive wisdom. The first realization of the fundamental. . . . if realization [of the transcendence of body and mind] were not first, then knowing and perception would be completely defiled. Know clearly that the autonomous [spontaneity of] knowing and perception is attained after that realization and is called successive wisdom.

When the mind does not activate on the basis of the eye's perception of form, this is fundamental wisdom. The autonomous [spontaneity of] perception is successive wisdom. When the mind does not activate on the basis of the ear's hearing of sounds, this is fundamental wisdom. The autonomous [spontaneity of] hearing is successive wisdom. The nose, tongue, body, and consciousness are also the same. With the fundamental and successive [wisdoms], the locations [*ch'u*] are distinct, the locations are emancipated. The senses do not activate, and the realizations are pure. When successive moments of mental [existence] are nonactivating, the senses are sagely [*sheng*].

Now, the terms "fundamental wisdom" (*mula-jñāna*) and "successive wisdom" (*prstha-labdha-jñāna*) are well known from the *Abhidharmakośa* and many subsequent texts, but they do not occur with any emphasis in the *Lotus Sūtra*, which is supposed to be the basis of this section of the *Five Expedient Means*.[33] Since this and other examples of Northern school literature revel in playing with and immediately discarding doctrinal formulations, there is little reason to speculate on why this particular pair of terms should occur here. The important issue is the congruence between this and other dyads used.

Scattered throughout the same section of the *Five Expedient Means* we find various statements involving this dyad:

If the mind does not activate, the mind is suchlike. If form does not activate, form is suchlike. Since the mind is suchlike the mind is emancipated. Since form is suchlike form is emancipated. Since mind and form both transcend [thoughts], there is not a single thing.[34]

The transcendence of mind is enlightenment of self, with no dependence (*yüan*) on the five senses. The transcendence of form is enlightenment of others, with no dependence on the five types of sensory data. The transcendence of both mind and form is to have one's practice of enlightenment perfect and complete [*chüeh-hsing yüan-man*] and is equivalent to the universally "same" *dharmakāya* of a Tathāgata.[35]

The transcendence of thought is the essence, and the perceptive faculties [*chian-wen jue-chih*] are the function. Serenity [*chi*] is the essence, and illumination [*chao*] is the function. "Serene but always functioning; functioning but always serene." Serene but always functioning—this is the absolute [*li*] corresponding to phenomena [*shih*]. Functioning but always serene—this is phenomena corresponding to the absolute. Serene yet always functioning—this is form corresponding to emptiness. Functioning yet always serene—this is emptiness corresponding to form. . . .

Serenity is unfolding; illumination is constriction (literally, "rolling up"). Unfolded, it expands throughout the *dharmadhātu*. Constricted, it is incorporated in the tip of a hair. Its expression [outward] and incorporation [inward] distinct, the divine function is autonomous.[36]

The meaning of enlightenment is that the essence of the mind transcends thoughts. Transcending the characteristic of craving, it is equivalent to the realm of space, which pervades everywhere. This is called enlightenment of self. Transcending the characteristic of anger, it is equivalent to the realm of space, which pervades everywhere. This is called enlightenment of others.

Transcending the characteristic of stupidity, it is equivalent to the realm of space, which pervades everywhere. The single characteristic of the *dharmadhātu* is the universally "same" *dharmakāya* of the Tathāgata. This is called complete enlightenment.[37]

These examples, which could easily be supplemented from later sections of the *Five Expedient Means* and other works, should suffice to reveal the basic Northern school concern for describing not only how one understands the abstract truth of the Buddha dharma, but also how one puts it into practice on behalf of sentient beings. This bimodal structure is certainly indebted to the *Treatise on the Two Entrances and Four Practices* attributed to Bodhidharma and may be taken as a basic characteristic of early Ch'an Buddhism.

It would be more convenient for our purposes, I suppose, if this bimodal structure explicitly involved masters and students, and if it stated clearly that one was first to become enlightened oneself and then inspire the enlightenment of others. Instead, as with all Ch'an literature at this time (not to mention the texts of other schools), the aspiring student is still invisible, and the recipients of the enlightened master's grace from the moment of successive wisdom onward are anonymous sentient beings. However, the importance of activity in the social or interpersonal realm (which is implicitly seen as temporarily subsequent but equal in value terms) is firmly established with these formulations.

The Use of Ritualized Dialogue between Teachers and Students

The mechanical formulations given above are not the only interesting feature of the *Five Expedient Means*. The text must have been something like a set of teacher's notes for holding initiation and training meetings according to an approved Northern school program, in which context it includes the following examples of ritualized dialogue. The first example is from the beginning of the text, just after the initiates are led responsively through a declaration of certain basic vows:

> THE PRECEPTOR ASKS: What do you see [literally, what thing do you see]?
>
> THE DISCIPLE(S) ANSWER: I do not see a single thing.
>
> PRECEPTOR: Viewing purity, view minutely. Use the eye of the Pure Mind to view afar without limit, without restriction. View without obstruction.
>
> THE PRECEPTOR ASKS: What do you see?
>
> ANSWER: I do not see a single thing.

D. View afar to the front, not residing in the myriad sensory realms, holding the body upright and just illuminating, making the true essence of reality distinct and clear.

> View afar to the rear . . . to both sides . . . facing upwards . . . facing downwards . . . in the ten directions all at once . . . energetically during unrest . . . minutely during calm . . . identically whether walking or standing still . . . identically whether sitting or lying down, not residing in the myriad sensory realms, holding the body upright and just illuminating, making the true essence of reality distinct and clear.

> E. QUESTION: When viewing, what things do you view?
>
> [ANSWER]: Viewing, viewing, no thing is viewed.
>
> [QUESTION]: Who views?
>
> [ANSWER]: The enlightened mind [chüeh-hsin] views.

Penetratingly viewing the realms of the ten directions, in purity there is not a single thing. Constantly viewing and in accord with the locus of nonbeing [wu-so], this is to be equivalent to a buddha. Viewing with expansive openness, one views without fixation. Peaceful and vast without limit, its untaintedness is the path of bodhi [p'u-t'i lu]. The mind serene and enlightenment distinct, the body's serenity is the bodhi tree [p'u-t'i shu]. The four tempters have no place of entry, so one's great enlightenment is perfect and complete, transcending perceptual subject and object.[38]

The second example is in the second section, which is nominally based on the *Lotus Sūtra:*

A. The preceptor strikes the wooden [signal-board] and asks: Do you hear the sound?

[ANSWER]: We hear.

[QUESTION]: What is this "hearing" like?

[ANSWER]: Hearing is motionless.

[QUESTION]: What is the transcendence of thoughts?

[ANSWER]: The transcendence of thoughts is motionless.

This motionlessness is to develop the expedient means of sagacity [hui fang-pien] out of meditation [ting]. This is to open the gate of sagacity. Hearing is sagacity. This expedient means cannot only develop sagacity, but also make one's meditation correct. [To achieve this motionlessness] is to open the gate of wisdom, to attain wisdom [chih]. This is called the opening of the gates of wisdom and sagacity.[39]

Here we find transcribed segments of ritual dialogue from a doctrinally specific Northern school context. When looking for antecedents for transcribed dialogues in early Ch'an texts, we should not overlook this type of material. That is, to what extent did encounter dialogue grow out of a monastic training and ritual context in which students responded to monkish ritual celebrants in thoroughly formalized manners? Elsewhere in the *Five Expedient Means* are other portions of this catechistic ritual, which demonstrate the same form of scripted recitation-and-response pattern. This material skillfully weaves Northern school doctrine into an intriguing mix of ritualized initiation, teaching catechism, and guided meditation practice. I have already discussed the relevance of some of the phraseology here for our understanding of Northern school doctrine and the construction of the *Platform Sūtra;*[40] other aspects of this material that deserve discussion include its bearing on the indebtedness of early Ch'an to T'ien-t'ai formulations.[41] Here I will focus on the following possible reading of the implications of this material: that Ch'an encounter dialogue derived not (or perhaps not solely) out of spontaneous oral exchanges but rather (perhaps only in part) out of ritualized exchanges. Given arguments already made by Griffith Foulk and Robert Sharf that spontaneity is merely "inscribed" within the heavily ritualized context of Sung dynasty Ch'an, this interpretation allows us to wipe out the distinction between the "classical" age of T'ang dynasty Ch'an, when encounter dialogue was spontaneous, and the subsequent ritualization of dialogue within Sung dynasty Ch'an. At the very least, the examples of transcribed dialogue above should break us loose from the preconception of "event" and suggest we look elsewhere for the origins of encounter dialogue as "text." I will come back to these points later.

The Widespread Use of Anecdote and Dialogue in Teaching

One factor that should not be overlooked is the widespread tendency within the developing Ch'an movement to use anecdotal material and dialogue transcriptions for teaching purposes. One can almost chart the ever-increasing anecdotal content of Ch'an literature. One interesting example is a story about an ignorant couple brewing rice wine, who have never seen a mirror and mistake their partners' reflections on the surface of the fermenting liquid for secret lovers; the moral drawn is that foolish ordinary people do not recognize that the entire world is a reflection of their own minds.[42] The growth of the Bodhidharma legend over time is once again relevant here but need not be discussed again. Then again, the most important individual contributor to this dimension of Ch'an was of course Shen-hui.

We do not have to accept the entirety of Hu Shih's characterization of Shen-hui's historical importance—which clearly projects Hu's own twentieth-century concerns onto his medieval subject—to recognize that Shen-hui transformed Chinese Ch'an. Whatever the doctrinal significance of Shen-hui's teaching of sudden enlightenment, whatever the factionalist impact of his outspoken criticism of the Northern school, one of the ways in which he changed Ch'an was in the extreme caution he imparted to his colleagues about describing their doctrinal formulations. I have labeled this impact Shen-hui's standard of "rhetorical purity," which mitigated against any expression using dualistic or gradualistic formats. That is, Shen-hui's vigorous attack on the dualism and gradualism of Northern school teachings had a chilling effect on other teachers.

Simultaneously, Shen-hui was a master storyteller, as he was a master public speaker. Many of the most famous stories of Ch'an appear first in the transcriptions of his sermons and lectures: Bodhidharma and Emperor Wu, Bodhidharma and Hui-k'o, but not, curiously enough, many stories about his own teacher Hui-neng. There is also a substantial amount of transcribed dialogue within the Shen-hui corpus, either between Shen-hui and his designated Northern school stand-in or between him and various famous laymen of his day. There is a palpable sense of fictional creativity here, such that some of the dialogues with famous laymen may have been made up out of whole cloth. On the other hand, the dialogues do not quite conform to our expectations of encounter dialogue: they are too clearly structured, too much of a logical pattern, to represent spontaneous exchanges.

The Fabrication of Enlightenment Narratives

Another tendency of early Ch'an writings is the tendency to compose fictionalized accounts of enlightenment experiences. This section will discuss the other examples of this tendency before we turn, in the next section, to the case of Hui-neng.

One of the best-known texts of early Ch'an is the *Treatise on the Transcendence of Cognition* of the Oxhead school, whose members were known for literary creativity. This text describes an imaginary dialogue between two hypothetical characters, Professor Enlightenment (*ju-li hsien-sheng*) and the student Conditionality (*yüan-ch'i*), of which the following is only the barest skeleton:

Professor Enlightenment was silent and said nothing. Conditionality then arose suddenly and asked Professor Enlightenment: "What is the mind? What is it to pacify the mind [*an-hsin*]?" [The master] answered: "You should not posit a mind, nor should you attempt to pacify it—this is called 'pacified.' "

Question: "If there is no mind, how can one cultivate enlightenment [*tao*]?" Answer: "Enlightenment is not a thought of the mind, so how could it occur in the mind?" Question: "If it is not thought of by the mind, how should it be thought of?" Answer: "If there are thoughts then there is mind, and for there to be mind is contrary to enlightenment. If there is no thought [*wu-nien*] then there is no mind [*wu-hsin*], and for there to be no mind is true enlightenment." . . . Question: "What 'things' are there in no-mind?" Answer: "No-mind is without 'things.' The absence of things is the Naturally True. The Naturally True is the Great Enlightenment [*ta-tao*]." . . .

Question: "What should I do?" Answer: "You should do nothing." Question: "I understand this teaching now even less than before." Answer: "There truly is no understanding of the Dharma. Do not seek to understand it." . . . Question: "Who teaches these words?" Answer: "It is as I have been asked." Question: "What does it mean to say that it is as you have been asked?" Answer: "If you contemplate [your own] questions, the answers will be understood [thereby] as well."

At this, Conditionality was silent and he thought everything through once again. Professor Enlightenment asked: "Why do you not say anything?" Conditionality answered: "I do not perceive even the most minute bit of anything that can be explained." At this point Professor Enlightenment said to Conditionality: "You would appear to have now perceived the True Principle."

Conditionality asked: "Why [do you say] 'would appear to have perceived' and not that I 'correctly perceived' [the True Principle]?" Enlightenment answered: "What you have now perceived is the nonexistence of all dharmas. This is like the non-Buddhists who study how to make themselves invisible but cannot destroy their shadow and footprints." Conditionality asked: "How can one destroy both form and shadow?" Enlightenment answered: "Being fundamentally without mind and its sensory realms, you must not willfully generate the ascriptive view [or, 'perception'] of impermanence."

[The following is from the end of the text.]

Question: "If one becomes [a Tathāgata] without transformation and in one's own body, how could it be called difficult?" Answer: "Willfully activating [*ch'i*] the mind is easy; extinguishing the mind is difficult. It is easy to affirm the body, but difficult to negate it. It is easy to act, but difficult to be without action. Therefore, understand that the mysterious achievement is difficult to attain, it is difficult to gain union with the Wondrous Principle. Motionless is the True, which the three [lesser vehicles] only rarely attain." [?]

At this Conditionality gave a long sigh, his voice filling the ten directions. Suddenly, soundlessly, he experienced a great expansive enlightenment. The mysterious brilliance of his pure wisdom [was revealed] no doubt in its counterillumination. For the first time he realized the extreme difficulty of spiritual training and that he had been uselessly beset with illusory worries. He then sighed aloud: "Excellent! Just as you have taught without teaching, so have I heard without hearing."[43]

I would not suggest that the preceding constitutes "encounter dialogue," because it is entirely too well structured and logical. This critique is also applicable to two texts that share a single rhetorical structure: the *Treatise on the Principle* and *Essential Determination*.[44] In each case, a single proponent of Buddhist spiritual cultivation is depicted as both enlightened Ch'an master and sincere lay seeker. That is, the same individual is depicted as both asking and answering questions concerning spiritual cultivation in his identities as monk and layman. The openings of these texts are amusing: after the dual identity of the speaker as both teacher and student is described, when the first question is posed by the student the teacher praises it as the most profound inquiry he's ever received in all his years as a monk!

The narratives found in the *Treatise on the Transcendence of Cognition, Treatise on the True Principle,* and *Essential Determination* are manifestly fictional, but it is reasonable to suspect that they were intended to model ideal teacher–student interactions and may in fact have resembled to some degree actual exchanges that took place between meditation masters and practitioners. The point here is not to speculate on the precise nature of such events, but to note that these texts represent an innovative use of text in the Ch'an tradition. The same may be said for the *Platform Sūtra,* of course. My study on the Northern school showed how the events described in this text could not have taken place, and the central point here is that the very fictionality of the Hui-neng story is of prime importance.[45]

The Genealogical Structure of Ch'an Dialogue

One other point about the example of Hui-neng—based not on the fictionality of the story per se but rather on the character of the protagonist—is that there is a profound similarity between the story of Hui-neng and that of the dragon king's daughter in the *Lotus Sūtra:* their total lack of the conventional accoutrements of spiritually gifted persons. On the one hand, she was female, nonhuman (although of high nonhuman birth), and severely underage, yet in a single moment she was able to transform herself into a male, pass through all the trials and tribulations expected of bodhisattva practitioners, and achieve perfect enlightenment. On the other hand, he was illiterate, from the very edge of civilization in the far south, lowborn (although his grandfather had been an official, albeit a banished one), and not even a monk, yet he had the intuitive genius to be selected as the Sixth Patriarch.

It is in the story of Hui-neng that we find the last key to the emergence of encounter dialogue transcriptions. The problem was not whether or not such dialogues were actually occurring between masters and students, and if so how and to what extent. Rather, the problem was the reluctance to transcribe what may have been an everyday occurrence in the back rooms of China's monastic compounds. There had to be some epistemic change that made it acceptable to transcribe not only the words of the gifted and famous master but those of the student as well. The example of Hui-neng may have been a significant factor in incurring this epistemic change, but the time was still not at hand.

It is generally believed that encounter dialogue first flourished in the faction of Ma-tsu Tao-i, which is known as the Hung-chou school. As indicated earlier, Ma-tsu and his disciples are depicted in Ch'an records as engaging in spontaneous repartee in an atmosphere of agricultural labor and other daily tasks. There are enough dialogues concerning a large enough number of figures that it would seem heresy to suggest that nothing of the sort "really" happened, that the encounters were all fictional. I will certainly not go that far here, but I cannot avoid noticing a certain problem, already introduced: whereas the encounters involving Ma-tsu and his disciples are supposed to have taken place in the latter part of the eighth century and the beginning of the ninth, they are not found in transcribed form until the year 952 with the appearance of the *Tsu-t'ang chi.*

We do have a much earlier text from the Hung-chou school, the *Pao-lin chuan* or *Transmission of Pao-lin [Monastery]*. Only parts of this text are extant, and scholars have generally assumed that the lost portions (which were devoted at least in part to Ma-tsu and his immediate disciples) must have been incorporated into, and thus were not substantially different from, the corresponding sections of the *Tsu-t'ang chi*. Unfortunately, I cannot accept this assumption, for the simple reason that the extant portions of the *Pao-lin chuan* do not contain encounter dialogue transcriptions. There is a great deal of dialogue transcribed in this text, virtually all of which is fictionalized representation of enlightened masters. However, none of this dialogue has the same lively feel as the exchanges of the *Tsu-t'ang chi.*

There is one feature of the *Pao-lin chuan,* though, that I believe to be of crucial importance: the rigid narrative structure of the text. This text describes the lives, and to a lesser extent the teachings, of the Ch'an patriarchs from Śākyamuni through Bodhidharma to Ma-tsu, and in each case the patriarch in question is described twice, first as a gifted student discovered by the current patriarch and second as a fully vested patriarch out searching for his own successor. It is curious that in no case (at least up to the account of Hui-k'o) is the enlightenment experience of the patriarch described; we have only the "before" and "after" images, not any reference to what should be the most crucial event in the process. For the present purposes, though, we may note the great significance placed on the patriarchs as students. This text creates a structural parity between the student as incipient patriarch and the patriarch as realized student.

I suspect that this structural parity played a role in making the transcription of encounter dialogue possible, that is, in making the transcription of both sides of the exchanges possible. However, it was not possible yet, and the reluctance of this text to describe enlightenment experiences may imply that it was used for popular teaching in the spread of Buddhism throughout the newly developing areas of Chiang-hsi, rather than for training within the context of the monastic meditation hall.

Final Ruminations

Because of the preliminary nature of this research, I will not add an integrated set of conclusions. Instead, one brief passage from the *Tsu-t'ang chi* will serve to indicate some of the considerations that can be applied to examples of Ch'an encounter dialogue transcription. The following is the famous story of Ma-tsu's first encounter with Huai-jang:

> Reverend Ma was sitting in a spot, and Reverend Jang took a tile and sat on the rock facing him, rubbing it. Master Ma asked, "What are you doing?" Master [Huai-jang] said, "I'm rubbing the tile to make a mirror." Master Ma said, "How can you make a mirror by rubbing a tile?" Master [Huai-jang] said, "If I can't make a mirror by rubbing a tile, how can you achieve buddhahood by sitting in meditation?"[46]

Did this really "happen"? There is obviously no way to prove that it did not, but since the event was first reported some two centuries after it was supposed to have taken place, we are certainly entitled to substantial skepticism.

More important than journalistic accuracy, though, is how the anecdote was recorded, edited, augmented, and transmitted through both oral and written media. First, we can clearly hear echoes of Vimalakīrti scolding Śāriputra for sitting in meditation in the forest in the *Vimalakīrti Sūtra*. This famous precedent has been recast in a contemporary mode by means of implicit reference to the "mind-verses" of the *Platform Sūtra*, which of course involve polishing a mirror. The material that immediately follows on the dialogue with Ma-tsu in the *Tsu-t'ang chi* contains other references to the mirror, which implies some sort of unified editorial inclination. Second, the reader should notice the primitive character of this rendition of the story: neither location nor time is specified—all we have is the simple nucleus of the words, with no effort to establish the context. Later versions of the story will add suitable detail, but it is the nature of the *Tsu-t'ang chi* to require its readers to use their imaginations to provide their own context; in Marshall MacLuhan's terms, this is a "hot medium" like radio, which makes the readers or listeners actively imagine what is happening, rather than a "cold medium" like television, which gives viewers enough sensory data to turn off their minds.[47]

Third, this story is usually cited as Ma-tsu's enlightenment story, or at least to indicate his identity as Huai-jang's student. Although this earliest version includes several lines of subsequent dialogue between the two men, it does not contain either statement explicitly. From this story, Ma-tsu is traditionally thought of as Huai-jang's successor, with Huai-jang understood as a successor to the Sixth Patriarch, Hui-neng. However, when we look more closely at the available sources, we see that Ma-tsu studied with other figures as well, and that Huai-jang's connection with certain Northern school figures is much more substantial than his problematic connection with Hui-neng.

The point is that, based on whatever may have happened during Ma-tsu's religious training, we realize that from some unknown point in time the Ch'an community developed this image of an encounter between him and Huai-jang. Whatever did or did not happen, the news of that encounter was dramatized and circulated in oral and/or written form. What we have in the *Tsu-t'ang chi* is something like the core of the story, with the reader, listener—or perhaps the teacher—left to supply the details. As T. H. Barrett has pointed out, this process resembles nothing so much as the circulation of jokebooks at roughly the same time. As with the formulaic notation of the *Five Expedient Means,* which seems to have provided the liturgical skeleton on which Northern school teachers could superimpose their own flourishes and interpretations, the encounter dialogue literature of Ch'an was prepared as skeletal notations upon which teachers and students could improvise. In order for this genre of literature to appear, though, it required a shared conception of Buddhist spiritual practice, some of the elements of which have been isolated in this chapter.

NOTES

1. For useful information on these anecdotes, see Heinrich Dumoulin, *Zen Buddhism: A History. Volume 1: India and China, With a New Supplement on the Northern School of Chinese Zen* trans. James W. Heisig and Paul Knitter (New York: Macmillan, 1988), pp. 92, 163, and 182–83, and James H. Sanford, *Zen-man Ikkyu* (Chico, Cal.: Scholars Press, 1981).

2. On this understanding of cosmology as what people in any culture feel is naturally true, see Mary Douglas, *Natural Symbols: Explorations in Cosmology,* 2nd ed. (New York: Pantheon Books, 1982). In the following I use either "orality" or the "Zen use of language" as shorthand for the tripartite combination of dialogue, narrative, and orality.

3. See Shunryū Suzuki, *Zen Mind, Beginner's Mind: Informal Talks on Zen Meditation and Practice* (New York: Weatherhill, 1970).

4. Yanagida Seizan, "The Development of the 'Recorded Sayings' Texts of the Chinese Ch'an School," trans. John R. McRae, in Lewis Lancaster and Whalen Lai, eds.,

Early Ch'an in China and Tibet, Berkeley Buddhist Studies, no. 5 (Berkeley, Cal.: Lancaster-Miller Press, 1983), pp. 185–205, esp. 192 and 204 n. 25, where the first compound (for "encounter") is defined.

5. See my "Encounter Dialogue and the Transformation of the Spiritual Path in Chinese Ch'an," in Robert E. Buswell, Jr., and Robert M. Gimello, eds., *Paths to Liberation: The Mārga and Its Transformations in Buddhist Thought* (Honolulu: University of Hawaii Press, 1992), pp. 339–69.

6. The following summary draws heavily from my *The Northern School and the Formation of Early Ch'an Buddhism,* Studies in East Asian Buddhism, no. 3 (Honolulu: University of Hawaii Press, 1986), although with the incorporation of more recently published analyses.

7. See David Chappell, "The Teachings of the Fourth Ch'an Patriarch Tao-hsin (580–651)," in Lancaster and Lai, *Early Ch'an in China and Tibet,* pp. 89–129; and Bernard Faure, *The Will to Orthodoxy: A Critical Genealogy of Northern Chan Buddhism,* trans. Phyllis Brooks (Stanford, Cal.: Stanford University Press, 1997), pp. 50ff. Although both Chappell and Faure take the section devoted to Tao-hsin in *the Leng-ch'ieh shih-tzu chi* as an authentic representation of his teachings, I have argued that it is unlikely to be so; see McRae, *Northern School,* p. 119.

8. I have intentionally oversimplified the definition of encounter dialogue and the issue of when it first came to be transcribed. Recently I have begun to consider hitherto unnoticed examples of Ch'an literature from Tun-huang that include dialogue transcriptions that may test the boundaries of the usage here.

9. Certain examples of Shen-hui's storytelling will be discussed below. The dialogues in his texts involving Shen-hui himself are formulaic and doctrinally oriented. I will defer documentation to my study of his teachings and translation of his extant works, which is now in progress.

10. In an unpublished manuscript on early Ch'an history, Jeffrey Broughton uses the term "metropolitan school" to refer to the Northern school. My use of "provincial Ch'an" is indebted to Broughton's usage. Yanagida, "Recorded Sayings," p. 192, suggests that the practice of recording Ch'an encounters probably began with Ma-tsu. This chapter attempts to address this issue with greater nuance.

11. For the explanation of "back room" activities, see Erving Goffman, *The Presentation of Self in Everyday Life* (Garden City, N.Y.: Doubleday & Company, 1959), pp. 106–40, esp. 109–13.

12. See the article cited in note 5.

13. Here I am drawing upon personal conversations with Professor Mei Tsu-lin of Cornell University.

14. One of the indications of this disconformity is that no encounter dialogue material has been discovered among the Tun-huang texts, even though a set of verses by the compilers' immediate teacher, Ching-hsiu Wen-teng, occurs there.

15. See McRae, *Northern School,* p. 36. It may not be precisely fair to suggest that these were the earliest such descriptions in Ch'an literature, since the same text (the *Ch'uan fa-pao chi*) simultaneously provides information about other teachers. Also the epitaph for Fa-ju, discussed immediately following, antedates the *Ch'uan fa-pao chi* by two decades. Nevertheless, Hung-jen was the earliest central figure around whom this sort of mystique developed.

16. The metaphor about Fa-ju is found in the *Ch'uan fa-pao chi;* McRae, *Northern School,* p. 264. For various stories about Lao-an and I-fu, see *Northern School,* pp. 56–59 and 64–65, and Faure, *Will to Orthodoxy,* pp. 100–105 (Huian, i.e., Lao-an) and 78–81 (Yifu, i.e., I-fu).

17. See Sekiguchi Shindai, *Daruma no kenkyū* (Tokyo: Iwanami shoten, 1967), which lists the various elements of Bodhidharma's hagiography and the texts in which they appear, arranged chronologically.

18. For the various texts revealing the evolution of Hui-neng's biography and legendary image, see Komazawa Daigaku Zenshūshi kenkyūkai, eds., *Enō kenkyū—Enō denki to shiryō ni kan suru kisoteki kenkyū* (Tokyo: Taishukan shoten, 1978).

19. See Philip B. Yampolsky, trans., *The Platform Sutra of the Sixth Patriarch: The Text of the Tun-huang Manuscript* (New York: Columbia University Press, 1967), p. 134. In the Tun-huang version of the text, Hui-ming is not challenged to lift the robe. This story is expanded considerably as the *Platform Sūtra* evolves. See *Enō kenyū*, pp. 142–49.

20. This section draws heavily on McRae, *Northern School*, pp. 91–95.

21. *Northern School*, pp. 92–93.

22. Simply put, this is the observation that any element that does not fit the polemical agenda of the text as a whole is more likely to be an inadvertent and thus potentially more accurate transmission from an earlier stratum of development. This approach can of course be overused, as is explained in David R. Catchpole, "Tradition History," in I. Howard Marshall, ed., *New Testament Interpretation: Essays on Principles and Methods* (Grand Rapids, Mich.: William B. Eerdmans, 1977), p. 175.

23. I have looked for similarities, to no avail, in Richard B. Mather, trans., *A New Account of Tales of the World,* by Liu I-ch'ing, with commentary by Liu Chün (Minneapolis: University of Minnesota Press, 1976).

24. See the definition in Ogawa Tamaki et al., *Shin-jigen* (Tokyo: Kadokawa shoten, 1994), p. 413a. Of course, this makes me wonder all the more about any actual connection with Bodhidharma's efforts to learn Chinese and teach the Dharma.

25. Cf. Sekiguchi, *Daruma no kenkyū*, pp. 335–43, and Yanagida Seizan, *Yaburu mono* (Tokyo: Shunjūsha, 1970), p.236.

26. See the *Kuan-hsin lun,* in McRae, *Northern School*, p. 235.

27. See *Northern School*, pp. 95, 294 n. 161, and 302 n. 243.

28. See *Northern School*, pp. 95–96 and 302 n. 244.

29. See *Northern School*, pp. 96 and 302 n. 245.

30. See *Northern School*, pp. 96 and 302 n. 246.

31. The best example of this is Hsiang-mo Tsang (d.u.); see McRae, *Northern School*, p. 63.

32. And of course their somewhat later successors had a great reluctance to explain their activities openly. Perhaps they were profoundly incapable of doing so, for reasons we have not yet thought to explore.

33. See references in Nakamura Hajime, compiler, *Bukkyōgo daijiten* (Tokyo: Tokyo shoseki, 1981), 81c–d, where the two terms are correlated with self-use wisdom and enlightening self, and other-use wisdom and enlightening others. Note that these terms are widely use in the *Five Expedient Means.* See Mochizuki Shinkō, *Bukkyō daijiten,* 10 vols. (Tokyo: Sekai Seiten Kankō Kyōkai, 1958–1963), 1269a–b and 1378b–c, 2689c–90a, and 4846b–c.

34. McRae, *Northern School*, p. 174 (from *Five Expedient Means,* section One, A).

35. *Northern School*, p. 175 (ibid., One, D).

36. *Northern School*, p. 178 (ibid., One, J).

37. *Northern School*, p. 179 (ibid., One, M). I have included only this one example of how a dualistic formulation is expanded into a tripartite one, but others occur. For example, on pp. 176–77 the text develops a different tripartite variation in which the initial nonactivation of the mind is correlated with the *dharmakāya,* knowledge of the

motionlessness of the six senses is correlated with the *sambhogakāya*, and perfect illumination through all the senses is correlated with the *nirmāṇakāya*.

38. *Northern School*, pp. 173–74 (*Five Expedient Means*, Introduction, C–E). For various minor comments on the terminology used, see *Northern School*, pp. 228–29 nn. 228–33.

39. *Northern School*, p. 180 (*Five Expedient Means*, Two, A).

40. See the conclusion to *Northern School*, p. 238.

41. Note Shen-hsiu's 25-year residence at Yü-ch'üan ssu, previously T'ien-t'ai Chih-i's (538–97) place of residence.

42. See the *Yüan-ming lun*, McRae, *Northern School*, pp. 169–70.

43. Cf. McRae, "The Ox-head School of Chinese Buddhism: From Early Ch'an to the Golden Age," in R. M. Gimello and P. N. Gregory, eds., *Studies in Ch'an and Hua-yen*, Kuroda Institute Studies in East Asian Buddhism, no. 1 (Honolulu: University of Hawaii Press, 1983); pp. 169–253.

44. These titles are abbreviations of *Ta-sheng k'ai-hsin hsan-hsing tun-wu chen-tsung lun* [Treatise on the True Principle of Opening the Mind and Manifesting the (Buddha)-nature in Sudden Enlightenment (According to the) Mahayana], and *Tun-wu-chen-tsung chin-kang po-jo hsiu-hsing ta pi-an fa-men yao-chüeh* [Essential Determination of the Doctrine of Attaining the Other Shore (of Nirvana) by the Practice of Adamantine Wisdom (According to) the True Teaching of Sudden Enlightenment]. I have discussed these treatises in "Shen-hui and the Teaching of Sudden Enlightenment in Early Ch'an Buddhism," in Peter N. Gregory, ed., *Sudden and Gradual: Approaches to Enlightenment in Chinese Thought*, Kuroda Institute Studies in East Asian Buddhism, no. 5 (Honolulu: University of Hawaii Press, 1987), pp. 227–78, and although now I would be very hesitant to make the historical assertions that form the heart of this article, the intriguing format of these two essays is still worthy of comment.

45. See, *Northern School*, p. 6. McRae's first law of Zen studies holds, "It's not true, and therefore it's more important." That is, historical events are trivial in comparison with how legends and myths live in the popular consciousness.

46. TTC, 72a14–b3.

47. See Marshall McLuhan and Quentin Fiore, *The Medium is the Message* (New York: Bantam Books, 1967).

3

Mahākāśyapa's Smile
Silent Transmission and the Kung-an (Kōan) Tradition

ALBERT WELTER

O NE OF THE most famous kung-an in the Ch'an tradition relates the story of how the Buddha's disciple, Mahākāśyapa, broke into a smile when the Buddha held up a flower to an assembly of the *saṃgha* on Vulture Peak. The standard version of this well-known story is recorded in one of the most widely used kung-an (kōan) collections, the *Wu-men kuan* (J. *Mumonkan*).

> The World Honoured One long ago instructed the assembly on Vulture Peak by holding up a flower. At that time everyone in the assembly remained silent; only Mahākāśyapa broke into a smile. The World Honoured One stated: "I possess the treasury of the true Dharma eye, the wondrous mind of *nirvāna,* the subtle dharma-gate born of the formlessness of true form, not established on words and letters, a special transmission outside the teaching. I bequeath it to Mahākāś-yapa."[1]

The episode exemplifies and openly affirms one of the cardinal features of the Chinese Ch'an and Japanese Zen traditions: the silent transmission of Buddhist truth between master and disciple as "a special transmission outside the teaching" (C. *chiao-wai pieh-ch'uan,* J. *kyōge betsuden*). Taken literally, the story suggests that this silent transmission outside the teaching originated with none other than Śākyamuni Buddha himself. According to Zen lore, the "special transmission" was passed down from master to disciple through a long list of patriarchs in India, conventionally fixed at 28, and was finally brought to China by the emigree monk Bodhidharma, whose descendants flourished, eventually forming several Ch'an lineages. The story thus plays a remarkably important role in Ch'an. The entire tradition is in some sense predicated on this episode. The identity and credibility of every Ch'an master and practitioner who believes in Ch'an as "a special transmission outside the teaching" derive from it.

The significance of this silent, "special transmission" is especially evident in the kung-an collections compiled during the Sung dynasty. The first case in the *Wu-men kuan,* "Chao-chou Cries *wu!*" (J. *mu!*), illustrates a basic principle of the kung-an Ch'an tradition.

A monk asked Chao-chou Ts'ung-shen: "Does a dog also have the Buddha-nature?" Chao-chou answered: "*Wu!*"[2]

The commentary by Wu-men Hui-k'ai (1183–1260) asserts that Chao-chou's *Wu* is the first barrier of Ch'an, and that those able to pass through this barrier will attain the same realization as Chao-chou and the patriarchs themselves. Wu-men compares this enlightenment experience, where "distinctions like inner and outer are naturally fused together," to a deaf-mute who has a dream. It cannot be communicated to anyone else.[3]

The analogy of the enlightenment experience to a dreaming deaf-mute underscores the degree to which the Ch'an kung-an tradition was predicated on the notion of silent transmission. The enlightenment experience, by its nature, cannot be communicated through rational, verbal means. Rather than a "statement," Chao-chou's *Wu* amounts to a categorical renunciation of the possibility of meaningful statements. Enlightenment is an inherently individual experience that is incommunicable in words.

As important as the story of dharma-transmission between Śākyamuni and Mahākāśyapa is for the Ch'an and Zen traditions, it has received remarkably little critical attention. Few have looked into the origins and veracity of this episode, freed of the influence of sectarian interpretation. The critical work of scholars who have investigated the Śākyamuni–Mahākāśyapa exchange has thus far received little attention, so the results are not widely known even in scholarly circles. Practitioners are similarly unaware of the true foundations upon which some of their most highly cherished notions are based.

This chapter examines the origins and development of the Śākyamuni–Mahākāśyapa story. The textual record indicates that the story was fabricated in China as part of an effort by Ch'an monks to create an independent identity within the Chinese Buddhist context. It also suggests that the Sung, rather than the T'ang, was the critical period in which this Ch'an identity crystalized. The most significant innovations in the Śākyamuni–Mahākāśyapa story are recorded in Sung documents. Such findings contradict the "golden age" hypothesis that has informed Ch'an and Zen studies in the modern period. This, hypothesis postulates the T'ang era as the critical period in the formation of Ch'an identity, and it interprets later developments in terms of "decline" or "stagnation," devoting little effort or space to post-T'ang Ch'an. The clear message in Ch'an and Zen studies has been almost unequivocal in suggesting that Sung Ch'an developments were insignificant compared with the accomplishments of the great T'ang masters.

The study shows how the development of the Mahākāśyapa, silent-transmission story parallels the growth of Ch'an identity as "a special transmission outside the teaching" during the Sung dynasty and is intimately linked to it in its conception. The kung-an or kōan collections that were produced during the Sung, such as the *Wu-men kuan* (*Gateless Barrier*)[4] and the *Pi-yen lu* (*Blue Cliff Record*),[5] represent the culmination of this Sung Ch'an search for identity as "a special transmission outside the teaching." They were compiled as testimony to the validity of this interpretation of Ch'an. The concern here, however, is not with these kung-an collections as such, but with the development of a Ch'an identity that the kung-an tradition served to affirm.[6] What is of interest is not the dynamics of kung-an as such, but the developments that made kung-an study viable as quintessential techniques for communicating the special status of Ch'an enlightenment as "a special transmission outside the teaching."

T'ang Ch'an and the Myth of Bodhidharma

The figure of Bodhidharma casts a large shadow over Ch'an and Zen studies as the founding patriarch and instigator of Ch'an teaching in China. The fact that little is known about Bodhidharma is hardly unusual in the history of religions, where historical obscurity often serves as a prerequisite for posthumous claims regarding sectarian identity. Indeed, one learns much about the nature and character of Ch'an through Bodhidharma, an obscure meditation master from India, around whose image the most successful challenge to Chinese Buddhist scholasticism was mounted.[7]

The history of Buddhism in China is generally presented as an evolutionary scheme involving several stages of development. It begins with the first trickle of Indian Buddhist texts and foreign monks into China in the early centuries of the common era.[8] Buddhism attracted few Chinese converts in its early years in China and was confined largely to emigree communities. The fall of the Han at the beginning of the third century and the sacking of the northern capitals of Ch'ang-an and Lo-yang a century later heralded an unprecedented crisis for Chinese civilization, bringing both a greater presence of Buddhism in China and a greater interest in the religion among native Chinese. As knowledge and interest regarding Buddhism grew, so did the translation and interpretation of Buddhist scriptures. This led to the presence of a number of essentially Indian-based Buddhist schools on Chinese soil.[9]

The next phase in the development of Buddhism in China is characterized by the formation of a native Chinese Buddhist tradition. While heavily indebted to the Indian scriptural tradition, Chinese monks began to reassess the conflicting claims and relative merits of the plethora of texts that had flooded into China as "the word of the Buddha." They did so by temporalizing the Buddha's teaching, assigning texts and teachings to different periods of the Buddha's preaching career, and assuming an evolutionary scale of development culminating in the final, perfect representation of the Buddha's message.[10] This method of hermeneutical or doctrinal taxonomy,[11] referred to as *p'an-chiao* ("dividing/classifying the teaching") in Chinese, had the combined benefits of being inclusionary on the one hand, awarding relative merit to all teachings promoted under the name of the Buddha, and comprehensive on the other, resolving apparent contradictions through a doctrinally conclusive scheme. Debates erupted over which scriptures represented the full, final version of Buddhist teaching, but the principle of interpreting Buddhism by assigning scriptures to a relative scale determined by doctrinal criteria became the norm.

Implicit in *p'an-chiao* interpretation was the assumption that the textual tradition was the sole legitimate vehicle for transmitting Buddhist teaching. This assumption was eventually challenged by a new tradition of Buddhist interpretation in China that came to be associated with Ch'an. Ch'an undermined the textual assumptions of established Buddhist schools and provided an alternate interpretation of how Buddhist teaching was legitimately transmitted. As a result, Ch'an was more than a new "school" formulated on the old model of textual interpretation: it was a "revolution" that undermined the entire scholastic tradition and rewrote the history of Buddhism in China according to new criteria.[12]

According to currently accepted views of Ch'an history, the successful assault of Ch'an on Buddhist scholasticism coincided with a period of vibrant dynamism, during which the activities of a core group of Ch'an masters, mostly descendants of Ma-tsu Tao-i (709–788), formed the basic components of Ch'an identity. Following this so-called "golden age," Ch'an dynamism was reduced to static formalism and lapsed into a state of gradual decline. Until recently, this view of the history of Buddhism in China has been pervasive to the point that it was universally accepted. According to this view, Sung Buddhism represents the "sunset period," the twilight glow of a once strong, vital tradition, reduced to a shadow of its former glory. From this perspective, the golden age of Buddhism in China, including Ch'an Buddhism, was unequivocally the T'ang dynasty (618–907). Sung Buddhism, especially Ch'an, represents the irrevocable process of decline.[13]

History rewritten from the Ch'an perspective posits Bodhidharma as champion of a "mind-to-mind transmission," focusing on the enlightenment experience occurring in the context of the master–disciple relationship, as an alternative to the exegetical teachings of the scholastic tradition. According to the Ch'an perspective, this true, nontextual transmission of Buddhist teaching originated in China with the arrival of Bodhidharma and was based on a lineage traced back to the Buddha himself. In one grand stroke, the long and well-established traditions and conventions of Buddhist scholasticism in China were turned on their head. Throughout the T'ang period, while Buddhist scholastics constructed ever more refined doctrinal systems, the true teaching of the Buddha was secretly being transmitted among the beleaguered and isolated descendants of Bodhidharma, battling the dark forces of establishment Buddhism, holding steadfastly to the truth.

So pervasive is this reconstruction of Buddhist history in China that virtually everyone who studies Ch'an or Zen Buddhism today has fallen under its spell. With all of the appeal of a good conspiracy theory, the Ch'an version of events replaces the syncretistic background of Ch'an history with a simple and straightforward message summarized through four expressions:

1. A special transmission outside the teaching (C. *chiao-wai-pieh-ch'üan*, J. *kyōge betsuden*)
2. Do not establish words and letters (C. *pu-li wen-tzu*, J. *furyū monji*)
3. Directly point to the human mind (C. *ch'ih-chih jen-hsin*, J. *jikishi ninshin*)
4. See one's nature and become a Buddha (C. *chien-hsing ch'eng-fo*, J. *kenshō jōbutsu*)

These slogans are known to those with even limited acquaintance with Ch'an and serve as a common starting point for the modern study of Zen.[14] The traditional position of Ch'an and Zen orthodoxy has been that the slogans originated with Bodhidharma and that they represent the implicit message of Ch'an teaching from its outset. Ch'an historians, following contemporary Zen school orthodoxy, regard the slogans as products of the T'ang period, reflecting the rise to prominence of the Ch'an movement in the eighth and ninth centuries during its so-called "golden age."[15] As a result, the slogans are typically regarded as normative statements for a Ch'an identity fully developed by the end of the T'ang. Ch'an kung-an collections, compiled in the Sung, expressed the principles contained in these slogans through dramatic encounters and riddle-like exchanges. What are the origins of these slogans, and how did they come to represent the Ch'an tradition of Bodhidharma?

Individually, the slogans are found in works dating before the Sung, but they do not appear together as a four-part series of expressions until well into the Sung, when they are attributed to Bodhidharma in a collection of the recorded sayings of Ch'an master Huai (992–1064) contained in the *Tsu-t'ing shih-yüan*, compiled by Mu-an in 1108.[16] In reality, three of the slogans—"do not establish words and letters," "directly point to the human mind," and "see one's nature and become a Buddha"—were well established as normative Ch'an teaching by the beginning of the Sung. The status of the fourth slogan, "a special transmission outside the teaching," as an interpretation of the true meaning of "do not establish words and letters" was the subject of great controversy throughout the Sung. The reason for this controversy is not hard to fathom. Of the four slogans that came to represent the Ch'an identity, this slogan sharply contradicted the textual basis upon which the Buddhist scholastic tradition in China was based. It met great resistance from Buddhist and Ch'an circles.

This chapter will explore how these slogans became accepted as integral features of Ch'an identity. It will focus on the first slogan, "a special transmission outside the teaching," and the controversy that erupted over its acceptance. In examining developments relating to this slogan, I will first review documents in which its acceptance in Ch'an circles is verified, and then look at controversial opinions surrounding its assertion. My contention is that without the acceptance of this first slogan, the Ch'an kung-an tradition would not have taken the form that it did, and might not have developed at all. More precisely, the kung-an tradition serves as vivid illustration of the principles expressed in the slogan "a special transmission outside the teaching."

The presentation will deviate from strict chronological order. First is a brief review of how the other three slogans were accepted. Then the *T'ien-sheng kuang-teng lu* (*Record of the Extensive Transmission [of the Lamp] compiled during the T'ien-sheng era*), compiled by Li Tsun-hsü and issued in 1036, is discussed as the primary document asserting Ch'an identity as "a special transmission outside the teaching" in the early Sung. Following this, an alternate view of the relationship between Ch'an and the teaching (*chiao*) as harmonious, or unified, is presented as a contrast to the view of Ch'an as "a special transmission outside the teaching." This alternate view was suggested by members of the Fa-yen lineage, dominant in the Wu-yueh kingdom during the Five Dynasties. It is presented here through a review of the prominent representatives of Wu-yueh Buddhism, Yung-ming Yen-shou (904–975) and Tsan-ning (919–1001). Finally, two prefaces are compared with regard to the important Sung transmission text that became known as the *Ching-te ch'uan-teng lu* (*The Transmission of the Lamp compiled in the Ching-te era*), issued in 1004—one by the original compiler, Tao-yuan, and the other by the Sung official Yang I, who helped reedit the text in the form by which it has become known to us. The terminology employed in each preface is reviewed in light of the debate over Ch'an identity as "a special transmission outside the teaching." Both of the transmission records discussed here, the *Ching-te ch'uan-teng lu* and the *T'ien-sheng kuang-teng lu,* provided numerous episodes that later found their way into kung-an collections.[17] Thus they served as primary sources for many kung-an cases as well as support for the growing identity of the Ch'an tradition as "a special transmission outside the teaching."

Ch'an Slogans and the Formation of Ch'an Identity

The notion that Ch'an represented a teaching within the Buddhist tradition advocating "do not establish words and letters," "directly point to the human mind," and "see one's nature and become a Buddha" was widely acknowledged by the ninth century. These three slogans are all documented in Ch'an works dating from the T'ang period. The slogan "do not establish words and letters" is recorded in the work of Tsung-mi and became a set phrase (along with "mind-to-mind transmission" [*i-hsin ch'uan-hsin*]) during the later half of the eighth century and the first half of the ninth.[18] According to Yanagida Seizan, the first recorded instance where the slogan "directly point to the human mind" appears as a set phrase is in Huang-po's *Ch'uan-hsin fa-yao,* compiled by P'ei Hsiu in 849.[19] "Seeing one's nature" was an old idea in China promoted by Tao-sheng (355–434), a disciple of Kumarajiva. Drawing from Mahayana doctrine, Tao-sheng advocated the notion of an inherent Buddha-nature in everyone, including *icchantika.* The full phrase *chien-hsing ch'eng-fo* (see one's nature and become a Buddha) first appeared in a commentary to the *Nirvāna Sūtra,* the *Ta-pan nieh-p'an ching chi-chieh,* in a statement attributed to Seng-liang: "To see one's nature and become a Buddha means that our own nature is Buddha."[20] In the *Ch'uan-hsin fa-yao,* the three slogans are even documented together, two—"directly point to the human mind" and "see one's nature and become a Buddha"—in the exact language with which they would later be appropriated, and the third—"do not rely on spoken words" (*pu-tsai yen-shuo*)—as a conceptually implicit form of the slogan "do not establish words and letters" (*pu-li wen-tzu*).[21] By the end of the T'ang period, Ch'an had an undisputed identity represented by these three slogans. This was the universally accepted image of Ch'an in the early Sung.[22]

The first use of the phrase "a special transmission outside the teaching" (*chiao-wai pieh-ch'uan*) that can be documented with historical certainty is in the *Tsu-t'ang chi* (*Collection of the Patriarch's Hall*), the oldest extant Ch'an transmission history to include a multibranched lineage, compiled in 952 by descendants of Ch'an master Hsüeh-feng I-tsun (822–908) at the Chao-ch'ing Temple in Ch'uan-chou.[23] Even here, the lone, insignificant appearance of the phrase *chiao-wai pieh-ch'uan* in the *Tsu-t'ang chi* is overshadowed by the repeated use of the other three slogans.[24]

The phrase is also included in a "tomb-inscription" of Lin-chi I-hsüan (?–866), the *Lin-chi hui-chao ch'an-shih t'a-chi* (*The Tomb Inscription of Lin-chi Ch'an Master "Wisdom-Illumination"*), attributed to Lin-chi's disciple, a certain Yen-chao of Pao-shou in Chen province. The tomb inscription was appended to the end of *Lin-chi lu,* the record of Lin-chi's life and teachings as a Ch'an activist.[25] According to this inscription, Lin-chi's use of the phrase was prompted by frustration after he mastered the Vinaya and widely studied the sūtras and śāstras: "These are prescriptions for the salvation of the world, not the principle of a special transmission outside the teaching" (*chiao-wai pieh-ch'uan*).[26] The historical authenticity of this inscription as the work of Lin-chi's disciple is highly dubious,[27] but the connection of the phrase "a special transmission outside the teaching" with the *Lin-chi lu* is highly suggestive of a Ch'an identity that developed in the Lin-chi lineage during the Sung, as we shall see.

While the *Lin-chi lu* professes to be the record of Lin-chi's words and deeds as recorded by his disciples, the current form of the text dates from an edition issued in 1120, accompanied by a new preface by a reputedly high-ranking (but otherwise unknown) Sung bureaucrat, Ma Fang.[28] This same edition is also the oldest extant source for Lin-chi's purported "tomb inscription" claiming Lin-chi's explicit use of the phrase "a special transmission outside the teaching."[29] This suggests that sometime around the beginning of the twelfth century or before, Lin-chi became associated with the Sung image of Ch'an as "a special transmission outside the teaching." This is also around the same time when the slogan "a special transmission outside the teaching" was added to the list of Ch'an slogans attributed to the Ch'an patriarch Bodhidharma in the *Tsu-t'ing shih-yüan*. The association of this slogan with Lin-chi and Bodhidharma was the culmination of a process through which the identity of Ch'an as "a special transmission outside the teaching" was transformed by members of the Lin-chi lineage, casting a strong shadow over both the T'ang Ch'an tradition and the image of Ch'an and Zen down to the present day. Sung kung-an collections compiled by monks belonging to the Lin-chi lineage memorialized the contributions made by Lin-chi, his teachers, associates, disciples, and heirs, by making them prominent subjects of kung-an episodes.

According to the oldest extant record of Lin-chi's teachings and activities, Lin-chi was a viable candidate for association with the new slogan.[30] In one of Lin-chi's sermons he is recorded as saying: "[I]n bygone days I devoted myself to the Vinaya and also delved into the sūtras and śāstras. Later, when I realized that they were medicines for salvation and displays of doctrines in written words, I once and for all threw them away and, searching for the Way, I practiced meditation."[31] The source of this record is the *T'ien-sheng kuang-teng, lu* of 1036. It is the primary source documenting a new Ch'an identity as "a special transmission outside to the teaching" in the early Sung.

The T'ien-sheng kuang-teng lu and Ch'an Identity as "A Special Transmission outside the Teaching" (chiao-wai pieh-ch'uan)

The *T'ien-sheng kuang-teng lu* is one of a number of important Ch'an transmission records (*teng-lu*) compiled in the Sung.[32] As their name implies, the purpose of these texts is to record the transmission lineages of important Ch'an masters, using a biographical format. In this way, lines of descent can be traced and links established between Ch'an masters. T'ang Ch'an transmission records had already succeeded in tracing the transmission lineage back to Śākyamuni through a line of Indian patriarchs (conventionally established at 28).[33] A major innovation of the Sung records was to establish lineal transmission with multiple branches.[34] This became the basis for the so-called "five houses" (*wu-chia*) of T'ang Ch'an. The much-heralded "golden age" of Ch'an (and Zen) history that the "five houses" represent is largely the product of this Sung-inspired revisionism and organization of the T'ang tradition.

Of the Sung Ch'an transmission records, the *Ching-te ch'uan-teng lu,* compiled by Tao-yüan in 1004, is regarded as the most important. It was the first to be accepted in official Sung circles and set standards that all subsequent Ch'an transmission records would follow. It helped establish a number of well-known Ch'an conventions: "great awakening" (*ta-wu*); the enlightenment experience as the culmination of Ch'an practice; confirmation of one's realization by a recognized master as the legitimate criteria for succession; and the transmission verse as a poetic account of one's experience. Many incidents involving Ch'an masters later memorialized in kung-an collections were recorded in the *Ching-te ch'uan-teng lu.* With its emphasis on Ch'an style dialogues and encounters between practitioners, the *Ching-te ch'uan-teng lu* became a primary source for Sung kung-an collections.[35] Some of the earliest versions of Ch'an *yü-lu* (*Recorded Sayings*) texts are also found within the *Ching-te ch'uan-teng lu.*[36]

The *T'ien-sheng kuang-teng lu* and other Sung Ch'an transmission records are usually accorded little importance alongside the *Ching-te ch'uan-teng lu.* Their contribution has frequently been ignored or minimized.[37] They are sometimes regarded in a dismissive tone as peripheral and imitative.[38] While it is true that the tendency of the transmission records to be comprehensive does make them repetitive, borrowing liberally from the *Ching-te ch'uan-teng lu* and earlier transmission records, this should not blind us from seeing the innovative features of each work. The tendency to regard the *Ching-te ch'uan-teng lu* as normative and later transmission records as imitations stems in part from the glorification of T'ang Ch'an and its masters as being representative of a Ch'an "golden age" while Sung Ch'an stands for a period of decline. On the basis of this interpretation of Ch'an history, it makes sense to see the *Ching-te ch'uan-teng lu* as the more important record, since it documents the activities of Ch'an masters during the "golden age" before the decline of the Sung had a chance to take hold. The further one moves into the Sung, the more serious the decline in Ch'an is presumed to be, leaving a dark cloud over subsequent transmission records.

In the present context, the *T'ien-sheng kuang-teng lu* assumes an importance that surpasses the *Ching-te ch'uan-teng lu.* As an "extensive record" of Ch'an transmission (*kuang-teng*), the *T'ien-sheng kuang-teng lu* was clearly intended to supplement and revise the claims of the previous transmission record, the *Ching-te ch'uan-teng lu*. The need for a new transmission record a mere 25 years after the *Ching-te ch'uan-teng lu* was compiled suggests that the earlier record was found lacking in some circles. In short, Ch'an masters associated with the Lin-chi lineage were transforming Ch'an in the early Sung, particularly in the early decades of the eleventh century. The *T'ien-sheng kuang-teng lu* was a tribute to the contributions of and to the novel styles being promoted by these new Ch'an masters, many of whom were still alive or only recently deceased when the *T'ien-sheng kuang-teng lu* was compiled. In order to highlight the importance of the *T'ien-sheng kuang-teng lu* and its importance in the rising self-definition of Ch'an as "a special transmission outside the teaching, "I will discuss this text before going back to explain the view of "harmony between Ch'an and the teaching" it attempted to displace, and the role played by the *Ching-te ch'uan-teng lu* in the debate.

One of the most important contributions that this "new breed" of Ch'an masters made was to establish Ch'an as "a special transmission outside the teaching." The phrase *chiao-wai pieh-ch'uan* does not appear in the *Ching-te ch'uan-teng lu*, except in an altered form in the preface by Yang I (discussed below).[39] It appears several times in the *T'ien-sheng kuang-teng lu* and is one of the prominent features of this work. Another important contribution was that it recorded important *yü-lu* materials, many for the first time, of masters associated with the Lin-chi lineage.

According to the *T'ien-sheng kuang-teng lu*, the interpretation of Ch'an as a "special transmission outside the teaching" was not the innovation of Bod-hidharma or Lin-chi, or any of a number of likely candidates associated with the T'ang Ch'an tradition. The first mention of "a special transmission outside the teaching" in the *T'ien-sheng kuang-teng lu* is in the biography of Ch'an master Kuei-sheng, recipient of a Purple Robe, from the Kuang-chiao Temple in Ju-chou.[40] The dates of Kuei-sheng's life are unknown, but the dates of contemporaries whose biographies are before and after his indicate that he was active in the early Sung period, in the last decades of the tenth century and the first decades of the eleventh.[41] Kuei-sheng uses the phrase in connection with a sermon in which he attempts to explain the meaning of Bodhidharma's coming from the West: "When Bodhidharma came from the west and trans-mitted the Dharma in the lands of the East [i.e., China], he directly pointed to the human mind, to see one's nature and become a Buddha. . . . What is the meaning of his coming from the West? A special transmission outside the teaching."[42] In this way, Kuei-sheng's reference to "a special transmission out-side the teaching" was directly connected to established slogans of the collec-tive Ch'an identity, the image of Bodhidharma, and the implicit meaning of his message.

This same link between Bodhidharma's message and the interpretation of Ch'an as "a special transmission outside the teaching" is also established in the biography of Ch'an master Shih-shuang Ch'u-yüan (987–1040) of Mount

Nan-yüan in Yüan-chou, active in the early decades of the eleventh century, he notes: "Therefore the Way [consists in] one saying: 'Bodhidharma came from the West, a special transmission outside the teaching.' What is this special transmission of the Way? Directly pointing to the human mind, seeing one's nature and becoming a Buddha.[43] This linkage pointed to the new, comprehensive direction Ch'an identity was taking in the early Sung. As Ch'u-yüan was the teacher of both Yang-ch'i Fang-hui (992–1049) and Huang-lung Hui nan (1002–1069), heads of the two branches that have dominated the Lin-chi lineage since the Sung, the influence of his interpretation was considerable. The question regarding the meaning of the phrase "a special transmission outside the teaching" even acquired kōan-like status in Sung Ch'an circles.

One of the preoccupations of the search for Ch'an identity in the early Sung was coming to terms with the meaning of Bodhidharma's arrival from the West.[44] In the *T'ien-sheng kuang-teng lu,* the question is asked by students with considerable frequency (over 70 times), as a test of a Ch'an master's mettle. It evoked a wide variety of responses, ranging from seemingly random observations about the weather and seasons, to nonsensical references to objects close at hand, as well as the infamous shouts and beatings for which Lin-chi-style Ch'an became famous. As the phrase "a special transmission outside the teaching" came to represent one of the central features of Bodhidharma's teaching (along with "directly point to the human mind, see one's nature and become Buddha"), the question: "What is [the meaning of] the one saying: 'a special transmission outside the teaching'?" came to be asked in the same manner as: "What is the meaning of Bodhidharma coming from the West?" as a test of a Ch'an master's understanding.[45]

In spite of the association between Bodhidharma and the interpretation of Ch'an as "a special transmission outside the teaching" by many Ch'an masters in the *T'ien-sheng kuang-teng lu,* there is no evidence for this connection in the record's biography of Bodhidharma. The biography does have Bodhidharma claim "seeing one's nature is Buddha,"[46] and "many people clarify the Way, but few practice it; many people explain *li* [principle], but few understand it,"[47] so that he is representative of principles summarized in later Ch'an slogans. The Bodhidharma of the *T'ien-sheng kuang-teng lu* is more aptly characterized as the conveyor of the "seal of the Dharma" (*fa-yin*),[48] or transmitter of the "seal of Buddha-mind" (*fo-hsin yin*).[49] In the biographies of Bodhidharma's descendants, Hui-k'o, Seng-ts'an, and Tao-hsin, the transmission is characterized in terms of "the Treasury of the True Dharma Eye" (*cheng fa-yen tsang*) (familiar to many in its Japanese pronunciation, *shōbōgenzō*), where it is described as the essential teaching passed to Mahākāśyapa from Śākyamuni, down through the line of Indian patriarchs to Bodhidharma.[50] This point is confirmed in the *T'ien-sheng kuang-teng lu* biographies of Śākyamuni and Mahākāśyapa, which make a point of stipulating that the "content" of the transmission between them was "the Treasury of the True Dharma Eye."[51] This constitutes the content of transmission from patriarch to patriarch through all the subsequent biographies of the Indian patriarchs in the *T'ien-sheng kuang-teng lu* as well.[52]

What the *T'ien-sheng kuang-teng lu* suggests, then, is that the depiction of Bodhidharma's message in terms of "a special transmission outside the teaching" was the product of early Sung interpretation, first affirmed in the *T'ien-sheng kuang-teng lu* text. The *T'ien-sheng kuang-teng lu* also alludes to the fact that this new interpretation was not universally accepted in Ch'an circles. Other Ch'an masters with biographies recorded in the *T'ien-sheng kuang-teng lu,* contemporaries of Kuei-sheng and Ch'u-yüan (who promoted Bodhidharma's Ch'an as "a special transmission outside the teaching"), retain a more traditional interpretation of Bodhidharma. Ch'an master Hsing-ming (932–1001) of the K'ai-hua Temple of Dragon Mountain in Hang-chou continued to maintain "the patriarch [Bodhidharma] came from the West claiming 'directly point to the human mind, see one's nature and become a Buddha, and do not exert one iota of mental energy',"[53] invoking standard Ch'an slogans without recourse to the new interpretation of Bodhidharma's message as "a special transmission outside the teaching." In doing so, Hsing-ming was confirming an accepted view of Ch'an in the early Sung, based on "official" interpretations of Ch'an in the T'ang, of "harmony between Ch'an and the teaching."

Two Interpretations of Ch'an: "A Special Transmission outside the Teaching" (*chiao-wai pieh-ch'uan*) versus "Harmony between Ch'an and the Teaching" (*chiao-ch'an i-chih*)

Until the *T'ien-sheng kuang-teng lu,* the prevailing view of Ch'an that was accepted in official circles was one of harmony between Ch'an and the Buddhist scriptural tradition. The phrase "a special transmission outside the teaching" had not gained standard currency. The situation began to change in the latter half of the tenth century, when some Ch'an monks began spouting their claim to be "a special transmission outside the teaching," independent of the scholastic tradition of Buddhism that preceded them. The new claim precipitated a conflict within the Ch'an movement over its proper identity. Advocates of Ch'an as a special transmission within the teaching—that is, Ch'an as the culmination of the Buddhist scriptural tradition—began to defend themselves against what they deemed to be pernicious, self-defeating claims. The story of this conflict is embedded in the rise of the Fa-yen lineage in the Wu-yüeh region and the evolution of Buddhism in the early Sung.

In the tenth-century period of the so-called Five Dynasties and Ten Kingdoms, China was without effective central control and the country was politically and geographically divided into several autonomous regions.[54] The fate of Buddhism fell into the hands of warlords (*chieh-tu shih*) who controlled these regions. Given the recent experience of dynastic collapse and the perception of Buddhist culpability for T'ang failings, most warlords continued policies established in the late T'ang designed to restrict Buddhist influence over Chinese society. As a result, support for Buddhism during this period was geographically restricted to a few regions. Ch'an lineages emerged as the principal beneficiaries of this regionally based support. The established schools of the T'ang, Hua-yen and T'ien-t'ai, had been highly dependent on imperial support, and they were left vulnerable when it was withdrawn. Campaigns against Buddhism during the T'ang were generally directed at obvious targets: the large, wealthy Hua-yen and T'ien-t'ai monasteries. Equally debilitating for Buddhism was the collapse of T'ang society, which deprived the aristocratic classes of wealth and position and Buddhism of its source of extra-governmental support. Ch'an lineages (such as the "Northern school" of Shen-hsiu and the "Southern school" of Shen-hui) located near the capital and dependent on imperial support suffered a similar fate.

As a result of the changing circumstances affecting Buddhism in the tenth century, Ch'an emerged as the dominant movement within Chinese Buddhism. At the same time, support for Buddhism varied from region to region, and this environment naturally produced different conceptions regarding the normative identity of the Ch'an school. These regionally based variations of Ch'an teaching became best remembered in the debate over whether Ch'an represented "a special transmission outside the teaching" (*chiao-wai pieh-ch'uan*) or "the harmony between Ch'an and the teaching" (*chiao-ch'an i-chih*),[55] that is, the controversy between the notion of Ch'an as an independent tradition and the view that sought to interpret Ch'an in terms of the Buddhist scriptural tradition. The debate is already implicit in the thought of Tsung-mi, the ninth-century Buddhist syncretist who interpreted Ch'an positions in terms of the doctrines of Buddhist scholasticism.[56] In order to understand the emergence of the Ch'an slogan "a special transmission outside the teaching," one needs to review the partisan reactions this debate generated in the early Sung.

The Buddhist revival in tenth-century China was dominated by supporters of the Fa-yen lineage.[57] Fa-yen Wen-i (885–958) hailed from Yü-hang (Chechiang province) and was ordained at the K'ai-yüan Temple in Yüeh-chou. Travel took him to Fu-chou and as far as Lin-chuan (Ssu-ch'uan province), but he eventually settled at the Pao-en Ch'an Temple in Chin-liang (Chiang-hsi province). His teachings attracted numerous students, many of whom achieved considerable fame in their own right.[58] The influence of Wen-i's disciples was especially strong in two kingdoms in the south, Nan-T'ang (Chiang-hsi) and Wu-yüeh (Che-chiang), where his disciples tended to congregate.[59] The rulers of these kingdoms were the strongest supporters of Buddhism during this period. The normative definition of Ch'an in Fa-yen circles, later summarized as "harmony between Ch'an and the teaching," directly countered the notion of "a special transmission outside the teaching," however articulated. A review of Buddhism in Wu-yüeh makes this point clear.

Broadly conceived, the promotion of Buddhism in Wu-yüeh envisioned solutions to the social and political turmoil plaguing China through the revival of past Buddhist traditions. Aside from spiritual concerns, the preservation of Buddhism in Wu-yüeh was linked to providing social and political stability. This was rooted in a T'ang vision of Buddhism as an indispensable force in the creation of a civilized society. As a result, the Wu-yüeh revival of Buddhism was broad-based. It depended on the reestablishment of Buddhist institutions as central features of Wu-yüeh society and culture, and to this end Wu-yüeh rulers made a concentrated effort to rebuild temples and pilgrimage sites and to restore the numerous Buddhist monuments and institutions that had suffered from neglect and the ravages of war. Historically important centers in the region, such as Mount T'ien-t'ai, were rebuilt. New Buddhist centers, like the Yung-ming Temple in Lin-an (Hang-chou), were established. Ambassadors were sent to Japan and Korea to collect copies of important scriptures no longer available in China. After several decades of constant dedication to these activities, the monks and monasteries of Wu-yüeh acquired considerable reputations. Monks throughout China, fleeing hardship and persecution, flocked to the protection and prosperity that Wu-yüeh monasteries offered. Rulers of non-Chinese kingdoms sought to enhance their reputations by sending monks from their countries to study under famous Wu-yüeh masters.[60]

The Buddhist revival in Wu-yüeh was largely carried out under the Ch'an banner, and the nature of the revival determined the traditional qualities of Wu-yüeh Ch'an. In addition to embracing Ch'an innovations, Wu-yüeh Ch'an identified with old T'ang traditions, and this identification with the larger Buddhist tradition became a standard feature in the collective memory of Wu-yüeh Ch'an. The distinguishing character of the Fa-yen lineage within Ch'an is typically recalled through the syncretic proclivities of its patriarchs, normally reduced to the harmony between Ch'an and Hua-yen in Wen-i's teachings, the harmony between Ch'an and T'ien-t'ai in Te-shao's teachings, and the harmony between Ch'an and Pure Land in Yen-shou's teachings.[61]

The reconciliation of Wu-yüeh Ch'an with the larger tradition of Chinese Buddhism was coupled with undisputed normative aspects of T'ang Ch'an self-identity. This is readily apparent in the Wu-yüeh Buddhist definition of itself in distinctly Ch'an terms. Even the writings of Tsan-ning (919–1001), a Wu-yüeh Vinaya master who became the leading Buddhist scholar-bureaucrat at the Sung court, reveal a definition of Buddhism in terms of a Ch'an identity that was compatible with conventional Buddhist teaching. In "The Transmission of Meditation and Contemplation Techniques to China" (*ch'uan ch'an-kuan fa*) section of the *Ta-sung seng shih-lüeh*, where Tsan-ning treats Ch'an from the perspective of the broader tradition of meditation practice in Chinese

Buddhism,[62] Bodhidharma is praised for having first proclaimed in China: "directly point to the human mind; see one's nature and become a Buddha; do not establish words and letters."[63] The "official" view of Wu-yüeh Ch'an presented to the Sung court asserted that these three slogans attributed to Bodhidharma were definitive of normative Ch'an teaching, along with a characterization of Ch'an as the quintessential teaching of Buddhism ("the *ch'an* of the Supreme Vehicle").[64] The fact that the fourth slogan, "a special transmission outside the teaching," was missing from this normative definition is closely connected to the view of Ch'an as the quintessential teaching of Buddhism, which presupposes harmony between Ch'an and Buddhist teaching. Rather than "a special transmission outside the teaching," Tsan-ning considered Bodhidharma's teaching as a branch of the larger tradition of Buddhism stemming from Śākyamuni.

> The Truth (*fa*) preached by the Buddhas of the three ages [past, present, and future] is always the same, and the learning imparted by the Sacred Ones of the ten directions is textually uniform. The teachings of Śākyamuni are the root [fundamental teaching]; the words of Bodhidharma are a branch [supplementary teaching]. How truly lamentable to turn one's back on the root to chase after the branches![65]

Implicit in Tsan-ning's definition of Ch'an was a criticism of Ch'an practitioners who denigrated Śākyamuni's teachings in favor of Bodhidharma's. Using language that Confucian trained-bureaucrats could easily identify with, Tsan-ning levels harsh criticism at those who view Ch'an as some kind of "special transmission outside the teaching."

> [The government minister] who does not follow the virtuous influence of his sovereign [*wang-hua*] is referred to as a rebellious minister. [The son] who does not carry on the legacy of his father is referred to as a disobedient son. Anyone daring to defy the teachings of the Buddha [*fo-shuo*] is referred to as a follower of demonic heterodoxies.[66]

Tsan-ning's aim was to provide an orthodox interpretation of Ch'an following the conventional understanding of Wu-yüeh masters. His message to those attempting to isolate Ch'an from Buddhist teaching is explicit: "based on an examination of the records and writings of those who have sought [meditation] techniques [*fa*] from the past down to the present, *ch'an* meditation in India is taught along with the vehicle of Buddhist teaching [*chiao-ch'eng*] [and not independently]."[67] Those who conceive of a Ch'an identity independent of Buddhist teaching do not understand that "the scriptures [*ching*] are the words of the Buddha, and meditation [*ch'an*] is the thought of the Buddha; there is no discrepancy whatsoever between what the Buddha conceives in his mind and what he utters with his mouth."[68]

The Wu-yüeh perspective on the harmony between Ch'an and the scriptures was not unprecedented but represented the "official" view in the T'ang. A century earlier Tsung-mi (780–841) promoted harmony or correspondence between Ch'an and Buddhist teachings, arguing that Ch'an teachings are in accord with the Buddhist canon, on the one hand, and with the doctrinal positions of Buddhist schools, on the other.[69] Tsung-mi's views provided the model for Wu-yüeh Ch'an, both for Tsan-ning[70] and for the teachings of Yung-ming Yen-shou (904–975), Wu-yüeh Ch'an's greatest representative.

It is beyond the scope of this chapter to delve deeply into either the complexity of Yen-shou's thought or his indebtedness to Tsung-mi.[71] Yen shou's commitment to the principle of "harmony between Ch'an and the teaching" is evident throughout his writings, as is his opposition to a conception of Ch'an isolated from Buddhist teachings and practices. Yen-shou's view of Ch'an, framed within the parameters of the Buddhist revival in Wu-yüeh, was of a teaching supportive of Buddhist ritual and conventional practices.

Yen-shou's view of Ch'an as the "Mind School" was firmly based on the theoretical assumptions of T'ang Buddhist scholasticism. The implication that Yen-shou drew from such standard Buddhist premises as "the myriad phenomena are mind-only" and the "interpenetration of *li* [noumena] and *shih* [phenomena]" was a radical phenomenalism: "It is unreasonable to assume that [any phenomena] is deprived of the essence of *li* [noumena]."[72] Taking the interpenetration of *li* and *shih* as a reasonable proposition, Yen-shou recommended pluralism as the guiding principle governing Buddhist teaching and practice. For Yen-shou, Ch'an suggested the principle of inclusion in which the entire Buddhist tradition culminated in a grand epiphany. Doctrinally, this meant that the entire scriptural canon became united in a great, all-encompassing harmony. From the perspective of practice, all actions, without exception, became Buddha deeds.[73]

Similar postulates became the pretext for licentious behavior in rival Ch'an lineages, where breaking the bounds of conventional morality was viewed as expressing one's true nature.[74] Yen-shou's reaction was the opposite. According to Yen-shou, "increasing cultivation with myriad practices [is required to] make the mind clear and lucid; . . . if the myriad dharmas are none other than mind, how can the mind be obstructed by cultivating them?"[75] The Ch'an experience, in Yen-shou's eyes, does not culminate in the mystic union of the sacred and profane where "everything that comes into contact with one's eyes is in the state of *bodhi;* whatever comes into contact with one's feet is the *tao*,"[76] expressions linked with Hung-chou Ch'an,[77] but in a concrete program of activities sanctioned by the Buddhist tradition: participation at Buddhist assemblies, ordination rites, prayers and rituals aimed at enlisting the blessings of the Buddhas, and so on.

Yen-shou thus clearly distinguishes Wu-yüeh Ch'an as distinct from Ch'an practitioners who "have become attached to emptiness, and [whose practice] is not compatible with the teaching."[78] For Yen-shou, Ch'an practice is firmly based in the scriptures and doctrinal formulations of the past, promoting conventional practices and rituals as requirements for actualizing enlightenment. Rather than "enslaving one's thought and wearing out one's body," as critics of Yen-shou charged,[79] conventional Buddhist activities (the myriad good deeds) are viewed positively, as "provisions with which Bodhisattvas enter sainthood, . . . gradual steps with which Buddhas assist [others] on the way [to enlightenment]."[80]

In the end, much was at stake over the two competing interpretations of Ch'an. The two conceptions of Ch'an as "harmony between Ch'an and the teaching" and "a special transmission outside the teaching" reflect different religious epistemologies. In essence, the distinction here is between a form of rationalism,[81] a view that reasoned explanation is capable of communicating the truth coupled with the belief that the vehicle of this reasoned explanation is Buddhist scripture, and a type of mysticism, a view that the experience of enlightenment is beyond reification, verbal explanation, or rational categories and that Buddhist scripture is incapable of conveying that experience. The debate in early Sung Ch'an was whether Ch'an is acquiescent with the tradition of Buddhist rationalism or belongs to an independent mystical tradition.

The history of Ch'an and Zen is generally presented as denying Buddhist rationalism in favor of a mysticism that in principle transcends every context, including even the Buddhist one. The "orthodox" Ch'an position maintains that the phrase "do not establish words and letters" is consistent with "a special transmission outside the teaching," treating the two slogans as a pair. In this interpretation, both phrases are said to point to the common principle that true enlightenment, as experienced by the Buddha and transmitted through the patriarchs, is independent of verbal explanations, including the record of the Buddha's teachings (i.e., scriptures) and later doctrinal elaborations. This interpretation was not acknowledged in Wu-yüeh Ch'an, which distinguished the phrase "do not establish words and letters" from the principle of an independent transmission apart from the teaching and which treated the two as opposing ideas. Wu-yüeh Ch'an acknowledged the validity of Bodhidharma's warning against attachment to scriptures and doctrines, but did not accept that this warning amounted to a categorical denial. As Ch'an became established in the Sung, monks and officials rose to challenge the Wu-yüeh interpretation and to insist on an independent tradition apart from the teaching.

The *Ching-te ch'uan-teng lu* and the *Fo-tzu t'ung-tsan chi*: A Tale of Two Prefaces

The view of harmony between Ch'an and the teaching exhibited in the writings of Yen-shou and Tsan-ning is oddly inconsistent with the *Ching-te ch'uan-teng lu,* the influential transmission record promoting the Fa-yen lineage compiled by the Wu-yüeh monk Tao-yüan.[82] The *Ching-te ch'uan-teng lu* was innovative in ways that signaled a departure from Wu-yüeh Ch'an. It became the model for the new style of Buddhist biography that became prevalent in Sung Ch'an, emphasizing lineage as the basis for sectarian identity (in contrast to Tsan-ning's *Sung kao-seng chuan,* conceived in the old, nonsectarian style based on categorical treatment). Moreover, through the prominence it gave to transmission verses and "encounter dialogues," it represented a style of Ch'an that seemed at odds with conventional Buddhism and "harmony between Ch'an and the teaching."

Other evidence, however, supports the Wu-yüeh view of a harmonious relationship between Ch'an and the scriptures, similar to that of Yen-shou and Tsan-ning.[83] The evidence is based on a comparison of the two prefaces with the work that became known as the *Ching-te ch'uan-teng lu:* the "standard" preface by Yang I (974–1020) and the original, largely forgotten preface by the compiler Tao-yüan. Yang I's preface shows, among other things, that Tao-yüan's original compilation was subjected to an editing process by leading Sung officials, headed by Yang I himself.[84] Since Tao-yüan's original compilation is no longer extant, it is difficult to assess the extent to which editorial changes were made to the text during this process. The two prefaces indicate that, at the very least, the conception of the work was significantly altered under Yang I's supervision. Tao-yüan's original title for the work, *Fo-tzu t'ung-tsan chi (Collection of the Common Ch'an Practice of the Buddhas and Patriarchs),* suggests harmony between Ch'an and the Buddhist tradition. The disparity between Tao-yüan's conception for the work he called the *Fo-tzu t'ung-tsan chi,* and Yang I's conception of the revised work, the *Ching-te ch'uan-teng lu,* is further reflected in the content of their respective prefaces.

The differences between Tao-yüan and Yang I's view of Ch'an is revealed in their prefaces in two ways. One concerns their view of the relation of Ch'an to Buddhist practices; the other relates to how the teaching of Bodhidharma is expressed in Ch'an slogans. Tao-yüan conceived of Ch'an practice in a way that was consistent with Wu-yüeh Ch'an, especially as promoted in the writings of Yen-shou.

> The best way of release from birth and death [i.e., *saṃsāra*] is to realize *nirvāṇa;* to instruct those who are confused, myriad practices [*wan-hsing*] are employed according to the differences among practitioners.[85]

Yang I's preface cast the meaning of Ch'an practice in an entirely different light. In contrast to Tao-yüan's interpretation of Ch'an as a teaching where "myriad practices are employed according to the differences among practitioners" (*wan-hsing i chih ch'a-pieh*), Yang I's preface insisted that the teachings of Ch'an masters be viewed in terms of "a special practice outside the teaching" (*chiao-wai pieh-hsing*). According to Tao-yüan, Ch'an teaching employed *wan-hsing,* the "myriad practices," while to Yang I Ch'an represented *pieh-hsing,* a "special practice (outside the teaching)." Not only did Yang I's phrase promote Ch'an exclusivity and implicitly undermine Ch'an pluralism, it paralleled the expression "a special transmission outside the teaching" (*chiao-wai pieh-ch'uan*), which came into vogue around the same time through the vehicle of the *T'ien-sheng kuang-teng lu.*

The different interpretations of Ch'an teaching held by Tao-yüan and Yang I were also reflected in the slogans that each attributed to Bodhidharma's teaching. According to Tao-yüan, "[Bodhidharma] did not make a display of verbal expressions [*pu-shih yü-yen*], and did not establish words and letters [*pu-li wen-tzu*]."[86] According to Yang I, [Bodhidharma taught]: do not establish words and letters [*pu-li wen-tzu*], directly point to the source of the mind [*ch'ih-chih shin-yüan*]; do not engage in gradual methods [*pu-chien chieh-ti*], attain Buddhahood immediately [*ching-teng fo-ti*]."[87] In spite of their different interpretations, Tao-yüan and Yang I both were in agreement that Bodhidharma's teaching was represented in the phrase "do not establish words and letters" [*pu-li wen-tzu*]. Their divergent views on the relationship between Ch'an practice and Buddhist practices were based on rival interpretations of this phrase.

Within the Ch'an tradition, the issue of whether Bodhidharma's teaching represented compatibility or incompatibility with Buddhist scriptures and practices depended on the interpretation of Bodhidharma's *Erh-ju ssu-hsing lun* (*Treatise on the Two Entrances and Four Practices*).[88] In the section of the Treatise where "entrance by principle (or reason)" (*li-ju*) is discussed, two characterizations are given. On the one hand, entrance by principle is said to "awaken one to the truth [*wu-tsung*] in accordance with [scriptural] teaching [*chi-chiao*]. Later, after realizing true nature (*chen-hsing*), one is said to "reside fixedly, without wavering, never again to be swayed by written teachings [*wen-chiao*]."[89] The two statements provided ample support for either interpretation of Bodhidharma's message. "Awakening to the truth in accordance with [scriptural] teaching" easily supports the position of "harmony between Ch'an and the teaching"; and "residing fixedly, . . . never again to be swayed by written teachings" serves similarly to support the position of "a special transmission outside the teaching."

In spite of the Sung emphasis on interpreting Bodhidharma's message as "a special transmission outside the teaching," the interpretation of it in terms of "harmony between Ch'an and the teaching" is more justifiable historically. John McRae has already pointed out that the distinction proposed by Bodhidharma in the *Erh-ju ssu-hsing lun* "is similar to the *Lankavatara Sūtra's* concept of *tsung-t'ung,* or 'penetration of the truth,' i.e., the true inner understanding of the ultimate message of the scriptures, as opposed to *shuo-t'ung,* or 'penetration of the preaching,' a conceptualized understanding of the words and formulae of the text and nothing more."[90] This distinction between "penetration of the truth" and "penetration of the preaching" was the favored method of interpreting Bodhidharma's phrase "do not establish words and letters" in T'ang Ch'an, and was adopted by Wu-yüeh masters. In this interpretation, "do not establish words and letters" was taken not as a denial of the recorded words of the Buddha or the doctrinal elaborations by learned monks, but as a warning to those who had become confused about the relationship between Buddhist teaching as a guide to the truth and mistook it for the truth itself.

Yang I's presence in the reinterpretation of Ch'an is a sure indication of the important role Ch'an played in the Sung as well as the role played by Sung literati in determining the shape of Ch'an ideology. The biography of Yang I in the *T'ien-sheng kuang-teng lu,* the transmission record compiled by Li Tsun-hsü, a son-in-law of the emperor, that consolidated the position of Ch'an as a "special transmission outside the teaching" suggests that Yang I's reinterpretation of Ch'an was closely linked to the Ch'an masters with whom he associated.[91] Yang I's initial associations with Ch'an masters were with descendants of Fa-yen Wen-i, Master An and Master Liang.[92] Later he developed close relations with Chen-hui Yuan-lien (951–1036), a descendant of Lin-chi.[93] Moreover, Yang I's adoption of a Lin-chi perspective on Ch'an intensified under the influence of Li Wei, a close cohort at the Sung court who was an avid follower of Lin-chi masters. In this way, Yang I's own biography parallels the changes occurring in early Sung Ch'an, changes that are reflected in his preface to the *Ching-te ch'uan-teng lu* and in the inclusion of his biography in the influential Ch'an transmission record, the *T'ien-sheng kuang-teng lu.* The Yuan edition of the *Ching-te ch'uan-teng lu* acknowledges Yang I's importance in establishing the new interpretation of Ch'an by appending the *T'ien-sheng kuang-teng lu* biography of Yang I to it.[94] Yang I, more than any other figure, was responsible for establishing Ch'an as "a special transmission outside the teaching" in official circles.

Mahākāśyapa's Smile: Silent Transmission and the Kung-an Tradition

The surge of recognition for Ch'an as "a special transmission outside the teaching" stimulated a number of ancillary developments to help give credence to the Ch'an claim. The most important of these was the story recounting how the "special transmission" was first conceived in the interchange between Śākyamuni and Mahākāśyapa. The credibility of the Ch'an tradition, as it took shape and began to assume a comprehensive form, necessitated that the "special transmission" originate with none other than Śākyamuni himself. It was the secret, esoteric enlightenment experience of Śākyamuni that Ch'an claimed as its unique possession, transmitted from mind to mind, not via writ-

ten texts, between master and disciple. Ironically, however, official acknowledgement of this tradition of secret, unwritten lore relied on written documents to substantiate Ch'an claims.

The most famous early Ch'an document to substantiate this tradition of
secret transmission is the *Platform Sūtra of the Sixth Patriarch.* This document
describes how the transmission was secretly passed from the Fifth Patriarch
Hung-jen to the Sixth Patriarch Hui-neng, over the rival claims of the learned
head monk Shen-hsiu. The following statement, attributed to Hui-neng, sum-
marizes the new meaning that Ch'an transmission had acquired.

> At midnight the Fifth Patriarch called me into the hall and expounded the *Dia-
> mond Sūtra* to me. Hearing it but once, I was immediately awakened, and that
> night I received the dharma. None of the others knew anything about it. Then
> he transmitted to me the dharma of Sudden Enlightenment and the robe, saying:
> "I make you the Sixth Patriarch. The robe is proof and is to be handed down
> from generation to generation. My dharma must be transmitted from mind to
> mind. You must make people awaken to themselves."[95]

Hui-neng, a supposedly illiterate peasant from the south without access to
written documents, became a fitting symbol of Ch'an "mind to mind transmission" (*i-hsin ch'uan-hsin*) and a "special transmission outside the teaching,"
freed of the alleged limitations of Buddhist doctrinal teaching.

The same forces that produced the *Platform Sūtra* were also questioning
the nature of transmission throughout the Ch'an tradition. It made no sense
that this "mind-to-mind transmission" began with Hui-neng, or even Bodhidharma. In order for a credible link to be maintained, the genesis of a secret
mind transmission had to originate with none other than the Buddha himself.
This requirement made the alleged transmission from Śākyamuni to Mahākāśyapa the first and crucial link in the chain, the prototype of mind to mind
transmission in the Ch'an tradition.

An important early Ch'an source addressing the issue of how the transmission took place between Śākyamuni and Mahākāśyapa is the *Pao-lin chuan,*
compiled in 801.[96] The *Pao-lin chuan* records Śākyamuni's words when transmitting the teaching to Mahākāśyapa as follows:

> I entrust to you the pure eye of the dharma [*ch'ing-ching fa-yen*], the wonderful
> mind of *nirvāṇa* [*nieh-p'an miao-hsin*], the subtle true dharma [*wei-mao cheng-fa*]
> which in its authentic form is formless [*shih-hsiang wu-hsiang*]. You must protect
> and maintain it. . . .
>
> > The dharma is at root a dharma of no dharma,
> > But that no dharma is yet the dharma.
> > When I now transmit the dharma,
> > What dharma could possibly be the dharma?[97]

According to Mahākāśyapa's biography in the same record, Mahākāśyapa was not present in the assembly when the Buddha entered *nirvāṇa,* but the Buddha made it known to his leading disciples that upon his return, Mahākāśyapa would clarify the treasury of the true dharma eye (*cheng-fa-yen tsang*), that is, the true teaching of the Buddha. Later, Mahākāśyapa verified that the treasury of the true dharma eye, the true teaching of the Buddha, was none other than the collection of sūtras preached by the Buddha, recited at the assembly by Ananda.

In this way, the *Pao-lin chuan* reflected an ambiguous understanding of the true nature of the Buddha's teaching transmitted to Mahākāśyapa. On the one hand, it contended that this teaching was "formless" and subtle, alluding to the mind-to-mind transmission that became the hallmark of Ch'an identity. On the other hand, it identified the teaching of the Buddha with the canonical tradition compiled through Ananda at the council of Rājagrha, as verbal rather than formless.

There is no hint of the story of Mahākāśyapa responding with a smile when Śākyamuni holds up a flower to the assembly in early Ch'an records. In the *Pao-lin chuan* the whole episode is implausible given Mahākāśyapa's absence from the assembly where his role in clarifying the Buddha's teaching after the Buddha passes into *nirvāṇa* is announced. Likewise the transmission between Śākyamuni and Mahākāśyapa is acknowledged in the *Ching-te ch'uan-teng lu* as a transmission of "the pure Dharma eye, the wondrous mind of *nirvāṇa,*" but there is no mention of the episode of the flower and Mahākāśyapa's smile.[98]

The first mention in Ch'an records of the transmission between Śākyamuni and Mahākāśyapa involving the presentation of the flower before the assembly and Mahākāśyapa's smile in response is in the *T'ien-sheng kuang-teng lu.* This comes as no surprise in light of the previous discussion highlighting the role of this text in establishing Sung Ch'an identity in terms of "a special transmission outside the teaching." In the *T'ien-sheng kuang-teng lu,* Śākyamuni presents the flower to the assembly as a test of the attendees' knowledge of the true nature of the dharma.

> When the Tathāgata was on Vulture Peak preaching the dharma, various devas presented him with flowers. The World Honoured One took a flower and instructed the assembly. Mahākāśyapa faintly smiled. The World Honoured One announced to the assembly: "I possess the treasury of the true dharma eye, the wondrous mind of nirvāna. I entrust it to Mahākāśyapa to spread in the future, not allowing it to be cut off.[99]

Acknowledging the nonverbal nature of the "formless" dharma, Mahākāśyapa responds in kind with a smile to the Buddha's challenge to the assembly, at which point the Buddha announces: "I possess the treasury of the true Dharma eye, the wondrous mind of *nirvāna.* I entrust it to Mahākāśyapa." The content of the treasury of the true Dharma eye (*cheng fa-yen tsang*), the essence of Buddhist teaching that Śākyamuni was said to possess, was not yet explicitly connected to the expression *chiao-wai pieh-ch'uan,* but the basis for identifying the two was clearly drawn. In the *T'ien-sheng kuang-teng lu,* the dharma transmitted from the Buddha to Mahākāśyapa is contrasted with the Buddha's preaching career, characterized in terms of the three vehicles. The implication is that the Ch'an dharma, transmitted secretly between master (the Buddha) and disciple (Mahākāśyapa), is superior to the exoteric message preached in the *Lotus Sūtra,* the teaching of the three vehicles, and particularly the supreme dharma in the *Lotus,* the "one vehicle."[100] Moreover, the *T'ien-sheng kuang-teng lu* was the first record to emphasize an interpretation of Ch'an as a tradition independent of Buddhist scriptural teaching associating the phrase "a special transmission outside the teaching" with the teachings of prominent Ch'an masters active in the early Sung. The inclusion of a story about how that independent tradition began forms a natural parallel to the kind of image that early Sung Ch'an masters were projecting about the unique and superior nature of the dharma they were transmitting. What is remarkable is that both of these developments, the story of silent transmission between Śākyamuni and Mahākāśyapa as unequivocally associated with a superior Ch'an teaching, and the identification of Ch'an as "a special transmission outside the teaching," were Sung rather than T'ang innovations.

The first version of the story involving the transmission of the dharma from Śākyamuni to Mahākāśyapa to make explicit what was only implicitly drawn in the *T'ien-sheng kuang-teng lu* is the one recorded in the *Ta fan-t'ien wang wen fo chüeh-i ching (The Scripture in which Brahman Asks Buddha to Resolve his Doubts).*[101] It is ostensibly part of the Buddhist canon, but there is no evidence that this "scripture" existed prior to the Sung. It is widely regarded as apocryphal, all the more so for the scriptural support it conveniently provided for the story involving Śākyamuni and Mahākāśyapa.[102] According to the *Ta fan-t'ien wang wen fo chüeh-i ching* version, when Śākyamuni sat before the assembly holding a lotus blossom that had been given him by Brahman, speechless and without uttering a word, Mahākāśyapa broke into a smile. The Buddha proclaimed, "I possess the treasury of the true Dharma eye, the wondrous mind of *nirvāṇa,* the subtle dharma-gate born of the formlessness of true form, not established on words and letters, a special transmission outside the teaching," and went on to entrust it to Mahākāyapa.[103] This proclamation established the origins of the Ch'an tradition in terms that directly linked the content of the Buddha's teaching, "the treasury of the true Dharma eye, the wondrous mind of *nirvāṇa,*" and so on, silently bequeathed to Mahākāśyapa, to the Ch'an identity as "a special transmission outside the teaching." It did so, ironically, under the pretext of scriptural authorization.

Subsequently the story of the transmission of the dharma from Śākyamuni to Mahākāśyapa as told in the *Ta fan-t'ien wang-wen fo-chüeh-i ching* began to appear in Ch'an transmission records. The *Lien-teng hui-yao,* compiled by Wu-ming in 1189, records this rendition of the story explicitly connecting the transmission with "a special transmission outside the teaching."[104] It also appears in a Ming dynasty collection of Ch'an biographies, the *Chiao-wai pieh-ch'uan,* compiled by the official Li Mei and others (preface dated 1633). This work organizes the lineages of the "five houses" around the motif of its title "A Special Transmission Outside the Teaching," suggesting that the entire Ch'an tradition be incorporated under this phrase.[105]

The full popularity of Ch'an that combined scriptural authorization with the interpretation of Ch'an as "a special transmission outside the teaching" was not realized through either the Ch'an transmission record where it originated or the scriptural account that supported it, but through the uniquely Sung literary from, the collections of kung-an case studies. The *Wu-men kuan* (*Gateless Barrier*), compiled at the end of the Sung in 1228, includes the story of the interaction between Śākyamuni and Mahākāśyapa as one of its case studies, following the version established in the apocryphal *Ta-fan t'ien-wang wen-fo chüeh-i ching.*[106] Through the inclusion of this story in the *Wu-men kuan,* the interpretation of Ch'an as "a special transmission outside the teaching" reached countless numbers of Ch'an and Zen students, continuing down to the present day.

In spite of the success the interpretation of Ch'an as "a special transmission outside the teaching" enjoyed, the history of Ch'an in the Sung reveals a mixed legacy. Even with the dominance of the Lin-chi line of Ch'an in the Sung, the interpretation of Ch'an as "a special transmission outside the teaching" was not universally acknowledged. There was a reluctance among Ch'an masters to deny the Buddhist scriptural tradition and to give voice to the interpretation of Ch'an as "a special transmission outside the teaching." In this respect, many masters continued to exhibit the influence of "scripture friendly" Ch'an, to see Ch'an in terms a basic harmony with the teachings of the scriptures, however much they fell under the sway of Ch'an rhetoric. Even in the Sung, when the Lin-chi branch rose to dominance, the interpretation of Ch'an as "a special transmission outside the scriptures" did not go unchallenged. Members of the Yün-men branch took the lead in this challenge. The record of Ch'an master Huai (992–1064), the *Huai ch'an-shih lu,* included in the aforementioned *Tsu-t'ing shih-yüan,* a collection of Yün-men lineage records compiled in 1108, contests the interpretation of "a special transmission outside the scriptures" promoted in Lin-chi circles. After citing the four slogans in connection with Bodhidharma, Ch'an master Huai remarks, "Many people mistake the meaning of 'do not establish words and letters.' They speak frequently of abandoning the scriptures and regard silent sitting as Ch'an. They are truly the dumb sheep of our school."[107]

There were limits to what Ch'an rhetorical claims to be "a special transmission outside the teaching" could, in practice, allow. These may be generally characterized as follows. The success of Ch'an in the Sung led to official recognition and support. The fledgling Ch'an movement of the T'ang came to dominate Chinese Buddhism in the Sung. The success of Ch'an institutions made them highly dependent on activities, rituals, ceremonies, and other forms of Buddhist practice rhetorically denied in the interpretation of Ch'an as "a special transmission outside the teaching." In short, the social reality of Ch'an was inconsistent with its rhetoric: the more successful Ch'an became institutionally, the more dependent it became on T'ang scholastic teachings. Sung Ch'an institutions inherited the rituals and conventions of T'ang Buddhist monasteries.[108]

Conclusion

This investigation into the origins of the Ch'an tradition as "a special transmission outside the teaching" and of the creation of the myth of silent transmission beginning with Śākyamuni and Mahākāśyapa raises some basic questions about the study of Ch'an. Rather than the standard view of a Ch'an "golden age" in the T'ang, the current study suggests that major components of the Ch'an identity were Sung, instead of T'ang innovations. In important respects, the so-called T'ang "golden age" must be treated as a product of Sung revisionism. The major sources for understanding T'ang Ch'an were, with few exceptions, compiled in the Sung. The fundamental "myths" of Ch'an's founding masters were crystalized in Sung imagination.

The possibility that Sung Ch'an masters were responsible for shaping our view of the Ch'an tradition, including the T'ang golden age, raises more fundamental questions about the way Ch'an history has been interpreted. In the first place, it undermines the entire Ch'an "golden age" hypothesis: was there such an era except in the retrospective vision of Sung Ch'an masters, who postulated it as a way to affirm their own identity? Rather than situating a hypothetical golden age in a particular historical period that demarcates sharply between T'ang and Sung Ch'an, it seems better to hypothesize Ch'an history during this important period of development on a T'ang-Sung continuum which acknowledges that our understanding of T'ang Ch'an is filtered through Sung memories of it.

In short, the whole "golden age" discussion presumes that such a period did, in fact, exist. This presumption has to a large degree influenced modern scholarship on Ch'an, directly and indirectly. It has influenced the way Chinese Buddhism and Ch'an have been interpreted, and established the agenda for Ch'an studies for some time. One need only look to the terminology of "Growth and Domestication" (pre-T'ang), "Maturity and Acceptance" (T'ang, "The Apogee"), and "Decline" (Sung, "Memories of a Great Tradition") employed in the leading English language text on Chinese Buddhism,[109] or to the preponderance of works, studies, and translations on T'ang Ch'an masters to confirm this impression. A prominent example is the attempt at "canon formation" in modern Zen, exhibited in collections such as the *Zen no goroku* (*Ch'an yü-lu*) series, which formally introduces works from the Chinese Ch'an tradition, focusing on works from the T'ang period and works and masters associated with the Lin-chi (Rinzai) branch.[110] This impression regarding the ideological assumptions of modern Zen scholarship has recently received critical attention. Regarding the scholarship of Yanagida Seizan, the leading luminary of modern critical scholarship on Zen and the guiding visionary behind the *Zen no goroku* series, Bernard Faure comments:

> For all its openness, Yanagida's scholarship remains under specific constraints: the importance of the doctrinal texts, the belief in a "pure" Zen, a tendency to focus on Zen (to the detriment of traditional and popular Buddhism), and on Rinzai Zen in particular. In many respects Yanagida remains close to the Kyoto school.... Yanagida's scholarship is still informed by an orthodox view of Ch'an/Zen. It is perhaps significant that he reserves his most severe criticism for the rival Sōtō tradition, and shares with his colleagues an interest in "classic Ch'an," to the detriment of other trends like Northern Ch'an, despite the fact that he was one of the first to reevaluate the teaching of this school.[111]

As long as one thinks in terms of a "golden age," one is bound by Zen orthodoxy and the "rhetoric of Ch'an." Like any successful religious tradition, Ch'an has gone through a process of development, but it is not important to isolate any one period as a "golden age" in this process. This may be of concern to a religious tradition searching for self-identity or attempting to reform or renew itself, but it is not an important debate for modern scholars to engage in (except as a reflection of debates within the tradition itself). More recent studies have broken from this framework, and current studies suggest that this trend will continue.[112]

Finally, a reconsideration of Sung Ch'an challenges the way that the history of Buddhism in China has been interpreted. Rather than an age lacking in creativity, where once dynamic teachings have degenerated into static formalism, the Sung dynasty needs to be approached as a period of intense, innovative reevaluation of the Buddhist experience in China in the face of strong new challenges.[113] The investigation here has shown that the identity of Ch'an summarized in its four slogans, a hallmark of "T'ang" Ch'an identity, emerged in complete and comprehensive form only through the interpretation of early Sung masters. Three of the slogans were acknowledged as the undisputed legacy of T'ang Ch'an. The acknowledgement of Ch'an as "a special transmission outside the scriptures" was a decidedly Sung innovation, however much it was inspired by earlier records. Likewise, the myth of a "silent transmission" between Śākyamuni and Mahākāśyapa, the prototypical transmission myth in the Ch'an tradition, was conceived in Sung Ch'an imagination as part of an effort to substantiate a unique identity. As such, it constituted a creative alternative to conventional ways in which the transmission of truth in Buddhism was conceived via textual means.

Notes

Portions of this chapter were originally presented at the American Academy of Religion conference in Philadelphia, November 1996, under the title: "Ch'an Slogans and the Creation of Ch'an Ideology: A Special Transmission Outside the Scriptures," and were published in a two-part series, the summer and fall 1996 issues of *Ch'an Magazine* (New York).

1. T 48.293c; Hirata Takashi, *Mumonkan, Zen no goroku,* vol. 18 (Tokyo: Chikuma shobō, 1969), pp. 37–41.

2. T 48.292c.

3. T 48.292c–293a. For the full text of Wu-men's commentary, see the first section of Ishii Shūdō's study in this volume (chap. 4).

4. T 48, no. 2005.

5. T 48, no. 2003.

6. On the development of the kung-an tradition in terms of the sinification of Buddhism, see Robert E. Buswell, Jr., "The 'Short Cut' Approach of *K'an-hua* Meditation: The Evolution of a Practical Subitism in Chinese Ch'an Buddhism," in Peter N. Gregory, ed., *Sudden and Gradual: Approaches to Meditation in Chinese Thought* (Honolulu: University of Hawaii Press, 1987), pp. 321–377.

7. On the current scholarly appraisal of Bodhidharma and his teachings, see John R. McRae, *The Northern School and the Formation of Early Ch'an Buddhism* (Honolulu: University of Hawaii Press, 1986), pp. 15–19 (on the legend and life of Bodhidharma), and pp. 101–117 (on Bodhidharma's teachings).

8. See, for example, Kenneth Ch'en, *Buddhism in China: A Historical Survey* (Princeton, N.J.: Princeton University Press, 1964).

9. The most noteworthy of these schools were the Mādhyamika (San-lun, or "Three Treatises") and the Yogācāra/Vijñānavada (Wei-shih, or "Consciousness-Only").

10. The T'ien-t'ai and Hua-yen schools were the most famous.

11. Borrowing the characterizations used by Robert E. Buswell, *The Formation of Ch'an Ideology in China and Korea: The Vajrasamādhi-Sūtra. A Buddhist Apocryphon* (Princeton, N.J.: Princeton University Press, 1989).

12. A view accepted in Chinese Buddhist circles as early as the beginning of the Sung dynasty; see Albert Welter, "Zanning and Chan: The Changing Nature of Buddhism in Early Song China," *Journal of Chinese Religions,* vol. 23 (1995). In truth, the evidence suggests a reality other than Ch'an rhetorical interpretation proclaims. Rather than a "revolution" against scholasticism, the success of Ch'an might better be viewed as an accommodation to the tastes of the rising literati class in the Sung. The famous *yü-lu* collections, dialogues of famous Ch'an masters, and the "transmission records" (*ch'uan-teng lu*), the biographies of Ch'an masters recorded according to lineage and including their sayings, conversations, and activities, were written to appeal to Sung literary tastes.

13. Evidence for this view can be seen in the way standard texts introduce Chinese Buddhism. In the fourfold evolutionary scheme ("Introduction," "Growth and Domestication," "Maturity and Acceptance," and "Decline") adopted by Kenneth Ch'en, *Buddhism in China,* the final section begins with ch. XIV, "Memories of a Great Tradi-

tion: Sung Dynasty." Another common text, Richard H. Robinson and Willard L. Johnson, *The Buddhist Religion: A Historical Introduction* (Belmont, Cal.: Wadsworth, 1982), pp. 190–191, says: "The Ch'an School, so vibrantly alive during the T'ang (618–907), began to fossilize during the Sung (960–1279). The spontaneous, witty interviews between master and disciple, the kung-an, became set texts for later generations. Ch'an began to look back to a golden age, its creativity drying up in the process." A survey of similar texts in Japanese reveals the same general attitude. It is interesting to note that the most recent edition (4th ed., 1997) of the Robinson and Johnson text has adopted a corrective approach, giving equal, fair-handed treatment to "Ch'an during the Five Dynasties" and "Ch'an in the Early Sung" (pp. 203–207), as well as "The Sung Dynasty" (pp. 207–210).

14. The slogans first became known in the West through the writings of D. T. Suzuki, *Essays in Zen Buddhism (first series)* (London: Rider, 1927; rep. New York: Grove Press, 1961), p. 176.

15. A position reflected in Heinrich Dumoulin, *Zen Buddhism: A History, Volume 1: India and China* (New York: MacMillan, 1988), p. 85, stemming from the works of Japanese Rinzai scholars like Furuta Shōkin and Yanagida Seizan.

16. The *Tsu-t'ing shih-yüan* is a collection of records of masters associated with the Yün-men branch of Ch'an. The four slogans are attributed to Bodhidharma in two places by Ch'an master Huai in ch. 5, ZZ 64.377b and 379a.

17. Of the 48 cases in the *Wu-men kuan,* for example, 25 are found in the *Ching-te ch'uan-teng lu* and 4 are found in the *T'ien-sheng kuang-teng lu;* see the chart by Ishii Shūdō in his review of Nishimura Eshin's translation of the *Mumonkan* in *Hanazono daigaku bungakubu kenkyū kiyō,* no. 28 (1996): 125–135.

18. Kamata Shigeo, ed., *Zengen shosenshū tojo, Zen no goroku,* vol. 9 (Tokyo: Chikuma shobō, 1971), p. 44 and note on p. 47.

19. Yanagida Seizan, *Shoki Zenshū shisho no kenkyū* (Kyoto: Hōzōkan, 1967), p. 475.

20. T 37.490c. Isshū Miura and Ruth Fuller Sasaki, *Zen Dust: The History of the Kōan and Kōan Study in Rinzai (Lin-Chi) Zen* (New York: Harcourt, Brace & World, 1966), pp. 228–230.

21. Iriya Yoshitaka, *Denshin Hōyō, Enryu roku, Zen no goroku,* vol. 8 (Tokyo: Chikuma shobō, 1969), p. 85. Even the usage here is suspect, since the section where the three slogans appear are not included in the earliest known redaction of the text contained in the *Ching-te ch'uan-teng lu,* ch. 9 (T 51.270b–273a). The compilation of the full text of Huang-po's teachings did not appear until 1036, when it was recorded in the *T'ien-sheng kuang-teng lu.*

22. This is the image provided in the "official" presentation of Ch'an in the early Sung by Tsan-ning, referred to in more detail below.

23. The *Tsu-t'ang chi* (K. *Chodong chip*) is noteworthy for promoting lineages descending from Ma-tsu Tao-i, including those descending from Lin-chi I-hsüan. An edition of this work was published by Yanagida Seizan based on the Korean edition contained in the library of Hanazono University (Taipei: Kuangwen shuchu, 1972). The phrase *chiao-wai pieh-ch'uan* appears in ch. 6, in the biography of Shih-shuang Ch'ing-chu (p. 130b). Regarding the circumstances surrounding the compilation and its connection to the lineage descended from Hsüeh-feng I-tsun (822–908), see chapter 6, by Ishii, in this volume (chap. 4).

24. See Yanagida Seizan, *Sodoshū sakuin,* 3 vols. (Kyoto: Kyoto daigaku jinbun kagaku kenkyūjō, 1984) v. 1, 67c; v. 2, 1087a; v. 3, 1276c.

25. T 47.506c. See Urs App, *Concordance to the Record of Linji (Rinzai)* (Kyoto: Hanazono University International Research Institute for Zen Buddhism, 1993).

26. Following Ruth F. Sasaki, trans., *The Recorded Sayings of Ch'an Master Lin-Chi Hui-chao of Chen Prefecture* (Kyoto: The Institute for Zen Studies, 1975), p. 62.

27. Yanagida Seizan, "The Life of Lin-chi I-hsüan," trans. Ruth F. Sasaki, *The Eastern Buddhist*, v. 5, no. 2 (October 1972): 71.

28. T 47.496a–b. The preface identifies Ma Fang as Scholar of the Yen-k'ang Hall, Gold and Purple Kuang-lu Official, Peace Keeping Envoy of the Chen-ting-fu Region, General Supervisor of Cavalry and Infantry Forces, and Director of Ching-te Military Prefecture.

29. T 47.506c.

30. Evidence of a growing distaste for the scriptures and doctrines of the Buddhist scholastic tradition is evident in the examples of Te-shan Hsüan-chien (780/82–865) and Hsiang-yen Chih-hsien (?–898) as well as Lin-chi (Yanagida, "The Life of Lin-chi I-hsüan," p. 73).

31. ZZ 78.471b; T 47.500b; Sasaki, *Recorded Sayings*, p. 24.

32. Aside from the *Ching-te ch'uan-teng lu* (compiled 1004; T 51, no. 2076) and the *T'ien-sheng kuang-teng lu* (compiled 1029; ZZ 78, no. 1553), there were the *Chien-chung ching-kuo hsü-teng lu* (compiled 1101; ZZ 78, no. 1556) by Wei-po, the *Lien-teng hui-yao* (compiled 1183; ZZ 79, no. 1557) by Wu-ming; the *Chia-t'ai p'u-teng lu* (compiled 1201; ZZ 79, no. 1559) by Cheng-shou (1146–1208); and the Wu-teng hui-yüan (compiled 1252; ZZ 80, no. 1565) by P'u-chi.

33. Early Ch'an chronicles with developed lineages of Indian patriarchs are the *Li-tai fa-pao chi* (Yanagida Seizan, *Shoki no Zenshi II, Zen no goroku*, vol. 3 [Tokyo: Chikuma shobō, 1976]), and the *Pao-lin chuan*, in Tokiwa Daijō, *Hōrinden no kenkyū* (Tokyo: Kokusho kangyōkai, 1973).

34. T. Griffith Foulk, "The Ch'an *Tsung* in Medieval China: School, Lineage, or What?" *Pacific World*, no. 8 (Fall 1992): 18–31.

35. See Ishii's book review of Nishimura Eshin's recent translation of the *Mumonkan*, mentioned in note 17, above.

36. The *Ch'uan-hsin fa-yao* is appended to ch. 9 of the Ching-te ch'uan-teng lu (T 51.270b–273a), and ch. 28 contains the *Nan-yang Hui-ch'ung kuo-shih yü*, the *Lo-ching Ho-tse Shen-hui ta-shih yü*, the *Chiang-hsi ta-chi Tao-i ch'an-shih yü*, the *Li-chou pao-shan Wei-yen ho-shang yü*, the *Yüeh-chou ta-chu Hui-hai ho-shang yü*, the *Fen-chou ta-ta Wu-yeh kuo-shih yü*, the *Ch'ih-chou Nan-ch'uan P'u-yüan ho-shang yü*, the *Chao-chou Ch'u-shen ho-shang yü*, *Chen-chou Lin-chi I-hsüan ho-shang yü*, the *Hsüan-sha Tsung-i Shih-pei ta-shih yü*, the *Chang-chou lo-han Kuei-ch'en ho-shang yü*, and the *Ta Fa-yen Wen-i ch'an-shih yü* (T 51.437c–449a).

37. Selections from the *Ching-te ch'uan-teng lu* have been available to English readers for some time through the introduction and translation of nineteen biographies by Chang Chung-yuan (selected *Original Teachings of Ch'an Buddhism [from the Transmission of the Lamp]* [New York: Vintage Books, 1971; orig. published by Pantheon Books in 1969]). There is no comparable selection for the *T'ien-sheng kuang-teng lu* or any later Sung collection. D. T. Suzuki, *Essays in Zen Buddhism* (second series) (New York: Samuel Weiser, 1970; orig. published in 1953) refers to the *Ching-te ch'uan-teng lu* numerous times (see the index, p. 365, entry for the *Transmission of the Lamp*), while failing to mention the *T'ien-sheng kuang-teng lu* or other collections. The *Ching-te ch'uan-teng lu* figures prominently in Philip Yampolsky, *The Platform Sutra of the Sixth Patriarch* (New York: Columbia University Press, 1967)—see entry in the Index,

p. 206—, but no mention is made of the *T'ien-sheng kuang-teng lu*. The prominence of the *Ching-te ch'uan-teng lu* warrants a mention in Etienne Balazs and Yves Hervouet, eds., *A Sung Bibliography (Bibliographie des Sung)* (Hong Kong: Chinese University Press, 1978), pp. 352–353; with the exception of the *Wu-teng hui-yüan* (pp. 354–355), other Ch'an tramission records like the *T'ien-sheng kuang-teng lu* are not mentioned. In contrast to the emphasis on the *Ching-te ch'uan-teng lu* and relative neglect of the other Sung collections in the works noted above, Heinrich Dumoulin provides an even-handed, if brief, introduction to each of the five major Sung transmission records, in *Zen Buddhism: A History*, Volume 1, pp. 8–9.

38. Jan Yün-hua, "Buddhist Historiography in Sung China" (*Zeitschrift der Deutschen Morgandländischen Gesellschaft*, no. 64 [1964], pp. 360–381), remarks that although the volume of the Sung transmission records is great, "most part (sic.) of these works were quoted and requoted from the first work done by Tao-yüan" (p. 366), and that the new material in the *T'ien-sheng kuang-teng lu* "was very limited," noting however that the references to the Lin-chi branch were "comparatively valuable" (ibid.). Similar comments are made by Jan in his entry on "*Ch'an yü-lu* (Dialogues of Ch'an Buddhists)" in William H. Nienhauser, Jr., ed., *The Indiana Companion to Traditional Chinese Literature* (Bloomington: Indiana University Press, 1986), p. 202, describing the *Ching-te chuan-teng lu* as "a dialogical history of Ch'an Buddhism which has had a long-lasting influence," and "the authoritative and sectarian history of the Southern School of Ch'an." In contrast, the "dialogical quality . . . declined consider-ably in the works which were compiled to supplement Tao-yüan's original." The point here is not to dispute such characterizations, but to highlight the unique and important circumstances surrounding the compilation of each transmission history. Until more painstaking research is carried out on each work, it is difficult to make broad general-izations regarding their respective importance.

39. T 51.196b.

40. ZZ 78.496b.

41. Based on the dates of Ch'an master Sheng-nien of Shih-ying Ch'an Temple in Ju-chou, 926–993 (ZZ 78.493c–495a), and Ch'an master Shan-chao of T'ai-tzu Temple of Ta-chung monastery, 947–1024 (ZZ 78.496b–499a). Many of the dates of Ch'an mas-ters recorded in the *T'ien-sheng kuang-teng lu* are unknown. The closer proximity of Kuei-sheng's biography to Shan-chao than to Shen-nien makes it likely that Kuei-sheng's dates were closer to Shan-chao's as well.

42. ZZ 78.496a–b.

43. ZZ 78.504c. The same statement is also recorded in the *Shih-shuang Ch'u-yüan ch'an-shih yü-lu* (ZZ 69.184c), which is contained in the *Tz'u-ming ssu-chia lu*, compiled in 1027. Ch'u-yüan was the disciple of Fen-yang Shan-chao (947–1024). The link be-tween Bodhidharma's teaching and the phrase "a special transmission outside the teaching" is also made in the *T'ien-sheng kuang-teng lu* biography of Ch'an master Chih-sung (ZZ 78.501c).

44. The meaning of Bodhidharma coming from the West is a question that is re-peated frequently in both the *Tsu-t'ang chi* and the *Ching-te ch'uan-teng lu*.

45. ZZ 78.516b. For other examples see 522c, 523b, 525b, and 534a.

46. ZZ 78.441c. This occurs in the context of a famous conversation between Bod-hidharma and the king of Liang, in which the king asks: "What is Buddha?" Bodhi-dharma answers: "Seeing one's nature is Buddha" [*chien-hsing shih fo*]. The king then asks: "Does the master see his own nature, or not?" Bodhidharma replies: "I see the Buddha-nature." The king asks: "Where does [Buddha-]nature exist?" Bodhidharma replies: "[Buddha-]nature exists in activity" [*tso-yung*].

47. ZZ 78.443a.

48. ZZ 78.443a.

49. ZZ 78.443b.

50. ZZ 78.443c, 444a, and 444c.

51. ZZ 78.428a, and 428c.

52. The transmission in these biographies is usually invoked with a standard formula: "In the past, Sākyamuni transmitted the Treasury of the True Dharma Eye to Mahākāśyapa. It continued to be transmitted from one to another until it came down to me. I now transmit it to you. Protect and uphold it so that it will flourish in the future. Do not let it become extinct. Receive my teaching, listen carefully to my verse." This is then followed by the master's transmission verse (as an example, see ZZ 78.429b). While there are variations to this formula, the content is remarkably consistent throughout. *Cheng fa-yen tsang* is sometimes written *ta fa-yen tsang* (Treasury of the Great Dharma Eye).

53. ZZ 78.559c.

54. Conventions dictating the preservation of imperial succession made it necessary for dynastic historians to label the northern states of Liang (907–923), T'ang (923–934), Chin (936–947), Han (947–951), and Chou (951–960) the "Five Dynasties" during this period. For the regional states that appeared in central and southern China, historians coined the label "Ten Kingdoms": Shu (907–925) and Later Shu (934–965) in Ssuch'uan; Nan-p'ing or Ching-nan (907–963) in Hu-pei; Ch'u (927–956) in Hu-nan; Wu (902–937) and Nan T'ang (937–975) based in Nan-ching; Wu-yüeh (907–978) in Chechiang; Min (907–946) in Fu-chien; Nan Han or Yüeh (907–971) based in Kuang-tung; and Pei Han (951–979) in Shan-hsi, a puppet state of Chi-t'an.

55. The expression *chiao-ch'an i-chih* was not used as a slogan in the same way as *chiao-wai pieh-ch'uan* but was a phrase coined later to indicate the positions of Buddhists who rejected the notion of Ch'an as an independent tradition and sought to interpret Ch'an in terms of the Buddhist scriptural tradition. It is implicit in the thought of Tsung-mi, the ninth-century Buddhist syncretist who interpreted Ch'an positions in terms of the doctrines of Buddhist scholasticism.

56. See Peter N. Gregory, *Tsung-mi and the Sinification of Buddhism* (Princeton, N.J.: Princeton University Press, 1991), pp. 224ff., and Jan Yün-hua, "Tsung-mi: His Analysis of Ch'an Buddhism," *T'oung Pao* LVIII (1972), pp. 1–54.

57. The other influential branch of Ch'an in the tenth century, Yün-men, was eclipsed by Fa-yen in the early Sung.

58. The biography of Fa-yen Wen-i is recorded in the *Ching-te ch'uan-teng lu* (T 51, no. 2076, ch. 24), a transmission record written to bolster the claims of the Fa-yen lineage. The biographies of Wen-i's disciples are recorded in ch. 25 (30 biographies) and ch. 26 (33 biographies). Wen-i's biography in the *Sung kao-seng chuan*, ch. 13 (T 50.788a–b), claims that his dharma-heirs numbered over 100 and that 14 achieved fame in their own right. See *Zengaku daijiten* (Tokyo: Taishukan, 1978), p. 1230a.

59. For Buddhism in Nan T'ang, see Tsukamoto Shungo, "Godai nantō no ōshitsu to bukkyō" (The Monarchy and Buddhism in the southern T'ang during the Five Dynasties), *Bukkyō bunka kenkyū*, no. 3 (November 1953): 81–88. The situation of Wu-yüeh Buddhism is discussed later.

60. For a discussion of the Wu-yüeh kingdom and translation of key documents, see Edouard Chavannes, "Le Royaume de Wou et de Yue," *T'oung Pao* XVII (1916): 129–164. An extensive discussion of Buddhism in Wu-yüeh is found in Abe Chōichi, *Chūgoku Zenshūshi no kenkyū* (Tokyo: Seishin Shobō, 1953), pp. 81–176. See also Hatanaka Jōen, "Goetsu no bukkyō—toku ni tendai tokushō to sono shi eimei enju ni

tsuite," *Otani daigaku kenkyū nempō,* no. 7 (1954): 305–365. The main features of Wu-yüeh Buddhism are outlined in Welter, *The Meaning of Myriad Good Deeds: A Study of Yung-ming Yen shou and the Wan-shan t'ung-kue chi* (New York: Peter Lang, 1993), pp. 26–32.

61. I have elsewhere (*The Meaning of Myriad Good Deeds*) challenged this characterization of Yen-shou as simplistic and misleading, only to conclude that Yen-shou's syncretism was more broadly based and much more encompassing than this traditional interpretation allows.

62. T 54.240a. The roles played by non-Ch'an school masters, Kumarajiva and Seng-jui, Buddhabhadra and Hui-yüan, in transmitting Ch'an to China are noted in addition to Bodhidharma's.

63. T 50.789b.

64. T 50.789c.

65. T 54.240a.

66. Ibid.

67. Ibid.

68. T 50.790a.

69. Following Yoshizu Yoshihide, *Kegon-zen no shisōshi-teki kenkyū* (Tokyo: Daitō shuppansha, 1985), Peter Gregory, *Tsung-mi and the Sinification of Buddhism,* pp. 225–226, suggests distinguishing Tsung-mi's efforts as *ch'an-ching i-chih* (harmony between Ch'an and the teaching) and *tsung-chiao i-chih* (harmony between Ch'an and doctrinal teachings) in order to do better justice to the complexity of Tsung-mi's thought. See also Jan Yün-hua, "Tsung-mi, His Analysis of Ch'an Buddhism."

70. Tsung-mi's influence on Tsan-ning is evident in borrowed phrases in Tsan-ning's prose. Tsan-ning's above quoted statement: "the scriptures are the word of the Buddha, and meditation is the thought of the Buddha; there is no discrepancy at all between what the Buddhas have in their mind and what they utter with their mouth" (*ching shih fo-yen, ch'an shih fo-i; chu-fo hsin-k'ou ting, pu hsiang-wei*) is found nearly verbatim in Tsung-mi's *Ch'an-yüan chu-ch'üan-chi tu-hsü* (Kamata, ed., *Zengen shosenshū tojo,* p. 44).

71. Jan, in "Two Problems Concerning Tsung-mi's Compilation of *Ch'an-tsung,*" *Transactions of the International Conference of Orientalists in Japan* 19 (1974), pp. 37–47, has suggested that major portions of Tsung-mi's no longer extant collection of Ch'an sources were absorbed into Yen-shou's *Tsung-ching lu* (T 48, no. 2016). A general comparison of some of the main features of Tsung-mi and Yen-shou can be found in Welter, *The Meaning of Myriad Good Deeds,* pp. 15–19, 147–149, 161 and 166–167.

72. T 48.958b.

73. Ibid.

74. A position typified by the behavior and sayings attributed to Ma-tsu Tao-i (709–788) and members of the Hung-chou lineage, and linked to the lineage of Lin-chi I-hsüan (d. 866). On Tsung-mi's characterization of Tao-i and the Hung-chou lineage, see Jan, "Tsung-mi: His Analysis of Ch'an Buddhism," esp. pp. 45–47.

75. T 48.958c.

76. T 48.961a. This phrase was used in Ch'an circles (e.g., *Ching-te ch'uan-teng lu,* ch. 19; T 51.356b).

77. The expression ("whatever one has contact with is *tao*") is attributed to the Hung-chou school by Tsung-mi (Kamata, ed., *Zengen shosenshū tojo,* p. 288; Jan, "Tsung-mi: His Analysis of Ch'an Buddhism," p. 45).

78. T 48.961b; following the words of Chih-i and the T'ien-t'ai school. According to Yen-shou, it is necessary to engage two types of practice to attain enlightenment:

practice which develops *li,* the abstract powers of penetrating insight; and practice which develops *shih,* provisionally engaging in concrete activities of worship and adoration, and so on. The "practitioners of emptiness" referred to here devote themselves exclusively to developing powers of penetrating insight at the expense of engaging in concrete activities.

79. T. 48.961a.

80. T 48.958c. In important respects, Yen-shou's position is reminiscent, of the religious philosophy of Northern school Ch'an. This is a topic with broad implications that can only be alluded to here with a couple of examples: (1) the Northern school text, the *Wu fang-pien* (Five Expedient, Means), connects the discussion of expedient means to the Buddhist scriptural tradition, a theme that also appears in Yen-shou's works, and (2) the list of religious activities enjoined in the scriptures according to another Northern school text, the *Kuan-hsin lun* (Treatise on Contemplating the Mind), including repairing temples, casting and painting images of the Buddhas, burning incense, offering flowers, burning memorial lamps, circumambulating stūpas, and sponsoring vegetarian feasts, are reminiscent of a list of activities deriving from Yen-shou's *Wan-shan t'ung-kuei chi* (T 48, no. 2017), or the record of his personal activities, the *Tzu-hsing lu* (ZZ 63.158–166). On the Northern school, see McRae, *The Northern School,* pp. 148–233, esp. 171ff., and 199–200; on Yen-shou see Welter, *The Meaning of Myriad Good Deeds,* pp. 131–142.

81. The use of the term "rationalism" here must be qualified. I am not imputing that the Buddhist use of language for arriving at truth be associated with the attempt to introduce mathematical methods to arrive at certainty, as in Descartes. The Buddhist conception, as in Augustine, acknowledges the mind's capacity to distinguish and connect things in a meaningful way, while stipulating that this rational activity is subordinate to the higher activity of the intellect, contemplation. The typical Buddhist way of appropriating rational activity is as "skillful means" (*fang-pien*), used for pointing to a truth that is essentially suprarational.

82. The details of Tao-yüan's life are largely unknown. He was a contemporary of Tsan-ning and a disciple of Te-shao. The circumstances are discussed by Ishii, *Sōdai Zenshūshi no kenkyū* (Tokyo: Daitō shuppansha, 1987), pp. 26–44.

83. My comments here are based on the versions of Tao-yüan's *Fo-tzu t'ung-tsan chi hsü* (Preface to the Collection of the Common Ch'an Practice of the Buddhas and Patriarchs) and Yang I's *Ching-te ch'uan-teng lu* (Preface to the Record of the Transmission of the Lamp compiled in the Ching-te era) in Ishii, *Sōdai Zenshūshi no kenkyū,* pp. 21–23, and on Ishii's discussion of them, pp. 8–21. The former is taken from *Ssu-k'u ch'uan-shu chen-pen,* vol. 8, *Wu-i hsin-chi,* ch. 7, 24a–26b; the latter from the Sung edition of the *Ssu-pu ts'ung-kan pen,* 1a–2b.

84. The other officials mentioned are Vice Director of the Bureau of Military Appointments (*ping-pun yüan-wai lang*) and [Han-lin Academy?] Drafter (*chih-chih-kao*) Li Wei, and Aide to the Court of Imperial Sacrifices (*t'ai-ch'ang ch'eng*) Wang Shu. Yang I held titles as Han-lin Academician (*han-lin hsüeh-shih*), Remonstrator of the Left (*tso-ssu-chien*), and Drafter (*chih-chih-kao*). Yang I's biography is contained in *Sung-shih,* ch. 305. For a discussion of Yang I's influence at the Sung court, see Peter K. Bol, *"This Culture of Ours": Intellectual Transitions in T'ang and Sung China* (Stanford, Cal.: Stanford University Press, 1992), pp. 161–162.

85. Ishii, *Sōdai Zenshūshi no kenkyū* p. 22a.

86. Ishii, *Sōdai Zenshūshi no kenkyū* p. 22a.

87. Ishii, *Sōdai Zenshūshi no kenkyū* p. 22b.

88. The text is recorded in the *Ching-te ch'uan-teng lu*, ch. 30 (T 51.458b–c); it is also contained in Yanagida Seizan, *Daruma no goroku: Ninyū shigyō ron, Zen no goroku*, vol. 1 (Tokyo: Chikuma shobō, 1969). For an English translation and discussion, see McRae, *Northern School*, pp. 101–117.

89. Yanagida, *Daruma no goroku*, pp. 31–32.

90. McRae, *Northern School*, p. 304, n. 14.

91. ZZ 78.511c–512a.

92. Nothing else is known of these masters. Ishii, *Sōdai Zenshūshi no kenkyū*, p. 19, speculates that they were disciples of T'ien-t'ai Te-shao.

93. The biography of Yuan-lin is contained in the *Ch'an-fin seng-pao chuan*, ch. 16.

94. Ishii, *Sōdai Zenshūshi no kenkyū*, p. 17.

95. Yampolsky, *Platform Sutra of the Sixth Patriarch*, section 9, p. 133.

96. Yanagida Seizan, ed., *Sōzō ichin: Hōrinden, Dentō gyokuei shū, Zengaku sōsho* no. 5 (Kyoto: Chūbun, 1983). I am also indebted here to a soon to be published study by T. Griffith Foulk, "Accounts of the Founding of the Ch'an Lineage: A Case Study of Sung Buddhist Historiography," in Peter N. Gregory and Daniel Getz, eds., *Buddhism in the Sung* (Honolulu: University of Hawaii Press, 1999); the manuscript consulted was submitted at the conference entitled "Buddhism in the Sung" held at the University of Illinois, April 20–22, 1996.

97. Yanagida, *Sōzō ichin: Hōrinden*, 10a–c; the translation is taken from Foulk, "Accounts of the Founding of the Ch'an Lineage."

98. Mahākāśyapa's biography is found in ch. 1 (T 51.205c–206b).

99. ZZ 78.428c.

100. Foulk, "Accounts of the Founding of the Ch'an Lineage."

101. ZZ 1, no. 27.

102. *Zengaku daijiten* (Tokyo: Daishukan, 1978), pp. 816c–817a, on the basis of its rendition of this episode, suggests that the *Ta fan-t'ien wang wen fo chüeh-i ching* postdates the *Ching-te ch'uan-teng lu*. The "Zenshūshi nenpyō" (Chronological Table of Zen History), *ibid.*, v. 3, p. 60a, claims that it was written in 1077.

103. ZZ 1.442a.

104. *Hsü-tsang ching* (Shin wen-feng reprint edition of *Zokuzōkyō*) 136.440b–441a.

105. The story of transmission between Śākyamuni and Mahākāśyapa, using the same language as the earlier precedents discussed above, is contained in ch. 1 (*Hsü-tsang ching* 144.27a).

106. T 48.293c. Hirata Takashi, *Mumonkan, Zen no goroku*, vol. 18 (Tokyo: Chikuma shobō, 1969), pp. 37–41. Another Sung Ch'an text, the *Jen-t'ien yen-mu*, compiled in 1188, follows a version of the Mahākāśyapa story that makes no mention of "a special transmission outside the teaching" (T 48.325b). For a list of the numerous texts in which the story appears, see Inoue Shūten, *Mumonkan no shin kenkyū*, vol. 1 (Tokyo: Hōbunkan, 1922), pp. 301–303.

107. ZZ 64.379a. T. Griffith Foulk, trans., "Myth, Ritual, and Monastic Practice in Sung Ch'an Buddhism," in Patricia Buckley Ebrey and Peter N. Gregory, eds., *Religion and Society in T'ang and Sung China* (Honolulu: University of Hawaii Press, 1993), p. 199, n. 17. Foulk reads the comments as those of the compiler of the *Tsu-t'ing shih yüan*, Mu-an. It seems clear to me that they are part of the *Huai ch'an-shih lu* and thus attributable to Ch'an master Huai. See also Foulk's comments on p. 151ff.

108. Foulk, "Myth, Ritual, and Monastic Practice in Sung Ch'an Buddhism," pp. 147–208.

109. Ch'en, *Buddhism in China: A Historical Survey.*

110. The *Zen no goroku* series (Tokyo: Chikuma shobō) contains twenty volumes of annotated translations of Ch'an works published in over a span of years from the late 1960s to the late 1970s. The volumes in this series are as follows:

1. Yanagida, *Daruma no goroku* (*Erh-ju ssu-hsing lun*).
2. ———, *Shoki no Zenshi I* (*Ch'uan fa-pao chi* and *Leng-chia shih-tzu chi*).
3. ———, *Shoki no Zenshi II* (*Li-tai fa-pao chi*).
4. Nakagawa, *Rokuso dankyō* (*Liu-tsu t'an-ching*)
5. Shinohara, *Jin'e goroku* (*Shen-hui yü-lu*).
6. Hirano, *Tongo yōmon* (*Tun-wu yao-men*).
7. Iriya, *Horo kyōshi goroku* (*P'ang chu-shih yü-lu*)
8. ———, *Denshin hōyō & Enryu roku* (*Ch'uan-hsin fa-yao* and *Wan-ling lu*).
9. Kamata, *Zengen shosenshū tojo* (*Ch'an-yuan chu-ch'uan-chi tu-hsu*).
10. Akitsuki, *Rinzai roku* (*Lin-chi lu*).
11. ———, *Jōshū roku* (*Chao-chou lu*).
12. Handa, *Tōzan roku* (*T'ung-shan lu*).
13. Iritani, *Kanzan ji* (*Han-shan shih*).
14. Shimada, *Hōkyō hen* (*Fu-chiao pien*).
15. Kajitani, *Setchō juko* (*Hsüeh-tou sung-ku*).
16. Kajitani and Tsujimura, *Jyūgyū zu* (*Shih-niu t'u*).
17. Araki, *Daie sho* (*Ta-hui shu*).
18. Hirata Takashi, *Mumonkan* (*Wu-men kuan*).
19. Fujiyoshi, *Zenkan sakushin* (*Ch'an-kuan ts'e-hsin*).
20. Iriya and Yanagida, *Goroku no rekishi* (History of *yü-lu*).

111. Bernard Faure, *Chan Insights and Oversights: An Epistemological Critique of the Chan Tradition* (Princeton, N.J. Princeton University Press, 1993), p. 110. Another interesting study of the ideological underpinnings of modern Zen, focusing on the works of D. T. Suzuki, is Robert Sharf, "The Zen of Japanese Nationalism," in Donald E. Lopez, Jr., ed., *Curators of the Buddha: The Study of Buddhism Under Colonialism* (Chicago: University of Chicago Press, 1995), pp. 107–160 (published originally in *History of Religions* 33/1 [1993]: 1–43).

112. In addition to the works already mentioned, one could include the works of a growing list of scholars, many of whom are contributors to this volume.

113. A viewpoint reflected in Gregory and Getz, eds., *Buddhism in the Sung.*

4

Kung-an Ch'an and the Tsung-men t'ung-yao chi

ISHII SHŪDŌ
(TRANSLATED FROM THE JAPANESE
BY ALBERT WELTER)

Kung-an Ch'an as a Unique Feature of Sung Dynasty Ch'an

T'ang dynasty Ch'an and Sung dynasty Ch'an are very different in character. Expressed in doctrinal terms, T'ang Ch'an represents "intrinsic enlighten-ment" (C. *pen-chüeh men,* J. *hongakumon*) and Sung Ch'an represents "ac-quired (or experiential) enlightenment" (C. *shih-chüeh-men,* J. *shigakumon*). In the case of "acquired enlightenment," the practitioner cultivates enlightenment after awakening from delusion to the true nature of reality. This form of culti-vation, unique to Sung Ch'an, is referred to as *k'an-hua Ch'an* (J. *kanna Zen*) or *kung-an Ch'an* (J. *kōan Zen*).[1] When we ask the question "What is a kōan?" the document commonly referred to for an explanation is the first *chuan* of the *Shan-fang yeh-hua* (*Night Talks in the Mountain Hut*), compiled by a Yüan dynasty representative of the Yang-ch'i branch of the Lin-chi lineage, Chung-feng Ming-pen (1263–1323).[2]

According to Chung-feng, *kung-an* was originally a legal term referring to judgments rendered by public courts of law. When Ch'an practitioners sought enlightenment, kung-an referred to as "enlightenment stories" served as mod-els in their search. Accordingly, the association of the term kung-an by Ch'an practitioners with the circumstances surrounding the enlightenment of the Buddhas and patriarchs was already established at the time of Chung-feng.

As a result, Ch'an practice that seeks enlightenment through the use of kōan is referred to as *k'ung-an Ch'an* (J. *kōan-Zen*) or *k'an-hua Ch'an* ("kōan introspection Ch'an"). The *k'an-hua* method refers to a form of cultivation intensely focused on enlightenment through the use of kung-an by referencing "enlightenment stories" in terms of the "crucial phrase" (*hua-t'ou*). *K'an-hua ch'an* is not a method of cultivation that dates from the early period of Ch'an development. There is no evidence at all of its existence during the T'ang dynasty. The *k'an-hua ch'an* technique was systematized by Ta-hui Tsung-kao (1089–1163), a master of the Lin-chi lineage during the Sung dynasty. Moreover, the kung-an technique of Ta-hui Tsung-kao originated in the *"Wu"* kung-an (*mu kōan*) involving Chao-chou. The *wu kung-an* of Chao-chou is the first kung-an in the *Wu-men kuan* (J. *Mumonkan*), the representative collection of 48 kung-an by Wu-men Hui-k'ai (1183–1260).[3] [Translator's note: The text of the *Wu-men kuan* is available in T 48, no. 2005. The kōan involving Chao-chou translated here appears on pp. 292c–293a.]

[KŌAN] A monk asked Chao-chou Ts'ung-shen: "Does a dog also have the Buddha-nature?" Chao-chou answered: *"Wu!"* [J. *Mu*].

[COMMENTARY BY WU-MEN] In studying Ch'an, one must pass through the barrier set up by the patriarchs. To attain inconceivable enlightenment [*miao-wu*], one must completely eliminate mental activity. Those who have not passed through the barrier of the patriarchs and not eliminated mental activity are all ghosts inhabiting plants and trees. Now, tell me, what is the barrier of the patriarchs? It is none other than the one word *"Wu!"* [*Mu*] spoken by Chao-chou here. This is the first barrier of the Ch'an school [*tsung-men*].[4] As a result, I have titled this work "The Gateless Barrier of the Ch'an School" [*Ch'an-tsung Wu-men kuan*]. Those who are able to pass through this barrier not only will meet with Chao-chou as a close friend, they will further be able to walk hand in hand with the patriarchs of history, intimately linked eyebrow to eyebrow. They will see with the same eyes as the patriarchs and hear with the same ears. What a wonderful thing this is!

Now, is there anyone who wants to pass through this barrier? If so, then with your 360 bones and 84,000 pores, you will produce one irresolvable doubt throughout your entire body—concentrate on what this word *"wu"* is, and absorb yourself day and night with this problem. Do not misunderstand the word *wu* either in terms of Taoist "nihilism" [*hsü-wu*] or as "nonexistence" conceived dualistically in terms of "existence" and "nonexistence" [*yu-wu*]. It is like swallowing a red-hot ball of iron and trying to spit it out, but without success. If you wash away completely the depraved knowledge and perverse theories studied previously, applying yourself earnestly over a long period, distinctions like "inner" and "outer" will naturally be fused together. Your experience is like a deaf-mute who has a dream. You yourself are the only one who knows about it. You cannot communicate it to anyone else. When suddenly the doubt is resolved (i.e., you break through the barrier), this event will astonish the heavens and shake the earth. It is as if you have snatched the great sword away from General Kuan-yü, met the Buddha and killed the Buddha, met the patriarchs and killed the patriarchs. Living in the world of birth and death [*saṃsāra*] you have attained complete freedom. Continually experiencing life according to the four modes of life on the six transmigratory paths, you wander joyfully in *samādhi*.

What then should one do to exert oneself with this word "*wu*"?

Exhausting all your spiritual energy in this constant pursuit, you must absorb this word "*wu*." If you succeed, without wavering for a moment, it will seem as if the light of the Dharma suddenly ignited in your mind.

[VERSE]   Does a dog have the Buddha-nature?
          The Buddhas and patriarchs have completely resolved
            this doubt.
          Whether you answer "yes" or "no,"
          Your fate is sealed.

In this way, Wu-men Hui-k'ai commented on the *wu kung-an* involving Chao-chou: "Those who are able to pass through this barrier not only will meet with Chao-chou as a close friend, they will further be able to walk hand in hand with the patriarchs of history, intimately linked eyebrow to eyebrow. They will see with the same eyes as the patriarchs and hear with the same ears." Accordingly, he claims that if one is able to solve this one kung-an, one can become the same as the Buddhas and patriarchs. The same kind of explanation for this kung-an appears in a "Dharma Lecture" (*fa-yü*) by Ta-hui, "Dharma Lecture Given to Officer Wang T'ung-p'an," as follows.[5]

[LECTURE TO OFFICER WANG T'UNG-P'AN]

The Officer's study of Buddhism does not extend beyond two intersecting paths. One refers to "forgetting feelings" [unconsciousness]; the other to "attachment to thought" [agitation]. "Attachment to thought" referred to here is what the elder of Tu-chuan called *kuan-tai* ["spiritual concentration"]. "Forgetting feelings" is what he called *mo-chao* ["silent illumination"]. If you can eliminate the two diseases of "spiritual concentration" and "silent illumination," you will be able to escape birth and death. The "birth and death" referred to here is originally without form. If people who study Buddhism do not break free of birth and death, they will be subject to rebirth in the cycle of transmigration. If the mind of birth and death is destroyed, the transmigrating original nature [*pen-hsing*] will achieve liberation just as it is. Transmigration and liberation are nothing more than provisional names and do not possess any substantial form. If you can constantly observe your everyday activity in this manner, as time passes you will surely make progress.

In the past, Bodhidharma told the second patriarch. "if you put an end to mental activity aimed at external objects, internally the mind will not become exhausted. If the mind becomes firm like a wall, one can enter the Way just as one is." The second patriarch spoke of nature [*hsing*] in terms of various types of mindfulness and explained it in reference to words and letters. He did not match Bodhidharma's intentions at all. He affirmed the aforementioned notions of "forgetting feelings" and "attachment to thought" as correct. When one does not affirm the concept of "attachment to thought," one puts an end to mental activity aimed at external objects. When one does not affirm the concept of "forgetting feelings," internally the mind becomes firm. When the mind becomes firm, it naturally becomes like a wall. Moreover, when one stops conjecturing with the mind, one will eventually become firm like a wall. As a result, one should try to practice correctly in order to eliminate uncertainty. But under no circumstances during one's practice should one hold that enlightenment is making the mind active. Holding that enlightenment is making the mind active has no bearing at all [on the matter].

When the mind of birth and death has not yet been destroyed, the self is completely seized with uncertainty. The following "crucial phrase" [*hua-t'ou*] case shows the uncertainty existing in the recesses of consciousness.

> A monk asked Chao-chou: "Does a dog have the Buddha-nature?"
> Chao-chou: "*Wu!*" [*Mu*].

Do not neglect this word "No!" during any activity, whether walking, standing, sitting, or lying down. When deluded thoughts arise, do not use the mind to restrain them, just grapple with the "crucial phrase." Even when one sits quietly [*ching-tso*], whenever the mind becomes despondent, one takes up this phrase to revive one's spirits. Doubts are eliminated as quickly as eyebrows and lashes are singed by fire, as quickly as the time it takes an old blind woman to blow out a flame. When one reaches this understanding, both "forgetting feelings" [unconsciousness] and "attachment to thought" [agitation] are valid, both quiet and noise are accepted. Even though completely confined to the cycle of transmigration, one is not subject to rebirth. Moreover, one can use transmigration as an opportunity for enjoying oneself just as one is. When one has reached this stage of understanding, one's mind is naturally sharp in a way that it is always perfectly focused. Furthermore, one can read about this throughout the three teachings which the sages have taught from the beginning. They taught it according to their own unique situations without adding or deleting a single word. If one does not follow this path, even though one spends an eternity cultivating austerities in anticipation of realizing "this great event of enlightenment," it will simply be wasted effort, plummeting one [into further rebirths]. [The methods of] "forgetting feelings" and "attachment to thought" will both pass you by [to no avail]. But what would it mean if you "forget feelings" and were not "attached to thought"? [Shout] YAH! What on earth is this? Officer Wang T'ung-p'an, you should simply study the meaning of this word. There is nothing that matters other than this.

It goes without saying that Ta-hui's references to kung-an were not confined to Chao-chou's word *wu*, but he did make frequent reference to it. As a representative kung-an of *k'an-hua Ch'an*, it exerted great influence on him.

When was *k'an-hua Ch'an* established? In Ta-hui's case, it was formed during his criticism of "silent illumination" (*mo-chao*) Ch'an while he was in Fu-chien province in the fourth year of the Shao-hsing era (1134).[6] As a result, Ta-hui's frequent references to Chao-chou's word *wu* occurred after this. The intrepretation of kung-an that developed after this is contained in the explanation of Chung-feng Ming-pen cited above.

What kind of kung-an did Ta-hui refer to besides Chao-chou's *wu kung-an?* Ta-hui Tsung-kao, compiled the *Cheng-fa-yen tsang,* (*Treasury of the True Dharma Eye;* J. *Shōbōgenzō*), a collection of 668 kung-an believed to have been completed in the seventeenth year of the Shao-hsing era (1147). Regarding the purpose of this compilation, Ta-hui himself commented on it following the first kung-an involving Lang-yeh Hui-chüeh.[7]

When I lived at Heng-yang in Ho-nan province, limited by the legacy of my sinfulness, other than shutting the door to repeatedly examine myself, I passed the days without worries. During the days spent living this way, Ch'an practitioners frequently appeared requesting instruction. Without fail, I answered their questions for them. Among the Ch'an practitioners there was one called Ch'ung-mi Hui-jan. In response to his questions, I took extracts [from Ch'an records] and over the days and months, through this process, I compiled a large text [of these extracts]. Ch'ung-mi and others brought it to me and asked that I give it a title. Thinking that it would preserve the treasury of the true dharma eye passed down between the buddhas and patriarchs to future generations of practitioners, I named it the *Cheng fa-yen tsang* [Treasury of the True Dharma Eye]. In other words, even though a story involving Lang-yeh Hui-chüeh happens to begin the collection, the order of the Ch'an teachers and distinctions regarding their lineages, etc., have no bearing at all on the fundamental position of the work. What they requested was simply to experience thoroughly the wonders of enlightenment, to be liberated from the bonds of confusion which rendered practitioners immobile, and to be furnished with eyes to see true enlightenment.

In this way, kung-an were, in effect, individual *hua-t'ou* or "crucial phrases" that were compiled and collected so that practitioners could be released from delusion and could experience enlightenment and be furnished with eyes to see what constituted the enlightenment of the buddhas and patriarchs.

In this regard, this chapter addresses a number of questions regarding the formation of the kung-an tradition. It seeks to clarify the process through which kung-an collections were compiled. In particular, it focuses on the important but overlooked role played by the *Tsung-men t'ung-yao chi* (J. *Shūmon tōyōshū*) in the compilation of kung-an. Finally, it considers the central status the *Tsung-men t'ung-yao chi* occupies among Ch'an sources. First it will review how the *Tsung-men t'ung-yao chi* has been overlooked by Ch'an scholars.

The Scholarly Neglect of the *Tsung-men t'ung-yao chi*

The study of Ch'an history advanced rapidly with the discovery of the Tun-huang manuscripts at the beginning of this century.[8] The study of early Ch'an history has been made clear through the Tun-huang sources and will continue to be clarified in more comprehensive ways in the future. However, there are historical limitations to the information that the Tun-huang sources provide. For example, it is impossible to understand the Ch'an community descended from Ma-tsu Tao-i (709–788), the master who exerted the greatest influence on the development of later generations of the Ch'an community, by studying Tun-huang sources. The Tun-huang manuscripts are likewise of no use as sources for studying Sung dynasty Ch'an. The period that the Tun-huang manuscripts are suitable for in the study of Ch'an is up until the rebellion of An Lu-shan in the middle of the eighth century. The greatest accomplishment in Ch'an research based on the Tun-huang manuscripts has been in clarifying the role played by Shen-hui (684–758) in Ch'an history.[9]

The sources used to conduct research on Ch'an history prior to the discovery of the Tun-huang manuscripts were the twin jewels of Ch'an transmission history texts issued in the Sung dynasty, the *Ching-te ch'uan-teng lu* (J. *Keitoku dentōroku*, issued in 1004) and the *Wu-teng hui-yüan* (J. *Gotō egen*, issued in 1252). The reason these two texts were used is that they concern the formation and development of Ch'an during the most interesting phase of its history. This rationale regarding their importance for the study of Ch'an is still applicable today. There are no better texts than these for the study of Ch'an history during this period. As was noted earlier, the history of Ch'an prior to the An Lu-shan rebellion was completely rewritten after the discovery of the Tun-huang manuscripts. In spite of this, the Sung transmission of the lamp records (*ch'uan-teng lu*) remains as important as ever for the study of Ch'an history after An Lu-shan.

As a source for the study of Ch'an from its formation until the development of the "five houses," the earliest of the transmission of the lamp records, the *Ching-te ch'uan-teng lu*, contains nearly all of the representative figures of Chinese Ch'an. In addition, it was included in the Chinese Buddhist canon by imperial order, a fact that shows it was an authoritative work. Its popularity was enhanced by the developments in printing technology in China around this time.

The other text, the *Wu-teng hui-yüan*, was compiled by the monk Hui-ming from the five previous Sung transmission histories, the *Ching-te ch'uan-teng lu*, the *T'ien-sheng kuang-teng lu*, the *Chien-chung ching-kuo hsü-teng lu*, the *Tsung-men lien-teng hui-yao*, and the *Chia-t'ai p'u-teng lu*. It is an extremely useful text containing the biographies and statements of Ch'an monks from the initial formation of Ch'an through the thirteenth century. The *Wu-teng hui-yüan* is representative of the Ch'an manuscripts consulted by philologists who investigated Ch'an in the Ch'ing dynasty. Zen adherents in Edo period Japan also began their investigations of Zen history by consulting the *Wu-teng hui-yüan*. As a source for the study of Ch'an, it has even been consulted by compilers of modern dictionaries of Buddhist terms and Chinese language dictionaries (in recent years it has been supplemented by materials found in the *Tsu-t'ang chi* issued in 952, discovered unexpectedly this century).

One of the problems that has plagued the study of Ch'an has been a reliance on easily available, later editions of Ch'an texts rather than on earlier, more original editions. In addition to the *Ching-te ch'uan-teng lu* and *Wu-teng hui-yüan*, many Ch'an records are contained in the Ming edition of the Buddhist canon. The Ming edition also served as the standard for modern editions of the Buddhist canon, *Taishō daizōkyō* and *Zoku zōkyō*. No effort was made to select earlier versions of Ch'an texts contained in Sung editions, the Japanese Gozan or "Five Mountains" editions, or assorted other manuscript versions. Professor Yanagida Seizan, an authority on the study of Ch'an history, has commented on this situation as follows.[10]

> Generally speaking, the inclusion of sectarian materials in *Taishō daizōkyō*, as in the case of Pure Land texts, shows the great potential impact that the old editions of the Buddhist canon may have. However, the full potential of older edition materials was not realized. In the case of Ch'an, Gozan edition materials were only used to supplement Ming edition texts which were used as if they were originals. No effort was made to put the true value of the older Gozan edition texts to practical use. This tendency prevails through all modern collections of the Buddhist canon, the *Shukusatsu zōkyō*, the *Zoku zōkyō*, and so on. It would be better to rely on Ch'an texts that survive in Sung or Gozan editions.

This is a very important observation, and one that must be heeded. It means that modern scholars who rely on *Taishō daizōkyō*, *Zoku zōkyō*, and so on, to carry out research on Ch'an continue this work without the aid of the most authentic versions of Ch'an texts available.

The subject of investigation here is the *Tsung-men t'ung-yao chi* (issued in 1093), known to most through the expanded text contained in the Ming canon, the *Tsung-men t'ung-yao hsü-chi* (*Shūmon tōyō zokushū*, issued in 1324).[11] The way the *Tsung-men t'ung-yao chi* and the *Tsung-men t'ung-yao hsü-chi* illustrate the problem associated with the proper use of sources for the study of Ch'an described above is as follows. Excerpts from the *Tsung-men t'ung-yao hsü-chi* were used in the 108 chapter *Sōden haiin*, a useful index of biographies of monks compiled by Taiso Gyōjo in the Edo period. However, the version of the *Tsung-men t'ung-yao hsü-chi* that Taiso Gyōjo used for his index was a Yüan edition by Ku-lin Ch'ing-mao (1262–1329), a version that added new fragments composed after the original *Tsung-men t'ung-yao chi*. The relation between the Sung text, the *Tsung-men t'ung-yao chi*, and the Ming edition version, the *Tsung-men t'ung-yao hsü-chi*, is illustrated in table 4.1.[12]

As the table makes clear, what the *Tsung-men t'ung-yao hsü-chi* added to the *Tsung-men t'ung-yao chi* notes was insignificant. It appended three chapters to the end of the work; the additions are for the most part confined to this ex-

Table 4.1 Contents of *Tsung-men t'ung-yao chi* and *Tsung-men t'ung-yao hsü-chi*

Tsung-men t'ung-yao chi	Tsung-men t'ung-yao hsü chi	→ Contents
ch. 1	ch. 1	S'ākyamuni
	ch. 2	Sages and worthies of India
ch. 2	ch. 3	4th–6th patriarchs
ch. 3	ch. 4	Nan-yüeh
		Nan-yüeh 1st–2nd generations
	ch. 5	Nan-yüeh 2nd generation
ch. 4	ch. 6	Nan-yüeh 3rd generation
	ch. 7	Nan-yüeh 3rd generation
ch. 5	ch. 8	Nan-yüeh 4th generation
	ch. 9	Nan-yüeh 4th generation
ch. 6	ch. 10	Nan-yüeh 5th generation
	ch. 11	Nan-yüeh 6th–11th generations
ch. 7	ch. 12	Ch'ing-yüan
		Ch'ing-yüan 1st–2nd generations
	ch. 13	Ch'ing-yüan 2nd–3rd generations
	ch. 14	Ch'ing-yüan 4th generation
ch. 8	ch. 15	Ch'ing-yüan 5th generation
	ch. 16	Ch'ing-yüan 5th generation
ch. 9	ch. 17	Ch'ing-yüan 6th generation
	ch. 18	Ch'ing-yüan 6th generation
ch. 10	ch. 19	Ch'ing-yüan 7th generation
	ch. 20	Ch'ing-yüan 8th–10th generations
	ch. 21	Nan-yüeh 12th–14th generations
	ch. 22	Nan-yüeh 15th–18th generations
	ch. 23	Ch'ing-yüan 11th–14th generations

panded framework. Concerning the descendants of the Nan-yüeh lineage added, the *Tsung-men t'ung-yao hsü-chi* notes as follows in ch. 22:[13]

From the 12th generation through the 18th generation descendants of Nan-yüeh, there are altogether 286 people whose encounters appear in the records, in over 212 cases.

Concerning the descendants of the Ch'ing-yüan lineage added, there is the following statement at the end of ch. 22.[14]

From the 11th generation through the 14th generation descendants of Ch'ing-yüan, there are altogether 120 people whose encounters appear in the records, in 47 cases. The descendants of the two lineages of Nan-yüeh and Ch'ing-yüan from the additional two chapters presented here, totals 406 people. . . . the encounters which appear in the records are contained in a total 259 cases, not counting any that have been unwittingly omitted.

According to the edition of the *Tsung-men t'ung-yao chi* contained in the library of the Tōyō bunko, the text originally contained 265 people from the Ch'ing-yüan lineage in 554 cases, and 249 people from the Nan-yüeh lineage in over 559 cases. Counting everyone mentioned from Śākyamuni onward, the *Tsung-men t'ung-yao chi* contained 614 people of the 859 total appearing in the 1,323 cases that form the *Tsung-men t'ung-yao hsü-chi*. Since the text is from the same era as the *Tsung-men t'ung-yao chi,* the structure of the *Tsung-men t'ung-yao hsü-chi* presents no major changes.

Consequently, one can hardly claim that the *Tsung-men t'ung-yao chi* is an unknown text, since its contents have become familiar to us through the *Tsung-men t'ung-yao hsü-chi.* Yet it is impossible to treat the *Tsung-men t'ung-yao chi* as a Sung dynasty Ch'an source when one's knowledge of it comes through the *Tsung-men t'ung-yao hsü-chi.* The reason is that the *Tsung-men t'ung-yao chi* has not been transmitted down to us in a single standardized form, and the version of the text in the *Tsung-men t'ung-yao hsü-chi* cannot be regarded as such. Consequently, even though we try to use the *Tsung-men t'ung-yao chi* for the study of Sung Ch'an, it cannot be easily used for such purposes. Had a Sung edition of the *Tsung-men t'ung-yao chi* been included in *Taishō daizōkyō,* legitimate research on the *Tsung-men t'ung-yao chi* would presumably have progressed further than it has.

The Importance of the *Tsung-men t'ung-yao chi* for the Study of Sung Ch'an

A recognition of the importance of the *Tsung-men t'ung-yao chi* for the study of Sung Ch'an developed gradually throughout my career. My initial recognition of the *Tsung-men t'ung-yao chi's* importance for the understanding of Sung Ch'an came about during Professor Yanagida Seizan's investigation of Sung Ch'an sources in the Kantō region around Tokyo. In 1973 Professor Yanagida published "A Report on Investigations of Sung Editions of Ch'an Sources," in which he addressed the topic of the Sung edition of the *Tsung-men t'ung-yao chi* contained in the library of the Tōyō Bunko institute. In his report Professor Yanagida pointed out that the *Tsung-men t'ung-yao chi* had been cited in chapter 10 of the *Ta-tsang i-lan chi* compiled by Ch'en-shih, thereby exerting influence on the *Kōzen gokoku ron* by Eisai (*Yōsai*).[15]

I originally began to study the *Tsung-men t'ung-yao chi* out of other interests. My graduate supervisor, Professor Kagamishima Genryū, completed a study on the sources cited by Zen Master Dōgen.[16] The effect of his research was epoch making for the history of Dōgen studies. Following Dr. Kagamishima's lead, I conducted research on sources cited in Dōgen's *Mana Shōbōgenzō* and published an article based on this research.[17] I knew at that time that citations from Ch'an sources in Dōgen's works were overwhelmingly taken from the *Ching-te ch'uan-teng lu.* I also knew that Dōgen cited frequently from the *Tsung-men lien-teng hui-yao,* a text with strong associations with the Ch'an lineage of Ta-hui. At this stage Dr. Kagamishima had concluded that there was no direct connection between Dōgen and the *Tsung-men t'ung-yao chi.* Because of this conclusion, I did not at that time consider the *Tsung-men t'ung-yao chi* as a source from which Dōgen might have cited.

Assisted to some extent by Professor Yanagida's investigation of Ch'an sources published in the Sung, I obtained copies of the *Tsung-men t'ung-yao chi* contained in the library of the Tōyō Bunko Institute. My research on the connection between the *Tsung-men t'ung-yao chi* and the *Tsung-men lien-teng hui-yao,* which was published after the *Tsung-men t'ung-yao chi,* made clear the close connection between the two works. The same year Professor Yanagida published his report, I published the results of my research in a study of the *Tsung-men t'ung-yao chi.*[18] The following year I published an article on the connection between the sources cited by Ta-hui in the *Cheng fa-yen tsang* (J. *Shōbōgenzō*) and the *Tsung-men lien-teng hui-yao.*[19] In it, I pointed out that Ta-hui Tsung-kao frequently cited from the *Tsung-men t'ung-yao chi* in his *Cheng fa-yen tsang* and that Ta-hui's *Cheng fa-yen tsang* exerted influence on the compilation of the *Tsung-men lien-teng hui-yao.* That same year, I published an article continuing my research on the *Tsung-men t'ung-yao chi,* comparing terminology used in the *Tsung-men lien-teng hui-yao* and the *Tsung-men t'ung-yao chi.*[20] It made clear that most of the citations in the *Tsung-men t'ung-yao chi* were from the *Ming-chüeh ch'an-shih yü-lu* by Hsüeh-tou Ch'ung-hsien (980–1052) of the Yün-men lineage. Through these studies I noticed that the *Tsung-men t'ung-yao chi* and the *Tsung-men lien-teng hui-yao* were different in character than the Ch'an transmission histories, the *Ching-te ch'uan-teng lu,* the *T'ien-sheng kuang-teng lu,* and the *Chien-chung ching-kuo hsü-teng lu.* The transmission histories documented the order of transmission of the dharma from generation to generation. The *Tsung-men t'ung-yao chi* and the *Tsung-men lien-teng hui-yao* were kung-an collections compiled for the purpose of establishing individual conversations between Ch'an practitioners as "cases for public examination" (kung-an). These kung-an were considered somehow to have meaning for practitioners independent of the context in which they appeared in the transmission histories, and it is evident that the *Tsung-men t'ung-yao chi* was the earliest such collection of kung-an.

In my *Sōdai Zenshūshi no kenkyū* (*Studies in the History of the Zen School in the Sung Dynasty*) I treated the problem of the origins of kung-an in Ch'an records, focusing on ch. 27 of the *Ching-te chuan-teng lu.* The thesis formed about this topic became the basic starting point for my research; it completely transformed my dissertation as a graduate student.[21] I was greatly influenced in my research by Professor Yanagida's study "The *Tsu-t'ang chi*'s Value as Source Material."[22]

From the beginning, the *Tsu-t'ang chi,* discovered at the beginning of this century from Haein-sa Monastery in a rendition of the Korean Tripitaka, proved a valuable document for the study of Ch'an. Advances in research on the *Tsu-t'ang chi* have come largely as a result of the work of Professor Yanagida. The *Tsu-t'ang chi* conveyed the unique charm of T'ang Ch'an in a way that the *Ching-te ch'uan-teng lu,* hitherto relied on by researchers, did not. Professor Yanagida serialized stories from the *Tsu-t'ang chi* in the journal *Zen bunka.*[23] Subsequently Professor Yanagida also published an abbreviated translation of the *Tsu-t'ang chi,*[24] and more recently he has published several works of stories from the *Tsu-t'ang chi.*[25] In 1984 a three-volume *Index to the Tsu-t'ang chi* was published, edited by Professor Yanagida.[26] Professor Yanagida's work on the *Tsu-t'ang chi* serves as a valuable contribution to research in the field of Ch'an and Zen studies.

In the original text of the *Tsu-t'ang chi,* the date of completion is given as "the tenth year of the Pao-ta era of the Southern T'ang" (952), a designation that has great significance. The compilation of the *Tsu-t'ang chi* was completed by two Ch'an masters known as Ching and Yün of the Chao-ch'ing monastery in Ch'üan-chou, currently in Fukien, province. The chief priest of the monastery at that time was Ch'an Master of Pure Cultivation Sheng-t'eng (884–972), who also wrote a preface for the *Tsu-t'ang chi.* It is also plausible to assert that Master Sheng-t'eng was in a position to act as supervisor for the compilation of the *Tsu-t'ang chi.* Chao-ch'ing Sheng-t'eng was a disciple of Pao-fu Tsung-chan (?–928), a member of the lineage of Hsüeh-feng I-tsun (822–908). Ch'üan-chou, where the *Tsu-t'ang chi* was compiled, had belonged to the country of Min, one of the ten kingdoms during the period of the so-called "Five Dynasties and Ten Kingdoms," prior to being subordinated to the Southern T'ang. Min was governed by the Wang family—the rulers of Wu-yüeh to the north (present day Hang-chou in Che-chiang province), including King Chung-I (also known as Wang Shen-chih, 862–925)—a family that had great admiration for Buddhism. Among the Ch'an groups that Wang Shen-chih protected most was the group descended from Hsüeh-feng I-tsun. Understanding the Hsüeh-feng branch is an important problem for the history of Ch'an at the end of the T'ang and during the Five Dynasties, and many of the sources for studying the Hsüeh-feng lineage are contained in the *Tsu-t'ang chi.* In this context, it is useful to analyze carefully Professor Yanagida's article "The *Tsu-t'ang chi*'s Value as Source Material," mentioned earlier.

From the close connection between the *Tsu-t'ang chi* and the Hsüeh-feng branch indicated by Professor Yanagida's research, I postulated that a similar case could be made for a connection between the *Ching-te ch'uan-teng lu* and the Fa-yen branch. In the *Tsu-t'ang chi,* a particular person's comments are recorded in response to certain topics. The types of comments vary, ranging from selecting certain aspects for comment (*chu*), making inquiries (*cheng*), offering critical remarks (*nien*), giving the commentator's own understanding of a monk's silence (*tai*), and describing how a matter may be otherwise understood (*pieh*). The purpose of the comments is to provide clarification and guidance. Commenting in this way reveals the preferred style of the commentator, and the favored way of acting in a Ch'an-like manner in the commentator's opinion. When Professor Yanagida analyzed these comments, he concluded that nearly all were made by people from the Hsüeh-feng lineage. Using the same method, I analyzed the comments in the *Ching-te ch'uan-teng lu,* completed in 1004, and determined that the comments were made by people belonging to the Fa-yen lineage. Because the compiler of the *Ching-te ch'uan-teng lu,* Tao-yüan, was a member of the lineage descended from Fa-yen Wen-i (885–958), this result could be anticipated, and the results of the analysis bore it out. The Fa-yen order developed in Wu-yüeh, receiving the support of the Ch'ien family, who held hegemony over the region. Facts and incidents relating to Wu-yüeh are frequently found in the *Ching-te ch'uan-teng lu* as a result.[27]

A problem remained, however, regarding Yanagida's research on the *Tsu-t'ang chi*. Although Professor Yanagida had argued in detail for the relationship between the *Tsu-t'ang chi* and the Min kingdom, he had not investigated the relationship between the *Tsu-t'ang chi* and the Southern T'ang kingdom. This I set out to rectify in a study of the newly discovered monastery record of the K'ai-yüan monastery in Ch'üan-chou (*Ch'üan-chou k'ai-yüan ssu-chih*), using as my lead the biography of Chao-ch'ing Sheng-t'eng.[28] The conclusion of this article made clear the close connection between the *Tsu-t'ang chi* and the Prefect of Ch'üan-chou, Liu Tsung-hsiao, and the numerous references to the Southern T'ang in ch. 12 of the *Tsu-t'ang chi*.

Regarding the basic character of the *Tsung-men t'ung-yao chi* as a kung-an compilation referred to above, we can look at the example of Yen-t'ou Ch'üan-huo (828–887) of E-chou.[29] By comparing the 27 cases pertaining to him in ch. 16 of the *Ching-te ch'uan-teng lu,* the 9 cases in ch. 8 of the *Tsung-men t'ung-yao chi* (abbreviated below as *t'ung-yao*), the 19 cases in ch. 21 of the *Tsung-men lien-teng hui-yao* (abbreviated below as *hui-yao*), and the 33 cases of ch. 7 of the *Wu-teng hui-yüan* (abbreviated below as *hui-yüan*), we can begin to see the great influence the *Tsung-men t'ung-yao chi* exerted over Sung Ch'an. To begin, we will look at the connection between the 27 cases in ch. 16 of the *Ching-te ch'uan-teng lu* in connection to the other works. (The numbers assigned in brackets to respective texts represent the order in which the case appears in that text.)

Ching-te ch'uan-teng lu Cases on Yen-t'ou Ch'üan-huo:

1. The story of Yen-t'ou's visit to Yang-shan → *hui-yüan* (1)
2. The story of Yen-t'ou's first visit to Te-shan → *hui-yao* (1), *hui-yüan* (2)

3. The story of Yen-t'ou stepping through the gate and asking: "Is it a common person, or a sage?" → *t'ung-yao* (1), *hui-yao* (2), *hui-yüan* (3)
4. The story of Yen-t'ou's affirmation following Te-shan's utterance → *hui-yüan* (4)
5. The story concerning the water and the moon involving Yen-t'ou, Hsüeh-feng, and Ch'in- shan → *t'ung-yao* (7), *hui-yao* (9), *hui-yüan* (5)
6. The story of Yen-t'ou and Hsüeh-feng leaving Te-shan → *hui-yüan* (6)
7. The dialogue concerning whether enlightenment is attainable without a teacher → *hui-yao* (18), *hui-yüan* (8)
8. The story of how rivals should be treated → *hui-yüan* (9)
9. The reason why Bodhidharma came from the West → *hui-yao* (14), *hui-yüan* (24)
10. The story of Yen-t'ou comparing the character for three dots with the teaching of the *Nirvāṇa Sūtra* → *t'ung-yao* (6), *hui-yao* (5), *hui-yüan* (10)
11. The story of a monk visiting Shih-hsiang and Yen-t'ou at the foot of Chia-shan → *hui-yüan* (11)
12. The story of Lo-shan questioning Yen-t'ou's criticism of Tung-shan → *hui-yüan* (12)
13. The dialogue concerning who can cut with a sword → *hui-yao* (19), *hui-yüan* (13)
14. The dialogue concerning whether there are cases that extend to the past and present → *hui-yüan* (14)
15. The story where Yen-t'ou asks: "Who picked up the sword after Huang-ch'ao left?" → *t'ung-yao* (2), *hui-yao* (6), *hui-yüan* (15)
16. The dialogue concerning which of two dragons snatched the pearl → *hui-yüan* (16)
17. What kind of thing is it when a monk sees his self-nature? → *hui-yüan* (17)
18. Who is master of the triple realm? → *hui-yüan* (18)
19. The story of Tuan-yen asking if Yen-t'ou is the teacher of Vairocana Buddha → *hui-yüan* (21)
20. What kind of master can be recognized within delusion? → *hui-yao* (16), *hui-yüan* ch. 7 [Pao-fu biography]
21. Question as to whether the arrow is useless when the bow is broken → *hui-yüan* (22)
22. What is the clear message in a cave? → *hui-yüan* (23)
23. What is the Way? → *hui-yüan* (28)
24. How can a staff reach to the bottom of a deep well? → *hui-yüan* (29)
25. The question whether to hoist the old sail → *hui-yüan* (30)
26. Yen-t'ou answers with a shout when asked about the Buddha, the Dharma, the Way, and Ch'an Practitioners → *hui-yüan* (32)

27. Yen-t'ou cries out once in a loud voice at the end of his life → *hui-yüan* (33)

When we compare the cases in the *Ching-te ch'uan-teng lu* with the *Tsung-men t'ung-yao chi,* the *Tsung-men lien-teng hui-yao,* and the *Wu-teng hui-yüan,* the main thing we notice is the similarity between the *Wu-teng hui-yüan* and the *Ching-te ch'uan-teng lu,* which presents the cases in essentially the same order. In comparison, only 4 of the 27 cases in the *Ching-te ch'uan-teng lu* appear in the *Tsung-men t'ung-yao chi,* and only 9 of the 27 cases appear in the *Tsung-men lien-teng hui-yao.* The order of presentation of the cases in these works is different than in the *Ching-te ch'uan-teng-lu* as well. Moreover, the *Tsung-men t'ung-yao chi* and the *Tsung-men lien-teng hui-yao* include cases not recorded in the *Ching-te ch'uan-teng-lu.* Even with these, the total number of cases in the *Tsung-men t'ung-yao chi* is only one-third of the total in the *Ching-te ch'uan-teng lu;* the total in the *Tsung-men lien-teng hui-yao* is only one-half the number of cases in the *Ching-te chuan-teng lu.* The significance of these numbers will become apparent from an examination of the contents of the *Tsung-men t'ung-yao chi.* The increased number of cases in the *Wu-teng hui-yüan,* or additions not contained in the *Ching-te ch'uan-teng lu,* have been taken from the *Tsung-men lien-teng hui-yao.* However, cases 7, 19, and 20 were clearly taken from the *Tsung-men t'ung-yao chi,* demonstrating the influence of the *Tsung-men t'ung-yao chi* on the *Tsung-men lien-teng hui-yao.*[30] This is a point that will also be raised later.

In contrast to the *Ching-te ch'uan-teng lu,* what about the section on Yen-t'ou in the *Tsung-men t'ung-yao chi?* A comparison of the nine cases regarding Yen-t'ou in the *Tsung-men t'ung-yao chi* with the same works as earlier, adding the *Ming-chüeh lu* and Ta-hui's *Cheng-fa-yen tsang* (Ta-hui) to the comparison, follows.

Tsung-men t'ung-yao chi Cases on Yen-t'ou Ch'üan-huo:

1. The story of Yen-t'ou stepping through the gate and asking: "Is it a common person, or a sage?" → *ch'uan-teng lu* (3), *Ming-chüeh lu* (ch. 3), *hui-yao* (2), *hui-yüan* (3)
2. The story where Yen-t'ou asks: "Who picked up the sword after Huang-ch'ao left?" → *ch'uan-teng lu* (15), *hui-yao* (6), *hui-yüan* (15)
3. The story where Yen-t'ou became Ch'üan-t'ou(?) → *hui-yao* (7), *hui-yüan* (7)
4. The story where Yen-t'ou tests two monks while holding an axe → *hui-yao* (8), *hui-yüan* (19)
5. The story where Yen-t'ou asks Jui-yen about the principle of permanence → *ch'uan-teng lu* (ch. 17) [Jui-yen section] *hui-yao* (ch. 23) [Jui-yen section] *hui-yüan* (ch. 7) [Jui-yen section]

6. The story of Yen-t'ou comparing the character for three dots with the teaching of the *Nirvāṇa Sūtra* → *ch'uan-teng lu* (10), Ta-hui, *hui-yao* (5), *hui-yüan* (10)

7. The story concerning the water and the moon involving Yen-t'ou, Hsüeh-feng, and Ch'in-shan → *ch'uan-teng lu* (5), *hui-yao* (9), *hui-yüan* (5)

8. The story of Yen-t'ou testing a monk who draws shapes of circles → *hui-yao* (10), *hui-yüan* (20)

9. The story of Hsüeh-feng attaining enlightenment on Mount Ao → Ta-hui, *hui-yao* (ch. 21) [Hsüeh-feng section], *hui-yüan* (ch. 7) [Hsüeh-feng section]

The *Tsung-men t'ung-yao chi* begins differently than the *Ching-te ch'uan-teng lu*, the *Tsung-men lien-teng hui-yao*, and the *Wu-teng hui-yüan*. It does not touch on Yen-t'ou's travels as a practitioner but starts right out in the first case with his stepping through the gate and asking: "Is it a common person, or a sage?" This story also appears in the *Ching-te ch'uan-teng lu* and the *Wu-teng hui-yüan*, but with the difference that in these latter works the comments of Hsüeh-tou Ch'ung-hsien are added. The activities of Hsüeh-tou Ch'ung-hsien (980–1052) postdated the compilation of the *Ching-te ch'uan-teng lu*. Naturally, Hsüeh-tou's comments would not be recorded there. As a result, it follows that the first case in the *Tsung-men t'ung-yao chi* is taken from an extract of ch. 3 of the *Ming-chüeh lu*.

What follows in the *Tsung-men t'ung-yao chi* is also found in the *Tsung-men lien-teng hui-yao*. They both have the second case, where Yen-t'ou asks: "Who picked up the sword after Huang-ch'ao left?" This case is also found in the *Ching-te ch'uan-teng lu* and the *Wu-teng hui-yüan*, but both the *Tsung-men t'ung-yao chi* and the *Tsung-men lien-teng hui-yao* have Ta-kuei Mu-che's (?–1095) commentary. Ta-kuei Mu-che was active later than Hsüeh-tou and exerted a great influence on the compilation of the *Tsung-men t'ung-yao chi*.[31] This commentary appears to have also been in the *Ta-kuei che ch'an-shih yü-lu*, but unfortunately this text is no longer extant. This suggests that the *Tsung-men t'ung-yao chi* probably includes fragments of Ta-kuei Mu-che's lost record. The case as it appears in the *Tsung-men lien-teng hui-yao* also includes Ta-kuei Mu-che's comments.

The *Tsung-men t'ung-yao chi* also includes cases 3, 4, 8, and 9, which are not contained in the *Ching-te ch'uan-teng lu*. The *Tsung-men lien-teng hui-yao* also includes these cases. The *Tsung-men lien-teng hui-yao* clearly records the number of cases recorded therein as "about 14," but when it is compared with other works, 19 can be counted. Among these, the cases appearing independently in the *Tsung-men lien-teng hui-yao* and not contained in the *Tsung-men t'ung-yao chi* appear to be from two nonextant works, the *Hsüeh-feng lu* and the *Yen-t'ou lu* (according to the postscript in ch. 21). Moreover, it is clear that the source for the long sermon to the assembly in case 4 is from Ta-hui's *Cheng-fa-yen tsang*.

As a result, the cases appearing in the *Tsung-men t'ung-yao chi* were subjects for kung-an used by many Ch'an practitioners at that time. The Ch'an records that served as sources for these kung-an included surviving works like the *Ming-chüeh lu* as well as nonextant species of "recorded sayings" such as the *Ta-kuei che yü-lu*.

The *Tsung-men t'ung-yao chi* as an Important Ch'an Record

My interest in the *Tsung-men t'ung-yao chi* was delayed for a time until 1981, when I had an opportunity to study at Kyoto University under the direction of Professor Yanagida. I participated in a seminar at the Institute for the Study of Zen Culture conducting research on Dōgen's *Mana Shōbōgenzō*. I discovered that several kōan cited in the *Mana Shōbōgenzō* were actually taken from the *Tsung-men t'ung-yao chi*, even though it was believed that Dōgen had not had direct access to this work. For example, case 102 of the 305-case *Mana Shōbōgenzō* is the famous "Pai-chang and the Fox," sometimes called "To Pai-chang, the Law of Cause and Effect Is Obvious."

Whenever the Ch'an Master of Great Enlightenment Huai-hai of Mount Pai-chang delivered a sermon, an old man always accompanied the monks to listen to him. When the monks left, the old man also left. One day, as it happened, he did not leave. Pai-chang asked: "Who are you, standing here before me?" The old man responded: "I am not a human being. In the past, at the time of Kaśyāpa Buddha, I lived on this mountain. When a student asked me, 'After someone masters great cultivation [i.e., attains enlightenment], will they again be subject to [the law of] cause and effect [i.e., karma],' I answered, 'No, they will be not subject to [the law of] cause and effect.' Since then I have been born five hundred times as a fox. Now, I beg you to give the transforming words to release me from being a fox." The old man then asked: "After someone masters great cultivation [i.e., attains enlightenment], will they again be subject to [the law of] cause and effect?" Pai-chang answered: "The [the law of] cause and effect is obvious."

As soon as the old man heard this he experienced a great awakening. He paid his respects to Pai-chang and said: "I have been emancipated from being a fox. My fox corpse can be found lying behind the temple. I have a favor to ask you. Please bury me as if I were a deceased monk."

Pai-chang ordered the director of monks to strike the gavel and inform the assembly of monks, "There will be a funeral service for a deceased monk following the midday meal." The monks wondered about this, saying, "Everyone is healthy. There is also no one sick in the Nirvāṇa Hall [i.e., Infirmary]. What is going on?"

After the midday meal, Pai-chang led the assembly of monks to the foot of a crag behind the temple. With his staff he he pointed out the body of a dead fox.

He then had the body cremated according to the rites for deceased monks. That evening Pai-chang gave a sermon in the [Dharma] Hall, telling the monks the story that preceded the day's events. Huang-po then asked: "Long ago, because the old man gave a wrong answer, he had to be reborn five hundred times as a fox. Suppose he had given the right answer. What would have happened to him then?" Pai-chang said: "Come here in front of me, and I will tell you." Huang-po came in front of Pai-chang and gave him a blow. Pai-chang clapped his hands and laughed: "I was thinking that the barbarian's beard was red, and lo and behold, here is the red-bearded barbarian!"

This story also appears in ch. 8 of the *T'ien-sheng kuang-teng lu*, the *Pai-chang yü-lu*, and ch. 4 of the *Tsung-men lien-teng hui-yao*, but when the use of terminology in these works is compared, it is apparent that the source of the story cited in the *Mana Shōbōgenzō* is ch. 3 of the *Tsung-men t'ung-yao chi*.

As a result of discovering a connection between the *Mana Shōbōgenzō* and the *Tsung-men t'ung-yao chi*, I reinvestigated all the kōan in the *Mana Shōbōgenzō* for their possible connection to the *Tsung-men t'ung-yao chi*. The surprising result was that out of the 305 kōan in Dōgen's *Mana Shōbōgenzō*, 129 were directly connected to the *Tsung-men t'ung-yao chi*. After more than ten years of study on this subject, I published an article, "The *Tsung-men t'ung-yao chi* and the *Mana Shōbōgenzō*," completely revising our view of the sources cited in Dōgen's *Mana Shōbōgenzō*.[32] The consequences of this pointed not only to a need to reexamine the sources Dōgen relied on in his works, but also to reconsider the importance of the *Tsung-men t'ung-yao chi* as a Ch'an source. This has been especially true for contemporary Dōgen scholars, who have had to take into account the influence of the *Tsung-men t'ung-yao chi* on Dōgen in their research.[33]

As is mentioned above, there are Sung editions of the *Tsung-men t'ung-yao chi* contained in the library of Tōyō Bunko. Professor Shiina Kōyū of Komazawa University published a study, "A Bibliographic Study of the *Tsung-men t'ung-yao chi*," introducing other Sung editions of the *Tsung-men t'ung-yao chi* in the library of Eizan Bunko, and a Yüan dynasty edition of the *Tsung-men t'ung-yao hsü-chi* in the National Cabinet Library (Naikaku Bunko).[34] The evidence assembled by Shiina Koyu suggested that the *Tsung-men t'ung-yao chi* was published no fewer than seven times in the Sung dynasty; his study clarifies the circumstances surrounding the publications and the connection between various editions. Shiina Kōyū pointed out what had been indicated by Professor Yanagida, that the *Ching-te ch'uan-teng lu* and the *Tsung-men t'ung-yao chi* issued in Ming-chou (Che-chiang province) in the twelfth century were the twin jewels among Ch'an sources, and the most important texts for Ch'an adherents at that time. After it was first published at the end of the eleventh century, the influence that the *Tsung-men t'ung-yao chi* exerted on the formation of *k'an-hua Ch'an* during its formative period in the Northern and Southern Sung is incalculable.

In spite of the importance of the *Tsung-men t'ung-yao chi* as a source for the study of Ch'an, scholars have thus far overlooked prominent aspects of the text's significance.[35] The famous collection of kung-an, the *Wu-men kuan,* was compiled by Wu-men Hui-k'ai in the first year of the Shao-ting era (1228). This is a well-known collection, particularly in Japan, where numerous translations and commentaries have been published. Among the works investigating the sources from which the kung-an in the *Wu-men kuan* are drawn, there are annotated translations by Furuta Shōkin, Hirai Kōshi, and Nishimura Eshin.[36] These works particularly focus on the connection between the *Wu-men kuan* and the *Wu-teng hui-yüan.* However, since the *Wu-teng hui-yüan* was compiled after the *Wu-men kuan,* it is impossible to consider it as a source for the contents contained in the *Wu-men kuan.* The possibility that the *Tsung-men t'ung-yao chi* might be a source for the kung-an contained in the *Wu-men kuan* had not even been considered.

The second case in the *Wu-men kuan* is the same case introduced above, "Pai-chang and the Fox," also case 102 of the *Mana Shōbōgenzō.* Noticing that the terminology used in this story was almost exactly the same in both the *Wu-men kuan* and the *Tsung-men t'ung-yao chi,* I compared these versions with versions of the story contained in other works: the *T'ien-sheng kuang-teng lu* ch. 8, the *Pai-chang yü-lu,* the *Tsung-men lien-teng hui-yüan* ch. 4, and the *Wu-teng hui-yüan* ch. 3. I determined from this comparison that the source of the second case, "Pai-chang and the Fox," in the *Wu-men kuan* was the *Tsung-men t'ung-yao chi.* I also compared case 28 in the *Wu-men kuan,* "Long Admired Lung-t'an" (or "Lung-t'an Blows Out a Candle"), with versions of the story in *Ching-te ch'uan-teng lu* ch. 15, Ta-hui's *Cheng-fa-yen tsang, Tsung-men lien-teng hui-yao* ch. 20, and *Wu-teng hui-yüan* ch. 7. This research confirmed that the source for this story in the *Wu-men kuan* was also the *Tsung-men t'ung-yao chi.* When all of 48 kung-an in the *Wu-men kuan* are compared in this way, the source for approximately half of them is found to be the *Tsung-men t'ung-yao chi.* Something else of great interest that has not been pointed out until now is that the appearance of these two stories ("Pai-chang and the Fox" and "Long Admired Lung-t'an") in the *Wu-teng hui-yüan* is also based on the *Tsung-men t'ung-yao chi.* As was stated earlier, it is generally agreed on that the *Wu-teng hui-yüan* was formed by Hui-ming Shou-tso from the five Ch'an transmission histories: the *Ching-te ch'uan-teng lu,* the *T'ien-sheng kuang-teng lu,* the *Chien-chung ch'ing-kuo hsü-teng lu,* the *Tsung-men lien-teng hui-yao,* and the *Chia-t'ai p'u-teng lu.* Wang-yüng's preface to the *Wu-teng hui-yüan* written in the first year of the Pao-yu era (1253) gives the same explanation regarding the origins of the name for the work, which refers to integrating five lamp records (*wu-teng*). In his preface there is no indication that the *Tsung-men t'ung-yao chi* was used as a source in its compilation. However, careful investigation clearly shows that the *Tsung-men t'ung-yao chi* was used in the compilation of the *Wu-teng hui-yüan,* based on the same style of the investigation as used with regard to the stories concerning Yen-t'ou Ch'üan-huo. In this way, the *Tsung-men t'ung-yao chi* exerted influence on both the *Wu-men kuan* compiled in 1228 and the *Wu-teng hui-yüan* compiled in 1253. This makes clear that the *Tsung-men t'ung-yao chi* was very popular among contemporary Ch'an groups in the thirteenth century. The details concerning the sources for the *Wu-men kuan* were published in my review of Nishimura Eshin's recent annotated translation of the *Wu-men kuan*.[37] Essential points made there are as follows.

The previously mentioned study by Shiina Kōyū, "A Bibliographic Study of the *Tsung-men t'ung-yao chi*," introduced other Sung editions of the *Tsung-men t'ung-yao chi* in the library of Eizan Bunko, and so on. Especially noteworthy among the results of that study was that the compilation of the *Tsung-men t'ung-yao chi* was far earlier than anticipated. From my investigations of the Sung edition of the *Tsung-men t'ung-yao chi* in the Tōyō Bunko, I had learned of a preface by Keng Yen-hsi written in the third year of the Shao-hsing era (1133). Shiina's study found a preface by Yao-tzu written 40 years earlier, making it clear that the *Tsung-men t'ung-yao chi* had been compiled sometime prior to the eighth year of the Yüan-yu era (1093). This meant that the *Tsung-men t'ung-yao chi* was compiled before the *Chien-chung ching-kuo hsü-teng lu* transmission history, which was compiled in 1101 by a monk of the Yün-men lineage, Fo-kuo Wei-po. The fact that the *Tsung-men t'ung-yao chi* was compiled more than 40 years earlier than previously thought suggests the possibility that it was composed around the period of the *Blue Cliff Record* (C. *Pi-yen lu*, J. *Hekiganroku*), a work influential in the earliest period of kung-an development.[38]

The *Blue Cliff Record* is one of the basic scriptures of Rinzai Zen (C. Lin-chi Ch'an). If the influence of the *Tsung-men t'ung-yao chi* as one of the earliest Ch'an *kung-an* texts can be ascertained, the importance of the *Tsung-men t'ung-yao chi* will clearly be even greater than previously thought.

As is well known, the *Blue Cliff Record* is a work consisting of 100 kung-an compiled by Hsüeh-tou Ch'ung-hsien (980–1052) of the Yün-men branch, with attached commentary by Yüan-wu K'o-ch'in (1063–1135) of the Lin-chi lineage. It goes without saying, therefore, that the fundamental source for Yüan-wu's comments was the work by Hsüeh-tou. As was noted previously, the sources used most in the *Tsung-men t'ung-yao chi* were the works of Hsüeh-tou, so the works of Hsüeh-tou were commonly used by both Yüan-wu and the compiler of the *Tsung-men t'ung-yao chi*. However, it is now clear that the *Tsung-men t'ung-yao chi* was compiled prior to the period when Yüan-wu was active. This fact raises the question of whether there is any connection between Yüan-wu and the *Tsung-men t'ung-yao chi*.

Yüan-wu lived first at the monastery of the Sixth Patriarch (*liu-tsu yüan*) in Ch'eng-tu. His whereabouts in the years following this are unclear. The next place he lived was the Chao-chüeh monastery. In the *Yüan-wu yü-lu* it is recorded that the name of the Chao-chüeh monastery was changed to the Ch'ung-ning wan-shou monastery. Since this change took place in the second year of the Ch'ung-ning era (1103), it is clear that Yüan-wu took up residence there from the first year of the Ch'ung-ning era (1102). The term "blue cliff" (*pi-yen*) from the *Blue Cliff Record* originated from the line of a poem by Chia-shan Shan-hui (805–881): "A monkey, embracing its son, returns home to its green peak; a bird, with a flower in its beak, drops it in front of the blue cliff." Yüan-wu also lived at the Ling-ch'üan monastery on Mount Chia, but that was after his period at T'ien-ning wan-shou monastery. The structure of the *Yüan-wu yü-lu* suggests that this was probably in the first year of the Cheng-ho era (1111). Following this, Yüan-wu moved to the Tao-lin monastery in Ch'ang-sha. Therefore, Yüan-wu certainly had an opportunity to be familiar with the *Tsung-men t'ung-yao chi.*

An investigation of the connection between the *Blue Cliff Record* and the *Tsung-men t'ung-yao chi* shows clearly that the source for case 5 in the *Blue Cliff Record,* with critical comments adopted to the story "Hsüeh-feng's Grain of Rice," is the *Tsung-men t'ung-yao chi.* In other words, the lines of influence showing a connection between Yüan-wu and the *Tsung-men t'ung-yao chi* may be reconstructed as follows. The *Hsüeh-tou sung-ku* quotes stories from the *Yün-men kuang-lu.* Yüan-wu adopted the commentaries of Yün-feng Wen-yüeh (998–1062) and Ta-kuei Mu-che (?–1095). That is undoubtedly the reason why all of their comments are recorded in the Hsüeh-feng I-tsun section, ch. 8, of the *Tsung-men t'ung-yao chi.* Moreover, Yüan-wu adopted the story about Ch'ang Wen (?) when Hsüeh-feng attained enlightenment on Mount Ao. The story contained in case 5 of the *Blue Cliff Record* is related in more detail in case 22. The story was discussed above, in connection with the nine cases in the Yen-t'ou section, ch. 8, of the *Tsung-men t'ung-yao chi.* Anyone who does a comparative analysis of the pertinent sources will acknowledge that the source for the story in the *Blue Cliff Record* is the *Tsung-men t'ung-yao chi.*

The connection between Yüan-wu and the *Tsung-men t'ung-yao chi* may also be verified from another perspective. The biography of Yüan-wu made reference to two of his influential disciples, Hu-ch'iu Shao-lung and Ta-hui Tsung-kao but the details of this biographical record are unknown.[39] In addition, the *Yüan-wu yü-lu* has no record of his final years when he returned to his native home in Ssu-ch'üan province. It includes nine temples where he served as chief priest, listed in the order in which he served at them: the monastery of the Sixth Patriarch (*liu-tsu yüan*) in Ch'eng-tu, Chao-chüeh (Ch'ung-ning wan-shou) monastery in Ch'eng-tu, Ling-ch'üan monastery on Mount Chia in Li-chou, Tao-lin monastery in Ch'ang-sha, T'ai-p'ing hsing-kuo monastery on Mount Chiang in Chien-k'ang, T'ien-ning wan-shou monastery in T'ung-ching, Lung-yu monastery on Mount Chin in Chen-chiang, Yün-chu chen-ju monastery in Nan-k'ang, and again at the Chao-chüeh (Ch'ung-ning wan-shou) monastery in Ch'eng-tu.

Yüan-wu's 100 kung-an cases, the *Yüan-wu nien-ku,* are contained in ch. 16, 17, and 18 of the 20-chapter *Yüan-wu yü-lu.* The locations where Yüan-wu used these while serving as chief priest are known from his own self-designated titles. Other than cases 53 and 100, where the location is given as Mount Chin (Lung-yu monastery), almost all of them date from before his tenure as chief priest at T'ien-ning wan-shou monastery in T'ung-ching. The first 50 cases can be said to be from the Ch'ung-ning wan-shou monastery period. The latter 50 cases are centered at the Tao-lin monastery in Ch'ang-sha. Case 70 is labeled as originating at "Blue Cliff," which is a term for Mount Chia (Ling-ch'üan monastery). As was noted earlier, the *Yüan-wu yü-lu* records that Yüan-wu served twice as chief priest at Chao-chüeh monastery in Ch'eng-tu. This is where the central figure connected with compiling the *Yüan-wu yü-lu*, Hu-ch'iu Shao-lung, who died the year following the passing of Yüan-wu, came to be associated with Yüan-wu. The preface to the *Tsung-men t'ung-yao chi* by Keng Yen-hsi was written two years before Yüan-wu's passing in 1135; the preface by Ch'ang-chun was written one year before. Yüan-wu's retirement lecture from Yün-chu chen-ju monastery is recorded at the end of the "Lectures" (*shang-t'ang*) section in ch. 8 of the *Yüan-wu yü-lu*. This further confirms that the kung-an cases date from before this period, also verified by the fact that no lectures are recorded from his second period of tenure as chief priest of Ch'ung-ning wan-shou monastery.

The first kung-an case in the *Yüan-wu nien-ku* recorded in the *Yüan-wu yü-lu*, "Pai-chang Goes Deaf for Three Days," is as follows.[40]

> Pai-chang Huai-hai again visited Ma-tsu. Ma-tsu, seeing Pai-chang coming, stood his whisk up on end. Pai-chang asked: "Are you in the use of it, or apart from the use of it?" Ma-tsu returned the whisk to its former position. Pai-chang stood for awhile off to the side. Ma-tsu said: "What kind of instruction will you give henceforth with those two lips of yours?" Pai-chang took the whisk and stood it straight up. Ma-tsu said: "Are you in the use of it, or apart from the use of it?" Pai-chang returned the whisk to its former position. Suddenly Ma-tsu shouted "WAH!" At that moment, Pai-chang attained great enlightenment. Later Pai-chang told the story to Huang-po: "When Ma-tsu shouted at me on that occasion, I couldn't hear anything for the next three days."

This story is also contained in Pai-chang's biography in ch. 6 of the *Ching-te ch'uan-teng lu*, but the story that Yüan-wu cites here includes the comments by Hsüeh-tou Ch'ung-hsien (980–1052), Fen-chou Shan-chao (947–1024), and Shih-men Yün-yen (965–1032). The *Ching-te ch'uan-teng lu* contains none of their comments. The *Ming-chüeh lu*, ch. 3, has only the comments by Hsüeh-tou. The only other place where the comments of all three are preserved seems to be the biography of Pai-chang in ch. 3 of the *Tsung-men t'ung-yao chi*. While the dating of the composition of the *Yüan-wu nien-ku* is unclear, the structure of the work suggests that it was done during Yüan-wu's tenure as chief priest at Ch'ung-ning wan-shou monastery.

On the face of it, it is possible that case 19 in the *Yüan-wu yu-lu*, "Hsüeh-feng Does Not Transcend Birth and Death," came from ch. 30 of the *Ming-chüeh-lu*, but the word order in the respective stories suggests that the source is the biography of Hsüeh-feng in ch. 8 of the *Tsung-men t'ung-yao chi*.[41] As said above, many passages from Hsüeh-feng's biography in ch. 8 of the *Tsung-men t'ung-yao chi* are cited in case 5 of the *Blue Cliff Record.* Yüan-wu himself referring to "Ch'ung-ning" in case 19 of the *Yüan-wu yü-lu* affirms that he already made use of the *Tsung-men t'ung-yao chi* during his tenure as chief priest of the Chao-chüeh ch'ung-ning monastery in Ssu-ch'uan province. As a result, the connection between the *Blue Cliff Record* and the *Tsung-men t'ung-yao chi* is corroborated.

As was suggested in the foregoing investigation, Yüan-wu already made use of the *Tsung-men t'ung-yao chi* before his tenure on Mount Chia (*Pi-yen,* or "Blue Cliff") at the Ling-ch'üan monastery. It is clear that Yüan-wu made use of the *Tsung-men t'ung-yao chi* soon after it was compiled in 1093. This fact suggests that the influence of the *Tsung-men t'ung-yao chi* extended over an extremely wide area, very early on in the development of kung-an collection literature.

There are still many uncertainties regarding the process by which the *Tsung-men t'ung-yao chi* was formed. The details surrounding the compiler, Tsung-yüng, are also unclear. According to the research of Shiina Kōyū, Tsung-yüng compiled the *Tsung-men t'ung-yao chi* at the Ta-yüan hermitage on Mount Kuei. He also indicates that according to the postface by Ku-lin Ch'ing-mao, Tsung-yüng acted as editor-in-chief. Furthermore he makes the comment that the chief priest at the time was Ta-kuei Mu-che. Ta-kuei Mu-che is known from his appearance in the *Yüan-wu yu-lu.* The preface to his no longer extant *yü-lu* collection has been preserved.[42] It is contained in ch. 16 of the "Collection of Prefaces" (*Hsü-ch'ang chi*) by Huang Ting-chien (1045–105). The title of the preface, "Preface to the Recorded Sayings of Ch'an Master Ta-kuei Mu-che" (*Ta-kuei che ch'an-shih yü-lu hsü*), suggests that it did not include events relating to Mu-che's tenure as chief priest of Chih-hai Ch'an temple at Ta hsiang-kuo monastery in his later years. We can also imagine a connection on Mount Ta-kuei between Tsung-yüng, compiler of the *Tsung-men t'ung-yao chi,* and the compilation of the *Recorded Sayings of Ch'an Master Ta-kuei Mu-che,* since the two works were compiled at almost the same time. It is also probable that the *Ta-kuei che yü-lu* (*The Recorded Sayings of Ch'an Master Ta-kuei Mu-che*) was in great use around the time when Tsung-yüng compiled the *Tsung-men t'ung-yao chi.* This means that although Hsüeh-tou Ch'ung-hsien's *Ming-chüeh lu* was the most important Ch'an source used for the compilation of the *Tsung-men t'ung-yao chi,* it is possible to imagine that the no longer extant *Ta-kuei che yü-lu* followed it in importance.

Conclusions

Regarding the *Tsung-men t'ung-yao chi* and its significance for Sung Ch'an, this study suggests two hitherto unexplored aspects that need to be addressed in a more systematic fashion. The first is the influence that it exerted. The second concerns the sources that it is based on.

Regarding the first aspect, the evidence that has been presented here suggests the large influence the *Tsung-men t'ung-yao chi* had on Ch'an during the Sung. The most important characteristic of Sung Ch'an is the development of the kung-an tradition. This tradition was established by Ta-hui Tsung-kao. At the time that the *Tsung-men t'ung-yao chi* was formulated, the *Chien-chung ching-kuo hsü-teng lu*, the *Tsung-men lien-teng hui-yao*, the *Chia-t'ai p'u-teng lu*, and the *Wu-teng hui-yüan* did not exist. Along with the *Ching-te ch'uan-teng lu* and the *T'ien-sheng kuang-teng lu*, the *Tsung-men t'ung-yao chi* is one of the important sources for the study of the early Sung Ch'an kung-an tradition. I indicated that Ta-hui cited kung-an from the *Tsung-men t'ung-yao chi* in my translation of the "Dharma talks" (*fa-yü*) of Ta-hui Tsung-kao.[43] As a result, the other "recorded sayings" (*yü-lu*) of Ta-hui need to be investigated to determine the extent of the *Tsung-men t'ung-yao chi*'s influence on them. In the same way comprehensive studies need to be done on other Ch'an sources compiled after the *Tsung-men t'ung-yao chi* (compiled in the eighth year of the Yüan-yu era, 1093) to determine the possible influence on them of the *Tsung-men t'ung-yao chi*. Among these, studies need to be conducted to examine its influence on the *Blue Cliff Record* and the *Wu-teng hui-yüan*, as suggested above.

Comprehensive studies are also necessary regarding the second aspect, the sources on which the *Tsung-men t'ung-yao chi* is based. Since stories that the *Tsung-men t'ung-yao chi* shares with the *Ching-te ch'uan-teng lu* use very different terminolgy, the *Ching-te ch'uan-teng lu* is not a likely source. Instead the versions of stories contained in the *Tsung-men t'ung-yao chi* are drawn from the various recorded sayings (*yü-lu*) of individual Ch'an masters. One of the works recording the sayings of individual Ch'an masters on which the *Tsung-men t'ung-yao chi* is based, the *Tsu-t'ang chi*, is of particular interest. It was initially thought that the *Tsu-t'ang chi* text had ceased to exist in China shortly after its compilation and that it was completely unknown in China during the Sung. However, recent research has made clear that the *Tsu-t'ang chi* was known in the Northern Sung.[44] Therefore the possibility of a close connection between the two works must be considered. As examples of this connection, there is the story of Hsüeh-feng I-tsun's enlightenment in ch. 8 of the *Tsung-men t'ung-yao chi* and the corresponding story in ch. 7 of the *Tsu-t'ang chi*,[45] the story about the transmission of the Dharma from Yün-yen T'an-sheng to Yao-shan Wei-yen in ch. 7 of the *Tsung-men t'ung-yao chi* and the corresponding story in ch. 16 of the *Tsu-t'ang chi*,[46] and the story about the meeting between Ch'üan-tzu Te-ch'eng and Chia-shan Shan-hui in ch. 7 of the *Tsung-men t'ung-yao chi* and the corresponding story in ch. 5 of the *Tsu-t'ang chi*.[47] Through extensive investigations like these, it will be possible to determine the place the *Tsung-men t'ung-yao chi* occupies in the history of Sung Ch'an.

The characteristics associated with Ch'an during the most important period of its development in the Sung, the end of the Northern Sung and beginning of the Southern Sung will become clear only through further, detailed research into the topics presented here. Regardless of the conclusions this research brings with respect to the influence of the *Tsung-men t'ung-yao chi* and the sources on which it is based, the *Tsung-men t'ung-yao chi* will now undoubtedly continue to be an important work for researching Sung Ch'an. The *Tsung-men t'ung-yao chi*, largely overlooked in scholarship thus far, must be added to the list of important sources for the study of Sung Ch'an. When this is done, the true character of Sung Ch'an can be ascertained in ways that have previously been lacking.

NOTES

1. Ishii Shūdō, *"Wanshi roku* to Dōgen zen" (The *Hung-chih lu* and Dōgen Zen), in *Sōdai Zenshūshi no kenkyū—Chūgoku Sōtōshū to Dōgen zen* (*Studies in the History of the Zen School in the Sung Dynasty—the Sōtō Lineage in China and Dōgen Zen*), (Tokyo: Daitō shuppansha, 1987), and Ishii, *Dōgen zen no seiritsu shiteki kenkyū* (*A Historical Study of the Development of Dōgen Zen*) (Tokyo: Daizō shuppan, 1991), pp. 742 ff.

2. Ishii, *Sōdai Zenshūshi no kenkyū*, p. 93.

3. Yanagida Seizan, "Mūji no atosaki—sono tekisuto wo sakanoboru," in *Zen to nihon bunka* (*Zen and Japanese Culture*) (Tokyo: Kōdansha gakujutsu bunko, 1985); Ishii, "Mūji no sekiken," in *Zen goroku* (Tokyo: Chūō kōron, 1992).

4. Translator's note: Although recent scholarship (T. Griffith Foulk, "The Ch'an Tsung in Medieval China: School, Lineage, or What?" *The Pacific World*, no. 8 (1992): 18–31) questions the translation of *tsung* as "school" (as opposed to "lineage") in the case of Ch'an, I have retained it here because it represents the well-developed self-understanding of Ch'an in the late Sung and seems to convey the intended sense here better than the alternative term "lineage."

5. In the fourth *chuan* of the four *chuan* edition of the *Ta-hui p'u-shuo*. Ishii, trans., "Yakuchū *Daie fukaku Zenshi hōgo, zoku,* ue" (*An Annotated Translation of the Ta-hui p'u-chüeh ch'an-shih* (continued), pt. 1), *Komazawa daigaku zen kenkyūjō nenpō*, no. 4 (1993): 29ff.

6. The process of Ta-hui's formation of *k'an-hua ch'an* is a conclusion I arrived at in earlier studies. See Ishii, "Daie sōkō to sono deshitachi—Shinketsu seiryō to no kankei wo megutte," *Indogaku bukkyōgaku kenkyū* vol. 23, no. 1 (1974); and "*Daie go-roku* no kisōteki kenkyū (shita)—Daieden kenkyū no sai kentō," *Komazawa daigaku bukkyōgakubu kenkyū kiyō,* no. 33 (1975).

7. Ishii, "*Shōbōgenzō* to wa nanika," contained in *Chūgoku Zenshū shiwa—Mana Shōbōgenzō ni manabu,* (Kyoto: Zen bunka kenkyūjo, 1988). [Translator's note: See HTC 118, *Cheng-fa-yen tsang,* ch. 1, 2c.]

8. Among the spectacular results in this field is Yanagida, *Shoki Zenshū shisho no kenkyū* (Kyoto: Hōzōkan, 1967).

9. Representative of these accomplishments is Ōgawa Takeshi, "Kazawa jin'e no hito to shisō," *Zengaku kenkyū,* no. 69 (1991).

10. Yanagida, "*Kozunsu goroku* kō," *Hanazono daigaku kenkyū kiyō*, no. 2 (1971).

11. [Translator's note: Available in ZZ 31.1–2.]

12. Ishii, "*Shūmon tōyōshū* ni tsuite (jō)," *Komazawa daigaku bukkyō gakubu ronshū*, no. 4 (1973).

13. *Chung-hua tai-tsang-ching* (J. *Chūka daizōkyō*) 19a; appearing after the later descendants of Nan-yüeh in ch. 22, beginning with Sung-yüan Ch'ung-yüeh (1132–1202).

14. Ibid., 28a.

15. Yanagida, "Sōhan zenseki chōsa hōkoku," *Zen bunka kenkyūjō kiyō*, no. 5 (1973). Other important studies of the *Tsung-men t'ung-yao chi* include the following:

   1. Nagai Masashi, "Settou no goroku no seiritsu ni kansuru hitotsu kōsatsu," *Komazawa daigaku daigakuin bukkyōgaku kenkyūkai nenpō*, no. 6 (1969).

   2. Ishikawa Rikizan, "Kanazawa bunkobon *Myō shū daibaisan jōzenji goroku* ni tsuite," *Komazawa daigaku daigakuin bukkyōgaku kenkyūkai nenpō*, no. 6 (1969).

   3. Yanagida, "Sōhan zenseki chōsa hōkoku," *Zen bunka kenkyūjō kiyō*, no. 5 (1973).

   4. Ishii, "*Shūmon tōyōshū* ni tsuite (jō)," *Komazawa daigaku bukkyō gakubu ronshū*, no. 4 (1973).

   5. ———, "Dai-e goroku no kisoteki kenkyū (chū)—*Shōbōgenzō* no shutten to *Rentō kaiyō* to no kankei," *Komazawa daigaku bukkyō gakubu kenkyū kiyō*, no. 32 (1974).

   6. ———, "*Shūmon tōyōshū* ni tsuite (ka)—*tōyō* to *kaiyō* no chogo no hikaku to shutten," *Komazawa daigaku bukkyō gakubu ronshū*, no. 5 (1974).

   7. Shiina Kōyū, "Sōgenhan zenseki kenkyū (5)—*Shūmon tōyōshū*," *Indogaku bukkyōgaku kenkyū*, no. 30–2 (1982).

   8. ———, "*Shūmon tōyōshū* no shoshiteki kenkyū," *Komazawa daigaku bukkyō gakubu ronshū*, no. 18 (1987).

   9. ———, *Sōgenhan zenseki no kenkyū* (Tokyo: Daitō shuppansha, 1993).

   10. ———, "Daizō ichiranshū," ibid., p. 130ff.

   11. ———, "*Meikaku zenji goroku* shobon no keitō," *Komazawa daigaku bukkyō gakubu ronshū*, no. 26 (1995).

   12. Ishii, "The *Zongmen tongyao ji* and the Distinctive Character of Song Chan Buddhism" (trans. Albert Welter), *Komazawa daigaku zenkenkyūjō nenpō*, no. 7 (1996).

   13. ———, "Shohyō Nishimura Eshin ju *Mumonkan*," *Hanazono daigaku kenkyū kiyō*, no. 28 (1996).

   14. ———, "*Shūmon tōyōshū* to *Hekiganroku*," *Indogaku bukkyōgaku kenkyū* (1997).

16. Kagamishima Genryū, *Dōgen zenji to in'yō kyoten goroku no kenkyū* (Tokyo: Mokujisha, 1965).

17. Ishii, "Mana *Shōbōgenzō* no motozuku shiryō ni tsuite," *Sōtōshū kenkyūin kenkyūsei kenkyū kiyo*, no. 3 (1971).

18. Ishii, "*Shūmon tōyōshū* ni tsuite (jō)."

19. Ishii, "*Daie goroku* no kisoteki kenkyū (chū)—*Shōbōgenzō* no shutten to *Rentō kaiyō* to no kankei," *Komazawa daigaku bukkyō gakubu kenkyū kiyō*, no. 32 (1974).

20. Ishii, "*Shūmon tōyōshū* ni tsuite (ka)—*tōyō* to *kaiyō* no chogo no hikaku to shutten," *Komazawa daigaku bukkyō gakubu ronshū*, no. 5 (1974).

21. Ishii, "*Keitoku dentōroku* no rekishiteki seikaku (jo) (ka)," *Komazawa daigaku daigakuin bukkyōgaku kenkyūkai nenpō*, nos. 4 and 5 (1970 and 1971).

22. Yanagida, "*Sodōshū* no shiryō kachi (1)—toki zenseki no hihanteki sochi ni kansuru hitotsu no kokoromi," *Zengaku kenkyū*, no. 44 (October 1953). Later Yanagida Seizan published an annotated translation, "*Sodōshū* no honbun kenkyū (1)" (A Study of the Text of the *Tsu-t'ang chi*), *Zengaku kenkyū*, no. 54 (1964).

23. Yanagida, "*Sodōshū* monogatari," *Zen bunka* 51–82 (1969–1976).

24. Yanagida, *Zen goroku* (Tokyo: Chūō kōronsha, 1974).

25. Yanagida, *Junzen no jidai—Sodōshū no monogatari* (Kyoto: Zen bunka ken-kyūjo, 1984); *Zoku Junzen no jidai—Sodōshū no monogatari* (Kyoto: Zen bunka ken-kyūjō, 1985); *Zen no sanga* (Zen bunka kenkyūjō, 1986); and *Sodōshū* (*Tsu-t'ang chi*), contained in *Daijo butten: Chūgoku, Nihon hen* (Tokyo: Chūō kōronsha, 1990).

26. Yanagida, *Sodōshū sakuin*, 3 vols. (Kyoto: Kyoto daigaku jinbun kagaku ken-kyūjō, 1980–1984).

27. An article on this subject written during my doctoral course work, "The Histori-cal Characteristics of the *Ching-te ch'uan-teng lu*" (*Keitoku dentōroku* no rekishiteki seikaku), was greatly influenced by Yanagida's work. It subsequently became the basis for the first chapter of my book *Sōdai Zenshūshi no kenkyū*.

28. Ishii, "Senshū fukusaki shokei-in no joshū zenji shoto to *Sodōshū*" (Ch'an Mas-ter of Pure Cultivation Sheng-t'eng of the Chao-ch'ing Monastery of Ch'üan-chou and the *Tsu-t'ang chi*), *Komazawa daigaku bukkyō gakubu kenkyū kiyō*, no. 44 (1986).

29. Initially I investigated the case of Hsüeh-feng I-tsun, but because of the great number of stories relating to him, 44 in the *Ching-te ch'uan-teng lu* and 42 in the *Tsung-men t'ung-yao chi*, I chose his contemporary Yen-t'ou Ch'üan-huo to avoid complica-tions. The conclusions would be the same in the case of Hsüeh-feng I-tsun, since they are in no way limited to any single disciple of Te-shan Hsüan-chien.

30. Ishii, "Shuka Nishimura Eshin yakuchū *Mumonkan*" (Book Review of Nishi-mura Eshin's Annotated Translation of the *Wu-men kuan*), *Hanazono daigaku kenkyū kiyō*, no. 28 (1996).

31. As indicated in Ishii, "*Shūmon tōyōshū* ni tsuite (jō)," the number of comments in the *Tsung-men t'ung-yao chi* is as follows: Hsüeh-tou Ch'ung-hsien 213, Ta-kuei Mu-che 79, Yün-men Wen-i 47, Ts'ui-yen Shou-chih 47, Wu-tsu Shih-chieh 41, and Lang-yeh Hui-chüeh 36.

32. Ishii, "*Shūmon tōyōshū* to *Mana Shōbōgenzō—Mana Shōbōgenzō* no shutten no zenmenteki hosei," *Shūgaku kenkyū*, no. 27 (1985).

33. Important studies on Dōgen's *Mana Shōbōgenzō* following the discovery of the connection between it and the *Tsung-men t'ung-yao chi* are as follows:

1. Ishii Shūdō, "*Giun ōshō goroku* no inyō shusseki ni tsuite—enbun ninen hon to *Mana Shōbōgenzō* to no kankei wo chūshin toshite," contained in *Giun zenji kenkyū*, Sozan kasamatsu kai (1984); later included in Ishii, *Dōgen zen no seiritsu shiteki kenkyū*, op.cit.

2. ———, "*Shūmon tōyōshū* to *Mana Shōbōgenzō—Mana Shōbōgenzō* no shut-ten no zenmenteki hosei," ibid.; later included in Ishii, *Chūgoku Zenshū shiwa*, op.cit.

3. Kawamura Kōdō, *Shōbōgenzō no seiritsu shiteki kenkyū* (Tokyo: Shunjusha, 1987).

4. Kagamishima Genryū, "Dōgen zenji no in'yō tōshi, goroku ichiran hyō," *Ko-mazawa daigaku bukkyō gakubu ronshū* 17 (1986), later included in the Sōtōshū shūgaku kenkyūjō volume, Kagamishima, ed. in chief, *Dōgen in'yō goroku no kenkyū* (Tokyo: Shunjūsha, 1995).

5. ———, "Dōgen zenji no in'yō tōshi, goroku ni tsuite—*Mana Shōbōgenzō* wo shiten to shite," *Komazawa daigaku bukkyō gakubu kenkyū kiyō*, no. 45 (1987).

6. Ishii, "*Mana Shōbōgenzō* no meo wo ou," *Chugai nippō* (June 24–July 3, 1987 issue); later included in Ishii, *Chūgoku Zenshū shiwa*, op.cit.

7. ———, *Chūgoku Zenshū shiwa*—*Mana Shōbōgenzō ni manabu.*

8. Kagamishima, "*Mana Shōbōgenzō* wo meguru shomondai," *Matsugaoka bunkō kenkyū nenpō*, no. 4 (1990); later included in Kagamishima, *Dōgen zenji to sono shūfu* (Tokyo: Shunjusha, 1994).

9. Tsunoda Tairyū, "*Kana Shōbōgenzō* to *Mana Shōbōgenzō*," *Komazawa daigaku bukkyō gakubu ronshū*, no. 24 (1993); later included in Kagamishima Genryū, ed., *Dōgen in'yō goroku no kenkyū.*

10. Mizuno Yaoko, "Tenkyo kara mita *Shōbōgenzō*—toku ni tōshi to mana sambyaku soku ni tsuite," *Matsugaoka bunkō kenkyū nenpō*, no. 8 (1994).

11. Ishii Kiyozumi, "*Mana Shōbōgenzō* no seiritsu ni kansuru ichi shiken—*ihei shōko*, *Kōshōji goroku* to no naiyō tairitsu wo chūshin to shite," *Sōtōshū shūgaku kenkyūjō kiyō*, no. 8 (1994).

12. ———, "*Mana Shōbōgenzō* no seiritsu ni kansuru ichi shiken," *Indogaku bukkyōgaku kenkyū*, vol. 43, no. 1 (1994).

13. Kagamishima, ed., *Sōtōshū shūgaku kenkyūjō*, Kagamishima, ed. in chief, *Dōgen in'yō goroku no kenkyū.*

14. ———, "Saishu kōgi' kongo no Dōgen zenji kenkyū wo tenbō shite," *Sōtōshū shūgaku kenkyūjō kiyō*, no. 9 (1995).

34. Shiina, "*Shūmon tōyōshū* no shoshiteki kenkyū," *Komazawa daigaku bukkyō gakubu ronshū*, no. 18 (1987).

35. A point first made in my presentation on the *Tsung-men t'ung-yao chi* at the annual conference of the American Academy of Religion (Philadelphia, 1995).

36. Furuta Shōkin, *Mumonkan* (Tokyo: Kadokawa bunko, 1956); Hirata Koshi, *Mumonkan* (Tokyo: Chikuma shobō, 1969); Nishimura Eshin, *Mumonkan* (Tokyo: Iwanami bunko, 1994).

37. Ibid.

38. Concerning this, I presented a paper at the 1997 conference, *Indogaku bukkyō gakkai.*

39. Ishii, "Kokyū Shōryū to Daie Shūko," *Bukkyō shigaku kenkyū* vol. 23, no. 1 (1982).

40. T 47.788c–789a.

41. The *Ming-chüeh*, ch. 3 (T 47.690c); *Tsung-men t'ung-yao chi*, ch. 8, Hsüeh-feng biography (Sung edition, 28b).

42. I have introduced the preface to his missing works in "Sōdai zenseki issho jobatsu kō (2)," *Komazawa daigaku bukkyō gakubu ronshū*, no. 9 (1978).

43. Ishii, *Zen goroku* in *Daijō butten: Chūgoku, Nihon hen*, vol. 12.

44. Yanagida Seizan, "*Sodōshū kadai*," *Sodōshū sakuin*, vol. 3.

45. *Tsung-men t'ung-yao chi* 8.41–42, and *Tsu-t'ang chi* 7.11:92–93.

46. *Tsung-men t'ung-yao chi* 7.19–20, and *Tsu-t'ang chi* 16. IV: 119–122.

47. *Tsung-men t'ung-yao chi* 7.24–25, and *Tsu-t'ang chi* 5.11:19–21.

5

Visions, Divisions, Revisions

The Encounter between Iconoclasm and Supernaturalism in Kōan Cases about Mount Wu-t'ai

STEVEN HEINE

On the Encounter between Iconoclasm and Supernaturalism

This chapter examines the role of popular religiosity expressed in several kōans dealing with the sacred mountain: Mount Wu-t'ai or Wu-t'ai-shan (J. Godaizan), especially case 35 in the *Pi-yen lu* (J. *Hekiganroku*) collection of 1128,[1] along with an alternative version in the Ch'ing dynasty collection, the *Yu-hsuan yü-lu* (J. *Gosen goroku*),[2] in addition to case 31 in the *Wu-men kuan* (J. *Mumonkan*) that is similar to case 10 in the *Ts'ung-jung lu* (J. *Shōyōroku*) as well as *Pi-yen lu* case 24. The *Pi-yen lu* kōan (see appendix to this chapter for a complete translation) focuses on a specific hieratic locale infused with cosmological symbolism. Mount Wu-t'ai, believed to be the earthly abode of Mañjuśrī (C. Wen-shu, J. Monju), was a primary pilgrimage site for popular, especially esoteric, Buddhism, where seekers traveled to attain visions of the bodhisattva of wisdom (*prajñā*), who often revealed himself either in a majestic way as a blazing ball of light or a youthful prince riding astride a flying golden-haired lion amid multicolored clouds, or in covert fashion as a beggar or old man mysteriously wandering the slopes.[3]

The mountain in Shansi province in northern China is sometimes referred to as Mount Clear-and-Cool (Ch'ing-liang-shan, which also refers to the name of the Fourth Patriarch in the Hua-yen sect, with which many of the temples were aligned), or as "snowy mountain" (*hsüeh-shan*) because of both its climate and its spiritual atmosphere. The name actually refers to a cluster of peaks with five main terraces (the literal meaning of *wu-t'ai*, including northern, eastern, western, southern, and central terraces) that once encompassed thousands of monks, including clerics from Mongolia and Tibet, who dwelled in hundreds of monasteries and temples that were depicted in cave murals at Tun-huang. Many of these continued to flourish throughout the T'ang and Sung eras, even while other forms of Buddhism underwent periods of suppression or deterioration.[4] Mount Wu-t'ai, particularly known for natural anomalies such as winter blossoms and multicolored hazes, was one of four sacred mountains in China where bodhisattvas were said to appear and perform miracles for those who came seeking visions.[5] These mountains were part of a general pattern of the transformation of the Chinese landscape pervaded by indigenous spirits that were assimilated and defined, decoded and reencoded, in terms of Buddhist sacred geography.[6]

Early Ch'an developed in an intellectual climate of competition with popular religion by further redefining, usually in a thoroughgoingly demythological way, spaces previously considered to be populated by autochthonic demonic and protector gods or dominated by cosmological principles such as esoteric Buddhist or yin/yang theory.[7] For example in the process of "opening a mountain" to pacify and purify the spirits in order to establish a temple in uncharted territory, Ch'an masters often tamed and converted magical beasts like tigers, snakes, or *nāga,* or outwitted and assimilated local hermits.[8] However, Mount Wu-t'ai was generally considered off limits for iconoplastic Ch'an monastics because of its emphasis on elaborate esoteric ritual performances to invoke the presence of Mañjuśrī, and the practice of pilgrimage was explicitly forbidden by prominent masters including Lin-chi, Yûn-men, and Chao-chou. In a scathing critique that echoes Confucian scholar Hsün-tzu's sharp contrast between the common folk who embrace rituals or ceremonies based on superstition and the *chün-tzu* who practice rituals because of their elegant ceremonial quality, Lin-chi directly refutes and forbids Mount Wu-t'ai pilgrimages from the standpoint of an internalization and humanization of the supernatural:[9]

There're a bunch of students who seek Mañjuśrī on Wu-t'ai. Wrong from the start! There's not Mañjuśrī on Wu-t'ai. Do you want to know Mañjuśrī? Your activity right now, never changing, nowhere faltering—*this* is the living Mañjuśrī. Your single thought's non-differentiating light—*this* indeed is the true Samantabhadra.

For Lin-chi, the true place is not outside of human experience but is located within authentically cultivated subjectivity. Yet Mount Wu-t'ai continued to appeal to and attract Ch'an seekers, some of whose pilgrimages are recorded in a large corpus of hagiographical literature about the mountain.

The *Pi-yen lu* collection diverges from Lin-chi's strict iconoclasm by including a kōan based on a passage in a text containing accounts of miraculous visits to Mount Wu-t'ai, the *Kuang Ch'ing-liang chuan* (*Extended Record of Mount Clear-and-Cool,* 1060).[10] In the source passage, a late eighth-century itinerant Ch'an monk, Wu-cho, meets and talks with Mañjuśrī in an apparitional monastery known as the Prajñā Temple, which the bodhisattva conjures to provide comfort during the pilgrim's difficult travels. According to the *Kuang Ch'ing-liang chuan,* Wu-cho was one of several visionary-builders of the period who sought to construct an actual temple on Mount Wu-t'ai based on one envisioned and inspired during a rendezvous with Mañjuśrī. The kōan case seems at first to read like a typical Ch'an "encounter dialogue" (C. *chiyüan wen-ta,* J. *kien-mondō*) between Mañjuśrī, often referred to as the Great Sage, who plays the role of the enlightened master, and Wu-cho, who is outsmarted in the conversation and ultimately fails to realize his vision of the temple proferred by the deity. But the case's dialogue, which deals with a variety of philosophical issues concerning the significance of Buddhist discipline in the Age of Decline (C. *mo-fa,* J. *mappō*), also expresses the encounter, characterized by a fundamental tension and sense of ambivalence, between two levels of Ch'an discourse, that is, the ideal theory of iconoclasm and antiritualism reflected in Lin-chi's injunction, and the appeal of practices based on supernatural visions and numinous experiences. Thus the case reflects a double sense of encounter: the personal encounter between disciple and master, who in this instance is an otherworldly being, in the story told in the kōan text derived in large part from popular Buddhist literature; and the larger, ideological encounter between Ch'an iconoclasm and supernaturalism in the story behind the story, or the contextual background of the text, which this chapter seeks to recover. The *Pi-yen lu* kōan commentary purposefully cultivates an ironic ambiguity that avoids taking a clear stand on accepting or refuting either the supernatural or antisupernatural quality of sacred space.

The Meaning of the "Encounter Dialogue"

To clarify the twofold nature of the meeting between Mañjuśrī and Wu-cho, it is first necessary to analyze the significance of the encounter dialogue as the basic literary unit of the great majority of kōan cases. Yanagida Seizan, the preeminent Japanese scholar in studies of the formative period of Ch'an Buddhism in China, has pointed out the crucial role played by encounter dialogues in the development of Ch'an/Zen discourse.[11] According to Yanagida, the dialogue is a spontaneous, intuitive repartee between enlightened master and aspiring disciple that formed the basis of the distinctive literary style of the records of Ch'an patriarchs. The dialogues, extracted from voluminous transmission of the lamp hagiographical genealogies, including the *Ching-te ch'uanteng lu* of 1004 as the first main example of the genre, were contained in the recorded sayings of individual masters as well as in kōan collection texts. Beginning with the records of T'ang era master Ma-tsu and his Hung-chou School lineage, credited by Yanagida with originating the encounter dialogue method of teaching, Ch'an literature's main thrust was not the formal articulation of doctrinal principles but the informal, oral expression of a dynamic, experiential pedagogical encounter. The encounter dialogue, or "oral instructions uttered in different specific situations" by which its participants "could grasp truth,"[12] took place at an intense and most likely foreshadowed meeting that was uniquely conducive to a spiritual breakthrough. The opportunity for the encounter occurred suddenly and unpredictably, yet the exchange was neither accidental nor predetermined by karma or fate but a consequence of a multiplicity of causal and conditioning factors that led the respective parties to participate in the highly charged interactive situation.

John McRae, who worked closely with Yanagida, has argued that the prototypical encounter dialogue associated with Ma-tsu may have had antecedents in pre-Hui-neng Northern school literature that contained rhetorical questions and pithy admonitions referred to as "questions about things" or "pointing at things and asking the meanings" (chih-shih wen-i).[13] Despite a relatively minor disagreement about the history of the origins of chi-yüan wen-ta as a literary genre capturing a key instructional device, Yanagida and McRae are in accord on the meaning of the dialogues, especially concerning the function of the encounter itself. Both stress that the efficacy of the encounter derives from the charismatic quality of the Ch'an master, who combines innovative pedagogical techniques with an irreverent, tables-turning outlook. McRae suggests that Ch'an came to distinguish its approach from that of other Buddhist schools because the master was by no means an isolated or aloof personage but was "defined almost entirely by the kind of interaction he had with his students."[14] The encounter dialogue, a genuinely concrete and personal rather than abstract or theoretical form of expression, is designed, according to Yanagida, to liberate "someone paralyzed and religiously impotent by his dependence on some predetermined religious position."[15] In the encounter, "an enlightened master displays an uncanny knack for exposing and overcoming the conceptual impasse of a disciple, often by using a rhetorical device, such as homophone, punning, paradox, absurdity, or non sequitur, or some nonverbal gesture such as the antiauthoritarian 'sticks and shouts' of Te-shan and Lin-chi."[16] In many cases the demonstrative nonverbal gesture is particularly exaggerated and even violent, such as putting shoes on one's head, kicking over a bucket of water, twisting a disciple's nose or ear, holding up a finger or cutting off the finger of a disciple who mimics the master, or jumping off a high pole. The impact of these actions forces a degree of humiliation, ridicule, or hazing that paradoxically enables the disciple to overcome the final psychological obstacle to liberation.

Thus Yanagida and McRae understand the dialogues to be a record of the psychology of the personal encounter between master and disciple engaged in the transition from unenlightenment to enlightenment. Following this line of interpretation, in his studies of the relation between Dōgen's Shōbōgenzō and the kōan tradition, Kawamura Kōdō has suggested that the encounter records can be referred to as "satori dialogues" because they depict an instructional process culminating in a breakthrough to an awakening experience.[17] However, this approach emphasizing the psychological, internal aspect may overlook another important dimension of encounters documented by the dialogues: the social, external aspect, or the encounter between Ch'an and otherness, or with forms of religiosity that are other than, different from, alien, or foreign, as well as challenging or threatening to the principles of Ch'an iconoclasm.

The standpoints of otherness that Ch'an contends with in the dialogues range from alternative Buddhist meditative disciplines, such as the T'ien-t'ai and Pure Land schools, and non-Buddhist philosophies to diverse forms of popular religiosity absorbing influences from Taoism and folk religions as well as Buddhist asceticism, or the extramonastic practices of *dhūtānga* (C. *t'ou-t'o heng*, J. *zudagyō*). The elements of folklore and popular religion that appear in the dialogues include dreams and visions, the worship of gods and the banishing of demons, the use of signs and symbols with talismanic properties, mountain veneration, and the spiritual methods of hermits and eccentric or irregular practitioners, influenced by indigenous shamanism and immortalism, who resemble but are challenged and exposed by authentic masters for the ways that they stray from the orthodox Ch'an path.[18] The dialogues give evidence of Ch'an encountering elements of diversity, division, disparity, or dissension, including the anomalous, strange, and perplexing. On these occasions Ch'an masters are eager to demonstrate that their own supernatural powers derived from meditative discipline (S. *abhijñā*, C. *shen-t'ung*, J. *jinzū*) were superior to those gained through other modalities.

The Yanagida/McRae model of interpretation focuses on the encounter dialogue as a philosophical record of a psychological technique for liberation within the confines of the Ch'an community's view of Buddhist theory and practice. The approach suggested here highlights the process of Ch'an interacting with diverse elements in the socioreligious environment, or of Ch'an testing and contesting with, defining, and defending itself in relation to experiences of the visionary, anomalous, miraculous, and apparitional. In these encounters Ch'an expresses ambiguity in striving for a balance between accepting and embracing or rejecting and refuting rival, supernaturalist standpoints. On the one hand, Ch'an seeks to establish its priority and superiority over local cults that rely on magic and folklore, but at the same time it tries not so much to eliminate but to transform these perspectives. Ch'an acknowledges a degree of validity in the alternative approaches, or at least it refashions their images and idioms to articulate its own stance.

A key example of the intersection of Ch'an philosophy and popular religiosity is case 2 in the *Wu-men kuan*, which absorbs folklore about magical, shapeshifting foxes into a narrative in which Pai-chang, known for creating the earliest code of monastic rules, restores order to his temple by expelling and burying a monk who has been punished by suffering endless reincarnations as a wild fox. Other examples are two kōans in the *Wu-men kuan* in which Chaochou tests his extrasensory mental faculties when investigating or "checking out" two hermits with whom he enters into dharma-combat (case 11), as well as an elderly laywoman (case 31), perhaps a witch or shamaness or at least a symbol of local, indigenous religious practice, who has been outsmarting monks struggling on their way at the foot of the Mount Wu-t'ai cultic center.

A case cited in Dōgen's *Eihei kōroku juko* no. 9.71[19] extends the theme of a contest between two masters, one a regular high priest or buddha and the other an irregular hermit or solitary practitioner, whose merit is questionable so long as he is not part of the lineal tradition. Here a monk who has not taken the tonsure builds a hermitage at the foot of Mount Hsüeh-feng and lives there for many years practicing meditation on his own outside the monastic system—that is, he is living as a wild fox in intertwined positive (symbolizing freedom) and negative (representing disorderliness) senses. Making a wooden ladle, the solitary monk draws and drinks water from a mountain torrent, his only daily ingestion. One day a monk from the monastery at the top of the mountain visits the hermit and asks the classic question, "What is the meaning of Bodhidharma's coming from the West?" The hermit responds, "A mountain torrent runs deep, so the handle of a wooden ladle must be appropriately long." The monk reports this to the abbot, who declares, "He sounds like a strange character, perhaps an anomaly. I'd better go at once and check him out for myself," using the same term uttered by Chao-chou in the two kōans cited earlier. The next day Hsüeh-feng visits the hermit while carrying a razor (i.e., he is prepared to tame the fox and incorporate him into the monastic system). He says, "If you can express the Way, I won't shave your head."[20] On hearing this, the hermit at first is speechless but then uses the ladle to bring water to have his head washed, and Hsüeh-feng shaves him. Dōgen's four-line verse comment deals with supernaturalism indirectly:

> If someone asks the meaning of Bodhidharma coming from the West,
> It is that the handle of a wooden ladle is long, and the valley torrent
>   plunges deep;
> If you want to know the boundless meaning of this,
> Wait for the wind blowing in the pines to drown out the sound of
>   koto strings.

The verse steers away from endorsing or disputing the spiritual powers of the irregular hermit, who has been adopted through the master's administration of the tonsure into the legitimate Ch'an lineage.

The Mount Wu-t'ai Kōan (Pi-yen lu Case 35)

Pi-yen lu case 35 is another prime example of a kōan recording the process of testing/contesting with the forces of popular religiosity in dealing with the theme of pilgrimage to the sacred mountain of Mount Wu-t'ai, considered the terrestrial dwelling place of Mañjuśrī, who is revealed to believers in a variety of numinous experiences, especially visions and miracles. In the main part of the kōan known as the "Dialogue between Mañjuśrī and Wu-cho" or "Mañjuśrī's Three in Front, Three in Back," Wu-cho, a Ch'an pilgrim to the mountains, is outwitted by Mañjuśrī in the pattern of an encounter dialogue taking place in atypical fashion on a supernatural level. According to the *Pi-yen lu* commentary, Wu-cho had wandered into rough terrain and Mañjuśrī produced a magical temple for him to stay the night, although this text makes no mention of the physical appearance of Mañjuśrī, whether supernal and majestic or mortal in a way that disguises his identity or deliberately diminishes his status. In the dialogue the bodhisattva first asks the monk where he comes from—a query, found in many Ch'an anecdotes, that inquires about a particular location but actually challenges an itinerant seeker to reveal immediately and fully his true self or level of spiritual attainment. Wu-cho replies rather naively from a literal standpoint, "The South," though this answer can be taken to represent the notion of southern Buddhism or even the Southern school of Ch'an in contrast to northern Buddhism or the Northern school. Mañjuśrī inquires about the state of the Dharma in the South, and Wu-cho admits that in the Age of Decline monks have little regard for ethics (*śila*) or the monastic rules of discipline (*vinaya*). When asked about the size of the congregations, Wu-cho offers another literal response: "Some are three hundred, some are five hundred."

Then the pilgrim asks Mañjuśrī the same questions. In contrast to Wu-cho's factual reply, Mañjuśrī responds from the standpoint of nonduality that on Mount Wu-t'ai "ordinary people and sages dwell together, and dragons and snakes intermingle." As for Wu-cho's query about whether the congregations on Mount Wu-t'ai are large or small, Mañjuśrī resorts to a Ch'an tautology expressing an overcoming of conceptual polarities that alludes to a passage in the *Hsüan-hsa kuang-lu* (J. *Gensha kōroku*): "In front, three by three; in back, three by three." Mañjuśrī, a supernatural ruler of the sacred mountain, "wins" this round of the dialogue by performing like a Ch'an master rather than a god in uttering an apparently inscrutable tautology. As Hsüeh-tou's verse commentary in the *Pi-yen lu* says of Wu-cho's inquiry, "It is laughable to ask, 'Are the congregations on Mount Ch'ing-liang [another name for Mount Wu-t'ai] large or small?'"—that is, he deserved to get outsmarted.

According to the commentary section of the *Pi-yen lu* as well as the *Yu-hsuan yü-lu,* after the main dialogue Mañjuśrī shows Wu-cho a crystal bowl used for drinking tea, which may refer to an ambrosial medicinal brew as found in Mount Wu-t'ai hagiographies, and the sight of the crystal bowl sends Wu-cho into a state of reverie. When Wu-cho acknowledges that there are no such bowls in the South, Mañjuśrī asks, "What do you use to drink tea?" Wu-cho is speechless and decides to take his leave. When he approaches the gateway, Wu-cho asks a servant boy, "When [Mañjuśrī] said, 'In front three by three, in back three by three,' does this mean [the congregations] are large or small?" The boy then calls out, "O Virtuous One," and Wu-cho calls back, "Yes." The boy asks, "Is this large or small?" Wu-cho inquires, "What are you referring to—this temple?" The boy points to a diamond-shaped opening behind the illusory temple, which is known in Mount Wu-t'ai lore as the miraculous Diamond Grotto (Chin-kang k'u), the primary though secret and secluded (or invisible) dwelling place of Mañjuśrī and his celestial attendants. But when Wu-cho turns his head to see this, suddenly the structure and the boy have completely disappeared. Recalling the *Lotus Sūtra*'s parable of the "illusory city," all that remains is an empty valley filled with trees and a mountain landscape lying beyond, as Wu-cho apparently realizes that the temple had been conjured by the bodhisattva.

However, in an anecdote also included in the commentary on the main dialogue, Wu-cho seems to turn the tables on Mañjuśrī. Some years later Wu-cho is serving as a cook in a temple in the deep recesses of Mount Wu-t'ai, where he has decided to spend his life, and when the bodhisattva appears in a diminutive form dancing above his cauldron of rice, the monk strikes him with his spoon, although the *Pi-yen lu* remarks that it is regrettable that Wu-cho had not taken such action much sooner, at the time of the original dialogue. In contrast to this remark, in the commentary in the *Yu-hsuan yü-lu* version, which differs in a number of key points from the *Pi-yen lu* although the main dialogue is identical, Mañjuśrī appears again as a beggar at the rice pot and the cook makes the bodhisattva an offering for which he receives the praise of master Yang-shan.

There are several crucial questions raised by the failure of Wu-cho as recorded in the kōan, which alters the source narrative contained in the *Kuang Ch'ing-liang chuan,* in which he is successful in realizing a vision of the temple, as well as by the critique of the pilgrim's act of sriking Mañjuśrī in the commentary section. What exactly does the put-down of Wu-cho indicate about the view of popular religiosity expressed by the kōan? Does it represent an ironic endorsement of the superiority of Mount Wu-t'ai practices that the itinerant monk is unable to comprehend or has not been initiated into, or does it reflect an appropriation or reencoding by Ch'an of the symbolism of Mañjuśrī? The kōan expresses an encounter with the problematics of belief or disbelief in the otherness of Mañjuśrī worship. It depicts a complex dialectical process that begins with a basic sense of disbelief grounded on the skeptical outlook of Ch'an and leads to a suspension of disbelief in that Wu-cho understands that he has been overwhelmed by the wit and majesty of Mañjuśrī. What is the basis of his doubt? Does the kōan suggest that his lack of success would have been overcome by a conquering of doubt? In the encounter characterized by the twofold attitudes of approach/avoidance and attraction/distrust, the issue of belief in the supernatural becomes a test for the monk, but it is not clear whether his downfall is based on succumbing to the temptation to believe or on an unwillingness or inability to give up his disbelief. Perhaps, in contrast to Lin-chi's radical refutation, the testing of belief should not be understood as antithetical to disbelief, which may in fact be deepened by the encounter in a way that marks the overcoming of another level of duality. The kōan's use of irony and playful ambiguity concerning a commitment or noncommitment to the supernatural is employed throughout traditional Ch'an records, including many passages in Lin-chi's text which emphasize the merit of internalizing rather than simply discounting the meaning of supernatural experiences. One of Dōgen's favorite sayings from the *Eihei kōroku* alludes to the episode in which Mañjuśrī appears not as a majestic being but as a diminutive god dancing on a rice pot: "The clouds above Mount Wu-t'ai steam rice."[21]

Historical and Literary Background of the Kōan Text

The efficacy of ambiguity as a central rhetorical strategy in Ch'an discourse— neither affirming nor denying supernaturalism while at once evoking yet disarming and disdaining it—revolves around the decisive issue in the kōan narrative: Why did Wu-cho not succeed in realizing his vision? According to the *Pi-yen lu* version, Wu-cho was unable to enter into the Diamond Grotto or to build an actual structure based on the design of the vision conjured by Mañjuśrī. This stands in contrast to several notable visionary-builders reported in the *Kuang Ch'ing-liang chuan* who either did enter the grotto or were able even without entering to realize their vision through the construction of an actual temple. Indeed, the *Pi-yen lu* has altered the story of Wu-cho in the *Kuang Ch'ing-liang chuan,* in which he does succeed like the others, apparently by conflating it, or perhaps by deliberately blurring the distinction, with the account recorded in the *Sung kao-seng chuan* (988) of another monk named Wu-cho who arrived at Mount Wu-t'ai a few decades later and failed to enter the grotto after it was revealed by a servant boy.[22] The version of the kōan in the *Yu-hsuan yü-lu* to some extent more closely follows the *Kuang Ch'in-liang chuan* in explaining that Wu-cho originally met Mañjuśrī in the form of a beggar and recognized that this was the bodhidsattva only after the apparitional temple vanished after the conversation with the servant boy, a common motif in the visionary-builder literature. (The vanishing of the apparition is also found in the *Pi-yen lu,* yet this version stresses the power of Mañjuśrī to conjure, but unlike the *Yu-hsuan yü-lu,* it does not delve into the issue of the initial mystery and subsequent revelation of his true identity.) Borrowing from the *Sung kao-seng chuan* account, in the *Yu-hsuan yü-lu* version Wu-cho has a second vision of Mañjuśrī riding off on a lion amid the "five-colored clouds." The differences between the two versions of the case deriving from two different accounts of monks named Wu-cho—one who succeeds and the other who fails as a visionary—indicate that the kōan narrative is situated on the discursive border between Ch'an iconoclastic rhetoric refuting Mount Wu-t'ai and popular Buddhist hagiographical literature extolling its virtues.

Ch'an Sayings and Kōans about Mount Wu-tai

Pi-yen lu case 35 is one of a small cluster of kōans, which are in turn part of a much broader body of writings, raising the issue of the appropriateness of experiencing Mount Wu-t'ai popular religiosity known for its emphasis on ecstatic, exotic masked ritual dance processions evoking the presence of the bodhisattva. The kōan commentary could be criticized for coming too close to an endorsement of supernaturalism, which would seem to go against the grain of the antiritual, demythological approach disdaining otherworldly symbolism, as exemplified by the Lin-chi lu passage cited above which is echoed by Yün-men.[23] However, while Lin-chi and Yün-men seem one-sidedly opposed to Mount Wu-t'ai pilgrimages, the understanding of Chao-chou, a contemporary of Lin-chi from a different lineage also known for his highly individualistic approach to Ch'an training, is more complicated, emphasizing ambiguity rather than a one-dimensional negative attitude toward mountain practices.

According to the Ching-te ch'uan-teng lu, during his early career as a priest after attaining enlightenment, Chao-chou spent many years traveling around the countryside. He was particularly fond of visiting remote mountains and encountering the masters or hermits living there. He was very much intrigued and planned a visit to Mount Wu-t'ai but was discouraged by another monk's verse:[24]

> What green mountain anywhere is not a place to learn the Way?
> Why bother to hike with your staff all the way to Mount Ch'ing-liang?
> Even if the Golden Lion [Mañjuśrī] reveals itself in the clouds,
> This is not auspicious when looked at with the Dharma-eye.

However, Chao-chou was apparently not dissuaded from making the journey, because his response to the verse was the challenging query, "What is the Dharma-eye?" to which the monk could not reply. Yet the record of Chao-chou makes no further mention of Mount Wu-t'ai in this context, so it is not clear whether or not he completed the trip.

Another Chao-chou anecdote concerning the mountain that seems to have taken place years later, after he was established as the permanent master of Kuan-yin temple near the mountains is the kōan referred to as "Chao-chou Checks Out an Old Woman." Like the Wu-cho dialogue, this case, originally an encounter dialogue extracted from the record of Chao-chou in the Ching-te ch'uan-teng lu, has two main versions; the identical encounter dialogue appears with different commentary in Wu-men kuan case 31 and Ts'ung-jung lu case 10.[25] According to this case, Chao-chou learns of reports of an elderly laywoman selling tea who has been giving directions to monks at the foot of the mountain and then ridiculing them behind their backs. When a monk asks how to get to Mount Wu-t'ai and heeds her advice, presumably misleading or simplistic, to "go straight ahead," she says, "Take a look at that monk; he just goes off." Chao-chou promises to test or "check her out" (C. *k'an-p'o*, J. *kanpa*) in order to determine whether this non-Buddhist is actually more advanced than regular practitioners. This is the phrase also used in *Eihei kōroku* 9.71 as well as in *Wu-men kuan* no. 11 when Chao-chou encounters two mysterious hermits, both of whom hold up a fist in response to his probing query, though he declares one a sage and the other bogus. But when Chao-chou receives the exact same treatment as the other monks from this Ch'an "granny," he still proclaims the encounter a success: "There, I've checked her out!" The *Wu-men kuan* prose commentary begins by praising him as a "skillful rebel who sneaked into the enemy barricades" but then declares that Chao-chou and the old woman "both had faults" and concludes by asking, "Now, tell me, in what way has Chao-chou checked out the old woman?"[26]

There is no direct connection between the old woman selling tea at the foot of the mountain and visionary experiences of Mañjuśrī, but it is likely that she is a representative of a form of local, popular religiosity who, like the bodhisattva, has the capacity to confound Ch'an monks during an encounter dialogical situation. The kōan commentaries argue that the earlier monks were just as successful (or unsuccessful) as Chao-chou, or they suggest that, rather than thinking that Chao-chou was checking out the old woman, it should be considered that the old woman was actually checking out Chao-chou. These comments reflect a rhetorical ambiguity that leaves it unclear who has been the victor in the encounter, or whether Chao-chou's final proclamation suggests a rejection or a begrudging acceptance of Mount Wu-t'ai. Another kōan, *Pi-yen lu* case 24, echoes the ambiguity as well as the association of Mount Wu-t'ai with female practitioners.[27] A nun known as Iron Grinder (or Grindstone) Liu arrives at Mount Kuei Temple, located in south central China very far from Mount Wu-t'ai, and asks the master, "Tomorrow there's a communal feast on Mount Wu-t'ai; will you be going?" Master Kuei-shan responds by lying down for a nap, indicating either that the question does not deserve a verbal reply or that he is incapable of giving one, and the nun immediately leaves, although it is not clear if she will try to travel the vast distance necessary to get to the mountain feast.

Literary History of Mount Wu-t'ai Pilgrimages

Pi-yen lu case 35 is distinctive in providing commentary on a complex imaginary conversation between Mañjuśrī and pilgrim Wu-cho which was not culled from Ch'an transmission of the lamp records but from Mount Wu-t'ai hagiographies. The sense of Ch'an confronting a source of spiritual otherness and mystery is considerably increased when the bodhisattva outsmarts the seeker, who is then denied access to the visionary realm. The visionary imagery is a rhetorical element not found, for example, in the Chao-chou anecdotes, though it clearly forms part of the context by which these are to be understood. Miraculous events at Mount Wu-t'ai were recorded in two main chronicles exclusively devoted to the topic, the *Ku Ch'ing-liang chuan* (*Old Record of Mount Clear-and-Cool,* 667) and the *Kuang Ch'ing-liang chuan,* as well as through references in dozens of other sources including the major monk biography text, the *Sung kao-seng chuan,* and the diaries of the Japanese monk Ennin, who traveled to China in the first half of the ninth century. The kōan plays off twin motifs expressed in these chronicles: (1) pilgrimage to the spiritual heart of Mount Wu-t'ai, the Diamond Grotto, which was completed successfully by the Kashmiri tantric monk, Buddhapāli (C. Fo-t'o po-li), who remained in Mañjuśrī's secret cave as his acolyte, and by the Pure Land pilgrim, Fa-chao, who was guided in by Buddhapāli and received the teachings but was eventually escorted out at the request of Mañjuśrī; and (2) visionary-builders who experienced an apparition which inspired their architectural planning and commitment to realizing an actual structure. In the case of both motifs, the underlying theme is that the pilgrim's disbelief was tested and overcome by a commitment to a belief in the power of an invisible, though visualizable, reality.

There were a number of temples founded on the basis of visions and revelations from Mañjuśrī, including the Clear-and-Cool Temple (Ch'ing-liang ssu) and the Buddha Light Temple (Fo-kuang ssu, an early temple on the mountain which was rebuilt by Chieh-t'ou based on a vision in the early seventh century), both of which were south of the Western Terrace.[28] The main visionary-builders of Wu-cho's period who designed, and realized as earthly replicas on the material plane, structures they envisioned in the invisible realm of sacred revelation were: Fa-chao, who built the Bamboo Grove Temple (Chu-lin ssu); the T'ien-t'ai monk Shen-ying, who built the Dharma-Blossom Cloister (Fa-hua yüan); and Tao-i, a Ch'an pilgrim who built the Temple of the Golden Pavilion (Chin-ko ssu, the original namesake of Kinkakuji in Kyoto) north of Ch'ing-liang ssu. The record of Wu-cho, who built the Prajñā Temple, is included in the same section of the *Kuang Ch'ing-liang chuan* as the three visionary-builders in addition to Buddhapāli. A common theme in these accounts that corresponds to the structure of the Wu-cho kōan narrative is the disappearance of the visionary temple, which becomes a crucial spiritual turning point testing the pilgrims' commitment that coincides with the realization that the appearance of old man or beggar is a manifestation of Mañjuśrī, as recorded in the *Yu-hsuan yü-lu* version of the kōan based on the *Sung kao-seng chuan* account. In addition, the Wu-cho narrative in both the *Kuang Ch'ing-liang chuan* and the kōan has a special resonance with the records of both Fa-chao, who was shown a crystal bowl by Mañjuśrī in the grotto, and Tao-i, who had an encounter dialogue with the bodhisattva near the Western Terrace concerning the state of the Dharma in the Age of Decline that was remarkably similar to Wu-cho's dialogue.

Mount Wu-t'ai, as a site of local Taoist cults through the fifth century, was particularly known for anomalies in the natural world, such as blossoms raining down from the heavens, hot springs on mountain peaks, crystal clear deep ponds or rainbow clouds. The strange and inexplicable sights attracted Taoist hermits and immortals who gathered medicinal herbs and communed with ever-present gods. By the middle of the sixth century the mountain became known as the abode of Mañjuśrī, who had been a popular object of worship in the capital in Ch'ang-an for over a century. The veneration of Mañjuśrī on Mount Wu-t'ai was based in part on a chapter in the *Hua-yen Sūtra* that enumerates the mythical dwelling places of bodhisattvas and mentions that Mañjuśrī resides on "Cold Mountain" in the Northeast, as well as passages in several apocryphal tantric texts. Although many of the temples were affiliated with the Hua-yen sect, the mountain practices were increasingly influenced by esoteric (C. *mi-chiao,* J. *mikkyō*) practices imported from Central Asia, including the recitation of the *Hua-yen Sūtra* to invoke the text's miraculous powers. By the eighth century Mount Wu-t'ai hagiographical beliefs and pilgrimage rites, which attracted countless followers from India and Central Asia, were associated with the theory of the Age of Decline and considered an antidote to pernicious conditions of an era tainted by endemic delusion.[29]

The key to Mount Wu-t'ai religiosity that influences the kōan's rhetorical approach to the notion of sacred place is frequent reports of visions of supernatural sites granted by Mañjuśrī. These visions were often associated with caves that were said to be connected by secret passages and energy flows, apparently borrowing from Taoist cosmology. Some caves were known as "grotto heavens" (*tung-t'ien*) or special caverns that opened for selected believers into a glorious radiance of the transcendent. The most prominent example was the famed Diamond Grotto, an invisible cave in Lou-kuan Valley west of the Eastern Terrace. The Diamond Grotto was Mañjuśrī's spacious paradise on earth containing temples, gardens, and a myriad of bodhisattva-attendants all listening intently to the Great Sage's pure teaching. It was also filled with miraculous phenomena bestowed by buddhas of primordial eras, such as supernatural musical instruments, exquisite calligraphic copies of scriptures in gold ink, and an infinitely high pagoda.

According to the *Kuang Ch'ing-liang chuan* as well as Ennin's travel diary, there were two pilgrims who entered the Diamond Grotto with varying degrees of success. One was the Kashmiri tantric missionary Buddhapāli, who came from India in 676 "empty-handed," seeking a vision of Mañjuśrī. He was met at the southern approaches to Mount Wu-t'ai by the bodhisattva in the guise of an old man, who sent him back to India to retrieve a copy of an esoteric sūtra believed to provide relief from rebirths in one of the three lesser realms of samsāra that were destined and deserved on the basis of prior karmic action. When he returned to Mount Wu-t'ai nearly a decade later with the Sanskrit text in hand, he was met again by the old man, who this time revealed his true identity. As reported by both the *Kuang Ch'ing-liang chuan* and Ennin, once Buddhapāli was led into the grotto by Mañjuśrī, the gate was closed off never to be opened again.[30] Buddhapāli was the only one of the pilgrims who provided a sacred object the bodhisattva required, which was perhaps a key to his success.

Yet there is another report about a late eighth-century Pure Land pilgrim, named Fa-chao, known for visions of Amitābha early in his career and for popularizing the recitation of the *nien-fo* (J. *nembustu*) later on. Fa-chao came to Mount Wu-t'ai in 770 and saw radiant lights and other auspicious signs, including a golden gate bridge and jeweled pagodas with bodhisattvas preaching the Dharma while seated on lion thrones. Then he approached and was ushered into the Diamond Grotto by Buddhapāli at the request of Mañjuśrī and Samantabhadra (C. P'u-hsien, J. Fugen) and was given the teachings. In the grotto Fa-chao had a vision of the spectacular Bamboo Grove Temple and he was also shown a precious crystaline medicine *vaiḍūrya* bowl that was incredibly ambrosial. But he was abruptly escorted out of the grotto by Buddhapāli at the behest of the deities. Although he pleaded to stay, Mañjuśrī told him that staying was impossible because of the defilement of his current corporeal existence.[31] When Fa-chao left, he "found himself back on the threshold at the entrance of the cavern. . . . all Fa-chao saw was a lone divine monk" who spoke a few words and then disappeared.[32] After this extraordinary event Fa-chao harbored reservations about the authenticity and value of his otherworldly experiences, but he continued to have visions of divine presences which reassured him. His faith reinvigorated by the new apparitions, he began a campaign to construct the monastery, which was completed by 805 with six magnificent cloisters, and he was permitted by the imperial court to perform clerical ordinations. Yet Fa-chao spent most of his life after his initial visit to Mount Wu-t'ai in the capital in Chang-an spreading the popularity of intoning the name of Amitābha.

These anecdotes are quite similar to the account of an eighth-century T'ien-t'ai monk, Shen-ying, who may have once met Shen-hui and, upon consulting with another Ch'an master, traveled from far in the south almost a thousand miles to reach Mount Wu-t'ai. Following a day of ritual abstinence at a grove near the Cloister of the Flower Ornament King, Shen-ying saw a miraculous cloister with marvelous, bright images and a divine and wondrous congregation of monks that included Mañjuśrī and Samantabhadra. However, like Fa-chao (and Wu-cho), he had doubts and started walking east away from the vision. Once again the motif of the vanishing manifestation is evoked: "After about thirty paces, hearing a sound, he turned his head to look at the cloister. Not even an outline could be seen."[33] However, like Fa-chao and Tao-i, but in contrast to Wu-cho, Shen-ying was successful in building a magnificent cloister (*yüan*) or subtemple, with a triple-gate (*san-men* or *shan-men*) entranceway just as in the visionary structure. The Dharma-Blossom Cloister was dedicated to the practice of repentance, perhaps based on the *Fa-hua san-mei ch'an-i* (*Rite of Repentance Resulting in the Attainment of the Dharma-Blossom Samādhi*).

The case of Tao-i, a Ch'an monk who started his pilgrimage in 736 and ended up founding one of the most impressive monasteries on Mount Wu-t'ai, comes closest to the Wu-cho narrative because of his kōan-like dialogue with Mañjuśrī.[34] Tao-i felt that in the Age of Decline only the bodhisattva's teachings could protect and redeem him. He saw an aged monk riding upon a white elephant attending an array of marvelous golden mansions which could be approached by a golden bridge, who suggested that Tao-i return at dawn the next day to gain a vision of Mañjuśrī. Tao-i then traveled to Ch'ing-liang ssu between the Western and Central Terraces, where he saw numerous additional magical signs and mystical objects, and he went off alone to meet the bodhisattva. He again saw the old monk riding an elephant and also met a youth who pointed out the visionary Golden Pavilion Monastery, which had a triple-gated structure and was filled with gold symbols. He then realized that the aged monk was Mañjuśrī, with whom he sat in the following conversation (italics indicate passages that are the same as those appearing in Wu-cho's dialogue):

GREAT SAGE: What is the *Buddha Dharma* like in the area you come from?

TAO-I: It is *the Age of Decline* that is *being upheld* there, so that *monks have little regard for ethics* (śila) *or the monastic rules of discipline* (vinaya). There is the view that if something is not proven by eyewitness it cannot be known with certainty.

GREAT SAGE: That is a good [attitude].

TAO-I (AFTER A PAUSE): What is the Buddha Dharma?

GREAT SAGE: *Unenlightened beings and sages dwell together* in a realm that is beyond form yet responds [by means of form] to the realm of causality in order to benefit all beings. This is the Great Vehicle.

TAO-I: The temples and lodgings of the monks here are vast. I have seen with my own eyes that they are made of bright gold. It is beyond the abilities of sentient beings to measure the extent; one can only say that it is inconceivable.

GREAT SAGE: That is so.

After this, Tao-i was served some marvelously fragrant food and then shown the twelve cloisters of the temple. In front of a large refectory he saw dozens of monks following the daily routine by observing the monastic rules of discipline and practicing sitting and active meditation. After reviewing the magnificent cloisters, Tao-i bid farewell, but after walking a hundred paces he turned around and saw that the temple had disappeared. The place was empty save for the mountains and trees, so he realized that it had been a manifested or apparitional temple all along. As the *Pi-yen lu* commentary notes, "The appearance [of the temple] reflects an opportunity to manifest the ultimate reality in the realm of provisional truth." Returning to Chang-an, Tao-i led a successful campaign to have an actual Golden Pavilion Temple constructed near the Central Terrace based on his design. Over 30 years later, in 767, the ministry granted approval of the completion of an earthly replica of the visionary temple with the considerable prodding of tantric master Amoghavajra (Pu-k'ung), a prominent religious and secular scholar and translator, one of three great T'ang tantric thaumaturges and proselytizers, who was apparently appointed the first abbot.[35]

Two Versions of Wu-cho's Encounter Dialogue

There are several important affinities between the dialogues with Mañjuśrī held by Tao-i and by Wu-cho: the contrasting of the role of Buddhism in different regions—or between "here" (Mount Wu-t'ai ritualism in the north) and "there" (the South, or Ch'an iconoclastic territory), with the implied superiority of the former and defensiveness of the latter; the question of how well the Dharma is being upheld in the Age of Decline, a condition acknowledged to exist by the Ch'an practitioners who normally deny the validity of this doctrine; the confession by the monks that the rules and codes of monastic discipline and conduct are not being followed in Ch'an monasteries because of the period of degeneration; and the assertion by Mañjuśrī of the unity of sages and dragons in the realm of the true Dharma. Yet a major difference is that Tao-i, even though he is given to skepticism based on an outlook that trusts only what is seen, maintains that he believes in Mount Wu-t'ai because he observes directly with his own eyes, through apparitions that are apparently taken to be real, the magnificence of temples and the upright behavior of monks. Tao-i moves beyond disbelief, but Wu-cho does not get involved, or is not invited by Mañjuśrī to participate, in this level of visionary experience or discussion about its significance. Nevertheless, there is an important affinity in the way that the disappearance of the vision functions as a critical turning point for both Tao-i and Wu-cho, as for Fa-chao and Shen-ying. Yet according to the kōan, Wu-cho is not successful in subsequently actualizing the vision, unlike the other pilgrims. That this was considered a very serious matter is indicated by the tale of a ninth-century pilgrim, Wu-jan, who upon losing his vision proceeded to mutilate and incinerate himself.[36]

The *Pi-yen lu* kōan instead highlights the dissolution as well as the unfulfilled state of the vision by combining elements from two accounts of monks named Wu-cho. According to the account in the *Kuang Ch'ing-liang chuan,* Wu-cho, like other visionary-builders, saw a vision of the Prajñā Temple conjured by Mañjuśrī appearing before him in the form of an old man.[37] He was able to build an actual structure after an encounter dialogue with the bodhisattva, similar to Tao-i's, that was adapted to form the heart of the kōan narrative. In this text, Wu-cho had a second encounter with Mañjuśrī before actualizing his vision. But according to the *Sung kao-seng chuan* there was another monk named Wu-cho, one of several pilgrims who approached the gate of the Diamond Grotto. Yet unlike some others, notably Buddhapāli and Fa-chao, he was not able to gain admittance.[38] This Wu-cho arrived at Mount Wu-t'ai looking for the Hua-yen Temple (Hua-yen ssu) and was told by an old man to enter the Diamond Grotto. He declined but saw the man go in, never to reappear. Then he saw a group of persons entering the grotto wearing clothes of red and purple. He first hesitated, not trusting what he observed, but then he realized that these figures were assistants to the bodhisattvas who go in and out of the grotto where Mañjuśrī lectures on the *Hua-yen Sūtra.* With his doubts and fears allayed, he steadied himself to try to enter the Diamond Grotto, but the opening narrowed suddenly and he was locked out. This Wu-cho understood that the old man had been Mañjuśrī, whom he saw one more time flying by amid five-colored clouds, an image used in the *Yu-hsuan yü-lu* version of the case, but he then retreated to a life of retirement in the mountains and was never to be heard from again.

Despite differences concerning the ultimate success or failure of Wu-cho as a visionary-builder (see table 5.1), both accounts emphasize how the dissolution of the pilgrim's vision is caused in part by his doubt or disbelief.

The two versions of the kōan combine the encounter dialogue taken from the *Kuang Ch'ing-liang chuan* with the negative outcome reported in the *Sung kao-seng chuan.* They both focus on the vanishing of the temple without a subsequent actual construction, as well as on the retirement of Wu-cho to an obscure life in the mountains, where he now serves as a monastery cook. In the *Sung kao-seng chuan* version Wu-cho glimpses the Diamond Grotto but hesitates, and in the *Pi-yen lu* he simply does not get in, whereas in the *Yu-hsuan yü-lu* his vision leads him to the realization of Mañjuśrī's true identity tinged with a sad awareness that he would never see the bodhisattva again, a sadness that was in turn softened by a vision of the multicolored clouds. In both versions of the kōan, Wu-cho's inability to succeed in the encounter dialogue is to some extent redeemed by an action taken year laters at the rice pot he tends in the monastery kitchen. This is achieved either through the striking of Mañjuśrī, who appears as a dancing god, an action that is criticized in the *Pi-yen lu* commentary for coming too late ("Right then and there [at the first dialogue] he should have given Mañjuśrī a shout. He would have hit the mark right off"), or through the giving of an offering to the bodhisattva who appears in the form of a beggar, an act that receives praise in the *Yu-hsuan yü-lu* com-

Table 5.1 Differences between the *Kuang Ch'ing-liang chuan* (KCLC) and the *Sung kao-seng chuan* (SKSC) Accounts of Two Pilgrims Named Wu-cho

KCLC	Common elements	SKSC
Enters into apparitional Prajñā Temple		Looks for Hua-yen Temple
	Greeted by bodhisattva appearing in form of old man	
Participates in dialogue with Mañjuśrī		Servant reveals Diamond Grotto
	"Wu-cho" experiences vanishing of initial visions	
Has a second important vision of Mañjuśrī		Visualizes Mañjuśrī in clouds but fails to enter the grotto
Builds actual Prajñā Temple like other visionaries of the period		Retreats to life of seclusion in mountain hermitage

mentary. Yet the evaluations, whether criticizing or praising the monk, are couched in irony and ambiguity so that their intentions vis-a-vis interpreting Wu-cho in relation to Mañjuśrī are either obscured or, more likely, purposefully disguised.

The common elements of the two versions clearly outweigh the disparate factors (see table 5.2). These include the core dialogue, which is similar to Tao-i's conversation with Mañjuśrī, the crystal bowl revelation, recalling Fa-chao's encounter, and the disappearance of the visionary site, which is something that happened to all the visionary-builders as a key turning point. The discursive elements in both versions highlight a sense of loss and failure that is captured in a fundamentally ambiguous manner in the prose and verse commentaries.

Assessing the Rhetoric of Ambiguity

Seen in light of the various legends of pilgrims successful and unsuccessful, the kōan narrative establishes the Mount Wu-t'ai cultic center as an important symbol in the encounter between two kinds of religion that is played out on several levels in the case commentaries. One kind, represented by the mountain in the north, cultivates esoteric practices based on experiencing a spiritual communion with the strange, extraordinary, anomalous, or Other that gener-

Table 5.2 Differences between the *Pi-yen lu* (PYL) and *Yu-hsuan yü-lu* (YHYL) Versions

PYL	Common elements	YHYL
Wu-cho in rough terrain		Wu-cho comes to see Hua-yen temple
[no mention of Mañjuśrī's form of appearance]		Wu-cho sees old man walking
Mañjuśrī conjures an unnamed temple		Mañjuśrī displays brilliant golden color
	Central dialogue on Age of Decline	
	Mañjuśrī shows crystal bowl	
	Servant reveals Diamond Grotto	Wu-cho realizes old man was Mañjuśrī
Wu-cho hesitates		Wu-cho sees five-colored clouds
[no mention of a second vision]	Disappearance of visionary site	Wu-cho is enlightened under Yang-shan
[no mention of Wu-cho's master]		
	Wu-cho becomes monastery cook	
Mañjuśrī appears above rice pot		Mañjuśrī appears as beggar
Wu-cho hits Mañjuśrī		Wu-cho serves Mañjuśrī rice
Wu-cho criticized in commentary		Wu-cho praised in commentary

ates a mysterium tremendum (C. *kuai*, J. *kai*). The second kind of religion, represented by pilgrims such as the two monks named Wu-cho in addition to Shen-ying and Tao-i migrating from the south, expresses a mistrust—a flirting with but finally a sense of the loss—of popular symbols, myths, and rituals in a way that appears close to the traditional Ch'an iconoclastic standpoint. For nearly all the pilgrims, including the one named Wu-cho cited in the *Kuang Ch'ing-liang chuan* though not the one cited in the *Sung kao-seng chuan* or in the kōan, there is a fulfillment of the vision. Yet the narrative of Wu-cho in the kōan culminates in a shunning of popular religiosity—or is it rather a disdaining of the Ch'an monk by Mañjuśrī?—due in part to his refusal or inability to surrender his disbelief.

However, the distinction between two kinds of religion is not so clear-cut, because the failure of the southern pilgrim to enter the Diamond Grotto is to some extent his own responsibility due to a lack of faith and resolve. According to the *Pi-yen lu* commentary, Wu-cho's inability to attain a supernatural vision of Mañjuśrī is coterminous with his being outwitted by the bodhisattva, who becomes the hero in the encounter dialogue. Furthermore, Mañjuśrī, the patron of the visionary's quest on northern, lamaist Mount Wu-t'ai, is also associated with the attainment of wisdom in southern, meditative Ch'an training so that his iconography and hagiography are integrated into the Ch'an monastic institution. Portrayed as a meditator wearing monk's robes, the bodhisattva is often assigned a room and acolyte-attendants in the compound.[39]

The critical question for the kōan is whether its use of Mount Wu-t'ai practices and the apparent encounter dialogue victory of Mañjuśrī come too close to embracing a supernatural belief about a sacred site in the process of refuting it. A skeptic might argue that the *Pi-yen lu* simply wishes to have it both ways: endorsing popular beliefs when doing so is convenient for evangelical purposes while demythologizing them on an abstract level for the sake of a clerical elite. But it is just this ambivalent attitude toward the sacrality of Mount Wu-t'ai as found in numerous recorded sayings texts that triggers the distinctiveness of Ch'an encounter dialogue rhetoric. Even the *Lin-chi lu*'s approach is double-edged with regard to the symbolism of Mañjuśrī. For the most part the message is straightforwardly negative: Mañjuśrī is located within, in one's own nature, and not actually on Mount Wu-t'ai. Elsewhere (2.3), however, Lin-chi proclaims that Mañjuśrī is irrelevant in a way that seems to acknowledge, at least in an ironic sense, his otherworldly status: "My discourse on Dharma is different from that of every other person on earth. Supposing Mañjuśrī and Samantabhadra were to appear before me, manifesting their respective bodily forms for the purpose of questioning me about Dharma. . . . I would have already discerned them through and through."[40] Furthermore, Lin-chi's own comment on the kōan supports the standpoints of both Wu-cho and Mañjuśrī, whom he sees expressing skillful means and the ultimate truth of discriminating wisdom, respectively: "How could Mañjuśrī permit Wu-cho's questioning!

How could expedient means go against the activity that cuts through the stream?"[41] This approach is similar to the commentary in the recorded sayings of Dōgen's mentor, Ju-ching, who maintains that the responses of both Mañjuśrī and Wu-cho should be considered transformative "turning words" (C. *chuan-yü*, J. *tengo*), or linguistic tools that have the power to bring about realization by turning or transforming ignorance into wisdom.[42]

This sense of ambiguity, which reflects the flexible multiperspectivism of the doctrine of the emptiness of all conceptual categories, is recovered and enhanced by the rich texture and playfully ironic literary style of the *Pi-yen lu*'s multilayered commentary, in which Yüan-wu offers various kinds of prose and capping phrase comments on the cases selected and verses written by Hsüehtou. Here the commentary moves in two directions simultaneously: toward an ironic refutation of supernatural beliefs concerning the sacrality of space, but without harsh polemic, which is intertwined with a rhetorical flirtation with those same beliefs. The aim of the discourse is to explore fully yet avoid a commitment to either perspective—to a popular belief in deities or to a philosophical view of causality rejecting supernaturalism—through a construction and deconstruction, or mythologization and demythologization, that continually plays the opposing beliefs off of one another. As Robert Gimello says of another Ch'an commentary dealing with Mount Wu-t'ai visionary experiences that reconciles the "disenchanting, demystifying spirituality of Ch'an with the enchantment and wonder of Wu-t'ai-shan," "There is a repeated pattern of significant alternation in all of this, a continuing movement back and forth between the profane and the hieratic, the ordinary and the stupendous, plain daylight and preternatural radiance."[43] But the *Pi-yen lu* takes this alternation a notch further not only by moving back and forth, but also by stepping away from and negating that very movement with irony and humor.[44]

Like the modern Japanese philosopher Nishida Kitarō, who formulates the logic of the place of absolute nothingness (*zettai mu no bashoteki ronri*), the *Pi-yen lu* seeks to capture through metaphor a paradoxical prelinguistic interior state. The instruction or pointer by Yüan-wu indicates that the kōan expresses what sounds like Nishida's notion of pure experience in referring to "right here and now your seeing and hearing are not obscured (C. *pu-mei*, J. *fumai*) so that sound and form are perceived without impediment," though he concludes with an ironic remark about this condition. Yüan-wu also writes, "If you can penetrate the meaning of this, then a thousand phrases, or even ten thousand phrases, will be realized through just this one single phrase." Other paradoxical expressions make an ironic reference to supernaturalism, including one in the kōan's dialogue: "ordinary people and sages dwell together, and dragons and snakes intermingle," and several in the commentary passages: "if you do not have an eye on your forehead or an amulet under your arm, you will keep on missing the point that is right in front of you over and over again"; "you will gain a natural ability to stay free from feeling hot whether you stand in a cauldron of boiling water . . . you will also not feel cold even if you stand on frozen ice"; "you will gain a natural ability to stay free from getting wet even if water is poured all over you, and also the wind will not penetrate you." Unlike Nishida, however, the *Pi-yen lu* makes no attempt at developing a formal logic; its concern is to clarify the quality of the metaphor in evoking subjective experience. The main rhetorical strategy of the kōan commentary is to turn what is literal, or at least what is generally taken as a physical entity, that is, the place (and visions) of Mount Wu-t'ai, into metaphor and simultaneously to deconstruct the metaphor. These are not two separable discursive movements but are interconnected as a single expression which undercuts and negates both sides of a literal view of the metaphorical and a metaphorical view of the literal. The *Pi-yen lu*'s approach is exemplified by its commentary on a verse dealing with the encounter dialogue attributed to the One-Eyed Dragon of Ming-ch'ao, a prominent Ch'an master who lived in a mountain hermitage:[45]

> Extending through the world is the beautiful monastery:
> The Mañjuśrī that fills the eyes is the one conversing.
> Not knowing to open the Buddha-eye at his words,
> [Wu-cho] turned his head and saw only the green mountain crags.

The final line can be read as a criticism of the pilgrim for not paying attention to the vision and words of the bodhisattva who "fills the eyes" and ears, thereby supporting a literal reading of the supernatural. But the commentary shows that the line can also be interpreted as the negation of the literal standpoint, or as a simple, descriptive *yūgen*-esque expression of nature beyond both literal and metaphorical that counteracts the supernatural claims: the mountain crags alone make up the universal/local place or topos of nothingness, to evoke Nishida's terminology, for Wu-cho, who no longer needs to rely on visions or dialogues with otherworldly beings to experience the true nature of the world.

Furthermore, the metaphor is not only negated but turned upside-down and topsy-turvy, especially when seen in light of the *Yu-hsuan yü-lu* version's ending that praises Wu-cho. According to Yüan-wu, "Later Wu-cho stayed on Mount Wu-t'ai and worked as a cook. Every time Mañjuśrī appeared on the rice pot, Wu-cho lifted the rice stirrer and hit him." Yet even here the *Pi-yen lu* adds an ironic comment, "Still, this is drawing the bow after the thief has already fled." Then Yüan-wu, recalling Dōgen's rhetorical style of refashioning traditional kōan dialogues, counsels that Wu-cho should have hit the diminutive Mañjuśrī right on the spine even before he is asked the question about the size of the southern congregations. Finally, Yüan-wu returns to Hsüeh-tou's comment, "It is laughable to ask, 'Are the congregations large or small on Mount Ch'ing-liang,' " but now this is used in the context of laughing at Mañjuśrī rather than Wu-cho. He also includes the anecdote that a monk inquired about the meaning Mañjuśrī's dialogue of master Feng-hsüeh, who said, "His phrase did not answer Wu-cho's query. He is still one who sleeps in the fields." Lest we think that the *Pi-yen lu* intends to support Wu-cho as the victor, it concludes: "There is a sword in Hsüeh-tou's laughter. If you can understand what he's laughing about, you will realize the meaning of 'In front, three by three; in back, three by three.' "

Therefore, the effectiveness of the last line of Ming-ch'ao's verse seen in light of the *Pi-yen lu* commentary lies in a multifaceted double-edged quality that is quite different from a logical standpoint of assertion and denial. Both versions of the Mount Wu-t'ai kōan reflect an ability to construct and deconstruct the multiple meanings of a sacred place through the use of ironic wordplay, ambiguity, ellipsis, tautology and paradox which purposefully subvert the text's own claims and fulfill what Roland Barthes refers to as the Ch'an "emptiness of language" based on a "loss of meaning" by signs and symbols. Barthes critizes "the ways of interpretation, intended in the West to *pierce* meaning, i.e., to get into it by breaking and entering—and not to shake it, to make it fall like the tooth of the ruminant-of-the-absurd which the Ch'an apprentice must be."[46] For the kōan this loss of meaning is accomplished through irony and ambiguity, or a reason of unreason that appears illogical and absurd from the standpoint of logic yet knows well the meaning of Hsüeh-tou's laughter, which according to Yüan-wu "exists prior to any discourse."

APPENDIX:
TRANSLATION OF *Pi-Yen Lu* CASE 35,
"THE DIALOGUE OF MAÑJUŚRĪ AND WU-CHO"

Introduction to the Translation

This case follows the typical seven-part structure of kōan commentary in the *Pi-yen lu* collection, which was based on a collection of kōans with verse comments by Hsüeh-tou that was edited and further commented on with capping phrases and prose commentary by Yüan-wu. The seven parts of the case are: (1) the opening instruction or pointer by Yüan-wu; (2) the main case originally selected by Hsüeh-tou with (3) capping phrase commentary by Yüan-wu; (4) prose commentary on the main case by Yüan-wu; (5) Hsüeh-tou's verse commentary on the main case with (6) Yüan-wu's capping phrase commentary; and (7) prose commentary by Yüan-wu on Hsüeh-tou's verse (which in this instance cites a verse by Ming-ch'ao).

Instruction (Yüan-wu)

Distinguish between dragons and snakes, discriminate jewels from stones, and separate the complex and simple decisively and without delay. But if you do not have an eye on your forehead or an amulet under your arm, you will keep on missing the point right in front of you over and over again. If right here and now your seeing and hearing are not obscured[47] so that sound and form are perceived without impediment, I will still ask you: "Is this black or white?" or "Is this crooked or straight?" Show me how you are able to discriminate.

Main Case (selected by Hsüeh-tou) with Capping Phrases (Yüan-wu)

Mañjuśrī asked Wu-cho, "Where are you from?"[48]
Under the circumstances, the question must be asked.
Wu-cho said, "The South."[49]
[Wu-cho's] head pokes up from his nest in the weeds, but why must he raise his eyebrows? There is nothing beyond the one vast realm, and yet there exists a place called "the South."[50]
Mañjuśrī asked, "How is the Buddha Dharma being upheld there?"
It would have been a terrible mistake to ask anyone but him. [The question] still lingers on his lips.
Wu-cho replied, "In the Age of Decline,[51] monks have little regard for ethics (śila) or the monastic rules of discipline (vinaya)."
It is hard to find such a truthful person.
Mañjuśrī asked, "Are the congregations large or small?"
Right then and there he should have given Mañjuśrī a shout. He would have hit the mark right off.
Wu-cho replied, "Some have three hundred, some have five hundred."
It's obvious from the way he said it that they are all nothing but wild fox spirits.[52]
Then Wu-cho asked Mañjuśrī, "How is [the Dharma] being upheld in these parts?"
What a blow! He pushes the spear in and turns it round and round.
Mañjuśrī responded, "Unenlightened people and sages dwell together; dragons and snakes intermingle."
The tide is turned. He's tripping over his own feet and his hands are flailing.
Wu-cho asked, "Are the congregations large or small?"
The phrase comes back to haunt me, [Mañjuśrī is thinking].[53] But [Wu-cho] couldn't hold it in any longer.
Mañjuśrī said, "In front, three by three; in back, three by three."[54]
An extraordinary statement! But, are the congregations large or small? Even a thousand arms of great compassion could not count all the people.[55]

Prose Commentary on the Main Case (Yüan-Wu)

Wu-cho was making a pilgrimage to Mount Wu-t'ai.[56] When he came upon a rough area on the road, Mañjuśrī conjured a temple so that he could spend the night. Mañjuśrī asked him, "Where have you just come from?"[57] Wu-cho replied, "The South." Mañjuśrī said, "How is the Buddha Dharma being upheld in the South?" Wu-cho replied, "In the Age of Decline, monks have little regard for ethics or the monastic rules of discipline." Mañjuśrī asked, "Are the congregations large or small?" Wu-cho replied, "Some have three hundred, some have five hundred." Then Wu-cho asked Mañjuśrī, "How is [the Dharma] being upheld in these parts?" Mañjuśrī responded, "Unenlightened people and sages dwell together; dragons and snakes intermingle." Wu-cho asked,

"Are the congregations large or small?" Mañjuśrī said, "In front, three by three; in back, three by three."

While drinking tea, Mañjuśrī held up a crystal bowl[58] and said, "Do you have anything like this in the South?" Wu-cho said, "No." Mañjuśrī said, "What do you use to drink tea?" Wu-cho was speechless, and he decided it was time to depart. Mañjuśrī told the servant boy, Ch'un-t'i, to escort him to the gates. When they approached the gate, Wu-cho asked the boy, "When [Mañjuśrī] said, 'In front, three by three; in back, three by three,' does this mean [the congregations] are large or small?" The boy called out, "O Virtuous One," and Wu-cho called back, "Yes." The boy asked, "Is this large or small?" Wu-cho inquired, "What are you referring to—this temple?" The boy pointed to a diamond-shaped opening behind the temple, but when Wu-cho turned his head to see it, suddenly the illusory temple and the boy had disappeared completely; all that remained was an empty valley. Thereafter, the site was known as the Diamond Grotto.

Sometime later, a monk asked Feng-hsüeh, "What about the master of Mount Chi'ng-liang?" Feng-hsüeh said, "His phrase did not answer Wu-cho's query. He is still one who sleeps in the fields."[59]

If you want to attain the ultimate truth with your feet set firmly on the ground, then realize the meaning of Wu-cho's words. You will gain a natural ability to stay free from feeling hot whether you stand in a cauldron of boiling water or in the embers of a stove. You will also not feel cold even if you stand on frozen ice. If you want to conquer all dangers, whether facing something steep or sharp, like the jeweled sword of the Diamond King, then realize the meaning of Mañjuśrī's words. You will gain a natural ability to stay free from getting wet even if water is poured all over you, and also the wind will not penetrate you.

Have you not heard about how Chi-tsang of Cheng-chou asked a monk, "Where have you just come from?" and the monk said, "The South." Chi-tsang asked, "How is the Buddha Dharma upheld there?" The monk replied, "They are constantly engaged in dialogues" [C. wen-ta, J. mondō] Chi-tsang said, "How does that compare with the way we sow paddy fields and reap in rice?"[60]

Now, let me ask, is this the same or different than Mañjuśrī's response [to Wu-cho]? There are many who consider Wu-cho's answers wrong, while Mañjuśrī's answers are said to enable one to experience the union of dragons and snakes, or of the unenlightened and sages. At least there is such a way of thinking. But can you clearly discern the meaning of "In front, three by three; and in back, three by three"? The first arrow hit the mark, but the second arrow probed deeper.[61] Now, let me ask you, are [the congregations] large or small? If you can penetrate the meaning of this, then a thousand phrases, or even ten thousand phrases, will be realized through just this one single phrase. If through this one single phrase you can cut off all attachments and maintain tranquility, then you will attain the unsurpassable realm.

Verse Commentary on the Main Case (Hsüeh-tou) with Capping Phrases (Yüan-wu)

A thousand peaks swaying with the color of indigo.
   Can you see Mañjuśrī?
Who says that it was Mañjuśrī that was conversing with him?[62]
   Even if it were Samantabhadra, it wouldn't matter. He's already slipped by.

It is laughable to ask, "Are the congregations on Mount Ch'ing-liang large or small?"
Let me ask, what's all this laughter about? It exists prior to any discourse.
In front, three by three; and in back, three by three.
Take a look and see it below your feet, but beware of the thorns in the muddy ground.[63] *A teacup falls on the ground and splinters into seven pieces.*

Prose Commentary on the Verse (Yüan-wu)

Of the lines, "A thousand peaks swaying with the color of indigo / Who says that it was Mañjuśrī conversing with him?" there are those who say that Hsüeh-tou was just reiterating a previous prose commentary passage without really adding an original verse commentary. But it is just like when a monk asked Fa-yen, "What is a drop of water from the source of the stream?" Or it is like when a monk asked Hui-chüeh of Lung ya, "How does fundamental purity and clarity give rise to the mountains, rivers, and great earth?" You cannot say these were just repetitions of earlier comments.

The One-Eyed Dragon of Ming-ch'ao also wrote a verse commentary that enveloped heaven and earth.

Extending throughout the whole universe is the marvelous monastery,
The Mañjuśrī that fills the eyes is the one conversing;
Not knowing to open the Buddha-eye on hearing his words,[64]
[Wu-cho] turned his head and saw only the green mountain crags.

The line, "Extending through the whole universe is the marvelous monastery," refers to the temple conjured up in the weedy caves. The appearance [of the temple] reflects an opportunity to manifest ultimate reality in the realm of provisional truth. Of the lines, "The Mañjuśrī that fills the eyes is the one conversing;/ Not knowing to open the Buddha-eye on hearing his words,/ [Wu-cho] turned his head and saw only the indigo mountain crags"—at the right moment this could imply the realm of Mañjuśrī, Samantabhadra, or Avalokiteśvara. The essence is not limited to any particular principle. Hsüeh-tou modifies Ming-ch'ao's phrasing to thread the needle when he writes, "A thousand peaks swaying with the color of indigo." He wields a sword without hurting his own hand. Within the phrase he uses there is the manifestation and the reality, the principle and the phenomena. Of the line, "Who says that it was Mañjuśrī that was conversing with him?"—it seems that even though they spent the night conversing, [Wu-cho] still didn't know that he was talking with Mañjuśrī.

After the dialogue, Wu-cho decided to stay on Mount Wu-t'ai and was serving as cook in a monastery. Every day Mañjuśrī appeared above his cauldron of rice, and each time Wu-cho struck him a blow with the bamboo stick used for churning the porridge. But that is like drawing the bow after the thief has already fled. At the right time, when asked "How is the Buddha Dharma being upheld in the South?" he should have hit Mañjuśrī on the spine—that would have accomplished something.

In the line, "It is laughable to ask, 'Are the congregations on Mount Ch'ing-liang large or small?' " there is a sword's edge in Hsüeh-tou's laughter. If you can understand what he's laughing about, you will realize the meaning of "In front, three by three; in back, three by three."

NOTES

1. In T 48:173b–74b, and in *Hekiganroku,* ed. Iriya Yoshitaka et. al., 3 vols. (Tokyo: Iwanami shoten, 1994) 2:49–57; a translation is in *The Blue Cliff Record,* 3 vols., trans. Thomas and J. C. Cleary (Boulder, Col.: Shambala, 1977), 1:216–20. The case also appears in the recorded sayings of Ta-hui (T 47:816a) and of Ju-ching (T 48, p. 127c), the *Mana Shōbōgenzō* collection by Dōgen (case 127), and the *Wu-teng hui-yüan* collection (J. *Gotō egen,* vol. 9), in addition to Dōgen's *Chiji shingi* and *Eihei kōroku* and the *Lin-chi lu* (J. *Rinzai roku,* vol. 1.9).

2. This version is in Charles Luk, trans., *Ch'an and Zen Teaching First Series* (Berkeley, Cal.: Shambala, 1970), pp. 139–42.

3. It is interesting to note that Mañjuśrī's manifestations are not always majestic or regal, for he also appears as an old man or beggar. Furthermore, as will be seen, Mañjuśrī is considered by Lin-chi to be purely internal, and in the Pai-chang record he is associated with Mind, though in the Ch'an monastic institution he is often venerated as a deity wielding a sword to cut through ignorance and enshrined in a special room in the compound. Also, in the Ritsu sect in Kamakura-era Japan, the bodhisattva is identified with outcasts (*hinin*) and beggars, for whom he strove to bring salvation.

4. The mountain was visited in modern times by the Ch'an master Hsü-yun in the 1880s. For an account of visionary experiences there in the 1930s, including a discussion of how these sights contradict a scientific outlook, see John Blofeld, *The Wheel of Life* (Berkeley, Cal.: Shambala, 1972, rpt. 1959), pp. 114–55. Also during the Maoist era, Mount Wu-t'ai, apparently once used by Mao as a hideout because of its caves, remained relatively popular and was the subject of afforestation campaigns in the 1950s.

5. The other three are Mount Omei in Szechuan in the south, the home of Samantabhadra (C. P'u-hsien, J. Fugen); Mount P'u-t'o on an island near Chekiang in the east, the home of Avalokiteśvara (C. Kuan-yin, J. Kannon); and Mount Chiu-hua in Anhui in the west, the home of Kṣtigarbha (C. Ti-tsang, J. Jizō). As is mentioned above, Mount Wu-t'ai is actually a group of five peaks (the literal meaning of the name) or terraces, with dozens of caves and grottoes.

6. For material on the mountain see Abe Chōichi, *Zenshū shakai to shinkō* (Tokyo: Shinkai shoseki, 1992), pp. 46–68 (which deals specifically with Ch'an during the Sung); Raoul Birnbaum, "The Manifestation of a Monastery: Shen-ying's Experiences on Mount Wu-T'ai in T'ang Context," *Journal of the American Oriental Society,* vol. 106, no. 1 (1986): 119–37; Raoul Birnbaum, "Secret Halls of the Mountain Lords: The Caves of Wu-T'ai Shan," *Cahiers d'Extreme-Asie,* no. 5 (1989–90): 115–40; Edwin O. Reischauer, trans. *Ennin's Diary: The Record of a Pilgrimage to China in Search of the Law* (New York: Ronald Press, 1955); Reischauer, *Ennin's Travels in T'ang China* (New York: Ronald Press, 1955), esp. pp. 194–211; and Edwin Birnbaum, *Sacred Mountains of the World* (San Francisco: Sierra Club Books, 1990), pp. 35–40. I also benefited from Rauol Birnbaum's slide presentation at the 1998 meeting of the American Academy of Religion in Orlando.

7. See Bernard Faure, *Chan Insights and Oversights: An Epistemological Critique of the Chan Tradition* (Princeton, N.J.: Princeton University Press, 1993), pp. 155–74.

8. See especially *Wu-men kuan* case 40 in T 48, p. 298a, which deals with Kuei-shan founding a mountain monastery, as well as the hagiographical background to the kōan case focusing on the role of geomancer Ssu-ma in the *Ching-te ch'uan-teng lu* in T 264b–266b.

9. *Lin-chi lu* (2.7) in T 47:498c26–29, and in *Rinzai roku,* ed. Iriya Yoshitaka (Tokyo: Iwanami shoten, 1991), pp. 65–66. This passage is also cited in Robert M. Gimello, "Chang Shang-ying on Wu-t'ai Shan," in *Pilgrims and Sacred Sites in China,* ed. Susan Naquin and Chün fang Yü (Berkeley: University of California Press, 1992), pp. 119–24, from *The Recorded Sayings of Ch'an Master Lin-chi Hui-chao of Chen Prefecture,* trans. Ruth Fuller Sasaki (Kyoto: The Institute for Ch'an Studies, 1975), p. 16—this translation uses a different system for numbering the passages.

10. In T 51:1111b–1112c.

11. Yanagida Seizan, "The 'Recorded Sayings' Texts of Chinese Ch'an Buddhism," trans. John R. McRae, in *Early Ch'an in China and Tibet,* ed. Whalen Lai and Lewis R. Lancaster (Berkeley, Cal.: Berkeley Buddhist Studies Series, 1983), pp. 185–205.

12. Yanagida, "The 'Recorded Sayings,' " p. 189.

13. John R. McRae, *The Northern School and the Formation of Early Ch'an Buddhism* (Honolulu: University of Hawaii Press, 1986), pp. 93–97. The main difference is that these were not conversations but monologues, or one-sided pronouncements of masters only without any interaction with disciples.

14. McRae, *Northern School,* p. 95.

15. Yanagida, "The 'Recorded Sayings'," p. 190.

16. Steven Heine, *Dōgen and the Kōan Tradition: A Tale of Two Shōbōgenzō Texts* (Albany, N.Y.: SUNY Press, 1994), p. 27.

17. See Kawamura Kōdō, *Shōbōgenzō no seiritsu shiteki kenkyū* (Tokyo: Shunjūsha, 1987).

18. Faure emphasizes the role of "dreams, thaumaturgy, death, relics, ritual, and gods . . . usually silenced or explained away—both by the tradition itself and by its scholarly replication—by means of notions of such as the Two Truths," in *The Rhetoric of Immediacy: A Cultural Critique of Chan/Zen Buddhism* (Princeton, N.J.: Princeton University Press, 1991), p. 305.

19. In *Dōgen zenji zenshū,* 7 vols., ed. Kagamishima Genryū et al., (Tokyo: Shunjūsha, 1999–1992), 4:230; the case is also cited by Dōgen in *Mana Shōbōgenzō* case 183. A common theme in Ch'an kōans, as in *Wu-men kuan* case 11, is the testing of irregular practitioners by Ch'an masters, who generally seek to prove their own superiority while acknowledging the insights attained by all those who do some form of zazen training.

20. In an extended commentary on this encounter dialogue in *Shōbōgenzō* "Dōtoku," Dōgen remarks that Hsüeh-feng should not and would not have asked or expected the irregular practitioner to "express the way" (*dōtoku*), unless he already knew that the hermit was enlightened. Yet the silent response indicates the superiority of Hsüeh-feng despite the hermit's own considerable spiritual attainment.

21. *Dōgen Zenji zenshū* 3:274; the saying is not unique to Dōgen but is found in earlier Ch'an/Zen records, especially *Pi-yen lu* case 96 citing a verse by Tung-shan, and is also used by Yün-men an Ikkyū, among others.

22. *Sung kao-seng chuan* in T 50, pp. 836c–837b.

23. T 47:548c8–15; and Urs App, trans., *Master Yunmen: From the Record of the Chan Teacher "Gate of the Clouds"* (New York: Kodansha, 1994), pp. 116–17.

24. In the *Ching-te ch'uan-teng lu,* vol. 10, in T 51:277a. An English translation is in Sohaku Ogata, trans., *The Transmission of the Lamp: Early Masters* (Wolfeboro, N.H.: Longwood Academic, 1990), p. 349.

25. This case, known as "Chao-chou Checks Out an Old Woman," first appeared in the transmission of the lamp history, *Ching-te ch'uan-teng lu* in T 51, p. 277b, and it is included in two kōan collections, the *Wu-men kuan* in T 48:297a and the *Ts'ung-jung lu* in T 48:233c.

26. This rhetorical strategy, used in many dialogues and kōans in the *Wu-men kuan* and other collections, combines tautology and paradox from an absurd, ironic point of view—so that identical answers get opposite responses, or opposite answers spark identical responses. Chao-chou is also known for offering tea to disciples regardless of how they reply to his queries.

27. In T 48:165a–165c. This case also included in *Ts'ung-jung lu* case 60.

28. On the latter temple see Marilyn M. Rhie, *The Fo-kuang ssu: Literary Evidences and Buddhist Images* (New York: Garland Publishing, 1977).

29. It is important to note that Mañjuśrī worship on Mount Wu-t'ai is not mentioned in the *Biographies of Eminent Monks* text of the sixth century and appears only briefly in the *Supplementary Biographies* text of the seventh century. But in the *Sung Biographies* text of 988, there are over a dozen stories, including many of those discussed in this chapter; see John Kieschnick, *The Eminent Monk: Buddhist Ideals in Medieval Chinese Hagiography* (Honolulu: University of Hawaii Press, 1987), pp. 105–6.

30. Reischauer, *Ennin's Travels,* p. 195; Birnbaum, "Secret Halls of the Mountain Lords," pp. 129–30; Gimello, "Chang Shang-ying on Wu-T'ai Shan," p. 130 n. 24. In addition to Ennin, a Japanese monk, Chōnen, arrived in the tenth century and later built Seiryōji Temple (Ch'ing-liang ssu in Chinese) in Kyoto after a vision of five-colored clouds.

31. Birnbaum, "Secret Halls of the Mountain Lords," pp. 130–31, citing *Kuang Ch'ing-liang chuan* in T 51:1114a–1115a; and Daniel Stevenson, trans., "Visions of Mañjuśrī on Mount Wutai," *Religions of China in Practice,* ed. Donald Lopez (Princeton, N.J.: Princeton University Press, 1996), pp. 203–22.

32. Stevenson, "Visions of Mañjuśrī on Mount Wutai," p. 218.

33. Birnbaum, "Shen-ying's Experiences on Mount Wu-t'ai," p. 128; and T 50, pp. 1112c–1113a and 52:422c. In a Noh play, *Shakkyō,* a Japanese priest traveling through India and China in search of Buddhist holy places visits the mountain and is about to cross over a great stone bridge when a boy warns him that the bridge stretches to the heavenly paradise of the bodhisattva but the valley below plunges as deep as hell. The bridge is impossibly narrow and slippery, but suddenly a golden lion appears dancing among flowers to lead the pilgrim on. See Carmen Blacker, *The Catalpow Bow: A Study of Shamanistic Practices in Japan* (London: George Allen and Unwin, 1975), p. 316.

34. In *Kuang Ch'ing-liang chuan* in T 51, pp. 1113a–1114b; *Sung kao-seng chuan* in T 50:843c–844a; and in Birnbaum, *Studies in the Mysteries of Mañjusrī* (Boulder, Col.: Society for the Study of Chinese Religions, 1983), pp. 14–16. Unlike the case of the two Wu-cho's, the Tao-i account is essentially the same in the *Kuang Ch'ing-liang chuan* and the *Sung kao-seng chuan* versions.

35. Stanley Weinstein suggests that the problems Tao-i had with completing the building of the temple stemmed from the An Lu-shan rebellion lasting from 765 to 73, in *Buddhism Under the T'ang* (New York: Cambridge University Press, 1987), p. 80.

36. *Sung kao-seng chuan* in T 50, pp. 855c–856b; see the discussion in Kieschnick, *The Eminent Monk*, pp. 37–39.

37. *Kuang Ch'ing-liang chuan* in T 51, pp. 1111b–1112c.

38. *Sung kao-seng chuan* in T 50, pp. 836c–837b; Birnbaum, "Secret Halls of the Mountain Lords," p. 131.

39. T. Griffith Foulk, "Myth, Ritual, and Monastic Practice in Sung Ch'an Buddhism," *Religion and Society in T'ang and Sung China,* ed. Patricia Buckley Ebrey and Peter N. Gregory (Honolulu: University of Hawaii Press, 1993), p. 183.

40. *Rinzai roku,* p. 49; Sasaki translation, p. 11.

41. *Rinzai roku,* p. 28; Sasaki translation, p. 6.

42. *Nyojō goroku,* ed. Kagamishima Genryū (Tokyo: Shunjūsha, 1983), pp. 291–93.

43. Gimello, "Chang Shan-ying on Wu-t'ai Shan," pp. 121, 122.

44. A prime example is the comment in Yüan-wu's notes on the kōan case in which he writes that "they are probably all wild fox spirits" about Wu-cho's response to the question about the size of the southern congregations; the fox-spirit criticism, often used in Ch'an texts, especially the *Lin-chi lu,* in which the term appears five times, seems to be a part of the Ch'an reaction to *mo-fa* (J. *mappō*) theory in which lazy or irresponsible monks are questioned as to whether they are legitimately of human status. For a related use of this kind of rhetorical device see *The Ch'an teachings of Hakuin,* trans. Norman Waddell (Boston: Shambala, 1994), pp. 9–18, 115 n. 3.

45. Ming-ch'ao is featured in *Pi-yen lu* case 48, which deals with a spirit that haunts stoves, and in the commentary on *Ts'ung-jung lu* case 55 about Hsüeh-feng working as a rice cook. His name also happens to be cited in the commentary on case 19 near a reference to master Mi-mo, who dwelled on Mount Wu-t'ai and is also cited in *Ts'ung-jung lu* case 62. Mi-mo, also mentioned in Dōgen's *Mana Shōbōgenzō* case 73, was known to carry a forked branch and demand of Mount Wu-t'ai pilgrims: "What kind of demons brought you on this path? You will die in the stocks whether you answer or not, so speak quickly!" Ming-ch'ao's verse alludes to the poem given to Chao-chou to discourage him from traveling to the mountain, and it is responded to in Hsüeh-tou's verse comments on the dialogue.

46. Roland Barthes, *The Empire of Signs* (New York: Hill and Wang, 1981), p. 72.

47. This phrase recalls the famous "Pai-chang and the wild fox" kōan in *Wu-men kuan* case 2.

48. Mañjuśrī was one of the four main bodhisattvas venerated in China and was said to make Mount Wu-t'ai his earthly abode.

49. This reply can be considered to imply southern Buddhism or, more specifically, the Southern school of Ch'an.

50. In other words, in the realm of nonduality how can distinctions between directions be made?

51. This notion is based on Buddhist prophecies that about 1,500 years after the life of Śakyamuni a period of degeneration would set in due to people's ignorance and karma. The Age of Decline (*mo-fa*) would last for a period of 10,000 years, during which no one could gain enlightenment through self-effort alone.

52. The term "wild fox spirits," borrowed from folklore about magical, shape-shifting foxes, is a conventional epithet used to refer to those who claim a false, inauthentic enlightenment. See Heine, *Shifting Shape, Shaping Text: Philosophy and Folklore in the Fox Kōan* (Honolulu: University of Hawaii Press, 1999).

53. The sentence structure is vague here, but it seems to imply that Mañjuśrī is

thinking that Wu-cho has turned the tables, at least momentarily, by asking him the identical question.

54. This saying alludes to a saying used in the *Hsüan-hsa kuang-lu* (J. *Gensha kōroku*), which could be interpreted to mean "six in front (or before), and in back (or behind)"—six may refer to the six senses, which are gateways for the perception of the world of external stimuli.

55. Yüan-wu is questioning, as echoed below in the anecdote about Feng-hsüeh, whether Mañjuśrī's response really answered Wu-cho's question, by referring to another bodhisattva, Kuan-yin.

56. This narrative is apparently based on records of two monks named Wu-cho who visited the mountain, one cited in the *Kuang Ch'ing-liang chuan,* who envisioned and later constructed the Prajñā Temple, and the other cited in the *Sung kao-seng chuan,* who saw but failed to enter the Diamond Grotto because of his doubt.

57. The passage in the commentary section adds the word "just" to the question as asked in the main case.

58. The crystal bowl may have been made, as in other Wu-t'ai tales, of *vaiḍūrya,* one of the seven precious objects in Central Asian (particularly Gandharan) Buddhist mythology.

59. Again there is a vagueness, so it is not clear whether the passage is criticizing Mañjuśrī or Wu-cho as the one sleeping in the fields.

60. This anecdote makes an interesting contrast between those monks who spend their time in encounter dialogues and those who adhere to Pai-chang's saying, "a day without work is a day without eating," by carrying out their chores with dedication and determination.

61. This line echoes in Hsüeh-tou's verse commentary in *Pi-yen lu* case 93.

62. This line can be considered an ironic response to the assertion in Ming-ch'ao's verse, cited below, that the identity of the mysterious supernatural being conversing with Wu-cho was the bodhisattva Mañjuśrī.

63. This line is echoed in the Yüan-wu's capping phrases on the main case in *Pi-yen lu* case 28.

64. The reference to the opening of the eye of wisdom alludes to a verse once given by a monk to discourage Chao-chou from visiting Mount Wu-t'ai, as recorded in the *Ching-te ch'uan-teng lu.*

6

"Before the Empty Eon" versus "A Dog Has No Buddha-Nature"

Kung-an Use in the Ts'ao-tung Tradition and Ta-hui's Kung-an Introspection Ch'an

MORTEN SCHLÜTTER

The Kung-an Introspection/Silent Illumination Ch'an Debate

A common view of the kung-an, implied in much of the literature on Ch'an available in English, is that its use is the special domain of the Lin-chi (J. Rinzai) tradition, in which kung-an were, and still are, used in the active pursuit of enlightenment. Along with this view is the depiction of the Ts'ao-tung (J. Sōtō) tradition as being rather passive while neglecting, or at least putting less emphasis on, the study of kung-an, instead pursuing a gradual approach enlightenment through long hours of meditation. These distinctions are furthermore understood to characterize the Lin-chi and Ts'ao-tung traditions from their very inceptions in China.[1]

This view is closely connected with the traditional understanding of the "debate" over Kung-an Introspection Ch'an (*k'an-hua ch'an*) versus Silent Illumination Ch'an (*mo-chao ch'an*) that unfolded in the twelfth century. In Western scholarship, it is still usually assumed that this was a controversy between the Ts'ao-tung and Lin-chi traditions and that the famous Ts'ao-tung master Hung-chih Cheng-chüeh (1091–1157) and the equally famous Lin-chi master Ta-hui Tsung-kao (1089–1163) were the main adversaries. As Heinrich Dumoulin expresses in the *Encyclopedia of Religion:*

> [In the twelfth century a] heated confrontation regarding the correct way of meditation broke out between the two schools, summarized in the catch-phrases *k'an-*

hua ch'an (J. *kanna-zen;* "Ch'an of reflection on the koan") and *mo-chao ch'an* (J. *mokusho-zen;* "Ch'an of silent illumination"). Ta-hui of the Lin-chi school took the offensive, warning against the false path of sitting in silent passivity. The literarily gifted Ts'ao-tung master Hung-chih mustered eloquent words in its defense: "Anyone who has arrived at silent illumination belongs to the house of our tradition. The silent illumination reaches up to the heights; it presses down to the depths." [Cited from Hung-chih's poem the *Mo-chao ming*].[2]

However, Ishii Shūdō and Yanagida Seizan, among other Japanese scholars, have in recent years argued that there are several indications of a cordial relationship between Ta-hui and Hung-chih,[3] and they have further presented evidence that Hung-chih's older fellow student Chen-hsieh Ch'ing-liao (1088– 1151) was the major target of Ta-hui's attacks.[4] It has now become accepted, at least among Japanese scholars, that Ta-hui did not mean to target the Ts'ao-tung tradition as such and that he did not have Hung-chih in mind when he made his attacks on Silent Illumination.[5] This understanding challenges the whole idea of a Silent Illumination/Kung-an Introspection Ch'an confrontation between the Ts'ao-tung and Lin-chi traditions.[6]

Certainly, extant sources offer no evidence that a "debate" was going on between the Ts'ao-tung and Lin-chi traditions. While Ta-hui very often in his sermons and writings attacks Silent Illumination vehemently, there are no clear indications, in the records of Hung-chih or any other Ts'ao-tung master, of a counterattack or even an attempt of a defense. Ishii has shown that Hung-chih's famous poem the *Mo-chao ming* (*Inscription on Silent Illumination*), which extols a silent awareness of the realm of Buddha-nature which Hung-chih refers to as Silent Illumination,[7] most likely was written *before* Ta-hui began his attacks on Silent Illumination and therefore cannot have been a response to them, as is commonly assumed.[8]

However, as much as the traditional view of the "debate" is clearly based on an inadequate understanding, I have argued elsewhere that it is really not so far off the mark after all, especially in the twelfth century.[9] Although Ch'ing-liao indeed was a major target for Ta-hui, Ta-hui's attacks on Silent Illumination were in fact aimed at the whole twelfth-century Ts'ao-tung tradition, including Hung-chih. The twelfth-century Ts'ao-tung tradition did put great emphasis on the notion of the original, inherent Buddha-nature of all sentient beings, and it did teach a type of still meditation in which the Buddha-nature would naturally manifest. Although the expression "Silent Illumination" is used only a few times in all of Ts'ao-tung literature, it is a convenient, and not unreasonable, term to characterize the twelfth-century Ts'ao-tung teachings. Ta-hui both exaggerates and distorts the Ts'ao-tung position, but it is still recognizable in his attacks.[10] Although Hung-chih probably never responded directly to Ta-hui, he was clearly aware of the attacks, and the whole affair gave rise to a sectarian atmosphere within Ch'an which was to last for many generations in China and which was also transmitted to Japan, where it is still alive and well.

The Silent Illumination/Kung-an Introspection "debate" was played out on the background of the state's policies toward monastic Buddhism during the Sung dynasty (960–1279). The Sung government from the beginning both encouraged and sought to control monastic Buddhism. Towards this end the government promoted a new kind of monastery known as "public (*shih-fang*) monasteries," the abbacies of which were open to any qualified candidate, who was often selected by secular officials and over which the state had considerable influence. The Ch'an school had a special association with the institution of public monasteries, and numerous ordinary "hereditary (*chia-i*) monasteries"—so named because here the abbacy stayed within a "family" of monks who held the rights to the monastery—were converted to public monasteries reserved for the Ch'an school.[11] The Sung policies thus had the effect of favoring the Ch'an school and allowing it to acquire an institutional framework which enabled it to develop a distinct identity and greatly expand its influence.

However, later in the Sung the state ceased to promote public monasteries, and so state support for Ch'an, and for Buddhism in general, was less forthcoming. Buddhism even experienced a brief suppression 1119–1120 under the emperor Hui-tsung (r. 1100–1126).[12] It was this less favorable political climate that set the stage for the development of Silent Illumination and the particular use of kung-an within the Ts'ao-tung tradition as well as Ta-hui's attacks on it and his own Kung-an Introspection Ch'an.

This chapter discusses the genuinely different approaches to kung-an use and enlightenment that are manifest in the twelfth-century Ts'ao-tung Silent Illumination and Ta-hui's Kung-an Introspection Ch'an. But it also seeks to show that these differences did not come about until the twelfth century and that they cannot be traced back to the "beginnings" of the Ts'ao-tung and Lin-chi traditions. Finally, it argues that Silent Illumination and Kung-an Introspection Ch'an can be fully understood only in the context of each other, as well as in the context of the political and social environment in which they took shape.

The New Ts'ao-tung Tradition of the Twelfth Century

Although government policies had enabled the Ch'an school to develop and dominate elite Buddhism throughout the Sung period, the Ts'ao-tung tradition had not been successful through most of the earlier part of the Sung dynasty, known as the Northern Sung (960–1127). In fact, the well-known scholar–monk Ch'i-sung (1007–1072) reported in 1061 that "the Ts'ao-tung tradition barely exists, feeble like a lonely spring during a great drought."[13] However, in the late eleventh and early twelfth centuries the Ts'ao-tung tradition underwent a great revival and renewal which over the span of just a few generations made it one of the most powerful groups of Sung-dynasty elite Buddhism. The active resurrection of the Ts'ao-tung tradition began with Fu-jung Tao-k'ai (1043–1118) and his dharma brother Ta-hung Pao-en (1058–1111), who both

did much to promote the Ts'ao-tung lineage and who became nationally famous Ch'an masters. Tao-k'ai and Pao-en were both heirs of the rather shadowy figure T'ou-tzu I-ch'ing (1032–1083), who himself was said to have received the Ts'ao-tung transmission of Ta-yang Ching-hsüan (942–1027).

Ta-yang Ching-hsüan was the last Ts'ao-tung master, and the only fifth-
generation descendant of the Ts'ao-tung "founder" Tung-shan Liang-chieh
(807–869), to be included in the famous and influential Ch'an transmission of
the lamp history the *Ching-te ch'uan-teng lu* (Ching-te [1004–1008] *Record of
the Transmission of the Lamp*).[14] However, I-ch'ing is said to have received the
transmission not directly from Ta-yang Ching-hsüan, but from the the Lin-chi
master Fu-shan Fa-yüan (991–1067), who had held the transmission "in trust"
for Ching-hsüan. The story goes that Ching-hsüan was about to pass away
without any living heirs, and with him the Ts'ao-tung lineage would die out.
But in the last minute Ching-hsüan managed to persuade the visiting Lin-chi
master Fu-shan Fa-yüan to take his transmission "in trust" and pass it on to
a suitable disciple in due time. Many years later Fa-yüan selected his student
T'ou-tzu I-ch'ing to be the recipient of Ching-hsüan's transmission, and in this
peculiar way the Ts'ao-tung lineage was saved.[15] The transmission of the lamp
histories, in fact, mentions several direct disciples of Ching-hsüan who seem
to have survived him,[16] but during the time of Fu-jung Tao-k'ai and Ta-hung
Pao-en the story became an accepted part of Ch'an lore and the two masters
were considered the only surviving lineage holders in the Ts'ao-tung tradition.[17]

Pao-en's lineage died out after a few generations, but Tao-k'ai's lineage was
highly successful and he had a number of famous disciples. However, the culmination of the Ts'ao-tung revival came with Tao-k'ai's two second-generation
descendants, Hung-chih Cheng-chüeh and Chen-hsieh Ch'ing-liao, who both
can be counted among the most famous Ch'an masters of the Sung dynasty.
Ch'ing-liao's lineage was later transmitted to Japan by the famous Sōtō
founder Dōgen (1200–1253), who also was deeply influenced by Hung-chih's
thought although at times critical of it.[18]

"Before the Empty Eon" and
"A Dog Has No Buddha-Nature"

In the following, I will distinguish between three types of kung-an in Sung
Ch'an. The first is the use of particular stories about, or dialogues involving,
a revered Ch'an figure of the past. Ch'an masters from the Sung dynasty onward would often use such stories in their sermons or in the instruction of
individual disciples. I will call this a "kung-an story." Second, a kung-an can
be in the form of a "catchphrase kung-an" which has no special association
with any particular Ch'an master, such as the various forms of the query
"What is the meaning of Bodhidharma's coming from the West?" The catchphrase kung-an about Bodhidharma's coming from the West is probably *the*
most common kung-an of all time, giving rise to numerous kung-an stories

about various Ch'an masters' answers to the question.[19] Third, "situation kung-an" are the unique questions or challenges posed by masters to students in particular situations.[20] Of course, such situation kung-an often became kung-an stories through their retelling and use by other Ch'an masters.

The awakening stories of Hung-chih and Ch'ing-liao, the two masters who were the most illustrious representatives of the Ts'ao-tung tradition in the Sung, must have been well-known among their contemporaries and must have had a special significance in defining the revived Ts'ao-tung tradition. In Hung-chih's epitaph, written shortly after his death, we are told that as a young man Hung-chih traveled around calling on various Ch'an masters (as was usual for a monk who aspired to receive transmission in the Ch'an lineage). While visiting the Ts'ao-tung master K'u-mu Fa-ch'eng (1071–1128), Hung-chih had a minor enlightenment experience, but Fa-ch'eng told him he had to go and see someone else for his enlightenment to be complete. Fa-ch'eng's fellow disciple under Fu-jung Tao-k'ai, Tan-hsia Tzu-ch'un (1064–1117), was a renowned master at the time and Hung-chih went to him. When they met, Tzu-ch'un asked Hung-chih:

> "How about your self before the empty eon?"[21] The master [Hung-chih] answered: "A toad in a well swallows up the moon; at midnight, we don't rely on curtains against the brightness of the night." [Tan] Hsia [Tzu-ch'un] said: "You are still not there, say some more." As the master [Hung-chih] was about to make a statement, Hsia hit him with his stick and said: "You still say you do not rely [on things]?" The master suddenly had an awakening and made obeisance. Hsia said, "Why don't you state something?" The master said: "Today I lost my money and was punished." Hsia said: "I don't have the time to beat you. Now leave."[22]

This was Hung-chih's enlightenment.

Ch'ing-liao was senior to Hung-chih, and the recognition of his enlightenment must have happened several years earlier. Ch'ing-liao seems to have had a profound influence on Hung-chih, although Hung-chih became the more famous.[23] In any case, Ch'ing-liao's epitaph, written by Hung-chih, relates that Ch'ing-liao traveled around for some time visiting various masters. Eventually he came to Tan-hsia Tzu-ch'un. His enlightenment took place after he had been with Tzu-ch'un for a while:

> One day Ch'ing-liao entered Tzu-ch'un's chamber and Tzu-ch'un asked him: "How about your self before the empty eon?" As Ch'ing-liao was about to answer, Tzu-ch'un slapped him with a hand. Ch'ing-liao had a great enlightenment.[24]

This account is strikingly similar to the account of Hung-chih's enlightenment. Not only do both involve the same catch-phrase kung-an, but in both instances Tzu-ch'un hits the student as he is about to answer, an action that finally triggers the student's enlightenment. The enlightenment stories of two famous monks like Hung-chih and Ch'ing-liao must have been in wide circulation during the lifetimes of their subjects, and since Hung-chih himself repeated Ch'ing-liao's enlightenment story in the inscription he wrote for him, Hung-chih sanctioned the story and its similarity with his own.

That the story was powerful enough to be used for both masters tells us much about the twelfth-century Ts'ao-tung tradition's self-understanding and self-representation. First of all, it contains a reaffirmation of what had become the main emphasis of the new Ts'ao-tung tradition, the Mahayana doctrine of inherent enlightenment.[25] This is expressed in the catchphrase kung-an "your self before the empty eon," which refers to a state before any creation takes place and therefore points to the Buddha-nature originally and inherently present in all beings. Furthermore, the teaching that ultimate truth cannot be expressed in words, not even in the metalanguage of the kung-an, is demonstrated when Hung-chih and Ch'ing-liao are about to speak and they are hit by Tzu-ch'un, an action that breaks their attachment to words and directly leads to their respective enlightenment experiences.

Not only are the Hung-chih and Ch'ing-liao enlightenment narratives almost identical, but they are clearly modeled on the story of Fu-jung Tao-k'ai's enlightenment, which again seems derived from that of T'ou-tzu I-ch'ing. Thus in the well-known Ch'an collection from 1123, the *Ch'an-lin seng-pao chuan*, Tao-k'ai's first encounter with I-ch'ing is described as follows:

[Tao-k'ai] said: "The words of the Buddhas and Patriarchs are like [bland] home-style food. Besides this, are there any other words that can help people?" I-ch'ing said: "Would you say that the orders of the emperor of a vast realm still have to rely on [the authority of the ancient sage kings] Yü, T'ang, Yao and Shun?" As Tao-k'ai was about to answer, I-ch'ing swatted him with his whisk and said: "Already when you first thought of coming here you deserved twenty blows of my staff."[26]

This was Tao-k'ai's enlightenment. Here, I-ch'ing's situation kung-an again points to the inherently enlightened nature of all beings, and as he is about to answer, Tao-k'ai is interrupted and enlightened with a blow from I-ch'ing's whisk.

I-ch'ing's own enlightenment is described in a similar way in the *Ch'an-lin seng-pao chuan*. Here we are told that one day Fu-shan Fa-yüan asked I-ch'ing about the story of the Buddha being questioned by a non-Buddhist,[27] and as I-ch'ing was about to answer, Fa-yüan covered I-ch'ing's mouth with his hand. This act triggered I-ch'ing's enlightenment.[28] The kung-an story here seems to be about the wordlessness of the true teaching, although it does not deal directly with inherent Buddha-nature. But in any case, I-ch'ing's enlightenment narrative appears quite similar to the enlightenment stories above.

It is interesting to note that the enlightenment narratives of Hung-chih and Ch'ing liao mirror that of their "grandfather" Fu-jung Tao-k'ai rather than that of their direct master, Tan-hsia Tzu-ch'un. Hung-chih and Ch'ing-liao were also known as Tao-k'ai's "great Dharma grandsons," further emphasizing their connection to Tao-k'ai, circumventing Tzu-ch'un.[29] Probably this was done partly because the twelfth century looked to Tao-k'ai as its main founding ancestor, and because Tzu-ch'un himself does not seem to have achieved any great fame, and he also died much earlier in his career.

Although the enlightenment story of Tan-hsia Tzu-ch'un also involves insight into the "empty eon," it was not cast in a form that was useful to Hung-chih and Ch'ing-liao, who lived at a time when Silent Illumination had come under attack. In his epitaph, dated 1118, we are told that Tzu-ch'un had visited several Ch'an masters before he came to Fu-jung Tao-k'ai. As soon as Tao-k'ai saw Tzu-ch'un, he realized that Tzu-ch'un had great potential. The inscription then reports that Tao-k'ai merely would teach that one should "retreat and get close to your own self, then there will not be one mistake in ten thousand," and "make the 'empty eon' your own responsibility and you will comprehend 'the time before a Buddha had come into the world.' "[30] Listening to these teachings, Tzu-ch'un is said to have been suddenly deeply enlightened and instantaneously to have gone beyond worldly concerns and discriminating thought.

Even though the vocabulary used here implies a sudden and complete enlightenment, the narration seems to suggest a more slowly maturing process, with no single transforming event. The story may very well reflect the teachings of Tzu-ch'un and the training of Hung-chih and Ch'ing-liao, but in the environment in which Hung-chih and Ch'ing-liao lived, such a passive narrative would not have served them well.

The audience for Hung-chih's and Ch'ing-liao's enlightenment stories can hardly have been shocked by Tzu-ch'un's catchphrase kung-an question. Indeed, anyone familiar with twelfth-century Ts'ao-tung literature would have heard much about "the self before the empty eon," as would the young students Hung-chih and Ch'ing-liao. As we have seen, the blow that both are given as they are about to answer also follows a well-established formula. So the entire unfolding of Hung-chih and Ch'ing-liao's enlightenment narratives follows a course already clearly mapped out. The enlightenment story of Hung-chih and Ch'ing-liao therefore must be understood as a performance which reenacts and reaffirms the wisdom and power of the tradition and its central tenets. The catchphrase kung-an "your self before the empty eon" is resanctified by the narrative as embodying the highest truth, which paradoxically cannot be expressed in words.

In fact, "your self before the empty eon" had a deep significance in the twelfth-century Ts'ao-tung tradition, and it is found in a number of places in its literature.[31] It is rarely found in a positive sense in the sayings and writings of Ch'an masters from other traditions, and it seems in the twelfth century to have been almost exclusively used within the Ts'ao-tung tradition. The similar catchphrase kung-an, "the time (or your face) before your parents were born" and "beyond the primordial Buddha"[32] and their variants, were also used much in the twelfth-century Ts'ao-tung tradition, although these two kung-an were also used by masters from other Ch'an traditions. The three catchphrase kung-an all invoke a state that is before and beyond any existence, which is the true state of Buddha-nature in which all sentient beings already dwell, although most are unaware of it.

A moving sermon by Tao-k'ai clearly lays out the meaning of "your self before the empty eon" in the twelfth-century Ts'ao-tung tradition:

> If you can awaken to and understand "your self before the empty eon" then it will be like hundreds or thousands of suns and moons whose radiance is inexhaustible, or like countless sentient beings all at once attaining liberation. But if you still don't understand, it is absolutely necessary that you retreat and come to a halt. You yourself must completely cease; you yourself should be completely at rest; you must be like a censer in an old shrine; the [instance of] one thought [of yours] should last for ten thousand years; and you should be like a man who doesn't take even a single breath. If you are able to be like this constantly for months and years, then, if you don't obtain the fruits of the Way, I am speaking nonsense and have been deceiving you all, and I will surely be born trapped in hell. I urge you all not to mistakenly apply your bodies and minds in trying to analyze the distance of the road ahead. Do not rely on an intermittent approach. It is necessary that you yourself put your strength into it; no one else can do it for you.[33]

This passage nicely sums up the twelfth-century Ts'ao-tung tradition's approach to enlightenment and practice. The message of "your self before the empty eon" here, as in Hung-chih's and Ch'ing-liao's awakening stories, is that the Buddha-nature that we all have, indeed are, is the single most important fact of existence. All a human needs for salvation is to recognize this fact, and the way to do so is through silent meditation. So Tao-k'ai here strongly advocates a silent and still meditation to be practiced for long periods. Such meditation is seen as necessary in order to truly awaken to the fact of one's own original Buddha-nature, but it is clearly not meant to be a passive and thought-suppressing practice. Rather this meditation requires strength and effort and will eventually lead to an awakening. Still, the moment of enlightenment is not particularly emphasized here, and it is not depicted as a sudden shattering event.

Tao-k'ai was the ancestor to most of the twelfth-century Ts'ao-tung tradition, and the teaching he outlines here can be said to characterize his whole lineage.[34] It was this teaching that came to be known as Silent Illumination. The notion of an inherent Buddha-nature in all sentient beings was of course

central to all of Sung Ch'an, and therefore in itself hardly controversial. However, Ta-hui Tsung-kao strongly attacked the Ts'ao-tung tradition and its favorite kung-an. Thus in one sermon he says:

> Nowadays heretical teachings have proliferated at every turn and have blinded
> the eyes of countless people. If [teachers] do not use the kung-an of the ancients
> to awaken and instruct [students], they (the students) will be like the blind per-
> son who lets go of the walking stick from his hand: not able to walk a single
> step. . . . [Some people] say that the Buddhist teachings and the way of Ch'an do
> not rely on words and writings. Therefore they point to all [kung-an] and con-
> sider them tall stories and ready-made.[35] [Such people] just eat their meals and
> sit like mounds in the ghostly cave under the black mountain. They call this
> "being silent and constantly illuminating," or call it "the great death," or "the
> matter before your parents were born," or "the matter before the empty eon," or
> the state of beyond the primordial Buddha." They just keep sitting and sitting
> until they get calluses on their buttocks, without daring to move at all. They call
> this "becoming skillful in self-cultivation (*kung-fu*) step by step."[36]

Here Ta-hui lists all the catchphrase kung-an commonly used in the twelfth-
century Ts'ao-tung tradition.[37] Ta-hui is objecting to these kung-an because
sees them as embodying a passive, unenlightened and unenlightening approach to Ch'an practice. To Ta-hui, the masters of the Ts'ao-tung tradition
were not using the kung-an stories of the ancient master as a key to opening
up the mind, but instead misused their catchphrase kung-an to justify a quietis-
tic type of meditation.

However, the twelfth-century Ts'ao-tung tradition in fact did use kung-an
stories extensively as a pedagogic device. Apart from the catchphrase kung-an
already discussed, Ts'ao-tung masters also commonly used kung-an stories in
their sermons and writings. As is the case with virtually all Sung-dynasty
Ch'an masters, much of the material in the extant recorded sayings of individual Ts'ao-tung masters consists of the master quoting ("raising," *chü*) a kung-
an story about a famous Ch'an figure and then offering his own comments on
the story.

A whole independent genre evolved out of the Sung Ch'an masters' practice
of commenting on kung-an stories. Many Ch'an masters (or their students)
would compile collections of, usually, 100 old kung-an cases with the master's
own brief comments attached to each of them. These collections were called
nien-ku ("picking up the old [cases or masters]") when a prose commentary
was attached, and *sung-ku* ("eulogizing the old [cases or masters]") when the
commentary was in poetic form. I-ch'ing, Tzu-ch'un, Ch'ing-liao, and Hung-
chih all have surviving collections in one or the other form, and Ta-hui himself
was the co-author of one.[38]

Hung-chih, for one, clearly expressed what he saw as the importance of
kung-an in the following statement:

If you have even a little Buddhist theory, then all kinds of concepts, illusions, and mixed-up thoughts will be produced in profusion. The kung-an is manifest right here before you. Penetrate it to the root; penetrate it to the source.[39]

On the other hand, there were also voices within the Ts'ao-tung tradition critical of the way kung-an were used in much of Ch'an, if not critical of kung-an themselves. In the entry on Tao-k'ai's student Ch'an-t'i Wei-chao (1084–1128) in the *Seng-pao cheng-hsü chuan,* Wei-chao is quoted as saying:

Worthy Ch'an meditation practitioners: There is no need to be all confused and muddled. Meditate so that you become enlightened. If you become enlightened you will be in a state of freedom twenty-four hours a day. You will not have to be concerned about Buddhas or patriarchs or even yourself. Even less do you have to listen to other people's instructions. The great master Bodhidharma came from the west to [teach] "pointing directly to the human mind" and "seeing your nature and becoming a Buddha." When was there [the need for] a lot of complicated words and phrases causing you to ponder and become confused? Today in the various monasteries of the realm there is no teacher who does not tell you to study Ch'an and study the way and to practice. . . . Furthermore, [they tell you to] examine the words [of the old masters], make commentary, and ponder kung-an cases, analyzing past and present. You just don't know the difference between good and bad. If you want to remain a [deluded] sentient being, then go and study with someone, and sit at a desk and record his words in your big and small notebooks.[40]

Wei-chao goes on to say that this deplorable situation is not the fault of the students but rather that of deluded masters who teach them to mull over kung-an stories, like the ones about the "cypress in front of the hall," the "cutting of the cat," the "washing your bowls," the "wild fox," and "investigating the old woman."[41]

Although most twelfth-century Ts'ao-tung masters seem to have recognized kung-an as pointing toward ultimate reality, especially the catchphrase kung-an discussed earlier, the Ts'ao-tung tradition strongly emphasized meditation as the way to realization. The point is rarely stated as unequivocally as Wei-chao does above, but there are many indications of this, as we have seen in the passage from Tao-k'ai's sermon quoted earlier.

When Ta-hui is objecting that the Ts'ao-tung masters were rejecting kung-an, he clearly did not mean that they were not using kung-an at all. Rather the issue was what should be the use and function of a kung-an, and ultimately what was the meaning of enlightenment. Thus in one of his letters Ta-hui writes:

Now the heretical teachers of Silent Illumination only consider being without a word or an utterance as the highest principle, and this they call the matter of "beyond the primordial Buddha" or "before the empty eon." They do not believe there is enlightenment: they call enlightenment madness, or they call it second-ary, or an expedient teaching, or an expression to attract [people to Ch'an teachings].[42]

There is no evidence that twelfth-century Ts'ao-tung masters called enlight-enment "madness" or any of the other terms Ta-hui mentions here, and it is clear that Ta-hui exaggerated and distorted the Ts'ao-tung position.[43] But it is perfectly true that a moment of enlightenment was not emphasized in the twelfth-century Ts'ao-tung tradition.

In other places Ta-hui complains that the followers of Silent Illumination called enlightenment "leaves and branches," an expression which he on one occasion specifically associates with Hung-chih.[44] And Hung-chih does, in fact, state poetically in a written sermon: "The naturally illuminated root, it does not follow from the leaves and branches."[45] Hung-chih here refers to the inherent enlightenment of all beings as the "root," and he asserts its indepen-dence of the "leaves and branches," that is, a moment of enlightenment in time and space. Hung-chih is clearly implying that such a moment is of secondary importance to the wonderful fact of inherent enlightenment.

But to Ta-hui, a moment of enlightenment was all important. The kung-an was a key to unlocking the potential of a human, or perhaps more appropri-ately, a hammer with which the delusions of person could be smashed and enlightenment achieved. Ta-hui, of course, did not deny the inherent Buddha-nature in all sentient beings, but without the breakthrough of enlightenment, this truth could never be realized. To facilitate the necessary but difficult, breakthrough enlightenment, Ta-hui devised what he saw as a simple and efficient way of using kung-an, known as Kung-an Introspection Ch'an.

Ta-hui's Kung-an Introspection Ch'an is too well-known to merit detailed discussion,[46] but in brief, Ta-hui advocated the intense concentration on the "punch line" or hua-t'ou, of a kung-an story, as a means to a breakthrough enlightenment. The kung-an story that Ta-hui almost always instructed his students to use is the now famous one of the T'ang Ch'an master Chao-chou Ts'ung-shen (778–897), who answered "no!" (C. wu, J. mu) to the question of whether a dog has the Buddha-nature. The hua-t'ou on which one should focus all one's energies is the "no/wu." Ta-hui explains in one sermon:

A monk asked Chao-chou: "Does even a dog have Buddha-nature?" Chao-chou answered: "No" [C. wu, J. mu]! When you observe it [the "no/wu"] do not ponder it widely, do not try to understand the word, do not try to analyze it, do not consider it to be at the place where you open your mouth [about to say it out loud], do not reason that it is at the place [in your mind] where you hold it up, do not fall into a vacuous state, do not hold on to "mind" and await enlighten-ment, do not try to experience it through the words of your teacher, and do not get stuck in a shell of unconcern. Just at all times, whether walking or standing, sitting or lying, hold on to this [no/wu]. "Does even a dog have Buddha-nature or not [*wu*]?" If you hold on to this "no/*wu*" to a point where it becomes ripe, when no discussion or consideration can reach it and you are as if caught in a place of one square inch; and when it has no flavor as if you were chewing on a raw iron cudgel and you get so close to it you cannot pull back—when you are able to be like this, then that really is good news![47]

Kung-an Introspection Ch'an was thus a meditative technique that aimed at pushing a person toward enlightenment. To Ta-hui, a shattering moment of enlightenment was absolutely crucial. Without such a moment, a person would forever remain a deluded being and any talk of inherent enlightenment, and of already being in a state of Buddhahood, would be meaningless. This is exactly the main point of Ta-hui's attacks on the Ts'ao-tung tradition. Ta-hui describes the difference he saw between himself and the Ts'ao-tung masters in this way:

> Everywhere people are saying that when you become still then you will be enlightened. But I say, when you are enlightened you will become still.[48]

Ta-hui therefore strongly opposed the emphasis on inherent enlightenment in the Ts'ao-tung tradition. Inherent enlightenment means nothing unless one can awaken to it, and so the greatest error made by the twelfth-century Ts'ao-tung masters is that they do not actively pursue a breakthrough enlightenment.

It is clear then, that the disagreement between the twelfth-century Ts'ao-tung and Lin-chi traditions was not over whether or not to use kung-an, but the role and meaning of kung-an in Ch'an training, as well as the nature of the ultimate goal of Ch'an practice.

Kung-an Practice and Ch'an in the Northern Sung (960–1127)

As was mentioned earlier, the extant Sung Ch'an literature shows that Ch'an masters of the eleventh century would frequently comment on old kung-an stories in their sermons. It is not clear exactly when the practice of commenting on old kung-an cases started, but the earliest Ch'an master to have such commentaries included in his recorded sayings is the "founder" of the Yün-men tradition, Yün-men Wen-yen (864–949).[49] A collection of Ch'an anecdotes, the *Ch'an-lin pao-hsün*, notes that the practice of gathering collections of kung-an commentaries began with the Lin-chi master Fen-yang Shan-chao (947–1024) but was popularized by the Yün-men master Hsüeh-tou Ch'ung-hsien (980–1052).[50] It is interesting to note that the early use of kung-an seems to have had a stronger connection to the Yün-men tradition than to the Lin-chi tradition. In addition to commenting on kung-an in their sermons, Ch'an masters also used kung-an in instructing individual students. There are, of course, nu-

merous instances in Sung Ch'an literature of a student experiencing enlightenment when a master asks him about his understanding of a particular kung-
an story.

The importance that kung-an stories took on in the enlightenment experiences of individual monks inevitably led to a great emphasis on kung-an study,
about which Wei-chao complained. At some point during the Northern Sung,
it seems to have become common that Ch'an masters gave their students a
particular kung-an story, or catchphrase kung-an, to reflect over for an extended period. This was supposed to lead the student eventually toward enlightenment.

For example, Ta-hung Ch'ing-hsien (probably 1103–1180), a second-
generation descendant of Ta-hung Pao-en, is said to have studied under a
master Wei-i (d.u.) who had him investigate (ts'an) the saying about "great
death but still living."[51] Unfortunately, this endeavor did not lead to an enlightenment for Ch'ing-hsien, but the hope was clearly that it would. Also, the
ancestor of the twelfth-century Ts'ao-tung tradition, T'ou-tzu I-ch'ing, is said
to have experienced enlightenment when he was thinking about (chü) a kung-
an story that Fa-yüan had earlier questioned him about.[52]

Ta-hui's master, Yüan-wu Ko-ch'in (1063–1135), who himself was very interested in the role of kung-an in enlightenment (as is discussed later), also
indicates that the practice of contemplating kung-an went back well before his
own time:

> For the neophytes or the senior students who wanted to practice [Ch'an] but who
> had no way to get the point, the former virtuous masters showed their kindness
> by asking them to investigate the ancients' kung-an.[53]

The earliest example of something akin to the Northern Sung Ch'an practice of kung-an contemplation that I have found is in the entry on the Ts'ao-
tung "founder," Tung-shan Liang-chieh (807–869), in the Ching-te ch'uan-teng
lu, compiled in 1004. Here a story is told of how Tung-shan Liang-chieh used
to say that just proclaiming that "fundamentally nothing exists"[54] did not earn
(the Sixth Patriarch Hui-neng) the robe and bowl (i.e., it was not proof that
he had received the patriarchy). Tung-shan Liang-chieh then urged his disciples to come up with a phrase that would have earned these insignia. An old
monk tried 96 times and finally had his answer approved by Tung-shan Liang-
chieh. Another monk wanted to learn the older monk's answer, and after trying to find out to no avail for three years, finally threatened the older monk
with a knife to make him tell.[55]

It is important to realize that the practice of contemplating kung-an stories
or catchphrase kung-an in the Northern Sung was by no means limited to, or
probably even especially typical of, Ch'an masters in the Lin-chi lineage. In
fact, although this idea cannot be pursued further here, I will suggest that

there are no clearly discernible and consistent differences in the teaching styles and doctrinal emphases between the different traditions of Ch'an as they appear to us in pre-twelfth-century materials.[56]

In this connection it should be noted that the well-known scheme of five different Ch'an traditions, or "houses," so dear to popular writers on Ch'an,[57] probably did not come into being until the mid-eleventh century.[58] The first mention of the five traditions by name is found in the scholar–monk Ch'i-sung's *Ch'uan-fa cheng-tsung chi* from 1061, and even here there is no indication that Ch'i-sung associated the different traditions with different teaching styles. In this text, Ch'i-sung points out that at the time he was writing, two of the traditions, the Fa-yen and the Kuie-yang, had already died out, while the Ts'ao-tung tradition was "feeble like a lonely spring during a great drought."[59] This is the only mention of the five traditions in any eleventh-century source, and it would appear that the scheme was not considered important until the twelfth century, when references to it become common.

It seems clear that the scheme of five traditions of Ch'an is one that was devised retrospectively, and all indications are that none of the "founders" of the traditions were conscious of founding anything. It is only in the preface to the *Chien-chung Ching-kuo hsü-teng lu,* written by the Emperor Hui-tsung (r. 1100–1126) in 1101, that we for the first time find an indication that the traditions were thought to differ in their teaching styles. Hui-tsung writes:

> After Nan-yüeh and Ch'ing-yüan [Ch'an Buddhism] has been divided into five traditions. Each developed its own tradition and taught according to the differences in the learner's talents. Although they differ in particular emphases their goal is still the same.[60]

It is noteworthy that this was written after Tao-k'ai and Pao-en had begun to revive and renew the Ts'ao-tung tradition and that both masters have laudatory entries in the *Chien-chung Ching-kuo hsü-teng lu.* In the decades after the publication of the *Chien-chung Ching-kuo hsü-teng lu,* references to the five traditions scheme become increasingly common, along with the increasingly high profile of the Ts'ao-tung tradition. Thus a sectarian awareness was developing within the Ch'an school.

Kung-an Use and Silent Illumination in the Early Ts'ao-tung Tradition

As was mentioned earlier, it is commonly assumed that the Silent Illumination teachings characteristic of the twelfth-century Ts'ao-tung tradition must have also characterized the earlier Ts'ao-tung tradition. To look for real evidence of Silent Illumination thought in the Ts'ao-tung tradition prior to T'ou-tzu I-ch'ing and the Ts'ao-tung revival of the twelfth century, one has to turn to the records in the Buddhist histories compiled before the twelfth century, since later sources could well have been influenced by developments since the revival. The relevant pre-twelfth-century Buddhist histories here are the 952 *Tsu-t'ang chi,*[61] the 988 *Sung kao-seng chuan,*[62] the 1004 *Ching-te ch'uan-teng lu,*[63] and the 1036 *T'ien-sheng kuang-teng lu.*[64] These works all exist in early editions, and we can be reasonably certain that the records of the masters in the Ts'ao-tung lineage they contain have not been subject to later modification.[65]

The first three of these works contain records of Tung-shan Liang-chieh. An examination of these makes clear that there is no indication that Tung-shan Liang-chieh taught a Silent Illumination approach similar to that of the twelfth-century Ts'ao-tung tradition. None of the catchphrase kung-an that are associated with twelfth-century Ts'ao-tung Silent Illumination are used, and there is no special emphasis on meditation and inherent enlightenment. Nor is there any evidence that Tung-shan Liang-chieh was deemphasizing enlightenment, as some writers have claimed.[66] Checking, for example, the records in the *Ching-te ch'uan-teng lu,* one finds that Tung-shan Liang-chieh and his famous contemporary Lin-chi I-hsüan (–866), who became the "founder" of the Lin-chi tradition, are both said to have experienced "great enlightenment" (*ta-wu*).[67] Furthermore, in the *Ching-te ch'uan-teng lu* two of Tung-shan Liang-chieh's disciples are said to have been awakened in dialogue with him, whereas the same is not reported for any of Lin-chi I-hsüan's students.[68] In sum, there is no evidence whatsoever that Tung-shan Liang-chieh founded a tradition of Ch'an based on some sort of Silent Illumination teaching.

One text that is sometimes cited as evidence for a Silent Illumination approach in the earliest Ts'ao-tung tradition is the famous *Pao-ching san-mei.* This beautiful poem does seem like a celebration of the inherently enlightened nature of all sentient beings and, in holding up the Buddha's contemplation under the tree as a model, it can be understood to advocate indirectly a meditation in which this enlightened nature becomes apparent.[69] The poem is commonly attributed to Tung-shan Liang-chieh,[70] although in his recorded sayings it is said that Tung-shan received it, secretly, from his master Yün-yen T'an-sheng (780–841).[71]

However, the text of the *Pao-ching san-mei* is not found in any source prior to Chüeh-fan Hui-hung's (1071–1128) *Ch'an-lin seng-pao chuan* (published in 1123), nor is it even mentioned in any earlier source.[72] Hui-hung states that the *Pao-ching san-mei* was kept hidden by the early worthies and that it could not be found in earlier Ch'an collections. However, Hui-hung says, in 1108 an unnamed old monk gave a copy of the *Pao-ching san-mei* to a certain official and eventually the text came into the hands of Hui-hung. Hui-hung then decided to disseminate it.[73] Given this explanation, we might surmise that the *Pao-ching san-mei* was a product of the new Ts'ao-tung school that had come into being at the end of the eleventh century and not a text that goes back to Tung-shan Liang-chieh or earlier.

A survey of the records of the pre-twelfth-century descendants in Tung-shan Liang-chieh's lineage in these same sources also, in general, does not turn up any indication of something one might call a Silent Illumination approach. Again, none of the catchphrase kung-an that are associated with the twelfth-century Ts'ao-tung tradition can be found, there is no special emphasis on sentient beings already being Buddhas, nor is there any emphasis on meditation.

The only exception is the entry on the Ts'ao-tung master Shih-men Hui-ch'e (d.u.) in the *T'ien-sheng kuang-teng lu,* from 1036.[74] Hui-ch'e is included in the *Ching-te ch'uan-teng lu,* where he has a short and unremarkable entry.[75] But in the *T'ien-sheng kuang-teng lu,* Hui-ch'e has a very long entry, where he uses the catchphrase kung-an "beyond the primordial Buddha" along with several other expressions associated with the Silent Illumination of the twelfth-century Ts'ao-tung tradition.[76] Hui-ch'e's lineage is somewhat unclear. In the *Ching-te ch'uan-teng lu* he is listed as the heir of Shih-men Hsien (d.u.) and is in the second generation after Tung-shan Liang-chieh. But in the *T'ien-sheng kuang-teng lu,* Hui-ch'e is said to be the heir of Liang-shan Yüan-kuan (d.u.), who was the teacher of Ta-yang Ching-hsüan.[77] This would put Hui-ch'e as the dharma brother of Ching-hsüan and close to the twelfth-century Ch'an lineage.

It seems quite possible that Shih-men Hui-ch'e's record in the *T'ien-sheng kuang-teng lu* was seen as a source of inspiration and legitimacy for the twelfth-century Ts'ao-tung tradition. It is also possible that his record reflects the beginning of a new vocabulary in the Ts'ao-tung tradition which perhaps started to take shape around the time of Ta-yang Ching-hsüan, although there is little indication that Ching-hsüan used it.[78]

Like other Ch'an masters, the early Ts'ao-tung masters do seem at times to stress the inherent Buddha-nature in sentient beings, and especially from the records of the third-generation Ts'ao-tung masters on, one often finds (fantastical) nature imagery which appears to be alluding to this.[79] However, very similar passages can be found in the records of masters in other Ch'an traditions.[80] So even if it can be argued that the Silent Illumination approach of the twelfth-century Ts'ao-tung could have found inspiration in the sayings of earlier Ts'ao-tung masters, there is no indication that a Silent Illumination approach characterized the Ts'ao-tung tradition from its beginnings. Again, there is simply no convincing evidence that there is a direct line of development from the teachings of the early Ts'ao-tung masters to the Silent Illumination of Hung-chih and Ch'ing-liao.

Maybe the best argument against the notion that there were substantial ideological differences between the Ts'ao-tung and Lin-chi traditions prior to the twelfth century is the story of T'ou-tzu I-ch'ing's transmission. As will be recalled, I-ch'ing is said to have received Ta-yang Ching-hsüan's transmission from the Lin-chi master Fu-shan Fa-yüan, who held the transmission in trust.

But I-ch'ing was not given the transmission until several years after his enlightenment under Fa-yüan, presumably much to his surprise, and there is no indication that he was trained in any special way or any differently than were Fa-yüan's other disciples. The historicity of the story may well be doubted, but the fact that it was accepted in the Ch'an community indicates that at the time neither the Lin-chi nor the Ts'ao-tung tradition saw the other as substantially different from itself. Of course, once the revival of the Ts'ao-tung tradition was well under way and it had started to manifest itself strongly, the story of I-ch'ing's tradition may have seemed less acceptable to both the Lin-chi and the Ts'ao-tung traditions, but at this point it was too well-known to try to modify.[81]

It is possible that the Ts'ao-tung Silent Illumination approach in fact began with I-ch'ing. In his recorded sayings, I-ch'ing in several places uses the catch-phrase kung-an "before the empty eon" and "beyond (or before) the primordial Buddha."[82] There are also several indications that I-ch'ing emphasized a still meditation in which the inherent Buddha-nature is revealed. This idea is most clearly expressed in the following passage:

> In the silent and profound world of *yin,* words fall into the deep pit. If you try to imitate it and hold on to it, then heaven and earth will be far apart; if you discard it, there will be endless rebirth. The turbulent waves are vast and extensive, the white billows fill the sky. The bright pearl that quells the ocean: who will receive it in his palm?[83]

The first part seems to be a description of the realm of still meditation which one must neither cling to nor relinquish. The turbulent ocean is an image of the deluded mind, while the pearl is a classic representation of inherent Buddha-nature, which is always present but which can be gotten at only when the waves of delusion have stilled. This passage suggests that I-ch'ing considered meditation essential in reaching enlightenment,[84] but it falls short of the emphasis on absolute stillness, and on inherent Buddha-nature being manifest in meditation, that one finds in the twelfth-century Ts'ao-tung masters.

The first Ts'ao-tung master whose sayings or writings exhibit a clear Silent Illumination approach is Fu-jung Tao-k'ai. The passage from his sermons quoted earlier can almost serve as a manifesto of the Ts'ao-tung Silent Illumination approach, but in Tao-k'ai's scant extant records several other passages also express a Silent Illumination approach. The following passage is a good example:

> The path to entering the Way is to be empty inside and tranquil outside, like water still and frozen. Then all things will brilliantly reflect [each other], and neither submerged nor floating on top all phenomena will be just thus. Therefore it is said that fire does not depend on the sun to be hot, and wind does not depend on the moon to be cool. A solid rock contains water, heaven and blindness are both radiance, brightness and darkness are naturally present [within

each other], dry and wet exist in the same place: if you can be like this then the withered tree facing the cliff will flower in the middle of the night, and the woman of wood carries a basket while in the fresh breeze under the moon the stone man will dance with floating sleeves.[85]

"Empty inside and tranquil outside" clearly refers to still meditation. The implication of the passage seems to be that once one can meditate like this, the whole world will be in harmony and all dualities will disappear. Tao-k'ai also has several references to "beyond the primordial Buddha" or its equivalents,[86] as well as to Bodhidharma and his nine years of wall-contemplation.[87]

In any case, it is perhaps not surprising that later students of Ch'an have projected a Silent Illumination approach back on the earlier Ts'ao-tung tradition. This process already began by the twelfth century. Thus, as we have seen, Tou-tzu I-ch'ing's extant recorded sayings has indications of what might be called a proto-Silent Illumination approach. But I-ch'ing's biography, probably written by a disciple of Tao-k'ai, is virtually teeming with expressions associated with the Silent Illumination of the twelfth-century Ts'ao-tung tradition, including references to "before the empty eon," and a rare mention of the term "Silent Illumination" itself.[88] In this way, the twelfth-century Ts'ao-tung tradition sought to firmly associate a Silent Illumination approach with its ancestor I-ch'ing.

Although there seems to have been no real attempt to associate Tung-shan Liang-chieh with a Silent Illumination approach, his (very late) recorded sayings do contain a passage in which he comments on "your self before the empty eon."[89] This passage cannot be found in any of the transmission of the lamp histories, and it seems to have been incorporated from Ch'ing-liao's recorded sayings, where the identical passage appears.[90] The compiler of Tung-shan Liang-chieh's recorded sayings must have felt that this particular catchphrase kung-an should have a place there, no doubt in honor of the famous twelfth-century exponents of Silent Illumination.

Kung-an Introspection Ch'an and Ta-hui

I have argued here that the mature Ts'ao-tung Silent Illumination approach cannot be traced back further than to Fu-jung Tao-k'ai. I have also argued that the use of kung-an before the twelfth century was not especially typical of the Lin-chi tradition. But the question remains to which degree Ta-hui's Kung-an Introspection Ch'an was a natural extension of kung-an use in the Lin-chi tradition, and to which degree it was truly innovative.

Several writers have argued that Ta-hui's teacher Yüan-wu K'o-ch'in was especially influential in the evolution of Kung-an Introspection Ch'an.[91] In several places Yüan-wu relates how he himself gained realization by contemplating kung-an stories. In a sermon, he says:

When I first came to Ta-kui to study with master Chen-ju[92] I sat silently all day facing a wall and contemplated (*kan*) kung-an stories of the old masters back and forth. After about a year I suddenly gained some insight.[93]

This passage is especially interesting because it implies that kung-an stories somehow were used in meditation. It must be assumed that Yüan-wu here was following the instructions of Chen-ju Mu-che, although I have found no other evidence that Chen-ju Mu-che advocated the use of kung-an in meditation.

Elsewhere Yüan-wu talks about his time with his teacher Wu-tzu Fa-yen (1024?–1104), whose dharma heir he eventually became. Yüan-wu reports that Wu-tzu Fa-yen told him the kung-an: "The verbal and the nonverbal are like vines clinging to a tree."[94] Yüan-wu tried to understand this in various ways, but Wu-tzu did not accept his answers, so Yüan-wu finally left. Two years later he returned.[95] He then relates:

It was first with the phrase, "She keeps calling out to [her maid] Hsiao-yü although there is nothing the matter,"[96] that the bucket was released and I then finally saw that what I had formerly been shown [by my teachers] was the true medicine.[97]

Here Yüan-wu is depicting his enlightenment being triggered by his contemplation of a kind of catchphrase kung-an.[98]

Yüan-wu's memory of his own enlightenment experience fits well with his emphasis on kung-an study. In instructing his students, Yüan-wu strongly emphasized that one should investigate the word and not the meaning of a kung-an, and that kung-an should be understood as live words and not dead words, that is, one should comprehend the kung-an directly without intellectual mediation.[99] Just as Yüan-wu's contemporary in the Ts'ao-tung tradition, Wei-chao, had criticized those who immersed themselves in intellectual kung-an study, Yüan-wu was concerned that Ch'an students were not approaching kung-an study correctly. But unlike Wei-chao, who seems to have wanted to relegate kung-an to a secondary importance, and perhaps do away with them altogether, Yüan-wu clearly felt that kung-an practice was of essential importance. In instructions to his students Yüan-wu would strongly stress the necessity of understanding kung-an stories in an intuitive or nonintellectual fashion as a crucial element in gaining enlightenment.[100] Thus in one sermon he says:

If you want to penetrate birth and death it is necessary to open up your mind. The kung-an is exactly the key to opening up your mind. You just have to understand the essential meaning beyond the words and only then will you arrive at the place where there are no doubts.[101]

Furthermore, Yüan-wu may have also been the first Ch'an master to state specifically that once one kung-an is truly understood, all kung-an are simultaneously understood.[102] Of course, the idea that truly understanding a kung-an story would be a moment of enlightenment was well established at the time of Yüan-wu, and therefore Yüan-wu's view cannot be understood to represent a real departure from the previous understanding of kung-an. Yüan-wu did not take the idea of understanding one kung-an to mean the understanding of all kung-an to its logical extreme, as did Ta-hui, who advocated that it was enough, or even preferable, just to concentrate on the punch line of one single kung-an.

Although Yüan-wu may have put stronger emphasis on understanding kung-an than did most of his contemporaries, his approach to kung-an contemplation does not seem radically different from that of other Sung Ch'an masters, and he can hardly be said to have revolutionized kung-an practice.

It is even difficult to maintain that Yüan-wu's stress on understanding kung-an was a direct influence on Ta-hui's development of Kung-an Introspection Ch'an. Yüan-wu's emphasis on investigating the live word of the kung-an is still quite different from Ta-hui's repeated insistence on the intense reflection on a single word or phrase of a kung-an story, the *hua-t'ou*. As will be discussed, Ta-hui did not begin advocating *hua-t'ou* meditation until almost ten years after his enlightenment experience under Yüan-wu, and I argue that he was motivated by forces quite different from the influence of his old master's teachings.[103]

It is sometimes claimed that Ta-hui, in telling his students to focus on Chao-chou's *wu*, was following an old tradition of Ch'an. As proof, Huang-po Hsi-yün (d. between 847 and 859) is cited. In a passage tagged on to the end of the Ming-dynasty (1368–1644) edition of the *Wan-ling lu*, Huang-po advocates contemplating Chao-chou's no/*wu* 24 hours a day, "whether sitting, lying, eating or defecating." He continues: "After a long time like this, one will inevitably have a breakthrough."[104] However, it has in the past been overlooked that this passage is almost certainly spurious, since the Sung editions of the *Wan-ling lu* do not include the passage.[105]

More difficult to refute are the indications that Wu-tzu Fa-yen (1024?–1104), the master of Ta-hui's teacher Yüan-wu, advocated the contemplation of Chao-chou's *wu.* Ta-hui may indeed himself have claimed that he was following Wu-tzu Fa-yen in advocating this practice. Thus in the very last of his collected letters, Ta-hui cites a letter that Wu-tzu Fa-yen is said to have written to a monk:

> [Wu-tzu wrote:] If this summer all the villages have nothing to harvest, that should not worry you. What should worry you is if in a hall of several hundred monks not one of them over the course of the summer [meditation period] pene-

trates and understands the story about a dog not having the Buddha-nature. I fear the Buddhist teachings are about to be obliterated.[106]

In Wu-tzu Fa-yen's recorded sayings, the following passage is indeed found:

[In a sermon, after quoting the story about a dog not having the Buddha-nature, Wu-tzu said:] All of you in the assembly, how do you understand this? This old monk always simply just holds up the word "no/wu." If you can penetrate and understand this one word, then no one in the whole world will have anything on you. How will you all penetrate this? Has any one of you penetrated and clearly understood? If so, come forth and speak out for all to see. I don't want you to say that [the dog] has [the Buddha-nature], I don't want you to say it does not have it, and I don't want you to say that it neither has it nor does not have it. What will you say?[107]

This passage could be seen as advocating a concentration on the one word *wu* that is extremely similar to Ta-hui's Kung-an Introspection practice, if not identical to it. However, nowhere else in Wu-tzu's recorded sayings have I found any other passage that recommends focusing on just one part of a kung-an story or that even maintains that the kung-an itself should be contemplated at length. Wu-tzu refers to the story about the dog's not having Buddha-nature at least twice more in his recorded sayings, but in neither case is there any emphasis on the word "no/*wu*" or on intense contemplation of the story.[108] The letter from Wu-tzu that Ta-hui quotes would seem to indicate that meditation on Chao-chou's dog kung-an was common at the time of Wu-tzu, but there is absolutely no evidence for this in the recorded sayings and writings of his contemporaries.

Considering the traditional Chinese praxis of attributing any system of thought or practice, however new, to a venerated and authoritative figure of the past, it is not surprising to find that Ta-hui wanted to show that Kung-an Introspection was advocated by Wu-tzu Fa-yen. Evidence of Wu-tzu's letter is found only in sources closely associated with Ta-hui. Wu-tzu's sermon on Chao-chou's *wu* could well be understood simply as urging his audience to grasp the essential meaning of the story, and not as advocating anything like Ta-hui's Kung-an Introspection Ch'an. But it is possible that the passage was an inspiration for Ta-hui's Kung-an Introspection Ch'an. Another possibility is that the passage is a later interpolation, designed to accommodate Ta-hui's claims.

Ta-hui's use of kung-an goes far beyond anything that is attested in Ch'an literature before him. His advocacy of the intense reflection on the *hua-t'ou,* the crucial point of a kung-an story, is really without precedent, and this aspect makes his Kung-an Introspection Ch'an unique.[109]

The Politics of the Kung-an

The development of Kung-an Introspection Ch'an can be fully understood only in the context of Ta-hui's opposition to the Silent Illumination of the Ts'ao-tung tradition and its use of kung-an. But what is more, the whole issue of Silent Illumination versus Kung-an Introspection Ch'an cannot be fully appreciated in a purely soteriological framework, but must be placed in the context of the political and social realities of its time.[110]

As was mentioned at the beginning of the chapter, during the Northern Sung state policies had favored the Ch'an school through the proliferation of public monasteries. This advantage allowed Ch'an to establish itself as a clearly defined "school" of Buddhism and contributed to its unprecedented growth. However, from the end of the eleventh century state support waned, and the environment became less favorable for monastic Buddhism in general and the Ch'an school in particular. Around the same time, the central government became less interested in local affairs and left much of local government in the hands of the local educated elite, that is, the class of scholar–officials, also known as the literati. Therefore, especially from the twelfth century onward, support from the literati became absolutely necessary for the success of any Ch'an lineage, or Ch'an master.[111] The development of Silent Illumination within the new Ts'ao-tung tradition can be seen partly as a response to the Ts'ao-tung tradition's need to differentiate itself from other groups of Ch'an and to offer a teaching that was appealing to members of the educated elite. The Ts'ao-tung tradition's use of the catchphrase kung-an "your self before the empty eon" and the related expressions functioned both to tie the Ts'ao-tung approach in with the rest of the Ch'an school and to set it apart and give it its own identity.

The considerable success of the twelfth-century Ts'ao-tung tradition can be credited in large part to its Silent Illumination approach with the emphasis on an original, inherent Buddha-nature of all sentient beings, and its teaching of a type of meditation in which the Buddha-nature would naturally manifest. The Silent Illumination teachings proved attractive to many members of the educated elite who were interested in Ch'an but who may have been discouraged by the difficulty of the kung-an study and contemplation commonly taught in Sung Ch'an.

It is easy to imagine that the sudden reemergence and flourishing of the Ts'ao-tung tradition, and the literati support it attracted, must have appeared very disruptive to other groups of Ch'an, particularly to the powerful Lin-chi tradition. The pool of interested literati must, after all, have been finite, and the success of the Ts'ao-tung tradition must have channeled support away from the Lin-chi tradition. There are indications that even before the time of Ta-hui, members of the Lin-chi tradition reacted against the new Ts'ao-tung tradition. Thus Yüan-wu was, in an oblique way, rather critical of the Ts'ao-tung tradition in his *Pi-yen lu.*[112] Also Ta-hui's older fellow disciple under Yüan-wu, Fo-hsing Fa-t'ai, (d.u.),[113] attacked Silent Illumination using a vocabulary very similar to that of Ta-hui.

But with his continued fierce attacks on the Ts'ao-tung tradition Ta-hui was the first to break the code of harmony that the Ch'an school had been able to maintain throughout the earlier part of the Sung. Interestingly, Ta-hui did not begin to attack Silent Illumination, nor advocate Kung-an Introspection Ch'an, until about ten years after his enlightenment. It seems to have been only when Ta-hui came to Fukien in 1134 that he realized the extent of the success of the Ts'ao-tung tradition and its Silent Illumination teaching among literati. Much of this success was due to Ch'ing-liao, who had been the abbot at the prestigious Hsüeh-feng monastery in Fu-chou since 1130. Ta-hui later described his experiences in Fukien in this way:

> Literati often have [the problem of] busy minds. So today, in many places, there is a kind of heretical Silent Illumination Ch'an. [The people who teach this] see that literati are obstructed by worldly concerns and that their hearts are not at peace, and accordingly they teach them to be like "cold ashes or withered wood," or like "a strip of white silk," or like "an incense pot in an old shrine," or "cool and detached." . . . This kind of teaching has in past years been especially abundant in Fukien province. When in the beginning of the Shao-hsing era (1131–1162) I lived at a small temple in Fukien I strongly rejected it.[114]

Ta-hui's special concern that literati were being ensnared by Silent Illumination is evident throughout his attacks on it. Almost all his Silent Illumination attacks are found either in letters to literati or in sermons that were given at the request or in honor of literati.[115] Ta-hui makes it very clear that he was greatly concerned with the appeal that the Silent Illumination teachings held for laypeople. But in an even more significant development, warnings against Silent Illumination and advocacy of Kung-an Introspection Ch'an are almost always found together in the letters and sermons that Ta-hui directed toward literati.[116] Ta-hui himself relates that it was in Fukien that he first began to use the Kung-an Introspection technique that "he now would always use to instruct people," after he had brought an old monk, who originally "didn't believe in enlightenment," to experience a great enlightenment.[117]

Therefore there is little doubt that Ta-hui developed his Kung-an Introspection method as a direct response to the Silent Illumination teachings of the Ts'ao-tung tradition, and mainly in order to entice literati away from these teachings. Ta-hui saw Kung-an Introspection Ch'an as an antidote to what he considered the passivity and lack of enlightenment of Silent Illumination. To Ta-hui, Kung-an Introspection Ch'an was a shortcut[118] to enlightenment, a technique that both simplified kung-an practice and amplified its power and efficacy. Although Ta-hui taught Kung-an Introspection Ch'an to his monastic disciples, he considered it especially useful in instructing literati. Because of its simplicity, Kung-an Introspection practice was especially suited to laypeople, who according to Ta-hui could practice it amid their busy lives.

Although developments in kung-an practice in the Northern Sung, both inside and outside the Lin-chi tradition, made Ta-hui's Kung-an Introspection Ch'an possible, it might well never have come into being had it not been for the inventive genius of Ta-hui and the need he perceived to find an easy and effective way to counter the Ts'ao-tung Silent Illumination teachings. And although Ta-hui and the twelfth-century Ts'ao-tung master speak to us with great sincerity, the context of competition for support from the literati cannot be ignored.

Kung-an Introspection Ch'an had an enormous impact on Chinese Ch'an and, by extension, Japanese Zen. Interestingly, although Kung-an Introspection Ch'an was of course closely associated with the Lin-chi tradition when Ta-hui began teaching it, it quickly became so influential that it was picked up in the Ts'ao-tung tradition, where Chao-chou's *wu* became a standard in meditation.[119] Thus, even if the particular use of kung-an in Kung-an Introspection Ch'an for a brief time was especially associated with the Lin-chi tradition, this association did not last long and kung-an use once again became the property of the whole Chinese Ch'an school.[120] On the other hand, Silent Illumination, at least as a term, had become so discredited through Ta-hui's attacks that the word was never used again in a positive sense.

The development of Silent Illumination in the Ts'ao-tung tradition, Ta-hui's ferocious attacks on it, created an atmosphere of sectarianism within Ch'an which was to last for several generations. However, eventually the differences were forgotten in China, and today Chinese monastics do not see Ts'ao-tung and Lin-chi Ch'an as opposed to each other. On the other hand, at the time Ch'an was transmitted to Japan, the sectarian climate still dominated and sectarianism became an integral part of Japanese Zen.[121] Writers like D. T. Suzuki did much to keep sectarianism alive in this century with his poorly hidden disdain for the Sōtō/Ts'ao-tung traditions.[122] The Japanese scholars, whose work has been so important for the study of Zen/Ch'an in the West, also have tended to read differences they found in Japanese Zen back into Chinese Ch'an. This legacy is still strong in the West, and I believe that it is for this reason that we have come to see the different traditions of Ch'an as distinct "schools" founded on different doctrinal emphases and methodology, just as kung-an practice has come to be associated with the Lin-chi school. Also, perhaps ironically, the origin of Kung-an Introspection Ch'an as primarily directed toward laypeople was forgotten, and it became seen as a practice that was best suited for monastics in strict, regulated settings. Only in recent years, and primarily in the context of Buddhism imported to the West, have both Kung-an Introspection Ch'an and the quiet sitting associated with Silent Illumination again become reclaimed by the lay community.

NOTES

1. For recent examples of such a view, see Daniel Overmeyer, "Chinese Religion," in *Encyclopedia of Religion*, ed. Mircea Eliade (New York: Macmillan, 1987), vol. 3, pp. 280–281, and Heinrich Dumoulin, "Ch'an," *Encyclopedia of Religion*, vol. 3, pp. 183–191.

2. Dumoulin, "Ch'an," p. 190.

3. See Satō Hidetaka, "Wanshi bannen no gyōjitsu nitsuite," *Sōtōshū kenkyūin kenkyūsei kenkyūkiyō*, no. 16 (1984): 219–248 for a detailed account of the interactions between Ta-hui and Hung-chih in their later years.

4. The notion of Ch'ing-liao as a target for Ta-hui's Silent Illumination attacks was first suggested in a little-noticed article by Takeda Tadashi, "Daie no mokushō zen hihan to Sōtō zen," *Tōhoku Fukushi daigaku ronsō*, no. 6 (1966): 237–256. This idea was later reintroduced in Yanagida Seizan, "Kanna to mokushō," *Hanazono daigaku kenkyū kiyō*, no. 6 (1973): 1–20, which does not mention Takeda's earlier article. Ta-hui's attacks on Ch'ing-liao have been further discussed in Ishii Shūdō, "Daie Sōkō to sono deshitachi (roku)," *Indogaku bukkyōgaku kenkyū*, vol. 23, no. 1 (1974): 336–339, and "Daie Sōkō to sono deshitachi (hachi)," *Indogaku bukkyōgaku kenkyū*, vol. 25, no. 2 (1977): 257–261.

5. However, Takeda, "Daie no mokushō zen hihan to Sōtō zen," does in fact suggest that the Ts'ao-tung tradition as such was the target for Ta-hui's attacks. Ishii Shūdō, *Sōdai Zenshūshi no kenkyū: Chūgoku Sōtōshū to Dōgen Zen* (Tokyo: Daitō shuppansha, 1987), pp. 331–354, seems to suggest that Ta-hui was reacting to Hung-chih's teaching, but also maintains that Hung-chih's Ch'an cannot have been the Silent Illumination that Ta-hui attacked. Satō, in his "Wanshi bannen no gyōjitsu ni tsuite," suggests that Ta-hui may have targeted several different Ts'ao-tung masters, perhaps even Hung-chih, at least before the two met.

6. This revised view is reflected in a few English sources such as Robert M. Gimello, "Mārga and Culture: Learning, Letters and Liberation in Northern Sung Ch'an" in *Paths to Liberation: the Mārga and its Transformations in Buddhist Thought*, ed. Robert E. Buswell, Jr., and Robert M. Gimello (Honolulu: University of Hawaii Press, 1992), pp. 371–437, n. 7, which refers to Miriam L. Levering, "Ch'an Enlightenment for Laymen: Ta-hui and the New Religious Culture of the Sung," Ph.D. dissertation, Harvard University, 1978, pp. 261–274. See also Carl Bielefeldt, *Dōgen's Manuals of Zen Meditation* (Berkeley: University of California Press, 1988), pp. 99–105, where Bielefeldt seems to suggest that Ta-hui's attacks on Silent Illumination may have been simply a device to accentuate his own position and that no one in particular was targeted.

7. The *Mo-chao ming* is translated in part in Morten Schlütter, "Silent Illumination, Kung-an Introspection, and the Competition for Lay Patronage in Sung-Dynasty Ch'an," in *Buddhism in the Sung*, ed. Peter N. Gregory and Daniel A. Getz, Jr. (Honolulu: University of Hawaii Press, 1999). See also the full translation in Taigen Daniel Leighton with Yi Wu, *Cultivating the Empty Field: the Silent Illumination of Zen Master Hung-chih* (San Francisco: North Point Press, 1991), pp. 52–54, and the free translation into modern Japanese in Ishii, *Sōdai Zenshū*, pp. 333–336.

8. See Ishii, *Sōdai Zenshū*, p. 333. This is based on the fact that the *Mo-chao ming* is found in the first section of the Sung edition of Hung-chih's recorded sayings, whereas all the other material is from Hung-chih's earliest career. The Sung edition is reproduced in Ishii Shūdō, ed., *Wanshi roku* (Tokyo: Meicho fukyūkai, 1984), vol. 1, pp. 1–467.

9. See Morten Schlütter, "The Twelfth Century Ts'ao-tung Tradition as the Traget of Ta-hui's Attacks on Silent Illumination." *Annual Report of the Zen Research Institute of Komazawa University,* no. 6 (1995): 1–35.

10. See Schlütter, "Silent Illumination and Kung-an Introspection" for a discussion and analysis.

11. For a discussion of Sung government polices toward Buddhism and their effect on the Ch'an sect, see Morten Schlütter, "Vinaya Monasteries, Public Abbacies, and State Control of Buddhism under the Sung Dynasty (960–1279)," in William Bodiford and Paul Groner, eds., *Going Forth: Vinaya and Monastic Power in East Asian Buddhism* (forthcoming). See also T. Griffith Foulk, "Myth, Ritual, and Monastic Practice in Sung Ch'an Buddhism," in Patricia Buckley Ebrey and Peter N. Gregory, eds., *Religion and Society in T'ang and Sung China* (Honolulu: University of Hawaii Press, 1993), pp. 147–208.

12. See Schlütter, "Vinaya Monasteries, Public Abbacies, and State Control of Buddhism."

13. *Ch'uan-fa cheng-tsung chi,* T 51, p. 763c8–9.

14. *Ching-te ch'uan-teng lu,* T 51, p. 421b–c.

15. The earliest version of this story is found in the *Chien-chung Ching-kuo hsü-teng lu* (published in 1101), ZZ 2B.9.1–2, pp. 176a–177a.

16. See, e.g., the 1036 *T'ien-sheng kuang-teng lu,* ZZ 2B.8.4–5, pp. 418a–426b, which has records of nine of Ching-hsüan's disciples. Later transmission of the lamp histories added several more.

17. It appears to have been as a result of Tao-k'ai's and Pao-en's influence that this and a number of other stories about the earlier Ts'ao-tung lineage became orthodox Ch'an history.

18. See Ishii, *Sōdai Zenshū,* pp. 355–383. See also Steven Heine, *Dōgen and the Kōan Tradition: A Tale of Two Shōbōgenzō Texts* (New York: State University of New York Press, 1994); and Carl Bielefeldt, *Dōgen's Manuals of Zen Meditation* (Berkeley: University of California Press, 1988).

19. See, e.g., cases 17 and 20 in the *Pi-yen lu,* T 47, pp. 157a–c and 160a–161c.

20. Cf. the definition in Richard Demartino, "On Zen Communication," *Communication,* vol. 8, no. 1 (1983): 53, "A kōan is a Zen presentation in the form of a Zen challenge," cited in Urs App, trans. and ed., *Master Yunmen: from the Record of the Ch'an Master "Gate of the Clouds"* (New York: Kodansha International, 1994), 53.

21. The "empty eon" refers to the last of the four great eons (*kalpa*) which each world cycle goes through, when everything has been destroyed and nothing yet has come into existence.

22. See the text of the epitaph in T 48, pp. 119c27–120a3.

23. Hung-chih served as head monk for Ch'ing-liao's congregation and, when Ch'ing-liao passed away, wrote his funerary inscription.

24. See the inscription in *Ch'ing-liao yü-lu,* ZZ 2.29.3, p. 317b12–13. Also in *Ming-chou Tien-tung Ching-te ch'an-ssu Hung-chih Chüeh Ch'an-shih yü-lu,* included in the second supplement to the Ming canon, see the reproduction in Ishii Shūdō, ed., *Wanshi roku,* pp. 508–510. A more elaborate account of Ch'ing-liao's enlightenment is found in his recorded sayings, which were published before 1132, *Ch'ing-liao yü-lu,* ZZ 2.29.3, p. 315b6–14, but Tzu-ch'un's question is the same.

25. The notion of "inherent enlightenment" was known to the Chinese most importantly from the *Ta-sheng ch'i-hsin lun* (*Awakening of Faith in the Mahayana*), where it is contrasted with "actualization of enlightenment," which refers to the moment when

one realizes one's own inherent enlightenment. The work is attributed to the Indian poet Aśvaghosa but was almost certainly written in China, where it became immensely popular. See T 32, p. 576b–c; cf. translation by Yoshito S. Hakeda, *The Awakening of Faith Attributed to Aśvaghosha* (New York: Columbia University Press, 1967), pp. 37ff.

26. *Ch'an-lin seng-pao chuan,* ZZ 2B.10.3, p. 256c (hereafter *Seng-pao chuan*),

27. This kung-an is case 65 of the *Pi-yen lu,* T 48, p. 195b26–c1, where it begins as follows:

A non-Buddhist asked the Buddha: "I am not asking about that which has words, I am not asking about that which has no words." The World-honored One was silent for a while. The non-Buddhist said in praise: "The World-honored One has great mercy and compassion, he has scattered the clouds of my deluded [mind] and enabled me to gain entrance [to the Way]."

28. *Seng-pao chuan,* p. 256b.

29. Among the "great Dharma Grandsons" is often included yet another disciple of Tzu-ch'un, Hui-chao Ch'ing-yü (1078–1140), who seems to have struggled, largely unsuccessfully, to have himself considered on a par with his famous Dharma brothers. No enlightenment narrative for Ch'ing-yü exists. See Ishii, *Sōdai Zenshūshi,* pp. 254–279.

30. See the inscription in *Hu-pei chin-shih chih,* 10, p. 25a6–7, in *Shih-ko shih-liao hsin-pien,* ser. 1.16. See also the text in Ishii, *Sōdai Zenshūshi,* p. 456.

31. See, e.g., Hung-chih's frequent use of this catchphrase kung-an, T 48, pp. 13a, 20b, 39c, 43c, 65a, and 69b. See also the records of twelfth-century Ts'ao-tung masters in the *Wu-teng hui-yüan,* Chung-hua shu-chü edition, 3, pp. 896.3, 898.5, 900.1, 900.14, 906.3, and 906.9.

32. Literally "beyond Bhīśmargarjitasvararāja" (Ch. Wei-yin wang), the Majestic Sound King. He appears in the *Lotus Sūtra* as a Buddha with a lifespan of billions of eons, who lived innumerable eons ago and who was followed by a series of two million Buddhas with the same name (see T 9.50c–51b; cf. Leon Hurvitz, trans., *Scripture of the Lotus Blossom of the Fine Dharma* [New York: Columbia University Press, 1976], pp. 279ff). Because of his antiquity, Bhīśmargarjitasvararāja came to be seen as the primordial Buddha at the beginning of time.

33. *Hsü ku-tsun-su yü-yao,* ZZ 2.23.4–24.1, pp. 453d11–16. This passage is translated slightly differently in my "Silent Illumination and Kung-an Introspection."

34. Some individual differences can be discerned in the teaching styles of Tao-k'ai's descendants, but I will address them only occasionally in the following.

35. Translation tentative.

36. *Ta-hui yü-lu,* T 47, p. 892a21–24. See also the translation of parts of this passage in Chün-fang Yü, "Ta-hui Tsung-kao and *Kung-an* Ch'an," *Journal of Chinese Philosophy,* no. 6 (1979): 211–235.

37. This is another indication that Ta-hui is indeed talking about the Ts'ao-tung teachings although, as is usual for Ta-hui's attacks on the Ts'ao-tung tradition, he does not openly say so.

38. See the collections by I-ching in ZZ 2.29.3, pp. 232b–238a, by Tzu-ch'un in ZZ 2.29.3, pp. 249d–257b, by Ch'ing-liao in ZZ 2.29.3, p. 328a, and two by Hung-chih in T 48, pp. 18b–35a. Ta-hui's collection is found in ZZ 2.23.4. Such collections themselves were sometimes further subject to another master's commentaries, resulting in a rather complex and somewhat confusing piece of literature, the most famous of which is the *Pi-yen lu* (*Blue Cliff Record*), which was Ta-hui's master Yüan-wu K'o-ch'in's commen-

tary on a 100-verse collection by the Yün-men master Hsüeh-tou Ch'ung-hsien (980–1052). Ta-hui is said to have later destroyed the wood blocks to this work because he found that students were relying on it too heavily. See *Ch'an-lin pao-hsün*, T 48, p. 1036b28. See Ogisu Jundō, "Daie zenji no *Hekiganshū* shoki ni tsuite," *IBK* 11 (1963): 115–118, cited in Levering, "Ch'an Enlightenment for Laymen," p. 32, n. 2.

39. *Hung-chih kuang-lu*, T 48.67a18–20. The translation is from Isshū Miura and R. F. Sasaki, *Zen Dust* (Kyoto: First Zen Institute of America in Japan, 1966), p. 172.

40. *Seng-pao cheng-hsü chuan*, p. 288c10–d1.

41. *Seng-pao cheng-hsü chuan*, p. 288d2–4.

42. *Ta-hui yü-lu*, p. 933c6–9; see also the modern edition of Ta-hui's letters found in Araki Kengo, *Dale sho, Zen no goroku*, vol. 17 (Tokyo: Chikuma shobō, 1969), p. 156.

43. See Schlütter, "Silent Illumination and Kung-an Introspection," for further discussion of enlightenment in the Ts'ao-tung tradition and Ta-hui's claims about it.

44. See *Ta-hui P'u-chüeh Ch'an-shih p'u-shuo, Dainihon kōtei daizōkyō* (*Manji daizō-kyō*) (hereafter cited as *Ta-hui p'u-shuo*) 1.31.5, p. 428d.

45. *Hung-chih kuang-lu*, T, pp. 48, 77a-29; also translated in Leighton, *Cultivating the Empty Field*, p. 28.

46. For discussions in English see Yü, "Ta-hui Tsung-kao and *Kung-an* Ch'an," and Robert E. Buswell, Jr., "The 'Short-cut' Approach of *K'an-hua* Meditation: The Evolution of a Practical Subitism in Chinese Ch'an Buddhism," in Peter N. Gregory, ed., *Sudden and Gradual Approaches to Enlightenment in Chinese Thought* (Honolulu: University of Hawaii Press, 1987). See also the discussion in several places in Heine, *Dōgen and the Kōan Tradition*.

47. *Ta-hui yü-lu*, pp. 901c27–902a6.

48. *Ta-hui p'u-shuo*, p. 425b11–12. Cited in Levering, "Ch'an Enlightenment for Laymen," p. 267.

49. See Furuta, "Kōan no rekishiteki hatten keitai ni okeru shinrisei no mondai," in *Bukkyō no kompon shinri*, ed. Miyamoto Shōson (Tokyo: Sanseidō, 1956), pp. 813–816. See the *Yün-men K'uang-chen ch'an-shih kuang-lu*, T 47, pp. 544–576.

50. T 48, pp. 1033c18–21, and 1036b19–22. See the *Fen-yang Wu-te ch'an-shih yü-lu*, T 47, pp. 594–629. Hsüeh-tou Ch'ung-hsien's kung-an commentary no longer exists as an independent work, but is incorporated in the famous *Pi-yen lu* commenting on the same 100 cases.

51. See Ch'ing-hsien's funerary inscription in the *Hu-pei chin-shih chih*, 12, pp. 7a–9b. An annotated and collated version is found in Ishii, *Sōdai Zenshū*, pp. 509–515.

52. See the *Chien-chung Ching-kuo hsü-teng lu*, pp. 176a–177a.

53. *Fo-kuo Ko-ch'in Ch'an-shih hsin-yao*, ZZ 2.25.4, p. 385a7–8. Translation adapted from Hsieh, "Yüan-wu K'o-ch'in's Teaching of Ch'an *Kung-an* Practice."

54. A reference to Hui-neng's famous verse found in the longer versions of the *Platform Sūtra;* see T 48, p. 349a. Of course, in the shorter and earlier Tun-huang *Platform Sūtra* a different verse is found, and the earliest occurrence of the verse that includes "fundamentally nothing exists" was probably in a version of the *Platform Sūtra* from 967, long after Tung-shan Liang-chieh had passed away. See Morten Schlütter, "A Study in the Genealogy of the *Platform Sūtra*," *Studies in Central and East Asian Religions,* no. 2 (1989): 53–114. This is yet another indication that the records in the transmission of the lamp histories are to be taken not as historical documents but as religious literature reflecting the concerns and needs of the age in which they were compiled.

55. *Ching-te ch'uan-teng lu*, p. 322c12–14.

56. Compare, e.g., records from masters in different lineages in the *Ching-te ch'uan-teng lu.*

57. A recent book by Thomas Cleary is *The Five Houses of Zen* (Boston: Shambhala, 1997).

58. The mention of some of the traditions in the *Tsung-men shih-kui lun,* attributed to Fa-yen Wen-yi (885–958) (see ZZ 2.15.5, pp. 439a–441c), is not a reflection of a five-tradition scheme, as is show by T. Griffith Foulk, "The 'Ch'an School' and Its Place in the Buddhist Monastic Tradition," Ph.D. dissertation, University of Michigan, 1987, p. 46. The five-tradition scheme is not mentioned in the *Ching-te ch'uan-teng lu,* but all masters in the last generations included here can be placed in one of the five traditions, and it is quite possible that this was what inspired the scheme.

59. See T 51, p. 763c. The version in the *Taishō shinshū daizōkyō* is based on a Ming edition, but a Sung edition is collated against it.

60. *Chien-chung Ching-kuo hsü-teng lu,* p. 19c. Adapted from the translation in Yü, "Ta-hui Tsung-kao and *Kung-an* Ch'an."

61. The entry on Tung-shan Liang-chieh is found in *Sodōshū,* pp. 2.49–2.71, his disciples are on pp. 2.117–2.156, and his second-generation descendants on pp. 3.109–3.118.

62. See the entries on members of the Ts'ao-tung lineage found in *Sung kao-seng chuan,* T 50, pp. 780a1–16, 781b9–c6, 786b16–c3, 883c16–884a20, 886b16–29, 898b20–c18, 788b17–c4, and 886c1–887a9.

63. See the *Ching-te ch'uan-teng lu,* pp. 321b–323b for the record of Tung-shan Liang-chieh, pp. 334c–340c for records of his disciples, pp. 361c–368c for records of his second-generation disciples, pp. 394c–396c for the records of his third-generation descendants, pp. 406a–407a for the records of his fourth-generation descendants, and p. 421b–c for his lone fifth-generation descendant, Ta-yang Ching-hsüan.

64. The records of the Ts'ao-tung monks included in the *T'ien-sheng kuang-teng lu* are found on pp. 418a–426b.

65. Or course it is uncertain to which degree, if any, the records in the histories reflect what these masters might actually have taught.

66. See, for example, Yanagida Seizan, "Chūgoku Zenshūshi," *Kōza Zen,* vol. 3 of Nishitani Keiji, ed., *Zen no rekishi: Chūgoku* (Tokyo: Chikuma Shobo, 1967), p. 77.

67. *Ching-te ch'uan-teng lu,* pp. 321c19 and 290b1.

68. *Ching-te ch'uan-teng lu,* pp. 337a21 and 337b14.

69. The text of this is most accessible in the *Jui-chou Tung-shan Liang-chieh ch'an-shih yü-lu,* T 47, pp. 525c24–526a19. See the translation into English in William F. Powell, *The Record of Tung-shan* (Honolulu: University of Hawaii Press, 1987), pp. 63–65.

70. The entries on the *Pao-ching san-mei* in the *Zengaku daijiten,* p. 1125a, the *Bukkyō kaisetsu daijiten,* vol. 10, p. 140, and the *Zenseki mokuroku,* p. 453, all give Tung-shan Liang-chieh as its author.

71. See the *Jui-chou Tung-shan Liang-chieh ch'an-shih yü-lu,* p. 525c23. This is a very late work, first published in the Ming dynasty (1368–1644).

72. *Seng-pao chuan,* p. 222b12–c13. Hui-hung also mentions the *Pao-ching san-mei* in his *Lin-chien lu,* p. 300b.

73. *Seng-pao chuan,* p. 224a18–b6.

74. *T'ien-sheng kuang-teng lu,* pp. 420a–422d.

75. *Ching-te ch'uan-teng lu,* p. 396a.

76. See *T'ien-sheng kuang-teng lu,* pp. 420b3, 420b6, 421d3, 422a6–7, and 422b1–2.

77. *T'ien-sheng kuang-teng lu*, p. 31c.

78. Ching-hsüan's entry in the 1123 *Seng-pao chuan* does include the expression "the time before your parents were born" in a poem Ching-hsüan is said to have composed upon his enlightenment.

79. See *Ching-te ch'uan-teng lu*, pp. 394c–396c and 406a–407a.

80. See, e.g., the record of the famous Lin-chi master Fen-hsüeh Yen-chao (887–973) in the *Ching-te ch'uan-teng lu*, T 51, pp. 302a–303c.

81. Thus the scholar Fan Yü in his 1113 inscription on Ta-hung Pao-en remarks, "Common people say that I-ch'ing did not receive [the transmission] personally. They do not understand that the saintly does not have before or after and that the transmission lies in awakening." See *Hu-pei chin-shih chih*, 10, p. 20b, and Ishii, *Sōdai Zenshūshi*, p. 438. This remark makes it clear that there were those who tried to discredit I-ch'ing's transmission. However, they do not seem to have been very successful, and there is no indication that the Ts'ao-tung tradition was commonly attacked on this point.

82. *T'ou-tzu I-ch'ing ch'an-shih yü-lu*, ZZ 2.29.3, pp. 222c3–4, 223a13, 224d11, 228a14, and 228b16.

83. *T'ou-tzu I-ch'ing ch'an-shih yü-lu*, p. 224a1–4.

84. That I-ch'ing may have emphasized meditation is also suggested by the fact that he has several references to Bodhidharma's nine years of wall contemplation. See *T'ou-tzu I-ch'ing ch'an-shih yû-lu*, pp. 222c14, 227c18–228a1, and 231c14.

85. *Hsü ku-tsun-su yü-yao*, p. 453c12–15.

86. *Hsü ku-tsun-su yü-yao*, pp. 453a13, 453a18, and 453b12.

87. *Hsü ku-tsun-su yü-yao*, pp. 453a14 and 454b12.

88. See the biography attached to *T'ou-tzu I-ch'ing Ch'an-shih yü-lu*, pp. 238b11–12, 238c1, 238c12–13, 238c16, and 238d12.

89. *Jui-chou Tung-shan Liang-chieh ch'an-shih yü-lu*, p. 511c14.

90. *Wu-teng hui-yüan*, 3, p. 900–1.

91. This notion seems first to have been advanced in Furuta, "Kōan no rekishi-teki hatten"; see especially p. 820. See also Buswell, "The 'Short-cut' Approach," and Ding-hwa Evelyn Hsieh, "Yüan-wu K'o-ch'in's (1063–1135) Teaching of Ch'an *Kung-an* Practice: A Transition from Literary Study of Ch'an *Kung-an* to the Practical *K'an-hua* Ch'an," *JIABS*, vol. 17, no. 1 (1994): 66–95. See also Hsieh's dissertation, "A Study of the Evolution of K'an-hua Ch'an in Sung China: Yüan-wu K'o-ch'in (1063–1135) and the Function of Kung-an in Ch'an Pedagogy and Praxis," Ph. D. dissertation, University of California, Los Angeles, 1993.

92. Ta-kui Chen-ju Mu-che (d.1095), a famous Lin-chi master whom several of the monks in the Ts'ao-tung lineage also studied.

93. *Yüan-wu Fo-kuo Ch'an-shih yü-lu*, T 47, p. 775a22–24.

94. According to Ta-hui himself, he worked on this same kung-an while studying with Yûan-wu. At some point he asked Yûan-wu: "I have heard that when you were with Wu-tzu you asked about this phrase. I wonder what he answered?. . . . [Yüan-wu] said: 'If you try to draw it you can't, if you try to paint it you can't.' I [Yüan-wu] then asked: 'What if the tree suddenly falls over and the vines dry up [and die]?' Wu-tzu said: 'You are following along with it.' " Hearing this, Ta-hui gained full enlightenment. See T 47, p. 883a27–b12. See also the *Manji* edition of the *P'u-shuo*, p. 421a10–16 which has a somewhat abbreviated version of the story. The passage is translated in Chün-fang Yü, "Ta-hui Tsung-kao and *Kung-an* Ch'an," p. 215. The story in this form is not found in any of Yüan-wu's recorded sayings.

95. *Fo-kuo Ko-ch'in Ch'an-shih hsin-yao*, ZZ 2.25.4, p. 355a17–b7.

96. See also *Yüan-wu Fo-kuo yü-lu*, p. 775b2–5, where the line continues: "it is only because she knows T'an-lang [her lover] will hear her voice." See the discussion of this poem in Hsieh, "A Study of the Evolution of K'an-hua Ch'an," p. 35.

97. *Fo-kuo Ko-ch'in hsin-yao*, p. 355b7–9. Cf. *Yüan-wu Ko-ch'in yü-lu*, p. 775b1–4. The whole passage is translated in J. C. Cleary and Thomas Cleary, trans. and eds., *Zen Letters: Teachings of Yüan-wu* (Boston: Shambala, 1994), p. 16. Cleary and Cleary in this work translate about half of Yüan-wu Ko-ch'in's *Hsin-yao*, fairly accurately, although many passages are shortened and paraphrased without any indication. There is also no indication of what passages are translated or indeed that the *Hsin-yao* is the work from which they are translating.

98. However, that is not how the story of Yüan-wu's enlightenment was remembered in the transmission of the lamp histories. Here Yüan-wu is said to have been enlightened during a discussion of the verse with Wu-tzu Fa-yen in a traditional encounter dialogue fashion that involved no prolonged contemplation of the saying. See the 1183 *Tsung-men lien-teng hui-yao*, ZZ 2B.9.3–5, pp. 346b17–c5, where the story first appears.

99. See Buswell, "The 'Short-cut' Approach," and Ding-hwa Evelyn Hsieh, "Yüan-wu K'o-ch'in's Teaching of Ch'an *Kung-an* Practice." See also Hsieh, "A Study of the Evolution of K'an-hua Ch'an."

100. See Furuta, "Kōan no rekishiteki hatten," pp. 821–823 for more examples of Yüan-wu discussing the uselessness and harmfulness of trying to understand kung-an intellectually.

101. *Fo-kuo Ko-ch'in hsin-yao*, p. 377a8–11. Cited in Furuta, "Kōan no rekishiteki hatten," p. 821.

102. See, for example, *Yüan-wu K'o-ch'in yü-lu*, p. 749b17–18. Cited in Furuta, "Kōan no rekishiteki hatten," p. 821.

103. See below. See also Schlütter, "Silent Illumination and Kung-an Introspection."

104. See T 48, p. 387b5–8.

105. See the Sung text in Iriya Yoshitaka, trans., *Denshin hōyō; Enryo roku. Zen no goroku*, vol. 8 (Tokyo: Chikuma Shobo, 1969), pp. 134–135 (where the passage should have been).

106. See *Ta-hui yü-lu*, p. 942c24–26; *Daie sho*, p. 239. Cited in Furuta, "Kōan no rekishiteki hatten," p. 830. This letter is also found in a rather different form in the *Ch'an-lin pao-hsün*, p. 1023a25–29.

107. *Fa-yen ch'an-shih yü-lu*, T 47, pp. 665b29–c5. Cited in Yanagida, "Chūgoku Zenshūshi," p. 102.

108. *Fa-yen ch'an-shih yü-lu*, pp. 660a3 and 666b28–c2.

109. The main argument in Buswell, "The 'Short-cut' Approach," is that Ta-hui's *hua-t'ou* practice was "the culmination of a long process of evolution in Ch'an whereby its subitist rhetoric came to be extended to pedagogy and finally to practice" (p. 322). However, although the development of Kung-an Introspection Ch'an was possible only because of previous developments in Ch'an, this characterization seems to underestimate the originality of Ta-hui's contribution.

110. See the discussion in Schlütter, "Silent Illumination and Kung-an Introspection."

111. For a detailed discussion of how political and social changes made literati support especially important in the twelfth century, see Schlütter, "Vinaya Monasteries,

Public Abbacies, and State Control of Buddhism." See also Schlütter, "Silent Illumination and Kung-an Introspection."

112. See cases 20 and 43, T 48, pp. 160a–161c and 180a–c.

113. See *Hsü ku-tsun-su yü-yao,* pp. 497c–498d.

114. *Ta-hui yü-lu,* p. 885a24–885a3. Also translated in Christopher Cleary, *Swampland Flowers: the Letters and Lectures of Zen Master Ta Hui* (New York: Grove Press, 1977), p. 124, with some inaccuracies.

115. See Ta-hui's *p'u-shuo* and *fa-yü* sermons in T 47, pp. 863–916, and his letters in T 47, pp. 916–943.

116. See, for example, T 47, pp. 884c–886a, 890a–892c, 901c, 923a, 933c, and 937a–b.

117. *Ta-hui p'u-shuo,* p. 443b–c; cited in Ishii, "Daie Sōkō to sono deshitachi (roku)," p. 338; see also Ishii, *Sōdai Zenshū,* p. 331.

118. See Buswell, "The 'Short-cut' Approach," for a discussion of this expression.

119. See recorded sayings by T'ien-t'ung Ju-ching (1163–1228), in Kagamishima Genryū, *Tendō Nyojō zenji no kenkyū* (Tokyo: Shunjūsha, 1983), p. 282. See also Pei-yi Wu, *The Confucian's Progress: Autobiographical Writings in Traditional China* (Princeton, N.J.: Princeton University Press, 1989), p. 77.

120. Even though Kung-an Introspection Ch'an may have been given a Silent Illumination twist in the Ts'ao-tung tradition. See the comments in Ishii Shūdō, "Wanshi Shōgaku to Tendō Nyodō," *Sōdai no shakai to shūkyō,* ed. Sōdaishi kenkyūkai (Tokyo: Gyūkō shoin, 1985), pp. 51–80.

121. There were of course internal reasons in Japan why this sectarianism was sustained so well. For background information see William M. Bodiford, *Sōtō Zen in Medieval Japan* (Honolulu: University of Hawaii Press, 1993).

122. See the discussion in Robert H. Sharf, "The Zen of Japanese Nationalism," *Curators of the Buddha: The Study of Buddhism under Colonialism,* ed. Donald S. Lopez (Chicago: University of Chicago Press, 1995), pp. 107–160.

7

Kōan History
Transformative Language in Chinese Buddhist Thought

DALE S. WRIGHT

Kōan Prehistory

What are kōans? Prior to its metaphorical extension into the realm of religious practice, the Chinese character combination *kung-an* referred to "public records" that document the precedent established by previous legal judgment. Just as the records of the legal tradition place into the public domain cases manifesting the criteria and principles of justice, the "public records" of the Ch'an tradition announce the criteria and principles of "awakening." As the *Extensive Record of Master Chung-feng* (discussed in depth in chapter 1 by Foulk and chapter 4 Ishii) extends the analogy, "the so-called venerable masters of Zen are the chief officials of the public law courts of the monastic community, as it were, and their words on the transmission of Zen and their collections of sayings are the case records of points that have been vigorously advocated."[1] In the same way that "public records" limit both the waywardness of the law and its arbitrariness, the "public records" of Ch'an "awakening" were thought to preserve the identity of enlightenment over time and to render refutable the assertions of impostors. Thus the *Chung-feng lu* repeatedly, as if to insist on the point, declares that "the word *kung,* or 'public,' means that the kōans put a stop to private understanding; the word *an,* or 'case records,' means that they are guaranteed to accord with the buddhas and patriarchs."[2] Parallel guarantees are offered by the text in both legal and religious domains: When "public records" are in order, both "the Kingly Way" and "the Buddha Way" "will be well ordered."[3] The Confucian rhetoric behind these assertions is certainly not accidental. Its intention is publicly to establish the kung-an as a set of standards—weights and measures—in juxtaposition to which all claims to religious attainment could be discernfully judged. Therefore the

Chung-feng lu completes this section by announcing that through the establishment of kung-an, "the intention of the patriarchs is made abundantly clear, the Buddha-mind is laid open and revealed."[4]

Which records would thus be made public as the standard of "awakened mind"? The selection process seems initially to have followed the unintentional consensus generated by Sung dynasty Ch'an abbots as favorite selections from the "discourse records," and "lamp histories" were repeatedly extracted for discussion and contemplation. The ultimately canonical choices, however, were made by compilers of explicit kōan collections like the classic *Gateless Barrier* (C. *Wu-men kuan*, J. *Mumonkan*) and *Blue Cliff Record* (C. *Pi-yen lu*, J. *Hekigan-roku*). What they chose were segments of discourse from the by then exalted masters of the "golden age" of Ch'an, segments which by Sung standards seemed to encapsulate and epitomize the experience of the world around them as seen from the perspective of awakening. These sayings were typically "strange," unusual, and sometimes paradoxical from the perspective of those who had yet to achieve this state of mind. Highlighting strangeness made it abundantly clear to everyone that "awakening" was something fundamentally other than the ordinary mental state of most practitioners. Strange sayings were signs of difference, formal disclosures of a qualitative distinction separating the original speakers of kōan discourse from those who would later contemplate it.

The purpose of these disclosures of difference appears to be twofold. The first is the maintenance of criteria in terms of which subsequent awakenings could be judged for authenticity. As Wu-men (J. Mumon) says in his first commentary on Chao-chou's (J. Jōshū) "Mu," "in studying Zen, one must pass the barriers set up by ancient masters."[5] Beyond their function as standards of judgment, however, Wu-men and the other early kōan masters regard their texts as expedients or means through which the attainment of those standards might be actualized. Why were the sayings of ancient masters thought to function in this capacity? Given that these sayings epitomize the mental state from which they have come forth, if the practitioner could trace back (*hui-fan*) the saying to its source, he or she would at that moment occupy a mental space identical to that of its original utterer.[6] D. T. Suzuki gave this traditional conception beautiful expression in English. He wrote that "the idea is to reproduce in the uninitiated the state of consciousness of which these statements are the expression."[7] Kōan language expresses or "presses out" into form the "empty" experience of the great masters. Or, once again from Suzuki, "When we reproduce the same psychic conditions out of which the Zen masters have uttered these kōans, we shall know them."[8] Wu-men claims further that those who succeed in this effort will have achieved identity with buddhas and patriarchs. Practitioners would then know the meaning or "intent" (*i*) of the strange kōan sayings and begin to speak similarly. "You will see with the same eye that they see with and hear with the same ear."[9]

Those who had experienced directly the intent (*i*) of the masters in their kung-an traditionally composed verses corresponding to, and thus "capping," the original kōan. These verses eventually came to be called "capping phrases" (C. *cho-yü*, J. *jakugo*). The most famous of these were appended to the kōans themselves, as alternative expressions of the same experience. Because they were regarded as expressions of the same, capping phrases were thought to possess the identical power of disclosure for those who might meditate on them. Later in the Japanese kōan tradition, Hakuin would systematically test the kōan answers of his students by their capacity to select a capping phrase to match the kōan from standard anthologies of Buddhist quotations. Essentially a multiple-choice exam rather than an act of composition, the test required the students simply to select a phrase from the source books to match the vision embodied in the kōan. The metaphorical language of "match" or "tally" that was employed in all these contexts shows further the intention of "mind-to-Mind transmission" contained in kōan study. These metaphors were drawn from numerous contexts such as commercial accounting and from the ancient Chinese practice of testing the authenticity of a messenger by seeing whether the broken piece of pottery in his possession matched that held by the receiver of the message. Since the linguistic expression of the kōan "matched" the mind from which it emerged, authentically to match that language in understanding indicated an identity of mind to some degree between kōan master and kōan meditator.

Interesting conclusions might be drawn from the universal assumption behind these conceptions that some kind of rational and predictable structure linked the language of the kōan with enlightenment. The relationships between kōan language and the mind of the master, and between kōan language and the mind of the practitioner, were thought to be far from accidental or random. Although they might be difficult to decipher from the vantage point of the unawakened, kōans were assumed to express directly and without distortion that state of mind from which they issued. Here, in the kōan, enlightenment has taken concrete form, form which, if meditatively pursued, could be traced back to the moment of its formation in emptiness.

These assumptions about the expressibility of enlightenment in linguistic form—regardless of their blatant conflict with Zen doctrine—were borrowed from earlier Chinese Buddhist traditions and their sources in India and Central Asia, where they were also widespread. Because they appear to contradict longstanding doctrine concerning the transcendence of *nirvāṇa,* these assumptions could not be articulated in theoretical form. Nevertheless, had the tradition lacked assumptions of this sort, neither kōan language nor sūtra language could have had the role that it did in Buddhism. If Buddhists could not assume that the word of the Buddha contained in the sūtras connected in some meaningful way with enlightened experience, then lacking both rationale and function, sūtras would have never been composed in the first place. Similarly, if the language of the kōans is not considered to be linked to the enlightenment of the great masters, no grounds for their use in contemplative practice remains. A complex prehistory of presuppositions about, and use of, religious language in the earlier Chinese Buddhist tradition has established conditions for the very possibility of the idea of the kōan.

The *gātha* recited in unison in Buddhist temples and monasteries before the sūtras are opened for ritual and contemplative use reads as follows:

> The Dharma, incomparable profound and exquisite
> Is rarely encountered even in millions of years
> We now see it, hear it, accept it and hold it
> May we truly grasp the Tathāgata's meaning.

These ritual words show the profound reverence and religious awe sought for the tradition's religious language. When the *gātha* is not just said but meaningfully heard, it reminds the practitioner that he or she has in hand words that have emanated from the enlightened mind of the Buddha, words compassionately intended to transmit enlightenment to them and thus to save them from suffering. The recital of these words enables practitioners to open themselves more resolutely and authentically to the appropriation of the Buddha's intention inscribed in the text. Although kōan language differs rhetorically from sūtra language in its abandonment of instruction, doctrinal assertion, and argumentative style, nevertheless behind this difference is the more fundamental identity that both kōans and sūtras express the mind of enlightenment and, on that basis, may be taken as a means to and measure of enlightenment.

The *Perfection of Wisdom Sūtras,* together with the *Lotus Sūtra,* widely disseminated several forms of religious language that came to serve as the practical background for the development of the kōan. We focus here on three of them: (1) *dhāranī* or sacred formulas, including *mantra,* practiced in esoteric Buddhism; (2) devotional recitation of the thought or name of the Buddha, the *nien-fo* used in the Pure Land School (J. *nembutsu*); and (3) the visualizations and conceptual "contemplations" (*kuan*) practiced by the Chinese scholastic traditions. These three linguistic phenomena established the conditions of possibility for the conception of religious language developed in the Ch'an *kung-an* tradition.

Dhāranī are sacred formulae customarily recited in original or classical languages that are not understood by those who intone them in memorized form for ritual purposes. Why recite a verse whose words are incomprehensible and whose meaning is unknown? To any devout practitioner it would be enough to reply that these were the most mysterious and sacred words emanating from the mind of ancient buddhas. Beyond that, presumably, these mysterious words must be thought to possess a power not transferable into Chinese through translation and therefore ungraspable in concept. They must, in short, function at a level more basic than the conceptual. They must work on the practitioner without the requirement that one think about their literal or metaphorical meaning. The parallel and precedent here should be clear: the later kōan tradition in Zen understood its language to emanate directly from the mind of enlightenment and, although still using Chinese records as sources, to surpass conventional comprehension by leaving an effect on the practitioner at a more fundamental level of mentality. The ritual aura and mystery of kungan practices in Ch'an monasteries by the end of the Sung were clearly parallel to the dhāraṇi and mantra practices in esoteric and tantric Buddhism.

The mystery and power of the Buddha's discourse as suggested in early Mahayana sūtras took only a slightly different form in the devotional, Pure Land tradition. Although the practice of *nien-fo*, "thinking Buddha," seems initially to have had the ethical force of edification, as Mahayana conceptions of the power and compassion of the Buddha and his teachings developed, the "other-power" implications of graceful, empowering language came to overshadow the ethics of Buddha imitation. Given the difference separating the Buddha from others, the practices of imagining the Buddha and reciting his name evolved away from imitative edification and toward the possibility that the merit and mind of the Buddha could be transferred through sacred language, or grace, without recourse to an ethics of achievement. Because the Japanese Zen that we have inherited in the West remained in sectarian competition with Pure Land Buddhism, trying to maintain its autonomy, we have also inherited the thought that the Chinese synthesis of Zen and Pure Land, kōan and *nembutsu*, constitutes a failure or fall. Although this unification was a complex historical phenomenon as, for example in the Japanese Ōbaku-shū sect, one condition of its occurrence may have been the widespread realization that whatever differences separated these two traditions in origin had either been sublated over time or simply "seen through." Just as the *nembutsu* exercise was a gift of the Buddha, kōans, as later Ch'an Buddhists would say, were transmissions to future generations by the buddhas of China's own age of enlightenment. To those who receive and cherish them through intense practice, they provide, aside from all claims to merit, a shortcut to that very same Buddha-mind. The language of intense practice of kōans and the *nembutsu* overlaps in surprising ways. The same terms that instruct kōan practitioners to "hold the words before the mind" also inform Pure Land Buddhists what to do with the name and thought of the Buddha.

Finally, the brief prehistory of the kōan sketched here includes the conceptually oriented contemplative exercises developed most fully in T'ien-t'ai and Hua-yen as well as the Mi-tsung or esoteric school. These exercises in the dialectics of "emptiness and form" were clearly developed out of images in the *Perfection of Wisdom Sūtras* of the Buddha's continual shifts in framework during conversations with disciples. The Chinese scholastic sects simply systematized the various realizations that could be seen in the "Wisdom" sūtras and extended them in directions that seemed most profound to the Chinese. These texts were commonly called *kuan*, "contemplations," and were used as guides for Chinese *vipaśyanā*. They were conceptual exercises that operated at the limits of thinking, challenging meditators to push further in their capacity to hold necessary but contradictory frameworks of thought together in the same exercise. Although they were indeed narrative and conceptual practices, often culminating in the command "think it!" (*szu-chih*), their rationale was to bring the mind thus prepared to the event of transconceptual disclosure called "sudden awakening." Like the Wisdom sūtras, Chinese *kuan* cultivated the sense of paradox, and over time paradox became a sign of depth or awakening. Some kōans, particularly those in Japanese master Hakuin's Tokugawa-era classification called *hosshin* kōans, retain the style of *kuan*, that is, they can indeed be thought even though such thinking is profoundly paradoxical because it is multidimensional. The explicit monastic exercise of *kuan* is thus a clear precursor to kōan practice. Both seek to move from intellectual perplexity to breakthrough.

"Public Cases" of Transformative Language

In the early Ch'an school, conceptions of religious language and corresponding practices developed in ways that, in retrospect, we can see pointing to the development of the kōan. The idea that religious language, particularly in paradoxical and strange forms, evokes enlightenment is fundamental to most early Ch'an texts. The phrase, "at these words, so and so was awakened," is perhaps the most common in late T'ang to Sung Ch'an literature. The quest to identify particular "turning words" used by the old masters became, in effect, the search for legitimate kōans. That potent phrases drawn from the discourse records of the masters might turn one's mind so thoroughly as to evoke enlightenment naturally led to the kind of intense focus on language that characterizes Sung Ch'an. When the ultimately triumphant lineage came to be identified by the name *k'an-hua* Ch'an, literally, "looking at language meditation," what we had was a Buddhist "rectification of names," because "looking at language in meditative ways" is exactly what they were doing.[10]

We might then ask: What were these ways? How was the language of the kōan, once extracted from the larger corpus of sacred literature and exalted, used in the meditative quest for the sudden breakthrough of awakening? We have already encountered the verb "to trace back" or "return" (*hui-fan*). Kōans were "traces" which monks could "track," tracing them back to their original source in enlightened mind. But *how* do you trace it back? Other verbs fill in some of this procedure: "to elevate," "to hold up," as if to bring into view; "to look at," "to inspect," that which has been held up before the mind; "to concentrate on," "to focus on," "to investigate," "to inquire," "to examine," all give the impression that the kōan was to be the sole object of contemplation and that all energies ought to be placed in the service of both the act of "holding in a fixed manner" and "concentration on" what has thus been centered in the mind.

One effect of this intense focus in meditation upon the language of the kōan would be an intensification of its strange and paradoxical character. Although one criterion in the selection of kōans in the first place was strangeness, nothing functions to bring about estrangement more thoroughly than does unnatural or disciplined concentration. For the most part, normality and common sense are maintained precisely in the fact that the everyday draws no attention to itself. On the rare occasions when we do focus on an element of everyday life and really examine it, recontextualized out of its unnoticed setting, it quickly begins to look odd, as when we suddenly become aware of the startling strangeness of a word that we have spoken hundreds of times without ever noticing it. It seems to me that kōan study would regularly have this effect—common words and common relations to language become deeply uncommon, almost to the point of bewilderment. The longer a monk would abide with a kōan, "holding it before the mind day and night," the less it must have seemed an expression in language at all. Crossing this threshold from the commonness of language into its startling strangeness seems to be fundamental to this mode of meditation.

One form that this estrangement seems to have taken is revealed in Ch'an monks' referring to a reversal of ordinary subject/object relations that occur in advanced kōan study. In the midst of meditating on the kōan as the object of contemplation, it may occur that the kōan has so occupied the practitioner's subjectivity that the language of the kōan takes the subject position while the self of the practitioner experiences itself as the kōan's object or effect. Ruth Sasaki expresses this on behalf of Isshū Miura as follows: "The kōan is taken over by the prepared instrument, and, when a fusion of instrument and device takes place, the state of consciousness is achieved which it is the intent of the kōan to illumine."[11] The monk's subjectivity is the prepared instrument. When the fusion of subject and object occurs, the kōan's subjectivity, its "intention," as Sasaki puts it, is the controlling factor.[12]

An interesting question comes up repeatedly in modern kōan interpretation. Were kōans, and the language of kōans, strange and paradoxical to the Zen masters who originally spoke them? Or is this language paradoxical only from our unenlightened point of view? Does kōan language express in a simple and straightforward way the new "common sense" attained in awakened vision? Is this the language that ultimately corresponds to the way things are in their "suchness"? It seems to me that traditional Ch'an texts will authorize both yes and no answers to these questions, depending upon which set of background ideas are being highlighted. When, for example, the complex interpenetration and interdependency of reality is being stressed as it was in Hua-yen Ch'an, then it makes sense that this language really does correspond to the way things are. When, however, the accent is placed upon the negative function of emptiness and upon the provisional and expedient nature of the bodhisattva's teaching methods, then no correspondence would be thought possible no matter how convoluted and paradoxical. Many elements in early Ch'an up through the writing of the initial kōan texts in the Sung seem to show a preference for the first of these: paradox is worth meditative exertion precisely because this language shows, from an enlightened point of view, something about how things really are. Later, critical developments seem to have made the second alternative more attractive. Noncorrespondence between kōan language and its goal is certainly a safer assertion, since it eludes the necessity of articulating the nature of the correspondence. The weakness of this view, however, is that, in the absence of an understandable relation, kōans take on the appearance of arbitrariness. Why should this language be thought to evoke that goal? In any case, the tendency in subsequent kōan exercises is to repudiate any role for thought and reflection in authentic kōan practice, thus implying that, in enlightenment, the Ch'an master does not necessarily think a deeper correspondence than that which is available to ordinary mind.

Two interesting controversies in the Sung dynasty have come to structure the way we think about these issues today. One of these, between masters Ta-hui and Hung-chih, establishes a dichotomy between the *k'an-hua* or kōan Zen of the Lin-chi (J. Rinzai) tradition and the "silent illumination" or zazen-only Zen of the Ts'ao-tung (J. Sōtō) tradition. The other controversy, also involving Ta-hui, was a disagreement over how kōans were to be handled. In opposition to the contemplative literary tradition that was developing around kōan study—what Ta-hui called "literary or cultured Zen," *wen-tzu Ch'an* (J. *monji Zen*)—Ta-hui proposed an essentially nonreflective kōan practice in which total concentration would be placed upon one word or element in the kōan, its *hua-t'ou* or "main phrase" or "punch line," the place where kōan language literally comes to a head in nonconceptual awareness. From my point of view, the marvelous irony of these divisions is that they would seem to be much more accurately described in reverse. That is, if we look closely at the kind of kōan practice advocated by Ta-hui, which repudiates any narrative, conceptual, or linguistic access to the meaning of the kōan, what we really have remaining is silent illumination. We will return to this point. If, on the other hand, we look at what develops in the Ts'ao-tung or Sōtō tradition, we find exceptional achievements in *k'an-hua Ch'an,* that is, a Zen of "looking at language," and of achievements in "literary Zen," or *wen-tzu Ch'an.*

This twofold divergence in orientation is evident in the two most famous kōan collections themselves. *The Gateless Barrier* foregoes literary and poetic development. Its language is stark and its rationale is the sublation of the conceptual order, breaking through the temptation to encounter the kōan intellectually. *The Blue Cliff Record* is itself a literary masterpiece of both refinement and complexity. The former collection, by its very character, encourages silent concentration on the intellectual barrier to awakening. The latter, by its very character, encourages contemplative and imaginative explorations into the unknown and as yet unexperienced. In *Dōgen and the Kōan Tradition,* Steven Heine rethinks this dichotomy. One thesis of the book is that Dōgen's *Kana Shōbōgenzō* is "thematically and stylistically remarkably similar to the *Blue Cliff Record*"[13] and that, if we stand back from the Rinzai claim that Ta-hui's "shortcut" method is the culmination of the kōan tradition, then we would recognize that Dōgen was himself a kōan master who has taken this genre of Zen literature off onto an entirely different line of development with fundamentally different consequences. Like the *Blue Cliff Record*, Dōgen reverses the direction of abbreviation and opens up the genre of commentary, erasing the distinction between primary source literature and secondary, interpretive commentary, or between text and self. In this genre, the "turning word" may show up anywhere, in Dōgen's criticism of the original kōans, or in the practitioner's own moment of reflection.

Nevertheless, in China, in spite of a historical milieu of enormous literary, philosophical, and cultural achievement in the Sung dynasty, Ta-hui's understanding of the kōan and of Ch'an won the day. Whereas conceptual sophistication would be the hallmark of the Sung in other dimensions of Chinese culture, Ch'an would resist this seduction and establish itself firmly in the nonconceptual. This development occurred primarily through the *hua-t'ou* (J. *watō*) or "critical phrase" style of kōan meditation. Ta-hui insisted that, although kōans may appear to promise advanced insight and understanding, this is not what they in fact offer. As an alternative to meditation on the full narrative of the kōan, therefore, Ta-hui advocated intense focus on one critical phrase, generally one word or element at the climax of the kōan. Furthermore, he maintained that the *hua-t'ou* had no meaning and that any intellectualization, any conceptual thinking at all, would obstruct the possibility of breakthrough. As a corollary to this, Ta-hui warned that the intellectuals who in his day were the ones most interested in kōan meditation would be the least likely to succeed at it, given their tendency to think.[14] His advice to them, therefore, was to cease completely any effort to resolve the kōan and "to give up the conceit that they have the intellectual tools that would allow them to understand it."[15] The primary effort required in this enterprise was a negative one, "nonconceptualization," which, as Robert Buswell explains, came to occupy "the central place ... in *k'an-hua Ch'an.*"[16] Otherwise, in Buswell's words, "there is nothing that need be developed; all the student must do is simply renounce both the hope that there is something that can be achieved through the practice as well as the conceit that he will achieve that result."[17]

Conclusions: On the Decline of the Tradition

The following four points are what I take to be the most important consequences of this development in Chinese Ch'an.

1. The tradition of *k'an-hua Ch'an,* which was generated by a fascination with the masters' linguistic expressions, became in effect silent illumination

Ch'an; the kōan was reabsorbed into zazen. This, of course, was never stated and, in fact, the opposite was what was generally assumed. My reasons derive from a simple comparison of descriptions of practice. After Ta-hui, kōan meditation drew as close to the nonconceptual as it could. No thinking was to be admitted into the exercise. The narrative structure of the kōan was eliminated in the focus on a single point, the *hua-t'ou* or "critical phrase." The critical phrase itself was declared to have no "meaning" (*i*). What remains is an intense, prolonged focus on a single point, whether one is sitting in the lotus posture or not. This description differs in no substantial way from zazen in its non-*vipaśyanā*—that is, in its *śamatha*—forms. Both "looking" (*k'an*) and "language" (*hua*) have been reabsorbed into the "silence" of meditation (*ch'an*).

2. With the ethics of achievement dismissed as a form of conceit, and also the functions of the intellect set aside in religious practice, the role of faith in Ch'an would come to be accentuated, thus bringing Ch'an closer to, and ultimately uniting it with, Pure Land Buddhism. Faith was an essential theme for Ta-hui, as it had been for several other Ch'an Buddhists, including Lin-chi. For Ta-hui, faith was required to make the leap into the nonconceptual. Pride, on the other hand, prevented the practitioner from realizing the futility of gradual awakening, a much maligned doctrine associated with the by then defunct Northern school that assumed substantial benefit from human effort and the quest for achievement. Although it is not clear to me how important a role was played in this doctrinal development by the influential idea of the declining dharma, or the "age of *mo-fa*" (J. *mappō*), the emphasis on faith and the rejection of pride in Ch'an and in Pure Land are strikingly similar. Both scorned intellectual practices and put their entire emphasis on overcoming the latent Confucian "ethics of achievement."

In retrospect, we can note an interesting doctrinal "intersection" that was encountered and determined in the Sung. During this period the notion of the prior "golden age" when many capable Ch'an Buddhists had been awakened was widespread. When they asked themselves what the great masters of the earlier era had in common, however, the universal answer was that they had all rejected their own earlier practice of sūtra study. That is, intellectual achievement was renounced in the end so that sudden breakthrough might occur. What this tended to mean for Sung practitioners was that they could obtain the benefit of the masters' realization by foregoing intellectual study in the first place. Why take it up if all the masters had come to reject it? Yet, another, apparently unnoticed, route that could have been taken from this intersection was the opposite one: they might have realized that what the great masters had in common was prolonged and serious study of the sūtras. Intellectual endeavor had, in fact, been common to all of them even if, at some point in their training, critique and negation of this learning were required. Although they did hold the act of critical rejection in common, they also held in common that which could be rejected but never lost.[18] Some extent of Buddhist learning could easily have been recognized as a precondition for sudden awakening in Ch'an. Sung masters, however, tended to take the rejection literally and nondialectically. In effect, what they instituted was a form of Zen fundamentalism: the tradition came to be increasingly anti-intellectual in orientation and, in the process, reduced its complex heritage to simple formulae for which literal interpretations were thought adequate. The increasing institutional unification of Ch'an and Pure Land Buddhism in the Yuan, Ming, and Ch'ing dynasties, although brought about by numerous factors, is less mysterious intellectually when seen in light of these doctrinal and practical conjunctions.

3. Even during the height of Ch'an in the Sung, but more so later, these developments would send the educated classes in China elsewhere, leading, in the final analysis, to the construction of a new tradition that would overwhelm Ch'an Buddhism by drawing several of its elements up into a more encompassing cultural framework. Already in the Sung an innovative *tao-hsüeh* tradition was gaining the upper hand in this stilted debate. Although this tradition benefited greatly from what Ch'an had to offer—meditative practices, sudden awakening, monastic retreat, and so on—it made more than ample room for intellectual practices as fundamental to the Way. Some of these intellectual practices were drawn from and modeled after earlier developments in Chinese Buddhism, doctrinal advances made in T'ien-t'ai, Hua-yen, and early Ch'an. Although it is now clear that the relationship of influence between Ch'an and Neo-Confucianism was multidirectional, with both traditions benefiting from the exchange, it is also clear that Ch'an drew the least benefit from this opposition because of its entrenchment in doctrines that condemned intellectual practice. Instead of regrouping to face the challenge of *tao-hsüeh* by probing ever more deeply into its own Buddhist and Chinese heritage, Ch'an opted for the silence of sudden illumination. This choice, however, had the effect of condemning Ch'an to its future marginal status in China; as the dynasties rolled by, the Ch'an contribution to Chinese culture would become increasingly insignificant.

4. Although Ch'an, for most practical purposes now merged with Pure Land Buddhism, would maintain itself in Chinese society through overwhelmingly conservative policies and practices, what creativity there has been in the tradition can be found precisely where, according to Ch'an theory, it should not be found: in the domain of Ch'an theory. What we find in some Yüan and Ming dynasty Ch'an texts is a reemergence of rational, metaphysical construction—the effort to "explain" how it is that Ch'an practices link up with reality.[19] No doubt this necessity was foisted upon Ch'an monks by historical circumstances that, for whatever reason, were allowing Neo-Confucianism to bypass Ch'an. Neo-Confucian critiques of Ch'an were widely successful, even when unsophisticated, because, for one thing, Ch'an Buddhists were by then so ill equipped to reason and argue in opposition to them. Eventually, however,

cultural decline did evoke a response; Ch'an Buddhists began to give reasons to justify their practice. These reasons naturally took metaphysical form: how is reality constructed such that it makes sense to focus all of your energies into meditation on a single "meaningless" phrase from the ancient masters? Psychological explanations were required too: how is the mind constructed such that is makes sense to drive yourself into a mental impasse? Neo-Confucian intellectuals, of course, argued that it made no sense, a conclusion applauded by mainstream advocates of common sense. Ch'an apologists thus had their work cut out for them, and their response was in fact a new wave of creative Ch'an literature. The creativity of this work is limited, however, because its authors could not see that their own writings in meta-kōan language went directly against the conclusions that they had set out to justify. They were unable—because of the power of doctrinal predilections to the contrary—to recognize that "the one who was right then doing the explaining," to borrow Lin-chi's phrase, was not the nonconceptual, nonnarrative self that their doctrine valorized. Although these doctrines concerning what a kōan is and what a human mind is were innovative, they could not encompass their own status as doctrinal assertions. They lacked the reflexive sophistication that had made many of the great Ch'an masters famous in the first place.

This split between kōans and the meta-discourse about kōans is heightened even further and modeled for us in English in the work of D. T. Suzuki. It is interesting to note that in his own writings about the kōan, Suzuki draws heavily upon this Yüan/Ming explanatory literature. This was naturally the literature most applicable to Suzuki's task, that of explaining to us in an entirely different cultural context why the great Zen masters said and did such "strange" things. Suzuki's own writings don't fit the definition of Zen that they propose. Transmitting Zen in the presence of Americans and Europeans in the mid-twentieth century called for some heavy-duty metaphysics and a lot of explaining. Too much "Zen Mind" would undermine the task. Instead of just giving us unadulterated "unreason" when he wrote about kōans, Suzuki was forced to step back and articulate "The Reason of Unreason," which is what he entitled his best essay on the kōan tradition. He knew in advance that he would have to give some very good "reasons" and that, unless Zen appeared to be the most reasonable alternative under the circumstances, it would simply be rejected. As it turns out, his reasoning was excellent and many of us were persuaded or at least influenced. Even now, when scholars regularly criticize the writings of Suzuki for their misrepresentation of the Ch'an/Zen tradition, we can see that Suzuki's task has been impressively accomplished. "Zen," whatever it is, still symbolizes for many some dimension at least of "the great matter." The reasons Suzuki provided for us may now be inadequate, but their one-time persuasiveness abides in the fact that we do not just drop the subject. Even if it takes a radically new form of metaphysics to pull it off, we would still like to learn how to hear "the sound of one hand clapping."

NOTES

1. *Chung-feng ho-shang kuang-lu,* trans. Isshū Miura and Ruther Fuller Sasaki, in *The Zen Kōan* (New York: Harcourt, Brace & World, 1965), pp. 4–6.

2. Ibid., p. 6.

3. Ibid., pp. 5, 6.

4. Ibid., p. 7.

5. Zenkei Shibayama, *Zen Comments on the Mumonkan* (New York: Harper and Row, 1974), p. 19.

6. I borrow this expression from Robert E. Buswell, "The 'Shortcut' Approach of *K'an-hua* Meditation: The Evolution of a Practical Subitism in Chinese Ch'an Buddhism" in Peter Gregory, ed., *Sudden and Gradual: Approaches to Enlightenment in Chinese Buddhism* (Honolulu: University Press of Hawaii, 1987), p. 347.

7. D. T. Suzuki, "The Kōan Exercise," in *Essays in Zen Buddhism,* Second Series (New York: Samuel Weiser, 1953), p. 94.

8. D. T. Suzuki, "The Reason of Unreason: The Kōan Exercise" in *Zen Buddhism,* ed. William Barrett (New York: Doubleday and Co., 1956), p. 151.

9. Shibayama, *Zen Comments,* p. 19.

10. Ironically, however, at precisely the time this name was coined, Ch'an Buddhists began to move in the opposite direction, toward a focus on the *hua-t'ou,* which, while still linguistic, was intended to sidestep language altogether.

11. Miura and Sasaki, *The Zen Kōan,* p. xi.

12. If this is what is meant, then Sasaki would be better off in English reversing the structure of the sentence before this one: "To say that the kōan is used as a subject of meditation is to state the fact incorrectly" (p. xi). Instead this would be "correct," if by "subject" Sasaki means "object," as we commonly and mistakenly do in English, then this statement makes sense of what follows. When we say "subject matter," we mean the "object" that will be taken up by the subject, the objective matter of concern to the subject.

13. Steven Heine, *Dōgen and the Kōan Tradition: A Tale of Two Shōbōgenzō Texts* (Albany, N.Y.: SUNY Press, 1994), p. 218.

14. "Training on this path is not bothered by a lack of intelligence; it is bothered by excessive intelligence. It is not bothered by a lack of understanding; it is instead bothered by excessive understanding" (*Ta-hui yü-lu* 29, T.47:935a23–24, cited from Buswell, "The 'Short-cut' Approach," p. 371).

15. Buswell, "The 'Shortcut' Approach," p. 350.

16. Ibid, p. 350.

17. Ibid, p. 351.

18. A similar point is made by Bernard Faure: "The point of these spiritual exercises is to go through all mental artifacts, through the conventional truths of *upāya,* before eventually discarding them upon reaching ultimate truth. But the process or itinerary is not irrelevant, for it is somehow inscribed in the arrival point," *The Rhetoric of Immediacy: A Cultural Critique of Chan/Zen Buddhism* (Princeton, N.J.: Princeton University Press, 1991), p. 53.

19. For example, from the Yuan dynasty, *The Extensive Record of Master Chung-feng,* and from the Ming dynasty, *The Mirror for Ch'an Studies* complied by T'ui-yin.

8

Ikkyū and Kōans

ALEXANDER KABANOFF

An Eccentric Monk of the Muromachi Era

Ikkyū Sōjun (1394–1481) was one of the most famous Zen monks in Muromachi-era Japan (1333–1573) because of his unconventional and eccentric behavior (not by chance he often called himself Kyōun, the "Crazy Cloud"), his unorthodox views, and his artistic abilities. His reputation as a popular hero of amusing stories has long been preserved, and his life story has been enriched by legends and anecdotes that are well-known among Japanese children today. We will examine Ikkyū's role as an original thinker and a versatile poet who left a collection of poems in Chinese writing or *kanbun,* the *Kyōun-shū* (*An Anthology of the Crazy Cloud*), many of which deal with traditional Zen kōans in innovative and creative ways.

Writing poetry in Chinese was a common practice for many Japanese monks, who left an enormous legacy known as *gozan bungaku* or the "literature of the Five Mountains" of medieval Zen monasticism. But Ikkyū's poetry contrasts strikingly with the typically formal works of *gozan* poets, who sought to pursue Chinese standards of secular poetry rather than to promote religious values. As a result, *gozan* poetry was often fossilized and artificial. In Ikkyū's poems, however, we find a somewhat clumsy and less refined, but at the same time a much more sincere and individualistic manner of writing. Robust and sometimes shocking revelations make Ikkyū's collection at once more attractive and more embarrassing than most of the works of his contemporaries. In particular, the treatment of traditional Buddhist subjects in the poems is original, highly personal, and paradoxical.[1]

Hardly anyone before or after Ikkyū used poetry to such an extent as an expression of the most intimate feelings, spiritual turmoil, or reflections on the meaning of life. His poems are not purely didactic considerations or admonitions, though in part they were written exactly for that purpose, as is apparent from some of the titles. Rather they are eloquent disclosures of his never-ending search for the Absolute, without any hope of finding a final solution, and they have no peer among *gozan* poetry. The poems are permeated with despair and anger, accusations against the vices of fellow monks and other countrymen, and nostalgic praise for the blessed, golden age of former Chinese or Japanese Zen masters. The *Kyōun-shū* as a whole may be labeled a "poetic confession of faith" or a "picaresque autobiography." It abounds in deep reflections on Zen philosophical principles and memorable events from the history of the sect, as well as self-criticism and even overtly erotic verses.

However, grasping the meaning of Ikkyū's poetry, composed in verses of four lines with a total of twenty-eight Sino-Japanese characters, sometimes seems quite difficult or nearly impossible because of the repeated use of the same characters with various meanings, as well as hidden allusions or uncommon expressions which seem to reflect an absence of any direct, logical connection between each of the four lines. Scholars and translators frequently argue about the intention and exact meaning of his poems and try to trace and dismantle possible sources by browsing through standard Zen writings or the verses of classical Chinese poets. However, even if certain lines are convincingly proved as intentional borrowings, the whole meaning may still remain elusive. Therefore only an exhaustive reading of famous Ch'an/Zen writings can provide a clue to the meaning of Ikkyū's poetry. These works include the *Lin-chi lu* (J. *Rinzai roku*), *Ching-te ch'uan-teng lu* (J. *Keitoku dentōroku*), *Wu-teng hui-yüan* (J. *Gotō egen*), and kōan collections such as the *Wu-men kuan* (J. *Mumonkan*) and *Pi-yen lu* (J. *Hekiganroku*), as well as the "recorded sayings" (C. *yü-lu*, J. *goroku*) of Hsü-t'ang (Ikkyū proclaimed himself the incarnation of Hsü-t'ang in Japan) or of Daiō or Daitō, the founders of the Daitokuji branch of the Rinzai sect to which Ikkyū belonged.

It is impossible in one short chapter to delineate even in a cursory manner all the possible ways that kōans were used in Ikkyū's poetry. I will provide only a few examples that show Ikkyū's attitude toward kōan practice, in addition to some cases for which allusions to certain traditional cases turn the poems themselves into kōans.[2]

Persistent Gratitude toward Yün-men and Kōan Collections

Ikkyū attained his first *satori* or Zen awakeing in 1418. At this time, he was reflecting on a kōan dealing with the 60 blows that Tung-shan was said to have promised Yün-men. Nevertheless, Ikkyū's satori apparently occurred when he heard a blind musician chanting a story from the *Heike monogatari* about Gio, a concubine of the powerful Taira Kiyomori; she lost his love and in distress became a nun. The extant sources do not reveal any connection between the Gio story, the aforementioned kōan, and Ikkyū's satori. Because Yün-men (864–949) was implicitly responsible for his first satori, throughout his life Ikkyū felt much indebted to the Chinese master and often included overt and covert allusions to him in his poems. For example, in the poem "Waves of Peach Blossoms" (no. 35 in the *Kyōun-shū*) Ikkyū wrote:

> Along the waves, together with the combers—a lot of red dust.
> I see again the peach blossoms—in spring of the third moon.
> Resentment flows by for three lives and sixty kalpas.
> Annually, dry gills and scales lay under the sun by the Dragon Gates.

The main images in this poetic kōan can be traced to popular Chinese concepts connected with seasonal changes. The phrase "waves of peach blossoms" indicates the third month, when falling peach petals cover the river water. According to Chinese beliefs, exactly at that time carps gather before the rapids known as the Dragon Gates, trying to jump over in order to change into dragons. The overcoming of the Dragon Gate in the Zen tradition became associated with "passing through a barrier," or the attainment of satori. Ikkyū also includes in his poem a quotation from Yün-men's "turning phrase," "Along the waves, together with the combers."

The poem pivots on the kōan from the *Pi-yen lu* (case 60) that deals with Yün-men, who raised his staff and announced that it was a dragon that would swallow heaven and earth. Later on Yün-men added, "Where will you be able to find mountains, rivers, and the great earth?" The kōan is followed by a verse:

> This staff swallows Heaven and Earth,
> Vain will be the chattering about "waves of peach blossoms."
> The parch-tailed ones will not grasp clouds and mists,
> For what purpose did those with dried gills lose their life
>   and soul?[3]

A poem (no. 47) under the title "The Hundredth Anniversary of Daitō Kokushi's Death" evidently hints at a verse in case 24 in the *Pi-yen lu:*

> Many of Buddha's descendants passed through the Main Gates.
> I alone am wandering among rivers and seas.
> Where will the next Communal Feast Festival be held?
> White clouds cook rice on the top of Wu-t'ai-shan mountain.

The case story is about the nun Liu Te-mo, who visited Kuei-shan Lin-yu and was greeted with a belittling question, "Is it you, old cow, who came to me?" (One has to keep in mind that Kuei-shan called himself "a water buffalo.") Mo answered, "Tomorrow will be the Communal Feast Festival (C. *ta-hui-chai,* J. *taiesai*) on Mount Wu-t'ai, and the teacher has just left that place." Kuei-shan lay down and fell asleep. Mo immediately left.[4] Since the Six Dynasties period Mount Wu-t'ai had been a popular pilgrimage site where official ceremonies beseeching for prosperity for the country were held annually. The last line of the verse alludes to a poem by Tung-shan preserved in the *Ku-ts'un-su yü-lu* (J. *Kosonshoku goroku*):

> Clouds cook rice on the top of Mount Wu-t'ai-shan.
> A dog urinates before the steps of the Buddha Hall.
> A banner-pole is used for frying rice flat-cakes.
> Three monkeys bolter daybreak through a sieve.

The first two lines in Tung-shan's poem are borrowed, in turn, from case 96 of the *Pi-yen lu;*[5] "Clouds on Mount Wu-t'ai-shan cook rice; a dog pisses to the sky before the old Buddha hall."[6]

Another poem in the *Kyōun-shū* (no. 45) is an illustration of case no. 83 in the *Pi-yen lu:*[7] "While Yün-men was addressing monks he asked, 'An old Buddha and a naked pole are communicating. What is the meaning of it?' He himself gave the answer, 'Clouds rise on the Southern Peak; it rains on the Northern Mountain.' " The verse reads:

> How can the "Small Bride" marry P'eng-lai?
> The "cloud-rain" this evening is like in a previous dream.
> In the morning he is on T'ien-t'ai, and in the evening on Nan-yüeh.
> I wonder, where could I find Shao-yang?

The "Small Bride" is a tiny island in the Yangtze River in Chiang-hsi province, and P'eng-lai (initially a mythic island where Taoist immortals abide) is also the name for a rock at the same place on the opposite bank. In the popular imagination the island and the rock were believed to be spouses. The second line contains complex allusive associations. The kōan pivots on the interrelation of two incompatible phenomena. As an answer to an illogical question Yün-men used an equally absurd phrase. Ikkyū further plays on images implying a love affair and shifts the content of the kōan into the sexual sphere. The word *sōkō* ("to communicate") in Yün-men's question also has the meaning "to copulate," while in the Chinese tradition the "cloud-rain" is a standard metaphor for a love-union, a phrase often exploited by Ikkyū in his poetry.

The third line contains the names of two sacred mountains in Chinese Buddhism, T'ien-t'ai and Nan-yüeh. It reverses the poetic flow from sexual associations back into a religious context. The former mountain was the abode of Chih-yi, the patriarch of the T'ien-t'ai school, while the latter was a dwelling place of his teacher Hui-ssu. As a result, the mountains are separated by a small geographical distance yet preserve a spiritual affinity between master and disciple. Modern interpreter Hirano Sōjō suggests that the line alludes to a story in the *Hsü-t'ang lu:* "A monk was asked, 'What is your strategy, if you cannot say anything?' The monk responded, 'If I am not on T'ien-t'ai mountain, I am on Nan-yüeh mountain.' "⁸ Also, Shao-yang was another name of Yün-men, the main character of the kōan that Ikkyū used as the subject for this poem.

Another poem (no. 51) has as an introduction a kōan story that was borrowed from case no. 82 in the *Ts'ung jung lu* (J. *Shōyōroku*) collection and that deals with the merciful bodhisattva Kuan-yin (J. Kannon) in one of her 33 manifestations: "Concerning the words, 'heard a sound and attained the Way, saw forms and purified the mind,' Yün-men said, 'The bodhisattva Kuan-yin took the money and went to buy millet-cakes.' Then he lost his heart and said: 'However, from the very beginning they were just ordinary dumplings.' "⁹ Ikkyū interprets the story in the following way:

> When Kannon was manifested in the shape of a servant-maid,
> She fed her spirit dumplings and millet-cakes.
> Unforgettable are things I "had seen and heard" in former days,
> Just before me is the person who played a flute in Shan-yang.

The poet tries to stress the lack of any essential difference between millet-cakes and dumplings, because their only purpose is "to feed the spirit" of an enlightened person who is not supposed to make a distinction between these two material objects. The last line recalls words from the poem "Listening to a Flute in the Fei-ch'eng Garden" by Tou Mu (742–822) and also alludes to an old story from the Chin dynasty days. Hsiang Hsü was one of the "Seven Bamboo Grove Wisemen." When he heard about the execution of his friend Hsi K'ang in Shan-yang, he broke his lute into pieces. Later on, when passing by Hsi K'ang's former dwelling in Shan-yang, he suddenly heard sounds of a flute, recollected his late friend, and composed the "Ode of Recollections on the Past" (*Wen hsüan*, vol. 16).

Implicitly Yün-men is also present in a poem (from an eight-verse cycle, nos. 432–439) about "Ch'en the Sandals-Maker":

> They babble about the Way, debate about Zen, multiply profits
>   and glory.
> During the uprising, by his own efforts he created a fortress of
>   lamentations.
> In vain he slammed the door to break Shao-yang's leg,
> But also broke the feelings of itinerant Zen monks.

Ch'en (real name: Chao-chou Tao-tsung, 780–877) inherited the Dharma from Huang-po and lived as a recluse at the Lung-hsing-ssu temple in Chao-chou. According to a tradition, he earned a living to support his aged mother by making straw sandals and selling them. The biography of Mu-chou Tao-tsung (another name was Ch'en Tsun-su) in the *Wu-teng hui-yüan* (vol. 4) reports that when the rebellious troops of Huang Ch'ao entered the city, Mu-chou produced huge straw sandals and hung them on the city-gate. Huang Ch'ao could not take the sandals off the gate, so he proclaimed Mu-chou a great sage and left the city. The Yün-men (Shao-yang) biography in the *Wu-teng hui-yüan,* as well as the case in the *Pi-yen lu* (case no. 6), contains a story about how he thrice came to Mu-chou asking for an instruction. When Mu-chou cried, "Speak, speak!" Yün-men got embarrassed and Mu-chou tried to push him out. Then the master slammed the door with such a force that it broke Yün-men's leg. At that moment, Yün-men made a loud cry and attained a "great awakening."[10]

Ikkyū's poem starts with a condemnation of Zen discourses and traditional kōan practice. In the next line he makes a shift to praise Mu-chou for his courage at a critical moment. Perhaps Ikkyū evaluates his behavior during the time of rebellion as being more appropriate when considered from the standpoint of Zen teaching. On the other hand, Mu-chou's arrogant attitude, glorified in many stories, is treated by Ikkyū with disgust as being unnecessarily cruel. In other poems Ikkyū consistently condemns similar rude methods of instruction. The last line ironically turns the statement upside down in calling the great spiritual experience the "breaking of the feelings of itinerant Zen monks." After many years of wandering and visiting a number of distinguished masters, Yün-men attained satori while staying with Mu-chou, but he still was rejected and sent to Hsüeh-feng, from whom he inherited the Dharma seal. The last line may also be interpreted as a capping phrase for the kōan.

Yün-men is mentioned again by Ikkyū in a reference to case 8 from the *Pi-yen lu,* which introduces poem no. 55: "At the end of summer retreat Ts'ui-yen addressed the community, 'Since the very beginning of the summer I have been talking to you. Look! Do I still have eyebrows left?' Pao-fu said, 'A person who becomes a robber has an uneasy heart.' 'They will grow anew,' said Ch'ang-ch'ing. 'Take care! A barrier [*kuan*]!' replied Yün-men."[11] Ikkyū provides an elucidation of the kōan and mentions Ts'ui-yen Ling-ts'an (d. ca. 950), Pao-fu Ts'ung-tien (d. 928), Ch'ang-ch'ing Hui-chi (854–932), and Yün-men Wen-yen (d. 949) in metaphorical form:

> "The kōan on eyebrows" is like a thorn inside mud:
> Pao-fu and Yün-men chose the same road.
> Ch'ang-ch'ing concealed his body, but manifested its reflection.
> To the south of the tower there is the moon of the third wake.

The Buddhists believed that a person who distorts the Buddhist Dharma or Teaching will become a leper, and the first symptom of the disease is the falling out of eyebrows. Thus Ts'ui-yen's question about his eyebrows is to be interpreted in this vein. Pao-fu hints that those who commit sins must become aware of this consequence Ch'ang-ch'ing tries to reassure the master by promising that the eyebrows will grow anew, while Yün-men abolishes the opposition by an indefinite exclamation "*Kuan!*" In the colloquial language of the T'ang and Sung periods, the word *kuan* also had the implication of "what the hell!" or "take care!" although the literal meaning of the character was "a border" or "an obstacle." Thus the two disciples shared their master's concerns, or as Daiō claims in his capping phrase to this kōan, "both of them followed the same road but not the same gauge." In contrast, by his indeterminate answer Ch'ang-ch'ing silently accepted the sins of Ts'ui-yen, and by assuring the teacher that his eyebrows would grow anew he feigned a stance of unconcern. Also, the first line alludes to Daiō's capping phrase, "Take care not to step on a thorn hidden inside mud," implying that the real meaning is hidden from ignorant persons. The last line contains a hint that for the person who grasped the meaning of the kōan "the moon of the third wake" will immediately appear in his enlightened mind.

Kōans in the Daitokuji Tradition

Ikkyū considered himself a follower of the transmission line of Japanese masters Daiō Kokushi and Daitō Kokushi that became the mainstream tradition of Daitokuji temple in medieval Kyoto. Daitō was known for his innovative capping phrase commentaries on kōans that were an important part of the Daitokuji oral tradition. Allusions to both of these spiritual predecessors are frequently found in Ikkyū's poetry.[12] The first poem in the cycle, " 'Three Turning Phrases'[13] of Daitō Kokushi" (no. 28), is prefaced by the phrase, "In the morning I 'connect our eyebrows' and in the evening 'join our shoulders.' What a person am I?"

> I have just passed a barrier, another one is before me.
> One cannot climb following only old samples and patterns.
> These strange lichih fruits have a heavenly taste.
> The name from the T'ien-pao era descended to people.

The verse focuses on the experience of Daitō, who as a disciple of Daiō grasped the meaning of the one-word kōan or "The Barrier" (*kuan*) and attained satori, only to face immediately another barrier. Ikkyū emphasizes the impossibility of realizing the highest truth only through textual sources and kōan training. He includes in the text a reference to delicious lichih fruits, the daily meal of Yang Kuei-fei, a consort of the T'ang Emperor Hsüan-tsung (712–756). The tragic fate of Yang Kuei-fei, murdered on the demand of soldiers who accused her of being the main source of turmoil brought on by the An Lu-shan rebellion during the T'ien-pao era (742–755), was repeatedly referred to by Ikkyū in his poetry as a classic example of a femme fatale and unhappy beauty at the same time. "The heavenly taste" of lichih put an end to the Heavenly Treasure (Tien-pao) era of rule.

Another example of this type of poetry is Ikkyū's reference (no. 157) to the "three turning phrases" of Chao-chou—"A clay Buddha can't pass across a river; a wooden Buddha can't pass through a fire; a metal Buddha can't pass through a furnace"—in which he tries to solve in a single blow the three problems of Chao-chou:

> A poem is finished: sorrowful thoughts resemble a love song.
> For many years I was listening to a night rain on a lonely bed.
> Who had produced a flute tune from the tower?
> The melody stopped abruptly; green peaks are across the river.

The "three turning phrases" of Chao-chou are mentioned in *Pi-yen lu* case 96,[14] although Ikkyū's poem contains no direct allusions or comments on the case. The more obvious explanation happens here to be the least intricate. Ikkyū compares three insoluble situations from the kōan with his own inability to combine a strict monastic lifestyle on the mountain slopes with his unceasing ties to earthly joys. He solves the kōan in the last line's words, "green peaks are across the river." The poem has been completed, the love tune has suddenly become silent, all "three turning phrases" are effectively "capped" by a magnificent landscape that delimits any mundane passions and invites one to commune with and dissolve into its beauty.

By introducing some of his poems with a kōan case, Ikkyū often turned the poems into condensed and allegorical comments on the source cases, as with the introduction to poem no. 44: "A monk asked Yen-t'ou, 'What will happen if an old sail will not be raised?' 'A small fish will swallow a larger one,' answered Yen-t'ou. 'And what happens after the sail has been raised?' asked the monk. 'A donkey is nibbling grass in the backyard,' Yen-t'ou replied." The main character of the kōan is Yen-t'ou (827–887), who initially belonged to the Lin-chi school but later turned to the Kuei-shan school. The kōan may be found in a variety of texts, including the *Ching-te ch'uan-teng lu, Tsu-t'ang chi, Wu-teng hui-yüan, Ch'an-men sung chi,* and *Ch'an-lin leichu;* Hirano argues that Ikkyū's version is closest to the last of these.[15] According to the Zen tradition, Hsü-t'ang (1184–1269), whom Ikkyū believed to be his spiritual Chinese forefather, attained satori after meditation on this very anecdote. Transmitted to Ikkyū by Daiō Kokushi, the kōan had great importance within the Daitokuji tradition.[16] Ikkyū comments on the kōan through allusions to a few other cases and supplants the original content with additional obvious and hidden connotations:

> Cold and heat, sufferings and pleasures bring shame to mind.
> Ears are originally only two pieces of skin.
> One, two, three—yes!—three, two, one.
> With a single twist of his hand Nan-ch'üan ripped the cat.

The first line alludes to the third of the "reflections" of Fo-yen Ching-yüan (1067–1120): "Sufferings and pleasures, anticipation and concordance—the Way is in between movement and immobility, cold and heat—I feel ashamed, repenting."[17]

Hirano, referring to an oral Daitokuji kōan tradition, considers that the questions asked of Yen-t'ou correspond to anticipation and concordance. When a sail is not raised, the wind prevents a boat's movement, whereas after it has been raised, the wind pushes the boat forward. I would like to stress another opposition: the first situation is associated with stillness, and the second one with movement. Then the whole poem may be seen as a cryptic solution of the kōan. The first line contains two of the four expressions mentioned in "Fo-yen's reflections," although logically they have no connection with the kōan, and the next two lines traditionally have been associated with this kōan. In the oral Daitokuji tradition, the words "ears are only two pieces of skin" were applied as a capping phrase to the first answer in the kōan, "A small fish will swallow a larger one," while the words "fangs and teeth are just bones" were a capping phrase to the second answer in the kōan.[18] However, this cannot be considered the only true answer.

According to the oral Daitokuji tradition, to the words "A small fish swallows a larger one" there is applied the capping phrase "Five, four, three, two, one." Sonja Arntzen considers the numerical image in its mirrorlike pattern to be an obvious illustration of the duality principle.[19] The *Daitō Kokushi goroku* or recorded sayings text states that one day, having ascended to the hall, Daitō announced:

> If one attains in his heart a state inexpressible in words, it will pertain. When one wishes to express in words something that is impossible to comprehend by the heart, it will be "seven, six, five, four, three, two, one." [Someone asked,] "And what will happen if one has attained something in the heart and may express it in words?" After a pause he added, "After flowers have blossomed no efforts are necessary to make them grow. A spring wind will take care of them."[20]

Perhaps in the above poem Ikkyū attempts to solve the problem by linking two figural sequences. The duality turns naturally into nonduality, and both number-orders conjoin into a single unit with an apex in the very middle of the line. The emphatic character *hsi* (translated here as "yes!" just to keep it in the translation) lacks any specific meaning and performs in Chinese poetry only an exclamatory function. The character *hsi* in the Japanese is also a homophone for the number "four" (C. *ssu*, but in Japanese both are pronounced as "shi"), becoming a pivot for the ascending and descending numerical order.[21]

The last line of Ikkyū's poem alludes to a famous kōan from the *Wu-men kuan* (case 14)[22] or the *Pi-yen lu* (case 63): "Once Nan-ch'üan noticed monks of the eastern and western halls disputing about a cat. Then he took the cat and announced, 'If anyone talks, I will not kill him.' Nobody pronounced a word. Then Nan-ch'üan ripped the cat apart."[23] A solution of the kōan is found in case 64 of the *Pi-yen lu:* "Nan-ch'üan related what happened to Chao-chou and asked what he would have done if he had been present at that time. Chou took off his straw sandals, put them on his head, and left the hall. 'If you had been there, the cat would still be alive,' Nan-ch'üan exclaimed."[24]

Respect for Chinese Patriarchs

The names of famous Chinese Zen patriarchs are often mentioned by Ikkyū, and the names of the early masters Lin-chi, Te-shan, Pai-chang, and Kuei-shan are found especially frequently. One of the poems, called "A Man But Not External Objects Has Been Grasped" (no. 14), is included in the cycle on the "Four Alternatives of Lin-chi":

> The names of Pai-chang and Kuei-shan still exist;
> Will not the fox and the water buffalo stay forever?
> In the temple of the past dynasty there are no more monks.
> Yellow leaves and autumn wind whirl above the tower.

This poem illustrates the state of mind after the subject has dissolved into the object: any trace of sentient beings has disappeared and only the purity of nature remains unchanged. Such a position was typical of the materialistic school of Sarvastivada Buddhism. Once Lin-chi said, "The spring sun shines and covers the earth with silk. A baby's hair hangs down in gray threads." That is, a person (subject) loses his self-importance when faced with the outer universe (object) embodied in the phenomena of nature. The subject tries to extrapolate himself into that illusory outer world, and such a view is as incredulous as gray hair for a baby. The world remains harmonious notwithstanding—or because of—the absence of human beings in it.

The names Pai-chang Huai-hai and Kuei-shan Ling-yu in the Ch'an tradition are associated with kōan stories about the wild fox and the water buffalo, respectively. The story about the wild fox is reproduced in *Wu-men kuan* case 2 and numerous other kōan collections. According to this case, whenever Pai-chang delivered sermons before his disciples, an unfamiliar old man appeared in the assembly. One day after the sermon was over, he did not leave the hall with the other monks. Pai-chang asked about his identity and the man answered that in the distant past he was a monk at this very temple, but because of his improper use of a turning word he was punished by being reborn for 500 lives as a wild fox. After the talk with Pai-chang the fox attained awakening and, as a result, became released from his wild fox transfiguration. He proclaimed that his corpse would be found behind the temple compound and asked that it be buried with the standard rite for Buddhist monks. That day the monks indeed found a dead wild fox and cremated him.[25] In a poem titled "Pai-chang's Wild Fox" (no. 48) the content on the surface appears completely dissociated from the case:

> A thousand mountains, ten thousand rivers, a monk's hut.
> This year I will surpass the fifth decade of my life.
> But thoughts on my pillow are not senile yet.
> As if in dreams I go on reading books of my youth.

Ikkyū juxtaposes his 50 years with the 500 lives of the monk in the case about Pai-chang and implicitly mentions his attachment to the traditional elegant (*fūryū*) style of aesthetics as represented in the "books of my youth" (which perhaps actually refers to erotic writings). The subject of karmic predestination and its compatibility with the content of the "wild fox" kōan are almost removed yet transferred into another level of sensual attachment to worldly pleasures that the poet has not yet completely suppressed.

On Three Categories of Handicapped Ones

The cycle of poems nos. 58–60 explicitly takes its roots in case 88 of the *Pi-yen lu*, where Hsüan-sha Shih-lei (835–908) mentions three categories of diseases: "Masters in different regions of China claim that they are spreading the Dharma and paying homage. But how can they instruct the three categories of deceased? The blind ones do not see the movements of their fingers, striking, putting down hands or sweeping the ground. The deaf ones do not hear the *samādhi* expressed by words. The mute ones cannot confirm that they had realized the Dharma. How can they be instructed? However, if such people cannot be instructed, it means that the Buddha's Law has no miraculous properties."[26]

The poem "Blindness" (no. 58) advises that one rely on the invisible and not be attached to visible phenomena:

> The writings from the Sacred Mountain were not inherited by the
>   Blind Donkey.
> Twenty-eight and six patriarchs are to be ashamed of it.
> How can he reach the place of glimmering light?
> His companion has a copper look and iron eyes.

Ikkyū often called himself "Blind Donkey" (*Katsuro*), hinting at the words of Lin-chi that after his death the Dharma will pass to a blind donkey. Perhaps Ikkyū, who refused to accept the "seal of enlightenment" (*inka*) from his teacher Kasō Sōdon, meant that he had obtained the real "transmission of the Dharma outside written words" in accord with the highly praised Zen practice of discounting and discarding scriptures. The second line mentions the transmission of the Dharma from 28 Indian and 6 Chinese Ch'an patriarchs (from Bodhidharma to Hui-neng). "The place of glimmering light" is obviously the Pure Land (*jōdo*) of Amida Buddha, where his believers were supposed to be reborn and to enjoy eternal bliss. The "copper look and iron eyes" mentioned in a commentary on the *gāthā* of case 1 in the *Pi-yen lu* is a valued trait of an unusual person.

The next poem in the cycle, "Deafness" (no. 59), praises those who can hear melodies of the "stringless harp" and appreciate them:

> Picked up a fly-whisk and made a cry like the hundred-times
>   melted gold.
> Because Huai-hai from his very birth had deep ears,
> Who else might have such perfect hearing abilities
> To listen to soundless melodies of a stringless harp?

The poem is pivoted on a story about Pai-chang in the *Ching-te ch'uan-teng lu* (vol. 6).[27] Once he visited his master Ma-tsu Tao-yi. Upon his arrival, the master took from the meditation seat a fly-whisk and raised it up. "Do you use it or not?" asked Pai-chang. Ma-tsu returned the fly-whisk to its place. Pai-chang kept silent, and then Ma-tsu produced a loud cry. For three days after this Pai-chang was nearly deaf and could not hear anything but Ma's voice, yet he was able to understand the meaning of Ma-tsu's illuminative cry because he naturally had exceptionally perceptive (literally "deep") ears.

In the poem "Muteness" Ikkyū once again insists that an enlightened person does not need any words to express his spiritual experience:

> With a single phrase he wished to let out the content of his heart.
> But the tongue stuck to the palate: only a weak "hi-hi"!
> Ling-yün did not respond to Ch'ang-sheng's answer:
> Who knows what golden words were in his heart.

Ikkyū's poem alludes to a story from Ling-yün's biography in the *Ching-te ch'uan-teng lu* (vol. 11): "Ch'ang-sheng asked, 'How could life appear before the chaos was separated?' 'In the womb of the hall pillar there is a fetus,' answered Ling-yün. 'And what was after the separation of the chaos?' 'A lonely cloud floating across the sky.' 'Was it put into motion by the sky?' The master did not give any answer. 'In this case, if water were pure, fish would not live there,' said Ch'ang-sheng. The master again kept silent." Ling-yün's silence is a wordless answer that cuts off any discrimination: "the chaos" means complete nonduality, "a fetus in the hall's pillar" corresponds to the state prior to differentiation, and "a cloud in the sky" refers to the level of provisional understanding by means of the realm of differentiation.

Ambivalent Attitudes toward Kōan Practice

Ikkyū's attitude concerning the use of kōans as well as the importance of famous kōan collections was rather ambivalent. Although kōan cases are often
used as sources for his poetry, the degenerate practice of using standard collections in Japanese monasteries in a routine, mechanical fashion was looked
on with great disdain. In the poem "Reading the Preface to the *Pi-yen lu*" (no.
138) Ikkyū postulates his views on one of the most voluminous and prestigious
of the kōan collections that is nearly inexhaustably exploited in so many of
his poems:

> Admonitions from Shen-shan cost a hundred golden pieces.
> Having burnt them, he hoped to save both the present and the
>   past ones.
> Stop your disputes about the cold ashes!
> The "merciful old hags" destroyed the Teaching.

The *Pi-yen lu* or *Blue Cliff Record* is perhaps the most famous and widely used
among the kōan collections, and Ikkyū seems to have known it by heart. The
collection of a hundred short cases accompanied by extensive comments, illus-
trative verses, and capping phrases was first compiled by a Sung monk, Hsüeh-
tou Ch'ung-hsien (980–1052). Later on, Yüan-wu K'o-ch'in (1063–1135) appended them with his own comments, a version that was said to have been
burned by Yüan-wu's main disciple, Ta-hui Tsung-kao (1089–1163). The edition of 1308 contains a few prefaces. Hirano insists that the poem by Ikkyū is
concerned mostly with the preface of Fang-hui Wan-li.[28] The third line alludes
to a phrase from that preface, "Chang-yen Ming-yüan warmed the cold ashes
and had the text printed anew." The "merciful old hag" (*rōboshin*) was also
mentioned in Fang-hui's preface, "Hsüeh-tou and Yüan-wu had the heart of a
'merciful old hag,' " that is, they combined a supreme sense of compassion
with extensive discourse.[29]

The phrase "Admonitions from Shen-shan" refers to the Ling-ch'üan yüan
monastery on Shen-shan Mountain, the place where Yüan-wu resided. Ikkyū
again combines an ambiguous praising of the editor who restored the burned
kōan collection with a straightforward accusation that he "destroyed the
Teaching." By citing the *Pi-yen lu,* Ikkyū in fact follows the way of his Chinese
predecessor and expresses a kind of self-flagellation for his own overadherence
to the practice that in other instances he himself had rejected.

In the poem "Master Ta-hui Burns the *Pi-yen chi*" (no. 72) Ikkyū praises
the conduct of Ta-hui, who according to a popular tradition protested against
an extreme reliance on the literary kōan tradition by destroying the original
woodblock of the famous *Pi yen lu:*

The name of the old man of Miao-hsi will pertain for a thousand years.
He had polished the Ch'an school and raised it above the others.
In old days Tzu-hsü ordered Wu-wang to cut out his eyeballs.
What a pity that a skull does not have shining eye-pupils!

"The old man of Miao-hsi" is Ta-hui Tsung-kao who once lived in a place of that name. The third line alludes to the biography of Wu Tzu-hsü in the *Historical Record* (*Shih chi*, section "Ch'un-ch'iu chang-kuo p'ien"). "When following the orders of Wu-wang, Wu Tzu-hsü was to commit suicide and said: 'Plant a catalpa tree on my grave, so that I would be able to make of it a coffin for Wu-wang. And furthermore, cut out my eyeballs and fetch them to the eastern gate of the Wu kingdom, to let me see how the Yüeh barbarians destroy the Wu kingdom.' "

The last line refers to a story in the *Ching-te ch'uan-teng lu* (vol. 11): "A monk asked Hsiang-yen about the Tao, and the master answered: 'A dragon sings on a dried tree.' The monk did not understand. Then Hsiang-yen added, 'A skull has shining eye-pupils.' " Ikkyū compares Ta-hui's posthumous fate with that of Wu Tzu-hsü, pointing out that neither happened to see his desires fulfilled after death. Ta-hui's attempt to eradicate the *Pi-yen lu* so as to prevent the degradation of the Ch'an spiritual essence and the ever-increasing formalization of kōan practice turned out to be a failure. In the ensuing centuries the *Pi-yen lu* became one the main devices used in Zen training, and Ikkyū's poetry abounds in allusions and quotations from this work. This fact is itself ample evidence of the popularity of the text in fifteenth-century Japan.

Sharp Admonitions against His Own Brethren

At the same time Ikkyū angrily accused those who considered kōan practice the only trustworthy expedient means to attain satori as, for example, in the following two verses, "Respectfully Addressing My Steady Disciples" (nos. 225–226):

> Round-headed profligates in monk's robes!
> They have a gorgeous appearance and people tremble on their
>   approach.
> Their main concern is to promote ancient cases.
> Be ashamed of fostering in vain your smugness!

> Do not claim that you had solved all the kōans.
> An octagonal millstone lays above the heart.
> You are unable to sense the smell of your own shit,
> But distinctly see in a mirror the misdeeds of others.

"An octagonal millstone" (*hakku maban*) was mentioned for the first time by Yang-yi (964–1020), "An octagonal millstone flies through the air," and is an indication of innate abilities that are not easy to realize. In 1325 during a dispute at the Imperial court between a Tendai monk and Daitō Kokushi, the latter used it as a capping phrase when answering the question, "What is the meaning of a special transmission beyond the Teaching?" The two last lines were borrowed by Ikkyū from a commentary on case 77 of the *Pi-yen lu*,[30] which stresses the difficulty in realizing the innate nature of a person (subject) as opposed to the ease of understanding the external world (object) of illusory phenomena.

Ikkyū goes on his attack against practices in vogue in the Japanese Zen monasteries in the poem "In Japan Comparisons Are Taken Literally" (no. 345):

> "Evaluating exams" involve people in lies, and they are permeated
> with a poison.
> They initially contain the spirit of humble people, not of gentlemen.
> Having found a metaphor in the mist they take it literally.
> Lo-t'ien sang about "a moss robe and a cloudy belt."

"Evaluating exams" (*kanben*) were a specific kind of Zen dialogue (*mondō*), when masters exchanged questions and answers to test the authenticity of satori experience. Lo-t'ien was another name of the poet Po Chü-i (772–846), whose poetry abounds with allegories and was highly popular among Japanese Zen monks. Ikkyū's irony is aimed at those who take allegoric expressions like "a moss robe and a cloudy belt" literally though they mean only "a moss-covered boulder" and "clouds on the mountainous peak."

Breaking Rules Brings Them to Life

Ikkyū's own unconventional conduct was often shocking. He drank wine, visited brothels, ate fish, and befriended mavericks of all sorts. He believed that strict adherence to the Buddhist precepts is nothing but a sort of hypocrisy, yet he firmly held the single principle, "Do not do evil, do only good things." His ironic smile is present in the poem "On the Precept 'Do Not Drink Wine' " (no. 331):

> He emptied three bowls of wine but did not moisten his lips.
> To compose poems when drunk is the only joy for Lo-t'ien.
> But Master Leng was wondering:
> Who on a nice day will be his companion in wine-drinking?

The first line alludes to the story from the *Ts'ao-shan lu* and the *Wu-men kuan* (case 10), "The monk Ch'ing Shui came to Ts'ao-shan and claimed that he was very poor and asked for alms. 'Acharya Shui!' called Ts'ao-shan. 'Yes, sir!' answered Shui. 'You have drunk three bowls of tasty wine in the famous wine shop of Ch'ing Yuan, but did not moisten yet your lips.' "³¹ "Master Leng" refers to Ch'ang-ch'ing Hui-leng. His name is connected with the following story in the *Ching-te ch'uan-teng lu* (vol. 18): "Once addressing the community Ch'ang-ch'ing said, 'Though my singing is clear, you still do not understand me. What will you do if I arrive from the darkness?' A monk asked, 'What does it mean to arrive from the darkness?' 'You have emptied your tea-bowl, now you can leave,' said Ch'ang-ch'ing. Chung-ta said, 'Master, let him be your companion in tea-drinking.' "

Ikkyū replaces the words "companion in tea-drinking" (*chaban*) with "companion in wine-drinking" (*shuban*), reversing in this way the supposedly well-known "Master Leng's kōan." The poem consists of two parts: the first part is really connected with the wine-drinking kōan and the poet Po Lo-t'ien (Po Chü-i) known by his love of wine; the second part alludes to the kōan that originally contained not a single mention of wine, but Ikkyū intentionally transfers it from a reference to tea into a verse about wine. The opposition between parts is demolished, and the whole poem transcends into an affirmation of wine-drinking that is incompatible with the title. An apparent paradox adds an ironic vein and turns it into a kind of kōan. The first line was reproduced in another poem by Ikkyū, "Pleasure in Suffering" (no. 46), but here he made it more explicit by including the name of Tung-shan in the second line:

> You emptied three bowls of wine but did not moisten your lips:
> With such words old Tung-shan consoled a lonely poor man.
> As soon as you enter a burning house,
> In a single moment an ache for ten thousand kalpas will
> appear.

Ikkyū's deep dissatisfaction with the existing state of affairs in the Zen community was expressed in the poem, "In Former Days I Worshipped the Image of Daitō Kokushi, but Now I've Changed My Garb and Entered the Pure Land School" (no. 228).

> The Crazy Cloud is Hajun of the Daitokuji tradition:
> I wish to put an end to the battles of demons in my community.
> Of what use are "ancient stories" and kōans?
> Instead of terrible sufferings I count now the treasures of others.

Ikkyū condemns the quarrels and doctrinal disputes between monks of Daito-kuji and equates himself (Crazy Cloud) with Hajun (S. *Pāpíyas*), the king of the demons who dwells in the Takejizai-ten heaven (S. *Paranirmita-vasavartin*) and who tries to create obstacles for buddhas striving to attain *nirvāṇa*. The name Hajun also recalls the name of the poet himself (Sōjun). The "terrible sufferings" may be interpreted as difficulties connected with the solving of kōans in Zen monasteries, while "counting treasures of others" is believed by some commentators to be the counting of rosary beads during the *nembutsu* recitations in the Pure Land tradition, which Ikkyū apparently practiced for a time.

We do not possess any reliable data about the reasons for Ikkyū's short-term conversion to the Amidist creed. Perhaps it lasted only a few months and was an expression of dissatisfaction with the standards of Daitokuji and especially with the activities of its abbot, Yōsō, whom Ikkyū scolded and damned in any number of ways. He even wrote a set of works, called "Jikai-shū," focused exclusively on condemning Yōsō. In the "Jikai-shū" he mentions that he converted to the Pure Land school in the sixth month of 1461, but before doing so he returned the image of the patriarch Daitō to the main temple of Daitokuji.[32] Nevertheless, his biographical "Chronicle" ("Nempu") contains not a single mention of such a conversion.

Ikkyū often pronounced self-accusations for his improper conduct based on an awareness that inevitable karmic retribution awaited him, as he claims in the poem, "Having Severed Ties with My Community, I Accuse Myself with This *Gāthā*" (no. 194):

> Addressed disciples, presided over a community, built "devil palaces";
> "Since old days sweating horses have made incredible efforts."
> A master and an ordinary disciple are both equally crooks.
> I feel pity for Han Hsin who lamented over a good bow.

The introductory words (*suiji*) to case 7 of the *Pi-yen lu* contain a phrase, "Since old days sweating horses had not had human knowledge, but wanted only to be retributed for making incredible efforts."[33] The lines allude to a poem in the *Tung-shan wai chi* that says:

> When pacifying the Six States,
> An immovable heart penetrates the eight cardinal points,
> People do not notice that horses are sweating,
> But want only to be retributed for making an incredible effort.

The poem implies a criticism of those soldiers who after a victory pay no attention to their sweating horses that actually brought them the victory. The line in the kōan shifts the image into the religious sphere to compare the effort of soldiers to that of monks striving to attain enlightenment. In both cases the auxiliary means are thrown away after the goal had been attained. Only a true master is able to keep in mind the real device that brought him to the final aim. The last two lines allude to a story from the *Historical Record* (*Shih chi,* section "Yüeh-wang chü-shi shih-chia") by Ssu-ma Ch'ien: "When Han Hsin was captured by Han-wang, he said, 'When fast-running hares die out, good dogs are used for soup; when high-flying birds disappear, good bows are left aside; when a state is defeated, faithful ministers are executed.' " Ikkyū expresses regret about the position of Han Hsin, who scapegoated innocents for any failures suffered.

In the poem "Lamentations on the Degradation of the Daitokuji School" (no. 486), Ikkyū condemns his own Zen tradition in the harshest manner:

> Who is the true master among descendants in the Eastern Sea?
> They do not distinguish true and false; their knowledge is distorted.
> Kyōun knows the smell of piss on his own body:
> They are his elegant messages and love-poems.

A comment on case 77 from the *Pi-yen lu* says, "The smell of own's shit is not sensed."[34] Later on Daitō used the words "he does not know the smell of his own shit" as a capping phrase. Ikkyū must have been aware of that expression, popular in the Daitokuji tradition, but preferred to turn it topsy-turvy to demonstrate his awareness of evil dwelling inside his lineage as well as in himself and his irresistible passion for composing verse.

Some of the major topics repeated consistently in the *Kyōun-shū* include the problem of keeping and breaking Buddhist precepts, praising the ancient Zen masters and paying tribute to some contemporaries, providing enigmatic comments regarding the authenticity of satori, or making casual remarks about current events. In fact, most of Ikkyū's poems demonstrate striking deviations from the rules of classical Chinese prosody. They were written not to demonstrate his erudition and knowledge of versification rules but to hint, strike, or push toward spiritual awakening in the tradition of Lin-chi or Te-shan. Due to his extensive use of kōan stories through frequently ambiguous or ironic allusions, Ikkyū managed to enlarge the semantic field of his 28-character verses and went far beyond the limits and conventions of the *gozan* poetry of his contemporary composers of verse as part of the literary technique of the Rinzai "Five Mountains" monastic institution very much influenced by Sung Chinese culture.

NOTES

1. I refrain from including Ikkyū's biographical sketch in this chapter. Interested readers can find a detailed biography in several English-language works, including Sonja Arntzen, *Ikkyū Sojun: A Zen Monk and his Poetry* (Bellingham, Wash.: Western Washington University Press, 1973); Arntzen, *Ikkyū and the Crazy Cloud Anthology: A Zen Monk of Medieval Japan* (Tokyo: University of Tokyo Press, 1986), pp. 3–61; J. H. Sanford, *Zen-Man Ikkyū* (Chico, Cal.: Scholars Press, 1981), pp. 1–117; and J. C. Co-

vell, *Zen's Core: Ikkyū's Freedom* (Seoul: Hollym International Corp., 1980). There are a great number of his biographies in Japanese, although most of them repeat the same "facts" that are contained in the official "Ikkyū's Cronicle" ("Nempu") and in his poems. A few of the best general biographical studies are Ichikawa Hakugen, *Ikkyū: Ransei ni ikita zensha* (Tokyo: Nihon hōsō shuppan kyōkai, 1970); Murata Taihei, *Ningen Ikkyū* (Tokyo: Kōbunsha, 1976); Nishida Masayoshi, *Ikkyū: Fūkyō no seishin* (Tokyo: Kōdansha, 1977); Minakami Tsutomu, *Ikkyū* Tokyo: Chūkō bunko, 1978); and Kamata Shigeo, *Ikkyū: Fūkyō ni ikiru* (Tokyo: Kōzaidō, 1995). A complete bibliography would amount to dozens of pages.

2. The *Kyōun-shū* was published in Japanese many times from different manuscripts that sometimes differ considerably. The critical revised text that contains all the poems from the existing manuscripts was published by Itō Toshiko in the journal *Yamato bunka* 41 (1964): 10–59. It contains 1,060 numbered pieces. Because it has became standard practice to refer to those numbers, I follow this system in this chapter. The best annotated edition is the two-volume *Kyōun-shū zenshaku* (hereafter KSZ), I, ed. Hirano Sōjō (Tokyo: Shunjūsha, 1976), and II, ed. Kageki Hideo (Tokyo: Shunjūsha, 1997). It contains 881 poems. In 1972 Ichikawa Hakugen published the most authoritative Okumura manuscript in *Nihon zenka no shisō* in the series *Nihon koten bungaku taikei* (Tokyo: Iwanami shoten, 1972), which provides extensive annotations for the first 231 poems. Yanagida Seizan selected 300 of Ikkyū's poems and published them accompanied by his interpretive renderings in modern Japanese and with detailed comments in Katō Shūichi and Yanagida Seizan, eds., *Ikkyū*, in *Nihon zen goroku*, vol. 12 (Tokyo: Kōdansha, 1983). The Western-language publications by Sanford, Arntzen, Covell, etc. as cited in note 1 provide translations for more than 200 poems from Ikkyū's collected verses accompanied by their own intricate interpretations and comments. These commentaries should be taken into account. Nevertheless, in most cases only a limited number of Ikkyū's poems are discussed repeatedly while a large section of the most complicated pieces still awaits interpretation. To stress the complexity of the problem, I would like to mention a book by Yanagda Seizan, *Ikkyū: Kyôun-shū no sekai* (Kyoto: Jinbun shoin, 1980), that amounts to 250 pages but offers a profound analysis of only twelve poems from the *Kyôun-shū*.

3. *Pi-yen lu,* T 48, p. 192b.

4. T 48, p. 165a.

5. T 48, p. 219b.

6. In a slightly modified form it was reproduced by Ikkyū in the poem "Wiping Filth with the Scriptures" (no. 70), "A dog pisses on the sandalwood old Buddha hall." The scatological theme combined with sacrilegious notions in fact was used by Ikkyū as an extreme demonstration of the absence of any distinction between sacred and profane, pure and impure, or the use of the scriptures for reading or simply as a paper to wipe an ass.

7. T 48, p. 209a.

8. KSZ, I:46.

9. *Ts'ung jung lu,* in T 48, p. 280a.

10. T 48, p. 145a–c.

11. T 48, p. 148b.

12. See Kenneth Kraft, *Eloquent Zen: Daitō and Early Japanese Zen* (Honolulu: University of Hawaii Press, 1992).

13. "Turning phrases" (*tengo*) were used by Zen masters to confuse disciples, push them toward awakening and reveal the innate essence of the Dharma. In his preface Ikkyū quotes only the first among the three turning phrases of Daitō.

14. T 48, p. 219a.

15. Hirano, in KJZ I:41. The *Ch'an-lin leichu* is in ZZ, 117, vol. 15, p. 187a.

16. KSZ I:41.

17. *Ku-ts'un-su yü-lu,* in ZZ, 118, p. 304a.

18. KSZ, I. 42–43.

19. Arntzen, *Ikkyū and the Crazy Cloud Anthology,* p. 103.

20. Hirano Sōjō, ed., *Daitō Kokushi goroku,* in *Zen no koten,* vol. 3 (Tokyo: Kōdansha, 1983), p. 113.

21. I thank Robert Duquenne at the Institute of Hōbōgirin, Kyoto, for suggesting this.

22. *Wu-men kuan,* in T 48, p. 294c.

23. T 48, p. 194c.

24. T 48, p. 195a.

25. See T 48, p. 293a–b. I refrain from an analysis of the kōan's original content. A sophisticated treatment of this kōan and its connections with the concept of causality in Zen may be found in the article by Steven Heine, "Putting the 'Fox' Back into the 'Wild Fox Kōan': The Intersection of Philosophical and Popular Religious Elements in the Ch'an/Zen Tradition," *Harvard Journal of Asiatic Studies,* vol. 56, no. 2 (1996): 257–317.

26. T 48, p. 212c.

27. KSZ I:138.

28. Cited from *Ching-te ch'uan-teng lu,* 30 vols., in T 51, 2076.

29. *Zengaku daijiten* (Tokyo: Taishūkan shoten, 1977), p. 1314.

30. T 48, p. 204c.

31. T 48, p. 294a.

32. *Jikai-shū,* in Minakami Tsutomu, *Ikkyū bungei shisho* (Tokyo: Asahi shuppansha, 1987), p. 80.

33. T 48, p. 147a.

34. T 48, p. 204c.

9

Transmission of Kirigami *(Secret Initiation Documents)*

A Sōtō Practice in Medieval Japan

ISHIKAWA RIKIZAN

EDITED AND TRANSLATED BY

KAWAHASHI SEISHŪ

(WITH ASSISTANCE FOR *KIRIGAMI*

TRANSLATION BY SUGUWARA SHŌEI)

Translator's Preface: Interpretive Problems

This chapter is Ishikawa's earliest attempt to explore the complex nature of a genre of medieval Sōtō Zen literature dealing with interpretations of kōans known as *kirigami*. It should be stressed that the field of *kirigami* studies was hardly explored at the time the essay was written in the early 1980s, and therefore it was nothing but Ishikawa's courage, passion, and painstaking efforts that opened up the field of studying these esoteric materials. Subsequent to this publication, Ishikawa produced dozens of important articles elaborating on this pioneering work.

The original text by Ishikawa is a highly condensed work and contains stylistic difficulties often shared with traditional Japanese sectarian scholarship. For this reason, in some cases the contents do not seem readily accessible to Western readers unless mediated and supplemented by additional remarks. I took the liberty of editing Ishikawa's text for the benefit of the Western audience. These additions are shown in brackets to distinguish them from the original text.[1]

Interpretive problems of this kind seem to be generic to the enterprise of translation. In working on this particular text, however, I was obliged to pay attention to the following issues. It is frequently pointed out that there is a significant stylistic difference between American and Japanese academic writing. For example, some Japanese scholarly texts lack question-proposing passages. Ishikawa's essay also lacks propositional segments. As translator, I was confronted with an interpretive gulf from the outset, and I had no choice but to read his essay thoroughly and add a plausible proposal to the original text. To complicate this problem further, Ishikawa offers insufficient explanations for the quotations he employs in the paper. *Kirigami* are essentially esoteric documents dealing with the tradition of kōans and, hence, their contents are hardly understandable, not only for a Western audience but also for Japanese readership outside the closed circle of the tradition. (If anyone is confident of his or her reading skills of these medieval esoteric sources, I hope that he or she will contribute to the development of *kirigami* studies.)

Clifford Geertz once remarked that the objective of the humanities is to extend the realm of human discourse. Benjamin Schwartz insists on the importance of making particular forms of Asian thought accessible to the Western audience based on a detailed knowledge not only of the language but of the cultural context underlying the thought forms (see Schwartz's foreword to Hoyt Cleveland Tillman's *Utilitarian Confucianism: Ch'en Liang's Challenge to Chu Hsi,* Harvard University Press, 1982). In pursuit of these goals, I either shortened the original text or added supplementary sentences to Ishikawa's text, and also have offered definitions for several key terms that Ishikawa overlooked, in order to make Ishikawa's argument more accessible and "extend the realm of human discourse." I have done my best for my Dharma friend Ishikawa Rikizan, who passed away on August 4, 1997.

Kirigami as a Style of *Shōmono*

There is a genre of historical sources called *shōmono.* These are one of the sets of documents that are especially useful for revealing the nature of Zen training in the medieval Sōtō school as well as the popular religious practice of lay and common people in this period. [This chapter attempts to provide not only a general definition of the *shōmono* genre, which involves detailed commentaries on traditional kōan collections like the *Mumonkan* and *Hekiganroku,* but also detailed philological data on secret initiation documents called *kirigami,* which are one of the varieties or subgenres belonging to *shōmono* literature, dealing especially with esoteric comments on specific kōan cases.]

Shōmono documents are medieval Sōtō teachers' colloquial commentaries on traditional Zen texts. [Medieval Sōtō teachers, instead of utilizing the recorded sayings of previous Zen masters as one of the training methods, adopted their own understanding of the traditional texts as a means to instruct their students. Since their thoughts and understanding were expressed in the form of so-called *shō,* or explanatory notes, these records were later called *shōmono.*]

The *shōmono* group is further classified into five categories according to content: *kikigakishō/gorokushō,* or phonetic transcriptions of "open lectures on kōans presented at medieval Sōtō monasteries";[2] *monsan,* or secret kōan manuals or documents of "the curriculum, questions, and expected responses for each kōan";[3] *daigo,* which refers to a teacher's correct answer, exegeses of *gorokushō,* anecdotes about a student's conversation with a master that provoked his enlightenment, and the answers to kōan questions;[4] *daigoshō,* or further commentaries and explanatory notes on *daigo;* and *kirigami,* or secret initiation manuals. [*Kirigami* literally means "paper strips" on which monks concisely recorded manuals of instructions for the performance of secret initiations and rituals. These instructions differed from traditional Chinese codes of monastic rules and regulations (*shingi*) because they referred to rituals conducted privately by particular abbots and reflected the assimilation of Japanese folk beliefs and magical practices. Among those things the monks recorded were closely guarded tips for daily rituals, explanations of the "three personal belongings" (*san-motsu*) to be transmitted from a master to a pupil, concrete illustrations of these personal items, and some *monsan* and *sanwa* (which are a particular type of *kirigami* providing questions and answers about a single kōan).]

A detailed analysis of these documents, however, leaves researchers with many difficulties, and a study of *kirigami,* which is the author's primary concern among the *shōmono* documents, is especially problematic. This is so partially because the project of researching *shōmono* in general, as well as *kirigami* in particular, is relatively new to the field of Japanese Buddhist history, despite the fact that the method of *kirigami* transmission was extremely popular among Sōtō monks and was practiced throughout the entire Sōtō organization, from generation to generation, and from the medieval to the modern period. [Questions still remain: Why has in-depth research on *kirigami* been overlooked thus far? What kinds of problems impede the process of analyzing *kirigami?*]

One of the problems in evaluating the *kirigami* is the magico-religious elements observable in some of the documents. Because the *kirigami* frequently contained occult ritual, such as Shinto–Buddhist syncretistic or pseudo-*yin/yang* types of divination, studies of *kirigami* in general came to be neglected and even despised in the later (that is, the early modern) Sōtō tradition. There were masters of Zen scholasticism who went further in stating that some *kirigami* notes merely demonstrate the original "scribbler's" own misconstrued ideas or their teachers' distorted views.

[In the Edo period, a tendency to look down upon *kirigami* was so exaggerated that some of them are believed to have been incinerated.] For instance, Menzan Zuihō in "Tōjōshitsunaidanshi renpi shiki," stresses the need to burn a *kirigami* in an essay titled "Shisho shōkyaku" ("Incineration of Transmission Certificate" [which apparently called for the destruction of transmission certificates, documents that were highly prized in Menzan's orthodox view of the monastic system]). Menzan asserts:

The *shisho* (transmission certificate) is the last document anyone should ever consider burning up. For instance, a scroll of a certificate that the founder of Eiheiji temple received at T'ien-tung ssu (J. Tendōji) temple is, in fact, kept in the master's room at Eiheiji temple. But in the medieval period a new, problematic concept of Buddhist lineage (*garanbō*)[5] was introduced. Due to the introduction of this rule, disciples easily received Dharma certificates from their masters, and the accession to abbacy at temples also became easy. *Shisho* was no longer of importance and was even returned to the previous master! [According to this practice], when there is no one or no place to return the certificate to, it should be incinerated.

The contents of *kirigami,* and also the making of them, are thus useless. They are the documents that must be burned up. ("Shicchū," *Sōtō-shū zensho*)[6]

With this assertion, Menzan points out the problem of the practice *garanbō,* by which the arbitrary custom, or rather the audacious practice, of the incineration of transmission documents came into effect. Therefore he strongly asserts that it is the *kirigami,* which records secret oral instructions for what he considers inauthentic practice, that must be destroyed in flames. Menzan, substantiating each flaw in the practice, further demanded that another collection of 145 *kirigami* of spurious origins be destroyed by fire.

In the *Eiheiji shicchū danshimokuroku narabini in,* Menzan goes on to negate the authenticity of a collection at Eiheiji temple (founded by Dōgen) containing 140 paper strips or *kirigami:*

> In the summer of 1746 (the second year of the Emperor Enkyō), I stayed at the Jôyô-an hermitage of Eiheiji temple for about fifty days to receive intimately the Dharma Treasure from the master in his room. When I looked around the room, I happened to come across as many as one hundred and forty *kirigami* lying about there. After having examined the list and contents of those documents I understood that all of them conveyed the past teachers' misconstrued and distorted ideas, and that none of them were useful to the Sōtō institution. ("Shicchū," *Sōtō-shū zensho*)

It is, indeed, true that every document Menzan takes up for discussion is of spurious origin, but at present these materials are being reexamined and reevaluated in the fields of religious studies and *kyōkagaku* (studies of the process of the propogation of Buddhism) as a rare source of information depicting the actual Zen missionary situation in medieval Japan, as well as the regional development of Sōtō organizations. In other words, there is no doubt that the *kirigami* are precious historical sources in spite of their apocryphal contents.[7]

[As was mentioned earlier, in-depth research on *kirigami* presents researchers with various difficulties.] More precisely, these difficulties include the problems of the diverse nature of the contents and the rare availability of *kirigami* documents of authentic origins. According to Sugimoto Shunryū in his *Tōjō shitsunai kirigami narabini sanwa kenkyū,* which was a path-breaking work for contemporary comprehensive studies of these documents, *kirigami* can be classified into nine groups [based on their function], these are *gyōji* (dealing with sustained practice and ceremonies), *tengen* (eye-opening rituals), *sōbō* (funerals), *kechimyaku* (lineage charts), *shihō* (Dharma transmission), *kuketsu* (secret oral instructions), *sanwa* (questions and answers about a single kōan), *kaji* (prayers and incantations), and *zōsan* (miscellanea). However, Sugimoto's taxonomy is still provisional, and there is a need for further critical evaluation of his approach.

It was not until the modern period of Japan that *kirigami* were collected and edited in bound volumes instead of taking the form of separate cut leaves or paper strips. This development has enabled some researchers to work with a complete set of *kirigami* derived from a single stream of a particular Sōtō community. However, originally the documents were in the form of discrete paper sheets that had been transmitted one by one. Therefore they easily became scattered as time went by. *Kirigami* from the medieval period are especially difficult to find and obtain. (It is beyond the scope of this study to discuss the special circumstances of the historical situation of the medieval period in which *kirigami* had their origins.)

It is noteworthy that most *kirigami* discovered in the process of recent research efforts are from following periods: Kan-ei era (1624–1644), Bunki era (1501–1504), Eishō era (1504–1521), Genki era (1570–1573), and Tenshō era (1573–1592). However, their recorded dates are more or less self-proclaimed or spurious records, and close scrutiny suggests that among these *kirigami* those deriving from the *Kan-ei* era are actually the oldest, in spite of the recorded ages of other documents. Documents like *kirigami* and *monsan* often trumpet their own authenticity by fabricating lineage charts that somehow trace back to certain key persons such as Dōgen and Ejō. Some even claim to trace back to Ju-ching, Dōgen's mentor in Sung China [in order to gain symbolic authority by evoking a direct transmission of the ancient tradition from China]. Among *kirigami* documents that are of the most plausible authenticity, those of the Kan-ei era were handed down in collected volumes to later generations. In contrast, there is no historical evidence available to indicate that the other documents claiming to derive from earlier eras were also collectively bequeathed to posterity.

Kirigami and Kōan Literature

Based on a philological analysis of the source documents, the development of various kinds of *kirigami* will be discussed, especially the category of *sanwa* that are directly related to instruction in the study of *kosoku-kōan,* or traditional kōan cases originally contained in Chinese sources. *Sanwa* are one of the various types of *kirigami* documents, as was mentioned in Sugimoto's taxonomy. The difference from other *kirigami* categories is that *sanwa* documents contain questions and answers specifically about kōans, often referring to a single, specific case, in addition to various doctrinal points. Other *kirigami,* however, are collections of manuals of instruction for the performance of cer-

$$Daigoshō \longrightarrow$$
$$\longrightarrow \quad \longrightarrow$$
$$Gorokushō \longrightarrow daigo \longrightarrow monsan \longrightarrow kirigami \ (sanwa)$$
$$\longrightarrow$$
Kōan Zen ------►

FIGURE 9.1. *Evolution of* Shōmono *literature. Translator's note: Genealogy of* Kirigami *as a variety of* Shōmono. *From the* gorokushō *and* daigo *that collected lectures on traditional kōans there arose* monsan *manuals, with* sanwa-kirigami *emerging as the final stage of commenting on the source dialogues. This figure also highlights the role of* daigoshō, *or further comments and notes on the* daigo, *influencing the development of the* kirigami. *Ishikawa's essay itself, however, which emphasizes that* sanwa *are a variety of* kirigami, *does not further develop this point.*

tain rituals, such as the animating of Buddha images through the eye-opening ritual, holding funerals, conferring precepts, and transmitting the Dharma.

There are numerous *monsan* documents available from diverse streams of the Sōtō tradition which are very similar in content to *sanwa[-kirigami]* documents. Many of the *monsan,* or secret curriculum manuals of acceptable responses to kōans, appeared in the medieval period accompanying the spread of "*Kōan Zen,*" or a kind of Zen training emphasizing the study of traditional kōan cases [usually based on the major Chinese Ch'an collections, such as the *Wu-men kuan* (J. *Mumonkan*), *Pi-yen lu* (J. *Hekiganroku*), and *Ts'ung-jung lu* (J. *Shōyōroku*), in addition to Dōgen's *Mana Shōbōgenzō* and *Eihei gen goroku* texts]. However, I believe that a majority of the *monsan* documents did not necessarily stem from a direct study of traditional kōans in the major Chinese collections, but rather originated as a form of commentary on *gorokushō* and *daigo* documents [that, in turn, were records of lectures, sermons, and spontaneous discussions of traditional kōans, as well as additional cases originating within the medieval Japanese sect]. Therefore, it is possible to speculate that the two groups of the *gorokushō* and *daigo* were actually forerunners of the *monsan,* which then gave rise to the development of the [*sanwa* variety of] *kirigami* (as suggested in fig. 9.1).

Daigo are a kind of exegesis appended or words "capped" (*jakugo*) as indirect, allusive comments onto *gorokushō*. Usually *gorokushō* commenting on traditional dialogues and kōan cases conclude with a section of acknowledgments and with the capping phrases of *daigo*. Generally, the latter introduce episodes of a student's conversation with his master which provoked the former into an experience of enlightenment, and they also include answers for the questions raised by the kōans themselves. Although the following suggestion is based in part on speculation, probably all of these *daigo* archives were sorted into an independent subgroup of records which then developed into *monsan* or secret kōan manuals.

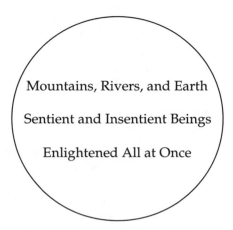

Mountains, Rivers, and Earth

Sentient and Insentient Beings

Enlightened All at Once

An ancient master said, "*Chōmongen* ('Eye on the head') is capable of casting a piercing light on all four lands around Mount Sumeru. What kind of eye is it?" The master pointed at a lamppost and said, "What an arrogant eye and ear it has!" The "Eye on the head" can be transmitted only when a master and his pupil have an eye-to-eye relationship. Original Heart (or Buddha Mind) can be transmitted only when they have heart-to-heart reciprocity. The "Eye on the head" has been transmitted from generation to generation until now.

FIGURE 9.2. *Part of the* Chōmon no manako kirigami *document*

The process of the evolution from the secret *monsan* manuals to the esoteric *kirigami* is more evident. [To illustrate this, we note that] among *sanwa* materials there is a document called *Chōmon no manako kirigami* (that Sugimoto groups in the category of *kuketsu* or secret oral instructions instead of *sanwa*), which is reproduced as figure 9.2.

The origin of the *kirigami* in question is found in a *monsan* document which is written on a scroll that Jakuen is said to have given to Giun [referring to two early, thirteenth-century patriarchs of the Sōtō sect at Hōkyōji temple]. It reads as follows:

The Sixth Patriarch said, "The 'Eye on the head' is capable of casting a piercing light on all four lands around Mount Sumeru. What kind of eye is it?" The master pointed at the nearest lamppost and said, "What an arrogant eye and ear it has!" He continued, "The 'Eye on the head' can be transmitted only when a master and his pupil have an eye-to-eye relationship. Original Heart can be transmitted only when they have heart-to-heart reciprocity. The 'Eye on the head' has been transmitted from generation to generation up until now."

Assimilating the words in the scroll, the Great Practitioner at Eiheiji said, "A head corresponds to eyebrows, and ears correspond to eyebrows. These relations

are called the 'Eye on the head.' It is the eye of the Dharma. . . ."[8]
Never let anyone else see this! This is the founder's authentic handwriting.

Bowing a hundred times to Ryūtengohōzenjin [a Buddhist guardian deity], Rev. Jakuen presents this to Rev. Giun.

(Document from Hōkyōji Temple, Ōno City, Fukui Prefecture, Japan)

According to the legend of Hōkyōji temple, the scroll containing the dialogue of the Sixth Patriarch commenting on the "Eye on the head" was first mentioned by Dōgen and was later recorded in Jakuen's authentic handwriting. If this is the case, there is no doubt that the *monsan* belongs to the Jakuen stream or faction of the sect. The question is how this came to be transmitted in the form of a *kirigami*. The difference between the two archives [of the *monsan* and *kirigami* (or *sanwa*)] is readily apparent from the style of the documents: the *kirigami*, which is the first record cited here, lacks the section known as *nentei*, or the passage that introduces a classic Zen dialogue or kōan in the manner of "taking up such-and-such a case." The *kirigami* also bears a diagram which reads, "Mountains, Rivers and the Earth; Sentient and Insentient Beings; Enlightened All at Once" (fig. 9.2).

There are similar diagrams observable in a *kirigami* called *Tsuki Ryōko* (reproduced as fig. 9.3):

Showing this *kirigami* to Gasan, Rev. Keizan said, "Unless you know there is a pair of moons you cannot be a blade of grass of the Sōtō tradition."

The *kirigami* in question is based on a kōan from the source titled, *Gasan oshō gyōjitsu*, which reads:

One evening Kin (Fourth Patriarch Keizan) was enjoying the beauty of the moon when he abruptly asked Gasan sitting behind him, "Do you happen to know that there is a pair of moons?" Gasan replied, "No." Keizan said, "Unless you know that, you cannot be a blade of grass of the Sōtō tradition." ("Shidenka," *Sōtō-shū zensho*)

This kōan was transmitted to Gasan's successors, especially to those in Mukyoku's clique, which branched off from Ryōan's faction. Mukyoku Etetsu founded the temple of Ryōtaiji in Gifu Prefecture. The temple possesses his own handwritten epistle to Gekkō Shōbun:

I will show an important thing of our school to Shōbun.
Beyond our general knowledge, there is a pair of moons. Where is there not such a pair?[9]
Abbot at Ryūsenji Temple, Etetsu

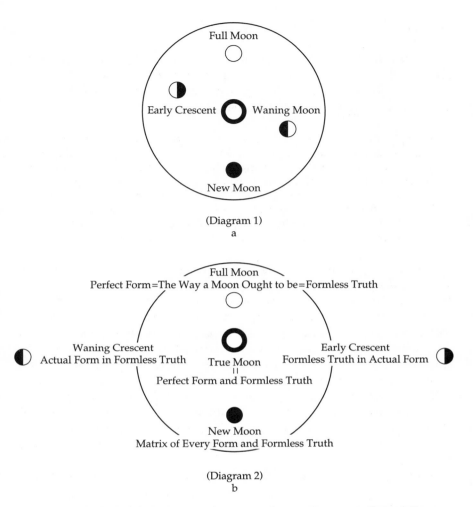

(Diagram 1)
a

(Diagram 2)
b

A full moon contains a new moon. A new moon contains a full moon. A full moon is to a new moon what a waxing crescent is to a waning one. Divide [fig. 9.3a] into two diagrams, and see [fig. 9.3b]. It seems that the Perfect Form of the moon (○: Full Moon) contains all phases as well as the hidden truth that a moon is circular (●). "The hidden truth (the Formless Truth) in the Actual Form (◐: Early Crescent)" is identical with "the Actual Form in the Formless Truth (◐: Waning Crescent)." The Perfect Form of the moon also exists in the Absolute Truth that contains both the Perfect Form and the Formless Truth (◎). A pair of moons, one existing in the physical sphere and the other in the metaphysical sphere, mutually reflect and interpenetrate one another to form one unified moon. This metaphor alludes to the relationship between a master and his successor, which is also like a pair of mirrors that mutually reflect each other so that neither one loses its brightness.

FIGURE 9.3. The Tsuki Ryōko kirigami

In addition to this epistle there is also a *monsan* of Mukyoku's stream that takes up the story of "two moons" for discussion. *Taisōha hisan,* which is the property of Kongōji temple in Tochigi Prefecture, similarly deals with the topic discussed in the above-quoted document. It says:

> A couple of moons sat before the master. The master made a brief commentary on an old text. The master, substituting for his pupil, replied to the commentary saying, "A lord illuminates an upper territory with this light, and his retainer illuminates a lower one with it. Reverand Fushū used to put his forefinger on the lower part of his thumb and say that a lord sheds this light on an upper place. Putting his thumb on the lower part of his forefinger, he also said that a retainer sheds this light on a lower place." [middle section omitted] *For more details, see the diagrams and the kirigami as well* [highlighting by Ishikawa].

Menzan Zuihō insisted that the pair of diagrams in the *kirigami* referred to as the *Tsuki ryōko* were the concoction of previous teachers' heathen views. However, it is clear that the formation of such a *kirigami* presupposes the popularity of the instructional technique of *kazoesan* among monks engaged in the practice of *daigo* in the medieval period. [*Kazoesan* is a teaching method devised by teachers of *daigo.* Usually a kōan of any kind consists of a few gradual levels of instruction. *Daigo* teachers added additional pedagogical steps to each level of instruction so that students might understand the kōan more smoothly. Those newly added steps were called *kazoesan.*[10]] A [well-known] *kirigami* on the saying "this very mind is Buddha" is a typical example of this technique. Thus the importance of *kirigami* in transmitting *daigo,* which interpreted the "main or critical phrases" (*watō*) of traditional kōans, cannot be denied.

But we must further clarify the relation between the *monsan* and the *kirigami* styles or genres of documents. For instance, in the above-quoted *monsan* called *Taisōha hisan* the master recommends that his pupil consult the *kirigami* for further interpretations of the source passage. As I have tried to show, these archives suggest the possibility that there was a strong sense of continuity and linkage in the process of the transition from *monsan* to *kirigami* in the medieval practice of kōan studies.

Final Thoughts

When one is considering the role of *monsan* as records of interpretations of traditional kōan cases in the medieval Sōtō sect, it is important to recognize that each stream transmitted its own unique *sanwa* documents, which were apparently distinguishable from those of different factions. But although there were many differences among the [*sanwa-*]*kirigami* transmitted by the various streams, many of the *kirigami* documents were virtually identical in terms of content and appearance. The only observable difference was often a slight variation in a few words that probably does not affect our understanding of the historical sources. Therefore we can conclude that *sanwa* were useful in disseminating the *monsan* of various streams but were a somewhat simplified genre of the overall *shōmono* literature that relied on using symbolic expressions, such as diagrams, transmitted in the form of cut leaves or paper strips (*kirigami*).

One of the main problems in investigating these records is the deterioration of the strips of paper. However, at a certain point in modern Japan, *kirigami* were compiled into collected, bound volumes. The tasks of determining the time and nature of this crucial turning point in the history of the *kirigami* and of clarifying the process of compilation still remain untouched. These await additional philological research comparing the different kinds of *kirigami* documents of the medieval [unbound] and modern [bound] periods.

TRANSLATOR'S NOTES

1. For a full listing of these articles, see the bibliography in Bernard Faure, *Visions of Power: Imagining Medieval Japanese Buddhism* (Princeton, N.J.: Princeton University Press, 1996), p. 311.

2. See William M. Bodiford, *Sōtō Zen in Medieval Japan* (Honolulu: University of Hawaii Press, 1993), p. 157.

3. See Bodiford, *Sōtō Zen in Medieval Japan,* p. 152.

4. In the Chinese Ch'an tradition, *daigo* referred to "an alternative answer to an old question or the master's own answer for a question to which no monk in the assembly would respond. In medieval Sōtō kōan literature, however, *dai* always indicated that the teacher is supplying the correct answer in order to instruct his student, not in order to replace the answer in the original text. . . . The students expected only to become conversant with the many nuances of each kōan. They did not have to create new responses." See Bodiford, *Sōtō Zen in Medieval Japan,* p. 153.

5. *Garanbō* was a new concept of Buddhist lineage that insisted on maintaining exclusive loyalty from generation to generation to the lineage of the founder of a temple. By so doing, the system could allow temples effectively to reject other able competitors from different lineages for the abbacy.

6. Ishikawa cites several passages from the compendium of sectarian literature, the *Sōtō-shū zensho* (Tokyo: Sōtōshū shūmuchō, 1970–1973).

7. Ishikawa cited these works, which were among the few available at the time of the composition of the chapter. Sakurai Shūyū, "Sōtōmonka ni okeru kirigami sōjō no ichikōsatsu," *Shūkyōgaku ronshū* vol. 9; Ishikawa Rikizan, "Chūsei Zenshūshi kenkyū to Zenseki shōmono shiryō," *Ida Toshiyuki hakase koki-kinen tōyōgaku ronshū;* and Ishikawa, "Chūsei ni okeru Zenshū kirigami no shiryōteki kachi," *Shūkyō kenkyū* vol. 246.

8. I have interpreted only a portion of Ishikawa's quotation, because *kirigami* documents were written in esoteric script and contain specialized terms and expressions that could be understood only within a particular group (that is, of course, what the documents were for). For the original *kanbun* or Chinese writing, see *Indogaku bukkyōgaku kenkyū* vol. 30–2, 1982, p. 744.

9. Only the first half of the quotation is translated here.

10. I owe this information to Daiten Iizuka, Ishikawa's successor at Komazawa University. In addition, I am deeply grateful to Dr. James Roberson at Sugiyama Women's College for his editorial assistance.

10

Emerging from Nonduality
Kōan Practice in the Rinzai Tradition since Hakuin

MICHEL MOHR

Recent debates on methodological issues applied to Buddhist studies[1] have both multiplied the approaches at our disposal and refined our perceptions of the domain under study by questioning some common convictions about the nature of the Buddhist tradition. The first steps in this direction have been critical assessments of how the tradition has presented itself as well as how many Westerners have wanted to interpret and epitomize it. However, this useful task of analyzing the tradition and its reception by the scholarly and nonscholarly audience leaves us with a number of new difficulties. For example, some interpreters have overlooked crucial issues in historical criticism by focusing instead on a questioning of the centrality of "awakening" in Buddhism, as if the word itself cannot be used without quotation marks, perhaps to show that nobody really gives credence to the "mystical claim" implied in what is actually a technical term used in a variety of ways in the source materials.[2]

The key historical issue in examining the Zen schools is based on a realization that the field of study is not as clearly divided into separable denominations as textbooks would suggest. It is more likely that the different sectarian units have actually overlapped and interacted for centuries, so that sectarian consciousness is a phenomenon whose crystallization in Japan in its present form can be attributed at least partially to post-Meiji developments.[3] For instance, the establishment of a "chief abbot system" (kanchōsei) in June 1873, which was then modified several times, represents the culmination of the institutional setting that is often attributed retrospectively to the Tokugawa era. Since 1876 this system has included the three Zen denominations: Sōtō, Rinzai, and Ōbaku; the Rinzai sect being later further divided into the present fifteen branches, each with its own administration.[4]

At any rate, although sectarian categories often fail to do justice to what actually happened or to account for the interwoven relationships among priests, Japanese Buddhist studies is still dominated by works that deal with only one particular school. This is especially the case for research on the figures who used kōans in their practice during the Tokugawa period. Despite the widespread image of kōan practice as the distinguishing feature of Rinzai, one cannot fail to notice that important Sōtō lineages also used kōans extensively. One example is the scholarly oriented lineage of Tokuō Ryōkō (1649–1709), represented in the fourth generation by the poet Daigu Ryōkan (1758–1831). The direct influence Tokuō had received from Ōbaku priests is still evident in his third-generation heir, Tetsumon Dōju (1710–1781), the ninth abbot of Entsūji. Tetsumon composed in particular a collection of kōans entitled *Tenchian hyakusoku hyōju* (*Verses and Commentaries on One Hundred Cases [by the Abbot] of Tenchian*), which was printed in 1771.[5] This text, typical of such anthologies, obviously has been read by Ryōkan and might even have inspired his *Hokkesan* (*Hymn to the Lotus Sūtra*).[6] In the succeeding years, however, kōan practice was largely expunged from the Sōtō school through the efforts of Gentō Sokuchū (1729–1807), the eleventh abbot of Entsūji, who in 1795 was nominated abbot of Eiheiji. Gentō's effort to "purify" his lineage of foreign influence seems to have contributed to Ryōkan's decision to leave Entsūji and choose a life of wandering.[7]

Although comprehensive studies on kōans in all three Japanese Zen sects are needed, this chapter will focus on the so-called "revival of the Rinzai school," credited to Hakuin Ekaku (1686–1769) and his followers, in order to highlight the fact that several distinctive orientations existed within the Rinzai tradition, especially in the theoretical background synthesized by Hakuin's line. Spotlighting this neglected aspect of Rinzai lineages will also entail asking to what extent the changes that occurred during the eighteenth century can be attributed to the work of a single person or in which respects they were produced by a conflux of historical circumstances.

Since we will be looking at some of the Tokugawa developments of a tradition that is still alive, the "filter" provided by contemporary interpretations must be examined. One might recall that religious congregations making extensive use of kōans constitute groups preserving an oral tradition. From this perspective, anthropological approaches deserve our attention, for they strive to describe what is generally lacking in textually based analysis: a live context.[8] Therefore this survey will be based on three sources of information: (1) documents left by Hakuin and his direct descendants, (2) the few published texts that describe the sequence of kōans,[9] and (3) observations from fieldwork.[10]

We will concentrate here on the specific tools called "kōans" and thus will travel the following course. After outlining the historical background concerning shifts in the meaning of the word "kōan," I will examine three events in the Tokugawa period that triggered innovation in the way training was conceived. A closer look at kōan practice will then lead to reflections on its somatic implications, its educational dimension, and its emphasis on the process of "going beyond" (*kōjō*).

Shifts in the Meaning of the Word "Kōan"

The Present Japanese Monastic Context

The word "kōan" has now become fully Anglicized, since there is no satisfactory translation.[11] Interpretations that emphasize paradox seem to overlook the cardinal purpose of this verbal device, which is presently used in the monastic context[12] as a specific tool for communication between teacher and student. It might be simpler to apprehend the way a kōan is dealt with by comparing it to a screen. This screen, on which students can focus their mind, serves as a surface onto which to project their understanding, called *kenge*. In their search for a "solution" to the problem presented by a kōan, at some point students are commonly advised to avoid *kenge* that fall into explicative discourse or general consideration: each *kenge* has to be sharp, inducing a definite impression in both the person who produces it and the teacher who takes it in.[13] Such an expression of the *kenge* during private consultation (*sanzen*)[14] subsequently allows the teacher to look at the meaning exposed on the screen, helping him to appreciate the depth of the student's meditative absorption or the factors hindering his or her progress. The teacher will in turn offer feedback, often verbal, in accordance with the student's state of mind or what he or she has expressed. This screen analogy is a very rough delineation of how such "topics" are concretely handled, a task that will be touched upon in the section concerning the somatic dimension of kōan practice. Although this analogy fails to account for how kōans function as catalysts for doubt, it is helpful as a first approximation.

It must also be noted that different kōans sometimes operate in distinctive ways and that using the word "kōan" as a generic term may be confusing. In addition, the use of kōans in the Japanese Rinzai tradition appears to be quite different from the Korean method, in which "Korean Sŏn meditators keep the same *hwadu* (C. *hua-t'ou* J. *watō*) throughout their careers, trying continually to deepen their sensation of doubt."[15] Within the mainstream Japanese Rinzai tradition,[16] where kōans belong to a multifaceted curriculum, it is first necessary to distinguish between "main cases" (*honsoku*) and "peripheral cases" (*sassho*).[17] Today most students begin their kōan practice by struggling either with "the word *mu*" (*muji*) or with "the sound of one hand" (*sekishu onjō*) kōan. Both are "main cases" that help condense existential doubts into one specific question, and months or years can be needed to solve the interrogation it implies, which is similar to a quest for one's fundamental identity. Once the kernel of one of these "main cases" has been discovered, the teacher directs his students to examine "peripheral cases," thus assisting them to apprehend their own comprehension from different angles without sticking to a single view. Then, when the complete range of peripheral cases associated with one main case has been exhausted, the student is instructed to work on a new main case. For example, Tōin alludes to 48 secondary cases associated with "the sound of one hand" kōan.[18]

These peripheral cases often take the form of direct challenges that arouse the spirit of the practitioner, such as "try to pass through the eye of a needle" (hari no mizo o tōtte miyo).[19] Such questions sometimes have a comical dimension, such as "try to hide yourself inside a pillar" (hashira no nakani kakurete miyo) or "try to save a ghost" (yūrei o saido shite miyo).[20] Hakuin himself indicates that "once [someone] has succeeded in hearing the sound of one hand, it requires [further] scrutiny" (sensaku ari), and he follows by enumerating some of the probes he used, such as "Mount Fuji being inside a pocket-sized medicine case" (inrō nai ni fujisan ari).[21]

Besides the aforementioned contour of the meaning of the word "kōan," one must note that it has not always been used in such a way. Changes in the historical context brought new understandings to this term, although its evolution obviously does not strictly follow the historical periods, which are mentioned in the next sections only as convenient reminders.

T'ang and Sung Dynasties

A quick review of T'ang dynasty sources shows that the word kung-an (Chinese pronunciation of kōan) was used in the vernacular with a meaning quite different from the one it takes in later texts. In The Recorded Sayings of Layman P'ang, for example, it can be rendered as "the point of your remark,"[22] whereas it takes a much more specific and weightier meaning in later records. The sayings of Yün-mén Wén-yen (864–949) also provide several early instances of the term "kōan" being used toward the end of the T'ang to mean a "case" including the juridical nuance, but still being devoid of associations with the contemplation of "test cases" often borrowed from ancient dialogues.[23]

In relation to the inner transformations associated with Ch'an practice, it is widely known that the technical term chien-hsing (J. kenshō) came to be used toward the end of the T'ang, after the publication of the Platform Sūtra, whose existence is attested at least since 847.[24] What is less known is that this term, often translated as "seeing into one's own nature," is already defined in early sources as an expression of nonduality:

QUESTION: How do you get to see the nature?

TA-CHU: Seeing is nothing else than nature, impossible to see without nature.[25]

Because the distinction between the verb (to see) and its object (the nature) introduces a dichotomy, it seems better to keep the term *kenshō* untranslated. In the Japanese context, insight into the first kōan is labeled *kenshō,* which corresponds to a turning point in one's training. However, there are considerable variations in the impact of this inner transformation, depending on each individual. In a sermon given on December 4, 1994, Daigu Sōkō (Morinaga 1925–1995) Rōshi commented on the expression "true understanding" (*chencheng chien-chieh,* J. *shinshō no kenge*) that appears in *The Sayings of Lin-chi.*[26] He confessed, "What I am eagerly waiting for in the consultation room is for someone to come in possessed by an irrepressible joy [*osaerarenai hodo no yorokobi*]; I am not looking for an answer to the kōan." If we take this statement in reverse, it also implies that practitioners may find the right answer to a kōan without being overwhelmed by its discovery. One notorious instance is the case of Nishida Kitarō (1870–1945), who inscribed in his diary on August 3, 1903:

> In the evening consultation, [my understanding of] the word *mu* was acknowledged [*muji o yurusaru*]. However, I was not so delighted [*hanahada yorokobazu*].[27]

Victor Hori also observes: "The remarkable point of the *kōan* method is that with concentrated effort, monks regularly do start to penetrate the *kōan* usually within six months of their arrival in the monastery" (1994, p. 29). As Hori says, his description aims first at "demystifying the notion of 'mystical insight,' " and "The entire monastery *kōan* curriculum operates on the assumption that beginning monks start with a slight insight which further training systematically deepens and makes intelligible" (1994, p. 6, n. 1).

Regarding this question of the "intensity" of a first breakthrough, Ta-hui stresses the idea that "at the footing of great doubt inevitably lies great awakening."[28] In other words, release is proportional to the preceding distress, although both ultimately are illusory from the perspective of intrinsic awakening.[29] This is not to say that doubt is equivalent to distress, since it implies a positive side (the capacity to mobilize the energy of the whole being), but rather suggests that release is somewhat conditioned by the process that leads to it. "Great doubt" further expresses an affirmation of the necessity to fall temporarily into a state "similar to trying to gulp down a ball of hot iron, which you cannot spit out either."[30] This function of the kōan is especially valued in the Korean setting, where "all *hwadus* are considered to be simply an expedient means of producing the doubt."[31]

In any event, while insisting on the necessity of the primary change of perspective accompanying *kenshō,* the Rinzai tradition of the Tokugawa period cautiously warns against attachment to this turn. As we shall see in section on "Going Beyond," the accent is put on the need to never be satisfied with incomplete achievements or the refinement of one's understanding and its thorough integration into daily behavior.

From the Chinese Sung to the
Japanese Kamakura Period

Among documents attempting to give a definition of the kung-an, the *locus classicus* remains a passage from the teachings given by Chung-feng Ming-pen (1263–1323), which dates back only to the Yüan dynasty.[32] An even more recent commentary of the *Ch'an-lin pao-hsün,*[33] the *Ch'an-lin pao-hsün yin-i* completed in 1635, has provided Japanese commentators with a handy simile, which forms the bulk of the *Zengaku daijiten* entry on *"kōan"* (p. 303a–b).[34] The Chinese commentary explains the two-character compound "kung-an" by expanding it to the five-character expression "case documents [for examination] by the official magistrate" (*kung-fu chih an-tu*).[35] Actually, this is just a remolding of the above-mentioned teaching of Chung-feng Ming-pen[36] and does not tell us anything about the way these cases were selected or used by the teachers.

Besides this elementary formulation, only limited concrete evidence can be gathered from earlier Chinese Ch'an sources on how kung-ans were used as a practical method in the teacher–disciple encounters. For instance, the scanty instructions contained in the *Ch'an-men kuei-shih* (*Regulations of the Ch'an Approach,* included in *Ching-te ch'uan-teng lu* completed in 1004) mention only the practice of "entering the [abbot's] room and requesting [his] guidance" (*ju-shih ch'ing-i*). The consultation apparently was left up to the dedication of the student, and the text does not spell out the importance given to it or describe how it was accomplished.[37] Even the more elaborate *Ch'an-yüan ch'ing-kuei* (*Pure Rules of the Ch'an Monasteries*), which has a preface dated 1103 and contains later additions, does not deal extensively with the contents of private consultations, although they appear central to practice. In the section devoted to "entering the [abbot's] room," it describes only formal behavior. When the acolyte has completed the preparation:

> The person who enters the room turns [toward the abbot] to salute him with folded palms [*wen-hsün*], while [other] monks advance in order, their hands superposed on the chest [*ch'a-shou*]. Do not proceed before [the others, since it would] affect the thoughts of the monks. Enter through the right side of the gate of the abbot's quarter. First lift your left foot [to enter]; when you are in front [of him] and have finished saluting him with folded palms, rotate with hands superposed on the chest, then salute with folded palms on the southwestern corner of the master's chair and remain standing. Saluting again with folded palms first, give vent to what you have to express [*t'u-lu hsiao-hsi*]. Avoid speaking for a long time or indulging in worldly idle talk, which would make other monks wait. When you have finished expressing yourself, withdraw with folded palms and make a prostration in front [of the abbot].[38]

The text goes on to give other minute instructions about how to behave properly, but this description is striking in its lack of emphasis on what is sought through such meetings with the teacher. Of course this document belongs to the genre of monastic regulations, making it more akin to a set of administrative rules than to a meditation treatise.[39]

Nevertheless, the author of this work, Ch'ang-lu Tsung-tse (n.d.), was a seventh-generation descendant of Yün-men; it is thus implausible that this lineage would not have been using kung-ans, especially since the kung-an anthology *Pi-yen lu* had been composed by his predecessor Hsüeh-tou Ch'ung-hsien (980–1052). In this particular Yün-men school, the blending of Ch'an practice with Pure Land teachings apparently became widespread around the Northern Sung,[40] but still it does not account for the muteness of Ch'ang-lu Tsung-tse concerning the use of kung-an at his time. As Martin Collcutt remarks, omitting a mention of some aspect of practice could also be interpreted as an indication that this aspect of monastic life was obvious:

> The *Ch'an-yüan Code*, likewise, does not specify times for meditation. We can perhaps assume from this silence that meditation practice was still sufficiently dedicated to need no special regulation.[41]

Among the monastic rules texts, the only one so far to mention kung-ans explicitly is the *Ch'ih-hsiu Pai-chang ch'ing-kuei* (*Pai-chang Code Compiled on Imperial Decree*), a relatively late work completed between 1336 and 1343.[42]

Aside from references to kung-an practice in monastic codes, the transformation experienced during the Sung dynasty, especially in the circle of Wu-tsu Fa-yen (1024–1104)[43] and his followers, appears to have played a cardinal role in developments that reached Japan and Korea. The movement led by Fa-yen's successors, which was centered around Huang-mei-shan in Hupeh, succeeded in receiving the patronage of the last emperor of the Northern Sung, Hui Tsung (reign 1100–1125). His heir to the throne of the Southern Sung, Kao Tsung (reign 1127–1162), further marked the confidence of his dynasty in this Ch'an lineage by awarding the title Yüan-wu Ch'an-shih to K'o-ch'in (1063–1135), Fa-yen's successor. What had momentous consequences for the subsequent transmission to Japan was the activity of the next successor, Ta-hui Tsung-kao (1089–1163), whom Hakuin took as a model in his efforts to revive the Tokugawa Rinzai lineage.

In comparison with other Sung teachers, Ta-hui gives more explicit descriptions of practice. In particular, his *Letters* provide a firsthand account of how lay practitioners were advised to handle the kung-an.[44] Ta-hui's emphasis on sharpening the spiritual inquiry while engaged in secular labor represents a significant departure from teachings centered on the purely monastic environment. This emphasis on integrating spirituality with secular activity was later also stressed by Hakuin when he addressed the lay community. In his *Orategama,* Hakuin writes that "Master Ta-hui too said that [meditative] work in movement is infinitely superior to that in stillness."[45]

Hakuin's words are faithful to the spirit of Ta-hui, who frequently used the expression "[meditative] work" (C. *kung-fu*, J. *kufū*) to stress the necessity of "not letting the [meditative] work be interrupted,"[46] that is, carrying it through in all activities. However, it does not appear in the works of Ta-hui with this exact wording. Ta-hui says in one of his *Letters:*

> Precisely if you like stillness and dislike agitation it is appropriate to exert your force (or to make a constant effort). When you clash head-on against agitation with the state [acquired in] stillness, the force [you exert] is infinitely superior to what [is obtained by sitting] on a bamboo chair or a cushion.[47]

The word for "agitation," *nao* in Chinese, suggests a noisy and busy environment, and Ta-hui writes to a layman, alluding to the activities of a person involved in public affairs. It is worth noticing that Ta-hui often addressed a Neo-Confucian audience. The difference with Hakuin's use of the word "movement" is admittedly minor, and the intention of the author is not betrayed, but the fact that Hakuin attributes to Ta-hui a sentence that he has himself devised is indicative of the liberty he sometimes takes with the Chinese tradition. Divergences between the Korean and Japanese Rinzai traditions, which both take Ta-hui as their paragon, show that the interpretation of Ta-hui's teachings represents a core issue for their respective understandings of kōan practice.

In this regard, one cannot fail to notice that transformations occurring within the Chinese Ch'an context itself are presumably not foreign to this cleavage. The Ming priest Yün-ch'i Chu-hung (1535–1615), for instance, showed considerable respect for Ta-hui's accomplishments. In his *Chu-ch'uang erh-pi*, Yün-ch'i uses Ta-hui to illustrate his comments on "great awakening and small awakening" (*ta-wu hsiao-wu*):

> According to the lore, the venerable Ta-hui [Tsung-]kao [underwent] great awakening eighteen times, [his] small awakenings being countless.[48]

Whether this represents Yün-ch'i's original interpretation or reflects Ta-hui's own understanding is a debate that is beyond the scope of this chapter. What is most interesting for our inquiry is that Hakuin and two of his disciples, Tōrei Enji (1721–1792) and Reigen Etō (1721–1785), mention this story, which otherwise appears only in the writings of Yün-ch'i.[49] They thus show their familiarity with Ming Buddhist thinkers, although they occasionally criticized Yün-ch'i.[50] This example is one limited illustration of the fact that, despite the Tokugawa Rinzai claim that it represents the unadulterated Sung Ch'an tradition, the Japanese clergy had in fact assimilated consciously or unconsciously many features characteristic of the Ming Buddhist developments.

From the Kamakura to the Tokugawa Period

There is little point in attempting to retrace in a few lines the history of Zen lineages spanning more than five centuries, but several events deserve attention because they are crucial for understanding changes that occurred prior to and at the beginning of the Tokugawa era.

Among the successive waves of transmission that reached Japan during the Kamakura period, the branches of Ch'an stemming from Wu-tsu Fa-yen and his disciples were the principal lines imported by the pioneers. Three varieties of kōans, namely *richi* (principle), *kikan* (functioning), and *kōjō* (going beyond), are already mentioned in the writings left by priests who journeyed to China, such as Enni Bennen (1202–1280, Shōichi Kokushi) and Nanpo Jōmyō (1235–1309, Daiō Kokushi).[51] Although Chinese sources do provide isolated examples of these technical terms, the returning Japanese monks' eagerness to clarify the teachings they had received seems to have given a special flavor to these expressions, which are for the first time arranged in such sequential categories. Aside from the comment that certain kōans correspond to certain stages of cultivation, this early classification can nevertheless hardly be considered a "system."[52]

It must be noted here that traditional accounts tend to underline the continuity between the Sung Ch'an lineages and their Japanese counterparts, this continuity being one of the foremost arguments to support their legitimacy. This claim, however, points to issues that have not yet been resolved. In particular, it is well-known that among the 24 early transmissions of Ch'an lineages reaching Japan,[53] only the branch of Nanpo Jōmyō (*Daiō ha*) survived beyond the nineteenth century. This means that, although fifteen branches of the Rinzai school formally exist, they actually are all emanations from the Myōshinji line.

There is another unavoidable problem concerning the two key persons at the origin of this transmission: Hsü-t'ang Chih-yü (1185–1269) and his Japanese disciple Nanpo Jōmyō. Philological research has demonstrated that the document traditionally regarded as the spiritual certification bestowed by Hsü-t'ang on Nanpo cannot possibly have been written by Hsü-t'ang.[54] Several explanations of the oddity of this document can be offered. In particular, I have suggested that Nanpo's disciple Sōtaku Zetsugai (d. 1334) might have created or misinterpreted the certificate in order to highlight the eminence of his master.[55] There is no question about the authenticity of Nanpo's travel to China or his disciple relationship with Hsü-t'ang,[56] but the forged certificate does spotlight a general propensity to adorn the chronicles of the pioneers. In any case, the authoritative and homogeneous character of this lineage increasingly appears to have been inflated through the toil of Nippō Sōshun (1368–1448), the thirty-sixth abbot of Daitokuji and the reviver of Myōshinji; this priest is now recognized even by Rinzai scholars as the author of several counterfeit "transmission of the Dharma certificates" (*inkajō*) hitherto attributed to his predecessors.[57]

Despite the haziness surrounding early developments of this blend of the Japanese Rinzai tradition, Daitokuji and Myōshinji unequivocally took advantage of the political, social, and economic changes that were reshaping religious institutions after the civil wars of the Ōnin era (*Ōnin no ran* 1467–1477). In short, the fortunes of these two lineages, which had not participated in the pomp of the official temples (*gozan*) after Daitokuji withdrew from this system in 1431, were completely reversed. They went from outsider status to authoritative status.

Additionally, it should be mentioned that in the Rinzai context the use of the word "monastery" (*sōdō* or *senmon dōjō*) as a special place for training monks goes back only to the eighteenth century. Around the fifteenth century, monastic compounds like Daitokuji or Myōshinji were still merely a complex of temples, in which practice generally depended on each abbot. It is only much later that the challenge of the Manpukuji presence, and the new religious policy posted by the eighth shōgun Yoshimune, known as the reforms of the Kyōhō era (1716–1735),[58] appear to have galvanized the Rinzai clergy. As a result, Tōfukuji, whose buildings had been spared from the devastation of civil war, was the first monastery to establish (in 1729) retreat periods devoted to collective practice (*kessei*).[59] In the same process, Hakuin's private initiative led to the construction of Ryūtakuji in Mishima, inaugurated in 1761, with Tōrei reluctantly accepting the post of abbot.[60] It was only in 1787 that Hakuin's disciple Shikyō Eryō (1722–1787) succeeded in launching Enpukuji in Yawata, the earliest "officially approved monastery" (*kōnin sōdō*) of the Myōshinji branch,[61] just before his death.[62] Shikyō was one of the many monks who came from the lineage of Kogetsu[63] to join Hakuin.

Going back to the pre-Tokugawa epoch, despite a relative lack of dynamism in monastic life, the sixteenth century saw a spectacular broadening in the lay support of both the Daitokuji and Myōshinji lines, which gradually came to dominate the Rinzai temple network. On the other hand, regardless of their relative success, temples associated with these lines evidently did not escape the consequences of the unification of the country following Ieyasu's seizure of power in 1600. Among the many changes that particularly marked the Rinzai milieu almost from the beginning of the Tokugawa, a few are especially important for delineating the backdrop against which its premodern transformation took place.

Three Events That Forced Innovation

Tightening the Grip on Buddhist Schools

The first series of events is closely associated with institutional history. Shortly after the beginning of his reign, Ieyasu issued several official ordinances (*hatto*) meant to secure firmer control over Buddhist temples, which were expanded under the rule of his successor, Hidetada. This set of regulations, known as the ordinances of the Keichō (1596–1615) and Genna (1615–1623) eras, are thought to reveal in particular the influence of Ishin Sūden (1569–1633) on Ieyasu and his son. Sūden, a Rinzai priest from the Nanzenji Branch who acted as the personal secretary for the first three Tokugawa shōguns, has often been depicted as the "éminence grise" of the Bakufu.[64] Although Ieyasu had formally retired, beginning in 1605 he was still assuming the control of the government, and it is a fact that Sūden was employed by Ieyasu in 1608, first to handle diplomatic correspondence. From 1610, Sūden began to arbitrate religious affairs, soon gaining the collaboration of Itakura Katsushige (1545–1624), who also held various key positions, such as Governor of Kyoto (*Kyōto shoshidai*). After Sūden's death, the Bafuku resolved to nominate in 1635 a specialized Magistrate of Temples and Shrines (*jisha bugyō*), a move intended to control clerical intrigue.[65] These developments during the early Tokugawa show one side of the intertwining of Buddhism and politics, which was systematized in the following decades. Other events, overlapping the borders of the emerging Japanese "nation," also played a decisive role in shaping the features of Zen schools.

Emergence of the Ōbaku Lineage

The second aspect to consider is the shock associated with the coming to Japan of Chinese monks who claimed to represent the authentic Rinzai tradition. Following the fall of the Ming dynasty in 1644, and the gradual consolidation of power by the new Manchu rulers, a considerable congregation of Chinese clerics chose to emigrate to Japan. In the first wave of newcomers to Nagasaki in 1651 were several priests such as Tao-che Ch'ao-yüan (1602–1662, J. Dōja Chōgen). Tao-che left lasting traces in Japan by certifying the awakening of Bankei Yōtaku (1622–1693) and exerting influence on other Sōtō and Rinzai reformers.[66] These priests could benefit from the support of the already well-established Chinese community, with figures who had settled in Japan before the collapse of the Ming dynasty. I-jan Hsing-jung (1601–1668, J. Itsunen Shōyū),[67] who came to Nagasaki in 1641 as a merchant and took the tonsure three years later, was particularly instrumental in welcoming his fellow countrymen. He is also credited with sending repeated invitations to Yin-yüan Lung-ch'i (1592–1673, J. Ingen Ryūki) and convincing him to make the journey to Japan in 1654.

Different speculations concerning the motivation that led Yin-yüan to accept the invitation have been formulated, but it is clear that the political dimension played a decisive role. Among those who resisted the Manchus and militated for restoring the Ming, the activity of Cheng Ch'eng-kung (1624–1662, known as Kuo-hsing-yeh by his peers and as Coxinga by the Dutch) is well appreciated, but his connection with Yin-yüan has not yet received the attention it deserves. Born Chinese with a Japanese mother, Cheng combined a flourishing shipping business with piracy, and in 1661 he succeeded in ousting the Dutch from Taiwan. His death the following year prevented him from realizing his dream of retaking the Chinese continent and marked the end of the resistance against the Manchus. A point that is most interesting for the history of Japanese Buddhism is that Cheng provided the ship that brought Yin-yüan to Nagasaki. It seems that Cheng hoped that Yin-yüan would convince the Bakufu to offer military assistance to his troops.[68]

Whatever the complicated military and political circumstances that had brought Yin-yüan to Japanese soil, the religious consequences of his arrival were enormous. Especially since the opening of Manpukuji in 1663, the very presence of Ōbaku monks, who considered themselves exemplars of the authentic Rinzai tradition, represented an unprecedented challenge to the existing Japanese Rinzai lineages. Although an incentive toward reforms had been emerging since the beginning of the seventeenth century, especially within the Myōshinji branch, the growing popularity of Ōbaku turned it into an emergency. One of the most conspicuous aspects of these interactions can be seen at the level of monastic regulations. The 1672 publication of the *Ōbaku Codes* (*Ōbaku shingi*)[69] led a few years later to a reaction from Myōshinji, in the form of a new set of regulations composed by Mujaku Dōchū (1653–1745), the *Shōsōrin ryakushingi,* which appeared at the beginning of 1685 and is still used as the basis of monastic conduct.[70] Areas where the influence of—or the reaction to—Ōbaku left an imprint on Japanese Buddhism are manifold, and its impact even reached the fields of Japanese cultural techniques, such as printing and painting. Regarding the way kōans were treated by Ōbaku teachers, no explicit information remains that allow us to distinguish the extent of differences with the Japanese Rinzai tradition. What is known is that an important change took place around the time of Ryōchū Nyoryū (1793–1868), who was appointed thirty-third abbot of Manpukuji in 1851. Ryōchū, though formally belonging to the Ōbaku lineage, was actually a product of Hakuin's line, having received his certification from Takujū Kosen (1760–1833).[71] Since then, it appears, kōan practice at Manpukuji has retained some of its typical Ōbaku flavor while being modeled mostly on its Rinzai equivalent.[72]

Manpukuji was, however, not the only source of dissemination of this new transplant of Chinese Buddhism. Nagasaki retained a prominent role in exchanges with the continent, while other areas in the Kyūshū region became important centers marked by the Ōbaku style. In this regard, the close relationship unfolding between Tao-che Ch'ao-yüan and Kengan Zen'etsu (1618–1697)[73] had enduring consequences. Kengan was later the teacher of Kogetsu Zenzai (1667–1751), a Rinzai priest whose influence spread throughout the western half of Japan. This flowering of a new blend of Rinzai teachings in the Kyūshū area had further consequences for the modern evolution of this school when the line of Kogetsu in the West commingled with the line of Hakuin in the East, especially after the demise of Kogetsu.

Partial Fusion of Kogetsu's and Hakuin's Lines

The development of an Ōbaku-influenced current that later merged with the still marginal group of Myōshinji monks following Hakuin is the third major event to consider before we turn to the subject of reforms attributed to Hakuin. Hakuin himself consulted the venerable Ōbaku teacher Egoku Dōmyō (1632–1721) at a critical phase in his practice. The meeting of the 29-year-old Hakuin with Egoku, who was already 82, represents a crucial event in Hakuin's biography which has not yet received the attention it deserves.[74]

Conversely, once Hakuin had gained some degree of recognition, priests from other schools, including Ōbaku, came to seek his guidance. An outstanding example is Kakushū Jōchō (1711–1790), who in 1786 became the twenty-second abbot of Manpukuji. He first consulted Hakuin in 1749 to resolve doubts he had concerning the teaching of "five positions" (goi) and subsequently contributed to introducing Hakuin's style into the Ōbaku lineage.[75] His role was pivotal in that he succeeded the last Chinese abbot of Manpukuji, Ta-ch'eng Chao-han (1709–1784, J. Daijō Shōkan) and his nomination marked a shift in the policy of the Bakufu, which seized the occasion to restrict the abbacy to Japanese priests.[76] Hakuin also had acquaintances among Sōtō priests, and in the same year that Kakushū Jōchō consulted him, Hakuin also met, for example, the young Genrō Ōryū (1720–1813).[77] Genrō is known for his Tetteki tōsui (The Iron Flute Blown Upside Down), a kōan collection edited by his disciple Fūgai Honkō (1779–1847), who also added his own capping phrases (jakugo).[78]

Thus a wide conjunction of circumstances converged in the direction of reforms well before the rise of Hakuin to the status of a "reformer." As to the particular figure of Hakuin, the movement he came to represent embodies dynamics that included Ōbaku influence and later incorporated the flood of monks coming from the line of Kogetsu.[79] These are some of the Buddhist factors that marked the movement led by Hakuin. In the next section we will see that Hakuin's personal interests extended beyond the Buddhist sphere.

Somatic Implications of Kōan Practice

We have already noted that kōan practice takes its significance from a specific context involving the encounter between teacher and disciple. Private consultations generally take place daily, or even more frequently during the intensive periods dedicated exclusively to zazen[80] known as sesshin. For practitioners residing in a temple or a monastery the everyday activities also include manual labor (samu), chanting or reading sūtras (kankin), in addition to zazen and sometimes the ritual begging for alms outside the monastic compound (taku-hatsu). Ideally the mind remains focused on the kōan while these activities are being carried out, in the manner described above by Ta-hui and Hakuin in their respective treatment of "[meditative] work."

But how does it happen in concrete terms? This facet of practice is related partly to the perception of the mind-body that appears to have been widespread in the Buddhist milieu, and in Japanese society at large.[81] Despite the gradual adoption of Western medical science, illustrated by the first human corpse dissection performed in 1754 by Yamawaki Tōyō (1705–1762) and his assistants, or the general anesthesia of a patient in 1805 by Hanaoka Seishū (1760–1835), learning about the body, especially before the eighteenth century, obviously was informed by Chinese medicine. As is well known, the pivotal concept of Chinese medicine is the idea of "vital energy" (ch'i, J. ki), circulating within the soma and in the outside world. This perception of the person not only in terms of a body-mind, but as an entity participating in a sphere of vital energy extending beyond the boundaries of an isolated "body," proves to be indispensable for understanding the legacy of meditation schools.

Now how does this concept apply to scrutinizing kōans? The technical term used today for "handling a kōan" is the compound nentei, which often appears in Chinese sources with the sense of "raising [a problem]."[82] The relationship between this compound and the use of kung-an already emerges in the *Wu-chia cheng-tsung-tsan* (*Hymns to the Authentic Principle in the Five Schools*), a text completed in 1254. In its section on Mi-an Hsien-chieh (1118–1186) this anthology relates how Mi-an one day "raised the case of the old lady burning the hermitage,[83] and said: 'In the monastery we are lacking people who handle (nien-t'i) this kung-an.' "[84]

In the Japanese context, the works of Hakuin contain at least one clear example where the author mentions "handling the word mu of Chao-chou."[85] Handling a kōan, however, does not imply simply mobilizing the mind. Hakuin stresses that it involves the whole person:

> Straighten your spine and adjust your body evenly. Begin by contemplating the count of your breaths [susokkan]. Among the innumerable samādhis this is the unsurpassable one. Having filled your lower-abdomen [tanden] with vital energy [ki], take one kōan. [Thus,] it is essential to cut the very root of life.[86]

The sequence given here is not arbitrary, the successive adjusting of the body, breath, and mind is one of the features shared by all Japanese Zen schools and is also fundamental to the Chinese tradition.[87] What appears original here is Hakuin's explicit use of the terms tanden (center of energy in the lower-abdomen) and ki (vital energy), a vocabulary closely associated with that in Taoist practices and Chinese medicine before becoming part of the general Chinese worldview. The other striking characteristic of this text is its mention of susokkan (contemplating breath-counts). Concerning the use of such concepts, Hakuin's taste for Taoist classics is acknowledged in most of his writings. He liked, for example, to quote from the *Su-wēn* (*Simple Questions*),[88] saying that when the sage is "composed and satisfied in nothingness, true vital energy follows him; innate nature and spiritual force being preserved within, from where could illness come?"[89] This peculiarity in his discourse reflects his personal history, which was marked by serious illnesses, but also represents an attempt to clarify the fundamentals of Rinzai practice in a way that would appeal to a broader audience than the traditional elite. While Taoist concepts had only reluctantly been used by Chinese Buddhists, it is conceivable that by Hakuin's time they had gained a new prestige, especially after exchange with China became restricted. In any event, Hakuin chose to use a literary artifice to transmit Taoist inklings about health, breathing, and the care of vital energy, by borrowing the enigmatic character of a hermit called Hakuyūshi.

The surname of Hakuyūshi designated the contemporary figure of Ishikawa Jishun (1646–1709), a disciple of the poet Ishikawa Jōzan (1583–1672). Hakuin first pretends to have met Hakuyūshi through the latter's commentary on Hanshan's poems, the *Kanzanshi sendai kimon,* published in 1746.[90] However, the narration of his encounter with Hakuyūshi is definitely fiction, although from Hakuin's perspective there seems to be no intent to deceive his readers. With his customary sense of humor, he might have assumed that the message was clear enough when he wrote that Hakuyūshi was more than 180 or 240 years old.[91] Furthermore, the title of the work *Yasenkanna,* in which he expanded this story, probably constitutes an allusion to the "night boat of Shirakawa" (*Shirakawa yobune*), a synonym for talking knowingly about nonexistent matters.[92] Finally, Hakuin explicitly confesses his stratagem in the postface to *Yasenkanna,* dated 1757, saying that this work "has not been *set up* (*mōkuru*) for those gifted persons who have already realized [the essential] in one hammer stroke."[93]

In that quotation Hakuin suggests that *susokkan* is the foundation upon which practitioners should handle their kōan. This instruction, still followed in contemporary practice, aims primarily at circumventing the tendency to tackle the kōan through analytical thinking.[94] Systematic counting of exhalations from one to ten first helps the mind focus on a bodily function and remain occupied by devoting some energy to sustaining the uninterrupted succession of numbers. It also serves to activate the circulation of vital energy that will in turn sustain the dynamic of the posture, until the distinction between the consciousness that is counting and the breaths that are counted fades away. Once the basic technique[95] of *susokkan* has been mastered to a certain extent, the practitioner is usually given a kōan, often with the recommendation to work on the kōan "with the belly, and not with the head," applying what has been learned through *susokkan*. This might appear strange to readers unfamiliar with the technique, but the handling of a kōan (*nentei*) in the front of one's consciousness with the support of vital energy originating from the *tanden* is usually taken for granted in the Japanese monastic context. One could say that the circulation of energy[96] activated by the bellows of breathing takes over from discursive consciousness and allows one to maintain a certain degree of awareness of the kōan while being engaged, for instance, in manual labor.

For Hakuin, promoting this practice as "the unsurpassable samādhi" also meant returning to the very roots of Indian Buddhism. One of the sources of inspiration Hakuin acknowledges in his writings is Chih-i (538–597) and his main treatises on meditation,[97] but, like many reformers, Hakuin also strove to return to the foundations of the Buddhist tradition to reinvigorate his own school. His frequent mention of the Āgamas indicates that he was looking at early sources to find a way to rejuvenate Rinzai teachings.[98] The correlation of Hakuin's own sermons with the Āgamas, however, often remains ill defined.[99] Additionally, despite the emphasis Hakuin put on *susokkan,* he did not explicitly formulate how this related to the early Buddhist practice of *ānāpāna-sati* (S. *ānāpāna-smrti*), a task modern interpreters have undertaken.[100] Dating from the Tokugawa period, the only clear attempt to enlarge the practice of *susokkan* to a pan-Buddhist dimension including Indian sources seems to be the voluminous *Commentary of the Ch'an-ching* by Tōrei.[101] In this work Tōrei argues that the kōan practice advocated in his Rinzai lineage is an adequate adaptation of practices such as the contemplation of the breath or the contemplation of the horrible (*aśubhā-bhāvanā,* J. *fujōkan,* a practice involving visualization of the different stages of the decomposition of a corpse), which were still widespread at the time of Hui-yüan (334–416), the author of the preface to the *Ch'an-ching.*

The Educational Dimension

Let us now make one last digression from the Zen Buddhist context to examine briefly some issues related to kōans from the perspective of the science of education. Caleb Gattegno (1911–1988), who began his career as a mathematician, apparently is still not a well-known educator in the West, where the works of Piaget or Montessori are more commonly discussed. What makes Gattegno's contribution relevant to our survey is the cardinal importance he accorded to awareness. The word "awareness" can have any of several meanings, but Gattegno uses it in an original way to indicate the smallest unit of measurement for learning—each "discovery" made by the learner (in his French writings he uses the phrase *prise de conscience*). In this sense, our daily functioning could hardly take place without repeated "awareness."[102] Consider the following two lines:

$$4 + 3 \times 6 = 42$$

$$4 + 3 \times 6 = 22.$$

A first reading of these formulas might makes us feel uneasy until we realized that something was missing: a set of parentheses would resolve the problem! This example shows a casual awareness, which results from the resolution of a problem that might have been set up deliberately so that beginners in mathematics could understand the usefulness of parentheses.[103] Yet an awareness can also open onto a totally new apprehension of reality, or even change the orientation of one's life. Gattegno stresses in particular the importance of "awareness becoming aware of itself"[104] as a field of study.

Gattegno's discoveries about how learning takes place resulted partly from his observation of early childhood and from his study of mechanisms involved in the acquisition of language. Careful investigation of how consciousness apprehends the unknown led him to formulate a comprehensive approach to teaching, which rejects purely theoretical constructs and always returns to the question, "How does it work in the learner's mind?" Gattegno expresses this perspective by saying that for teaching to become realistic, it has to be subordinated to learning.[105] Educators must use their skills to mobilize the presence of their students here and now, the aim always being to "force awareness." This is how Gattegno envisions this exigency:

> Awareness is neither automatic nor constant. In fact, most people go through life only aware of a very small fraction of what could have struck them had they been uniformly and constantly watchful. There are, therefore, two meanings to "forcing awareness." One is concerned with what we do to ourselves, and the other with what can be done to us so that we become aware of what has escaped us, or might escape us.[106]

Moreover, Gattegno came to the meaningful conclusion that "education of awareness is the only possible and the only worthwhile education."[107]

This succinct picture of Gattegno's approach, also called the Silent Way, might sound familiar to readers acquainted with texts on Zen teachings. Yet I am not interested in establishing some shallow comparison, and Gattegno himself was careful "neither to claim any affiliation to a way of thinking with a venerable past, nor to enhance the Silent Way in a setting which brought Zen to life a long time ago."[108]

The purpose in mentioning Gattegno's work is to invite reflection on the role of "awareness" in the function of kōans, an avenue that seems more promising than the frequently emphasized "experience."[109] As was asserted before, kōans direct students to work on different problems, although the contents are never stated explicitly beforehand, and they can thus be considered elaborate pedagogical tools.[110] To express this more traditionally, kōans represent expedient means (*upāya*). One of their few common premises is that every problem, even the worst existential agony, carries its own solution. This is additionally supported by the basic Buddhist assumption of impermanence. Gattegno would simply say "there is always an entry into the problem."

Concerning the contents of the problem epitomized by a kōan, one might say that it carries both a universal and a personal dimension. The personal dimension can be described in terms of projections by the person, who is hindered by her own history or issues that she might be facing at the time she receives a kōan. The universal dimension, although sometimes tinged with cultural premises, implies that there is a rationale behind the problem and that the kōan is not a nonsensical question devised to befuddle the student. Even though every *kenge* is "original," since it bursts from an awareness reached through each disciple's struggle, the amazing fact is that everyone finally falls upon a common truth, which could otherwise hardly be acknowledged by the teacher. When this happens, the teacher sometimes indulges in explaining how the new awareness that has just occurred and has been demonstrated in front of him relates with other elements.

An example should help make this point clearer. *The Sayings of Lin-chi* contains a popular passage describing four types of circumstances, known as "the four measures" (C. *ssu-liao-chien,* J. *shiryōken*). This teaching depicts distinctive situations in which subject (the practitioner) and object[111] (his environment, or the other party) are placed in different relationships:

Sometimes one withdraws the person but does not withdraw the object.
Sometimes one withdraws the object but does not withdraw the person.
Sometimes one withdraws both the person and the object.
Sometimes one withdraws neither the person nor the object.[112]

The Chinese verb "*to,*" translated here as "to withdraw," refers to the negation or absence of negation of the protagonists in this strategical tetralemma.

Imagine that one evening you are coming home and you find a tiger crouched on your doorstep. You can choose to retreat carefully. Another choice might be to produce an unshakable confidence and ignore the tiger. The third situation might correspond to both of you vanishing, probably in this case as a result of surprise or terror. The last option here would amount to finding a modus vivendi, perhaps by succeeding in taming the tiger, so that your mutual presence would be affirmed. Besides its function as a Buddhist instructional device, this fourfold arrangement can be seen in light of the science of education as a sample of decisions the educator has to make when facing the problem of how to help students reach an awareness.

In the kōan curriculum followed by most Japanese Rinzai practitioners, these "four measures" are dealt with when the student is instructed to study key passages of *The Sayings of Lin-chi.* What is interesting from the pedagogical perspective is that an identical scheme had already been used in the peripheral cases assigned since the early stage of kōan study. In other words, enacting situations corresponding to the above four measures foreshadows the later understanding of this section of Lin-chi's teachings. Such an architecture of the sequence in which kōans are given implies a long-range intent, apparently refined through centuries of trial and error in instructing students. Although the

actual order followed in giving kōans varies according to lineages or to different individuals in the same lineage, a fundamental common thread is the emphasis on "going beyond" (kōjō) and never resting on an awareness, even if
one is left breathless by its contents.

Going Beyond: The Significance of "Kōjō"

Aside from its implications in scholastic Buddhism, the Chinese word *hsiang-
shang* (J. *kōjō*) is a colloquial expression that was used around the T'ang dynasty, chiefly in Ch'an recorded sayings, with the meaning of "upward."[113] Following the later evolution of Ch'an lineages, and their transmission to Japan,
this expression became a technical term associated with the advanced stages
of practice. It is difficult to demarcate a precise timing for this shift in meaning,
but a first step in this direction apparently had already been taken at the time
of the Kamakura pioneers.

The next stage in the evolution of the understanding of *kōjō* coincides with
the Tokugawa Rinzai transformations, since Hakuin and his disciples continually underlined the need to master this phase of practice. For example, Zenso
Tenkei (n.d.) writes in a preface to Hakuin's work *Sokkōroku kaienfusetsu* (*Introduction to the Sayings of Hsü-t'ang*) dated 1743: "After penetrating unexpectedly the [arcane] of the activity in favor of people [taught by his teacher]
Shōju Rōnin, [Hakuin] always used the ironhanded method of going beyond
when instructing others."[114]

Likewise, Tōrei Enji in his major work, *Shūmon mujintōron* (*Treatise on the
Inexhaustible Lamp of Our Lineage*),[115] gives a detailed exposition of what is
meant by "going beyond." The ten chapters of this treatise can be divided into
three parts.[116] The first part consists of the first four chapters. Chapters 1 to 3
constitute a kind of "preparation" for the fourth chapter on "true realization."
This chapter brings about a turn, in the sense that awakening, which was first
envisioned as a goal to reach, becomes manifest once the practitioner has overcome this major change of perspective. This transformation is described by
the traditional metaphor of "great death":

> When the crucial moment (*jisetsu*) comes, everything crumbles at once: You will
> know what it looks like. This is what is called "Dropping the hands hanging from
> the cliff, and coming back to life after having expired."[117]

After recounting the joy associated with this event, Tōrei warns against satis-
faction that might impede further progress:

> You, practitioners, don't discontinue [your inquiry] by stagnating in the unique
> principle of *kenshō*![118]

Far from being the terminus, this phase marks for Tōrei the beginning of real practice, actually "crossing the threshold" (nyūmon). Interestingly, Tōrei does not present the necessity of surpassing the first achievements of practice as being unique to Zen teachings. He quotes extensively from the sūtras to show that Buddhist classics imply a similar requirement. With this intent, Tōrei refers twice to the simile from the Lotus Sūtra in which the Buddha urges his traveling companions to advance further:

> The place [where lies] the treasure is at close hand; do not linger in the magic city [kejō]![119]

Tōrei basically advocated the oneness or inseparability of Buddhist canonical teachings and the meditative approach (kyōzen itchi).[120] He advised, for instance, the regular reading of sūtras and canonical commentaries and comparing their teachings with one's own comprehension. He adds: "If there are discrepancies with the sūtras and commentaries, [it signifies that] your comprehension is not only biased and dried up, but also shallow and sketchy!"[121]

Yet Tōrei had a precise idea about what made his school original. There are several passages in his treatise in which he enunciates this originality by identifying it with "going beyond."[122] In the second part of Tōrei's treatise, chapters 5 to 9, each chapter presents a different theme, but the idea of "going beyond" stands as their common denominator, summed up by chapter 6, which is entitled "Going Beyond." In contrast to the T'ang Chinese context, where this expression was used as an adverb or a preposition, by Tōrei's time the word kōjō had become substantivized, as is also indicated by nominal variants such as the ironic saying "the tiny matter of going beyond" (kōjō no shashi), or the more suggestive "decisive move of going beyond" (kōjō no ichijakusu).[123] To make this point clearer, Tōrei even resorted to formulating his own new "doctrinal classification" (hankyō), inspired by the Treatise of the Ten [Stations of the] Heart (Jūjūshinron) by Kūkai (774–835),[124] and by the model found in Tendai doctrinal classifications. Not surprisingly, Tōrei places Zen teachings at the top of his hierarchy, just above the esoteric teachings characterized by "the heart of hidden splendor" (himitsu shōgonshin), and he qualifies the Zen superiority by its explicit formulation of "going beyond" (kōjō).[125] The third part of Tōrei's treatise consists mainly of his discussion of the "diffusion" of the essential teachings beyond the borders of Buddhist sects. In an innovative manner, he reviews religions of which he was aware—Shintō, Confucianism, and Taoism—with a special emphasis on Shintō, which he knew best through personal acquaintance.[126]

This summary description of Tōrei's major work should have suggested an unambiguous picture of his principal theme: "going beyond" as the pivotal feature of Rinzai practice and doctrine. In comparison, he regarded kenshō as not the single property of Zen-related lineages but rather belonging to all Buddhist schools and even shared by non-Buddhist religions:

> In the teachings of the *kami,* of Confucius, or of Lao Tzu, it is by realizing first *kenshō* that one obtains to achieve [one's true nature], and it is by deepening all aspects of the Buddhist Dharma that one can say that [one's true nature becomes] fully actualized.[127] . . . Therefore, it is not only our school that founds itself on *kenshō,* [since] all the essential principles of other schools necessarily are founded on *kenshō.*[128]

This perspective leaves us with a picture of Rinzai practice significantly different from that presented in most published accounts aimed at popularizing Zen teachings. Tōrei quickly shifts emphasis from the importance given to a first breakthrough to a heavier stress on the need to go further. This dimension, also generically known as "post-awakening practice" (*gogo no shugyō*), corresponds to an essential part of the kōan curriculum, not to say its main component. I used Tōrei's formulation of this dimension, because it is often more straightforward than the writings of his teacher Hakuin, but there is no doubt both of them laid emphasis on the same point. For instance, in a letter to his lay disciple, the doctor Ishii Gentoku (1671–1751), Hakuin describes the state of someone who has gone through a first breakthrough but still fails to gain real autonomy in regard to differentiations and activity:

> When getting to the great matter of going beyond [taught by] the patriarchs, it is as if he were deaf or mute.[129]

Here an objection might arise. As those conversant with the few publications introducing the Japanese "kōan system" know, their authors assert that the reorganization of the kōan curriculum attributed to Hakuin involves the extension of the three aforementioned categories (*richi, kikan,* and *kōjō*) into five successive types of kōans: *hosshin* (dharmakāya), *kikan* (functioning), *gonsen* (verbal expressions), *nantō* (difficult to penetrate), and *kōjō* (going beyond).[130] These reports accurately describe trends that are used in most current monastic lineages, but their assumption of a perfect identity between kōan practice at the time of Hakuin and the *sanzen* as it is performed today is not supported by any clear evidence. In other words, they take for granted that the Rinzai tradition fundamentally has not been altered for three centuries.

Of course the existence of a continuity in this tradition is evident, but oversimplifications that neglect the historical context are insufficient. Given the seal of secrecy, which prevents disclosure of the contents of the dialogue taking place in the abbot's room, textual evidence cannot be the only criterion. It is nevertheless surprising to notice that no text by Hakuin or his direct disciples mentions five categories of kōan that should be practiced in sequence. While the necessity of realizing one's true nature (*kenshō*) indeed is emphasized in Hakuin's writings, this emphasis is surpassed by the frequency of reiterated exhortations not to be satisfied by such realization. The kōans "difficult to penetrate" are, for example, cited as efficient tools for avoiding this danger of stagnation. In *Sokkōroku kaien fusetsu* Hakuin advises his students: "Individuals of strong resolve, you must fiercely mobilize your energy and see your nature once. As soon as you realize an unequivocal *kenshō,* drop it and resolve [this matter] by practice on the cases difficult to penetrate."[131] According to this passage, *kenshō* (corresponding to *hosshin* kōans in the above categories) would appear to be directly followed by the *nantō* kōans.

Concerning the fact that neither Hakuin's nor his direct disciples' works mention an explicit sequence of kōans, two rationales could be offered to explain this silence. First, given the accent on oral transmission and direct guidance from teacher to disciple, Hakuin, even if he did actually use these categories to teach disciples, might have chosen not to commit such a rigid pattern to paper, since doing so could impede the optimal adaptation to individuals and circumstances. If written records of a particular sequence of kōan existed, they were noted down individually and these notes were not intended for public disclosure. However, such information about Hakuin's practices and those of his direct disciples has not been divulged yet, if it exists. Nevertheless, the idea commonly held by living teachers, attributing the paternity of these transformations to Hakuin, cannot be entirely discarded either, since results from information transmitted by the oral tradition.[132]

Second, successors of Hakuin may have devised this sequence of kōans, drawing on their master's teachings. Here again, the lack of documents precludes a definite conclusion. Proceeding by negative elimination, it is possible to ascertain that nothing close to a "system" appears in Tōrei's writings. As was mentioned before, his central treatise does describe in detail the stages on the path of cultivation but carefully avoids delineating a rigid structure of the way kōans should be used. The date of publication of Tōrei's treatise, 1800, therefore allows us to contend that at least until the end of the eighteenth century Rinzai teachers avoided formulating anything resembling a system with a definite set of kōans. They presumably resorted to some types of blueprints for their own purposes, but the danger of falling into stereotyped patterns of teaching apparently prevented them from leaving public traces of these resources.

A prominent matter of concern, which goes beyond the scope of this chapter, is the extent of transformations that occurred in the Rinzai clergy during the last 70 years of the Tokugawa period and after the Meiji Restoration.[133] One might wonder in particular to what extent the crucial concept of "going beyond" survived the Meiji transition. Although this question remains open, the contemporary voice of Kajitani Sōnin Rōshi (1914–1995) suggests some degree of continuity in that regard, since he maintained that the aim of the whole kōan "system" is to avoid stopping halfway by being satisfied with one's accomplishments—in other words, to go beyond.[134]

Conclusion

The diverse facets of kōan practice described here have presented a complex picture which challenges the common image of a homogeneous Rinzai tradition. Considerable shifts in the interpretation of key terms should caution us to avoid quick generalizations and to refer always to a specific historical context, especially when referring to "kōans." Areas in which the dynamics inherent to the various branches of the Rinzai sect interacted with political events, or with other schools, have indicated that the "reform movement" credited to Hakuin and his followers also must be situated in this broader context, which was generally inclined to direct and indirect interactions with the Ōbaku movement that were an important and often overlooked catalyst for change within Rinzai lineages.

Discussing the specific contribution of Hakuin and his followers in the Tokugawa transformation of Rinzai teachings necessarily involves taking into account the angle of "somatic implications." The abundant background from which Hakuin derived his inspiration suggests a much wider intellectual profile than what is usually credited to Tokugawa Buddhist thinkers. The dynamism demonstrated by Hakuin and his disciples in their systematic "takeover" of most Japanese Rinzai monasteries within a few decades presumably is not unrelated to the insistence they placed on breathing and vital energy and their rejection of the use of kōans as a literary exercise.

A brief excursion into the field of education has allowed us to stand back from the purely Buddhist context for a moment and suggested that we might examine the function of kōans from the perspective of "awareness" (in the sense defined by Gattegno). This concept furnishes a tool for envisioning the transformations of consciousness accompanying practice while avoiding the pitfalls associated with the inevitable discourse on "Zen experience." In that regard, the above indications should also have provided some evidence that the idea of "a Rinzai emphasis on *satori* as a once-and-for-all goal to be reached in the future," still often heard, is a groundless misconception. Cultivation pursued in this tradition, at least as it is presented by its major Tokugawa proponents, intends precisely the opposite: constantly going beyond a first awareness of nonduality and aiming at integrating this insight into daily life until no trace of transient exalted states remains.

NOTES

1. I am thinking in particular of publications inspired by postmodern approaches and of those touched by the so-called "Critical Buddhism" current. Reflections on method applied to Buddhist studies in general can be found in particular in Ruegg (1995) and Gomez (1995), while the state of the field concerning Ch'an studies is reviewed in Foulk (1993a). Concerning "Critical Buddhism" and its reception by Japanese and Western scholars, see the volume edited by Hubbard and Swanson (1997). A reaction against reductionist interpretations is found in Kirchner (1996).

2. I shall use the word "awakening" rather than "enlightenment," because it is a more felicitous rendering of the Sanskrit *bodhi*. "Enlightenment" also seems to suggest a stronger contrast between darkness and light than the idea of sliding naturally from sleep to wakefulness.

3. This represents the outcome of a long process beginning in the Kamakura period. Tokugawa developments are discussed in Mohr (1994).

4. Statistical data on the number of temples, priests, and believers for each branch or each school can be found in the yearly publication *Shūkyō nenkan,* edited by the Bunkachō. Its 1995 (Heisei 7) edition describes the Zen schools on pp. 72–73, and its edited translation forms appendix C in Mohr (1997, pp. 767–774).

5. ZGD, p. 896c–d.

6. This text has been edited by Nakamura Sōichi (1987). For the hypothesis of a relation between Tetsumon Dōju's work and Ryōkan's redaction of the *Hokkesan,* see Yanagida (1989, p. 105).

7. Yanagida (1989, p. 263).

8. Such an approach has been successfully followed in Ueda (1983) and Hori (1994).

9. I shall in particular mention three kōan collections published by Akizuki Ryōmin: *Gasenshū* (Collection of Tiles and Keepnets), anonymous (Akizuki 1979, pp. 259–324); "Ekkei—Kasan ka shitsunai kōan taikei" ("The Kōan System in the Sanzen Room of the Ekkei-Kasan Lineage"), based on a manuscript list of kōans (*anken*) in the line of Kasan Genku (Suga 1838–1917), (Akizuki 1987, pp. 257–332), and "Hakuin ka kōan Inzan Bizen ha: Shitsunai issantō" (Kōan under Hakuin, the Bizen Branch in Inzan's Lineage), (Akizuki 1986). I will not mention the more famous anonymous *Gendai sōjizen hyōron* (*Criticism of Today's Mock Zen*) or its English translation by Yoel Hoffmann, which not only are full of inaccuracies but also could be harmful to inexperienced practitioners. The charges found in this book, first published in 1916, mostly lack justification and seem to be the product of an embittered monk who sought revenge for his negative experience. Rikugawa Taiun (1886–1966) has done justice to this polemic text in his *Shinzenron* (About Authentic Zen, posthumous work published in 1968), see pp. 225–292.

10. In several areas of the history of thought, such as that of sectarian consciousness, we cannot deny the existence of gaps between patterns emerging during the Tokugawa period and today's perception of the same categories. The contents of kōan practice, however, are often viewed by the clergy as a product of the tradition's continuity, a claim that adds significance to fieldwork. For example, Thomas Kirchner, a Rinzai monk, claims that "For better and for worse, the methods and goals of Zen teaching have remained largely the same as they were in the Tokugawa period—the same Inzan and Takujū teaching lines continue, the same kōan systems are used, and the same basic texts and interpretations shape the direction of monastic training" (Kirchner 1996, p. 49). Although *sanzen* practice suggests a reasonable amount of continuity, it can also

be examined from the perspective of the slight mutations that necessarily followed the post-Hakuin evolution of the Rinzai school. In my opinion, positing a working hypothesis that circumspectly challenges this basic assumption of continuity might better encourage research centered on what happened between the eighteenth century and today.

11. To take just one example, the *Longman Dictionary of the English Language* (1991 edition) gives the following definition of "koan" (p. 878): "A paradox to be meditated on that is used to train Zen Buddhist monks to abandon reason and develop intuition in order to gain enlightenment [J. *kōan*, from *kō* public + *an* proposition]." This definition contains at least four inaccuracies: (1) The expressions used in kōans are not necessarily paradoxical; (2) this practice is not limited to monks, and many laypersons engage in it; (3) the goal of kōans is certainly not to "abandon reason," and many texts warn against "irrational understanding" (*muri no e*); (4) the purpose of this practice is not only "to gain enlightenment" (it would be more precise to speak of rediscovering enlightenment) but, as will be emphasized in this chapter, to go beyond it. The dictionary's explanation of the compound kōan by the simple combination of the two characters that compose it is also erroneous. On the accepted etymology, see the discussion later of *kung-fu chih an-tu,* or "case documents."

12. The "monastic context" refers here to a place dedicated to practice, which might be an ordinary temple or a Zen center. Likewise it is not restricted to monks but obviously includes laypersons.

13. Technically the "inner state" expressed through each *kenge* is often depicted by the Buddhist term *kyōgai*. Its Sanskrit equivalent *gocara* first designated a pasture (for cows) before being used as a technical term for the "objects" that can be apprehended by consciousness, sometimes also translated as its "sphere" or "range" (Edgerton 1953, p. 215a). Within the Sino-Japanese context, it is often understood as alluding to the fact that such an inner state is the outgrowth of cultivation, differing from a mere transitory "state of mind" and rather carrying the quality of a "cultivated field."

14. Consultation in the teacher's room (*sanzen*) generally is divided into the usual individual consultation (*dokusan*), which is optional, and the consultation for all practitioners in turn (*sōsan*), which is compulsory and held on the first, fourth, and seven days of the intensive periods of meditation (*sesshin*).

15. Buswell (1992, p. 158). For the definition of *hwadu* (J. *watō*), as the "essential theme" or "critical phrase" of the kōan, see also Buswell (1992, pp. 150–151).

16. An exception would be the perspective of Hisamatsu Shin'ichi (1889–1980), who instructed his students to work on "the fundamental kōan" (*kisoteki kōan*).

17. The word *sassho* literally indicates an action that presses someone to react, which is used to test (*tamesu*) her understanding. To my knowledge this expression does not appear in Chinese sources. The commentary on case 28 in *Pi-yen lu* uses the close compound *ai-tsa-ch'u* (J. *aisatsu no tokoro*), meaning "hitting home" or "pressing hard" (T 48 no. 2003, p. 169a09; see the entry on *aisatsu* in Koga 1991, p. 5). In Japanese, since the word *aisatsu* already had the meaning of "a salutation" in the Tokugawa period, the compound *sassho* may have become necessary later (see for instance HZS, edited by Gotō, vol. 5, p. 53). One of the few written examples of the use of *sassho* in the sense of a "peripheral case" appears in a passage of *Zoku kinsei zenrin sōbōden;* it describes how Shinjō Sōsen (Kobata, then Sakagami [1842–1914] reached a breakthrough after hearing a bird singing at dawn. When he entered the consultation room of Gisan Zenrai (1802–1878), "[Gisan] gave him a sequence of peripheral cases, but Sōsen's answers were just flowing" (Obata 1938, vol. 3, p. 334). The absence of this

compound in earlier sources, including HZS, suggests late origins. On the other hand, the verb *sasshite iwaku*, with the meaning of "say for testing," frequently appears in HZS (for example in vol. 1, p. 58).

18. Iida (1943, pp. 23–26).

19. Akizuki (1986, no. 86, p. 170). The character used by Akizuki for *mizo* is a phonetic approximation (*ateji*). The proper compound is in the *Kokugo daijiten*, p. 2268e.

20. Akizuki (1987, no. 19, p. 263 and no. 22, p. 264).

21. HZS, vol. 1, p. 261. Based on this, one concrete formulation of the question asked to the student is "try to take out Mount Fuji from the second layer of a pocket-sized medicine case!" (*inrō no nijūme kara fujisan o dashite miyo*), found in Akizuki (1986, no. 94, p. 171).

22. Iriya (1973, pp. 200–202); Translation by Sasaki et al. (1971, p. 55).

23. T 47 no. 1988, pp. 547a12, 551c29, and 570c09. Two of these three passages are translated by App (1994, pp. 107 and 143).

24. Yanagida (1976, p. 459). This is the year Ennin (794–864) presented to the court his catalogue of texts brought back from China. It mentions the *Platform Sūtra* (T 55 no. 2167, p. 1083b07–b08) and constitutes safer evidence than the Tun-huang manuscripts, the dates of which are uncertain.

25. This passage appears in *Tun-wu yao-mēn* (*The Essential Gate to Immediate Awakening*), attributed to Ta-chu Hui-hai (n.d., a successor of Ma-tsu Tao-i). It is included in T 51 no. 2076, p. 443a20–a21; see also Hirano (1970, p. 186). A similar dialogue takes place earlier in the same text, T 51 no. 2076, p. 247c09–c12; Hirano (1970, p. 138).

26. This expression occurs several times in *Lin-chi lu*, T 47 no. 1985, pp. 497b01, 497c26, 498b23, 498b25, 498c04, and 502c15. It has been variously translated as "true insight" (Sasaki 1975), "true and proper understanding" (Watson 1993b), or "la vue juste" (Demiéville 1972).

27. Ueda, ed. (1996, p. 269).

28. T 51 no. 1998A, p. 886a27. This sentence also figures in the teachings of Hakuin, with a slight alteration, without mentioning the author (HZS vol. 2, p. 414).

29. Debates about whether the philosophy of intrinsic awakening (*hongaku shisō*) is or is not a Japanese innovation seem to have neglected an obvious bit of evidence: the Korean tradition. Since the Korean perspective on this question seems to be the same as its Japanese equivalent, speculation about the Japanese originality appears quite sketchy (see Buswell 1992, p. 152).

30. Commentary on the first case in *Wu-men kuan* (*Gate without Barriers*), T 48 no. 2005, p. 293a04–a05.

31. Buswell (1992, p. 158).

32. Translated in Miura (1965, pp. 4–7, and 1966, pp. 4–7).

33. A text completed in 1185, which is included in T 48 no. 2022. The passage suggesting "they quote the kung-ans of the ancients and request their disciples to appraise them" is a critique of such behavior, found on p. 1033b21–b22.

34. ZGD relies on the work of Mujaku Dōchū (1653–1745), who provides all main sources in his *Zenrin shōkisen* (Zengaku sōsho edition, pp. 606–607) and *Kattō-shū* (*Zengaku sōsho edition, pp. 957–958*).

35. HTC 113, p. 264b05–b10. See also the separate definitions of *kung-fu* and *an-tu* in Morohashi's *Daikanwa jiten*, vol. 2, p. 40c–d no. 1452–652 and vol. 6, p. 328c no. 14762–57. For the compound *kung-fu*, Hucker proposes the more rigorist translations "Three Dukes" or "Ducal Establishment" (1995, p. 292b no. 3426).

36. MZ 60, p. 193a018–b02.

37. T 51 no. 2076, p. 251a15.

38. Kagamishima et al. (1972, p. 67).

39. Foulk even considers "entering the [abbot's] room" in this context to represent a mere ceremony (1993b, pp. 181–182).

40. Kagamishima et al. (1972, p. 4).

41. Collcutt (1981, pp. 142–143).

42. This mention is found in T 48 no. 2025, p. 1154a06. For the date of completion of this text, I have followed Yanagida (1976, p. 501).

43. The birthdate of Wu-tsu Fa-yen is not known with certainty, but I have followed Ishii (1987, pp. 229 and 566).

44. The original is accessible in the edition included in the *Recorded Sayings of Ta-hui* (T 47 no. 1998A, pp. 916b–943a) and in the abridged version included in *Chih-yüeh lu* (HTC 143, pp. 676b–736). The former has been edited by Araki (1969a), and the latter has been partially translated by Cleary (1977).

45. HZS vol. 5, p. 111. See also Izuyama (1985, pp. 35 and 38, n. 6) and Yampolsky (1971, p. 33).

46. See for instance the *Recorded Sayings of Ta-hui* (T 47 no. 1998A, p. 868c22).

47. *Ta-hui shu* (T 47 no. 1998A, p. 918c21–c23; Araki 1969a, p. 25).

48. *Chu-ch'uang erb-pi* (The Second Volume of Writings by Chu-ch'uang [surname adopted by Yün-ch'i]), p. 64a of the Japanese woodblock edition of 1653 (Shōō 2), kept in the Sekisui Fund of the Zen Bunka Kenkyūsho at Hanazono University. This text is also included in the more comprehensive *Collection of Dharma [Sayings] by Yün-ch'i (Yün-ch'i fa-hui)*. Concerning this author see Araki (1969b and 1985), and Yü (1974 and 1981).

49. This story is found in Hakuin's *Itsumadegusa* (HZS vol. 1, pp. 193–194 and 226) and *Yasenkanna* (HZS vol. 5, p. 364), in Tōrei's *Shūmon mujintōron* (T 81 no. 2575, p. 587c02; translation in Mohr 1997, p. 163), and in Reigen's *Dharma Talks (Kaisan Reigen) oshō hōgo zatsushū*, HZS vol. 8, p. 53).

50. This is in particular the case of Tōrei, who reprinted in 1762 (Hōreki 12) the *Ch'an-kuan-ts'e-chin (Exhortation to Proceed through the Ch'an Gates)*, a work by Yün-ch'i. He did so in memory of the inspiring effect this text had had on his master Hakuin. The postface by Tōrei contains a virulent critique of Yün-ch'i (T 48 no. 2024, p. 1109a20–c13).

51. See for example T 80 no. 2544, p. 20b17–b20 for Enni, and *Zenmon hōgoshū* vol. 2, p. 438 for Nanpo.

52. Chinese antecedents of the words *richi* and *kikan,* and the views of Musō Soseki (1275–1351) on this question, are discussed in Yanagida (1985, pp. 578–586). Haskel presents another facet of the early Japanese patterns of kōan study (1988, pp. 52–99).

53. The 24 transmissions of Zen lineages (*Zenshū nijūshi ryū*) include 10 branches founded by Japanese monks and 14 established by Chinese immigrants. They begin with Myōan Yōsai (1141–1215) returning to Japan in 1191 after his second trip to China and conclude with Tung-ling Yung-yü (J. Tōryō Eiyo 1285–1365), who arrived in 1351. This traditional list, which is far from exhaustive, was compiled at the beginning of the Tokugawa. It is reproduced in ZGD, p. 689b.

54. Iriya (1985). Further comments on this in Mohr (1997, n. 928).

55. This clue is supported by the appendix to the sayings of Hsü-t'ang, which bears the signature of Sōtaku (T 47 no. 2000, p. 1062a10).

56. Yanagida has given a clear account of this encounter within the tense context of the Kamakura period, marked by the threat of a Mongol invasion and the rise of Nichiren nationalism (Yanagida 1959).

57. Katō (1995).

58. On these reforms, see the monograph by Ōishi (1995).

59. Katō (1969, p. 256).

60. Nishimura (1982, p. 180).

61. Katō (1969, p. 261). The date given by Katō, sixth year of the Tenmei era, twelfth month, eight day, conforms with HZS vol. 8, p. 261 or p. 289, with the day added. This corresponds to January 26, 1787 (or 1786 without taking into account the gap between lunar and solar calendars), and not to 1768, as misprinted in his article.

62. Shikyō died on the March 12, 1787 (seventh year of the Tenmei era, first month, thirty-third day), HZS vol. 8, p. 268. Curiously, there is no mention of this event in Tōrei's biography, although Tōrei lived until 1792.

63. Akiyama (1983, p. 153). Shikyō was a disciple of Kogetsu's successor, Kangan Kaikai (d. 1744), whose biography is included in *Kinsei zenrin sōbōden* vol. 2, pp. 160–163.

64. Tsuji (1944–1955, vol. 8, p. 260) and Takenuki (1989, p. 183). A whole chapter of Tsuji's monumental work is devoted to Sūden's biography (1953, vol. 8, pp. 26–88).

65. Tsuji (1944–1955, vol. 8, pp. 29–32). This function existed during the Kamakura and Muromachi periods, but its establishment by the Tokugawa Bakufu began in 1635 (Kan'ei 12, see Takayanagi and Takeuchi, *Kadokawa nihonshi jiten*, pp. 432 and 1148).

66. The role played by Tao-che is partially described in Ogisu Jundō (1958, pp. 34–35); See also Schwaller (1989, pp. 8–10). For Tao-che's dates and other invaluable references see OBJ, p. 263.

67. OBJ, pp. 17b–18b.

68. See Ono (1987) and Takenuki (1993, pp. 424–426).

69. T 82 no. 2607.

70. T 81 no. 2579. The preface and publication were completed in January 1685 (first year of the Jōkyō era, twelfth month).

71. ZGD, p. 995d, OBJ, pp. 388a–89a, and Murase (1982, pp. 72–77).

72. Personal communication from Rev. Tanaka Chisei, Chief Executive of the Ōbaku Culture Research Institute (Ōbaku Bunka Kenkyūsho).

73. Kengan Zen'etsu died on January 8, 1697 (ninth year of the Genroku era, twelfth month, sixteenth day, see ZGD, p. 672c–d, and OBJ, p. 106a–b).

74. *Itsumadegusa,* HZS vol. 1, p. 182; Katō (1985, p. 137); Rinoie (1981, pp. 217–222); Waddell (1983, p. 109).

75. Katō (1985, pp. 228 and 231, n. 16), OBJ, pp. 59b–60b. This episode is also mentioned in *Keikyoku sōdan,* HZS vol. 1, p. 144.

76. OBJ, p. 60a.

77. Rikugawa (1966).

78. This text has been partially translated into English as *The Iron Flute* (Senzaki 1964). *Tetteki tōsui* is found in *Sōtō-shū zensho: juko.*

79. Fourteen important figures among Hakuin's prominent disciples had first practiced under Kogetsu before joining the ranks of Hakuin (Akiyama 1983, p. 153).

80. *Zazen* is another word that should, as much as possible, remain untranslated, since the character "*za*" of *zazen* is often understood in the sense of an inner unmovable "seated" posture. Akizuki asserts this point in his encouragement to practice every-

where: "Because it is not only *zazen* with legs folded that is *zazen*" (1986, p. 160). The term "seated zen" coined by Bielefeldt does not appear satisfactory either (1995, p. 198).

81. Analysis of this aspect can for instance be found in Yuasa (1987) and in the volume by Kasulis et al. (1993).

82. Koga (1991, p. 370b).

83. This case, known in Japan as "basu shōan," is included in *Lien-teng hui-yao* 29, HTC 136, pp. 930b17–931a02, and in *Wu-teng-hui-yüan* vol. 6, HTC 138, p. 226a17–b02.

84. HTC 135, p. 952b03.

85. *Usenshikō,* HZS vol. 6, p. 144.

86. *Rōhatsu jishu,* teachings by Hakuin written by Tōrei. T 81 no. 2576, p. 615a22–a25, and HZS vol. 7, p. 233. This text, recited in the monasteries every year on the occasion of the December *sesshin,* can be considered the Tokugawa Rinzai reformulation of the rules for *zazen.*

87. See Bielefeldt (1988).

88. This is the first part of *The Yellow Emperor's Inner Classic* (*Huang-ti nei-ching*) followed by the *Ling-shu* (*The Spiritual Pivot*), considered to be "the acupuncturist's bible."

89. *Huang-ti nei-ching su-wēn,* first fascicle, second section, edited by Jen Ying-ch'iu (1986, p. 8). Compare with the translation by Veith (1966, p. 98). This passage is quoted in the third volume of *Itsumadegusa* (HZS vol. 1, p. 221), twice in the first volume of *Kanzanshi sendai kimon* (HZS vol. 4, pp. 108 and 116), and in *Yasenkanna* (HZS vol. 5, p. 359).

90. HZS vol. 4, p. 109.

91. Three or four sexagesimal cycles, as mentioned in *Yasenkanna* (HZS vol. 5, p. 350).

92. For the details, see Izuyama (1983, p. 114).

93. HZS vol. 5, p. 365. See also Katō (1985, p. 21). The expression "realized in one hammer stroke" is common in Chinese Ch'an sources. See, for instance, the *Ching-te ch'uan-teng lu,* fascicle 15 (T 51 no. 2076, p. 319b09–b10). Koga (1991, p. 18a).

94. Contemporary descriptions are given in Osaka (1969, pp. 129–134), Ōmori (1972, pp. 63–71), and Ueda (1993, pp. 235–240).

95. *Susokkan* is "basic" in the sense that it is necessary to acquire some familiarity with this mediation technique at the beginning, but it remains an essential tool at all stages. People who have completed their kōan training eventually return to *susokkan.*

96. Most teachers of the Ch'an or Zen Buddhist traditions have been careful not to present the circulation of vital energy as a goal in itself, in particular to distance themselves from Taoist teachings. However, parallels between *zazen* and the Taoist technique of the "small celestial revolution" (*hsiao-chou-t'ien*) are quite obvious. These analogues, and mutual borrowings from both traditions, need further investigation.

97. Chih-i's biography is mentioned in *Keisōdokuzui,* HZS vol. 2, p. 105; *San'in shishūjo sendai kimon,* HZS vol. 4, p. 9; *Kanzanshi sendai kimon,* HZS vol. 4, p. 332; and *Orategama,* HZS vol. 5, p. 168. Chih-i's main work, the *Mo-ho chih-kuan,* is referred to chiefly in *Itsumadegusa,* HZS vol. 1, p. 220, in *Orategama,* HZS vol. 5, pp. 108 and 118, and in one of Hakuin's letters, HZS vol. 6, p. 445. Hakuin appended to his *Kanrin'ihō* a key section of the introduction to the *Mo-ho chih-kuan* by Kuan-ting, which he entitled "Endonshō" ("The Chapter on Perfect and Sudden [Calming and Contemplation]"). This section corresponds to T 46 no. 1911, pp. 1c23–2a02 and is included in HZS vol. 4, p. 379. See the lecture by Yamada Mumon (Taishitsu Mumon 1900–1988) (1974)

and the translation by Donner and Stevenson (1993, pp. 112–114). A brief commentary on the same section by Tōrei, with capping phrases added, is also found in HZS vol. 8, pp. 419–422. Hakuin also mentions the *Hsiao-chih-kuan* in HZS vol. 5, p. 359.

98. We find for example, mentions of the Āgamas in *Itsumadegusa*, HZS vol. 1, p. 220, in *Keisō dokuzui*, HZS vol. 2, p. 117, and in *Kanzanshi sendai kimon*, HZS vol. 4, pp. 106, 115, and 137. In this last allusion, Hakuin considers the Āgamas to be expedient means intended to simplify Buddhist teachings that were too arduous in their first expression, but he evidently considers them to be the Buddha's words. In another text full of irony, the *Anjin hokoritataki* (*Dusting off the Heart in Peace*), he even ventures to compare these teachings to a "mass credit sale on cheap articles" (*yasumono urikake*) (HZS vol. 6, p. 245).

99. It is in particular the case of his "soft-butter method" (*so o mochiuru no hō*), a relaxation technique which Hakuin describes as if it were from the Āgamas (*Kanzanshi sendai kimon*, HZS vol. 4, p. 115, and *Yasenkanna*, HZS vol. 5, pp. 358 and 361). To date no similar passage in the Āgamas has been located.

100. See, for instance, the publications by Muraki Hiromasa (1979, 1985, 1988) or Kamata Shigeo (1996).

101. Commentary of the *Ta-mo-to-lo ch'an-ching* (T 15 no. 618) entitled *Darumatara zenkyō settsūkōsho*. This text, first published in 1784, remains only in the form of a woodblock edition. One of the few original copies is kept at the Jinbun Kagaku Kenkyūsho in Kyoto.

102. Although unusual in English, the plural "awarenesses" is common in the writings of Gattegno.

103. I am indebted to Dr. Roslyn Young for this example, and for many insights into Gattegno's approach, received during a workshop in Osaka in October 1996.

104. Gattegno (1987, p. 38).

105. Gattegno (1973, p. 132; 1987, p. 168).

106. Gattegno (1987, p. 210).

107. Gattegno (1973, p. 130).

108. Gattegno (1985, p. 3).

109. I have sought to show some of the limitations inherent in the word "experience" applied to Buddhist awakening, due in particular to its vagueness (Mohr 1993).

110. Mentioning the educational aspect of kōans is not new: "The selection of pithy sayings from the ancient records to be used *pedagogically* as kung-an, or "test cases" was a Sung innovation." (Foulk 1993b, p. 148, italics are mine).

111. The character *ching* is a common Chinese translation for the Sanskrit *visaya* or *ālambana*, which designate the objects of the mind (Nakamura Hajime 1981, p. 238).

112. *Lin-chi lu*, T 47 no. 1985, pp. 497a22–a23; compare my translation with that of Sasaki (1975, p. 6), Watson (1993b, p. 21), and Demiéville (1972, p. 51).

113. Iriya (1986, pp. 81–82). Nagao, although he acknowledges that no Sanskrit term corresponds to this concept, argues that "the basic connotation was already developed rather elaborately in Indian Mahāyāna" (1991, p. 202). Ueda has given his own interpretation of "ascent" and "descent" (1983).

114. HZS, vol. 2, p. 365. See also Tokiwa (1988, p. 10). Preface not included in Waddell's translation (1994c).

115. T 81 no. 2575. First woodblock edition was printed in 1800. Complete French translation is in Mohr (1997).

116. These divisions do not appear in the original text. For the details of the analysis that brought me to identify three main sections, see Mohr (1997, pp. 81–91). I may

just suggest here that Tōrei uses the threefold scheme that is usually applied to commentaries of sūtras, an introduction (*jobun*), the main purpose (*shōshūbun*), and the part dealing with diffusion (*ruzūbun*), a format he uses in other works.

117. T 81 no. 2575, p. 588a13–a14. An example of this classical expression is found in *Pi-yen lu,* case 41, with a slightly different wording, T 48 no. 2003, p. 179a12.

118. T 81 no. 2575, p. 589c27.

119. T 81 no. 2575, p. 587a25. The same image is used in a different context on p. 603b04. Tōrei does not mention his source, since he gives a free narration of the original passage. The Buddha's utterance in the *Lotus Sūtra* reads: "The place [where lies] the treasure is at close hand: this city is not real, it is only [a mirage that] I made up" (T 9 no. 262, p. 26a24; compare with Watson 1993a, p. 137).

120. I mention the more commonly known expression of *kyōzen itchi,* but Tōrei uses here the compound *fugō,* which also indicates coincidence (T 81 no. 2575, p. 590a14).

121. T 81 no. 2575, p. 590a14–15.

122. The four most relevant passages establishing this distinctiveness are found in T 81 no. 2575, pp. 582c02–c06, 584c09–c11, 592c24, and 600b28–b29.

123. Main instances of this compound are found in T 81 no. 2575, pp. 581b08, 583b18, 584c10–c11, and 584c13. The expression *ichijakusu* derives from "a move" in the Chinese chess game (see the entry *itchaku* in Koga 1991, p. 15).

124. The complete title of this work is *Himitsu mandara jūjūshinron,* T 77 n° 2425. The same classification is also included in Kūkai's *Precious Key to the Secret Treasury* (*Hizōhōyaku,* T 77 no. 2426).

125. More details on this in Mohr (1997, pp. 102–106).

126. Tōrei was most familiar with Watarai Shintō, into which he was initiated. His interpretation of the "primordial chaos" (J. *konton,* Ch. *hun-tun*) as related to *kenshō* is unique, to my knowledge. I analyzed some of its implications (Mōru 1995). Recent English translations of most of the original texts have appeared in Teeuwen (1996).

127. T 81 no. 2575, p. 603c13–c14.

128. T 81 no. 2575, p. 603c28–c29.

129. Included in *Keisō dokuzui,* HZS vol. 2, p. 175. There are dozens of other examples of the use of the word *kōjō* by Hakuin. What makes this letter especially interesting is that it is addressed to a layperson. On the whereabouts of this doctor, see Katō (1985, p. 181, n. 1).

130. A detailed exposition of these categories can be found in Akizuki (1985, pp. 138–188, and 1987, pp. 77–109), Miura (1965 and 1966, pp. 46–76), and Shimano (1988). These categories generally are further followed by the kōans dealing with the *goi* (five positions), *jūjū kinkai* (the ten essential precepts), and *matsugo no rōkan* (the last barrier).

131. HZS vol. 2, p. 389. See also Mineo (1977, pp. 97–100) and Tokiwa (1988, p. 52). Compare with the translations in Miura (1965 and 1966, p. 58) and Waddell (1994c, pp. 29–30).

132. This idea is, for example, clearly expressed by Kajitani Sōnin (1914–1995), former abbot of Shōkokuji, who stated that Hakuin "created (*tsukutta*) a kōan system" including five categories (1968, p. 263).

133. The 1998 special issue of the *Japanese Journal of Religious Studies* is centered on this topic.

134. Kajitani (1968, p. 266).

References

Abbreviations

HZS   *Hakuin oshō zenshū.* 8 vols. Gotō Kōson and Mori Daikyō, eds. Tokyo: Ryūginsha, 1934–1935 (reprint 1967).

MZ   *Manji zōkyō,* Kyoto 1902–1906, pagination is given for the Taiwanese reprint *Wan cheng tsang-ching.* Taipei: Hsin-wen-feng, n.d.

OBJ   *Ōbaku bunka jinmei jiten.* Ōtsuki Mikio, Katō Shōshun, and Hayashi Yukimitsu, eds. Kyoto: Shibunkaku, 1988.

ZGD   *Zengaku daijiten,* new ed., Zengaku daijiten hensansho, ed. Tokyo: Taishūkan, 1985.

Main sources

Hakuin oshō zenshū. 8 vols. Gotō Kōson and Mori Daikyō, eds. Tokyo: Ryūginsha, 1934–1935 (reprint 1967).

Kinsei zenrin sōbōden. Ogino Dokuon, 1890, and *Zoku Kinsei zenrin sōbōden.* Obata Buntei, 1938, 3 vols. Kyoto: Shibunkaku, facsimile edition 1973.

Tenchian hyakusoku hyōju. By Tetsumon Dōju, block-print edition of 1771, also known under the title *Dōjuroku.*

Zenmonhōgoshū. 3 vols., Yamada Kōdō and Mori Daikyō, ed. Tokyo: Shigensha, 1921, facsimile edition 1973.

Publications Cited

Akiyama Kanji, 1983. *Shamon Hakuin.* Shizuoka: Akiyama Aiko.

Akizuki Ryōmin, 1979. *Zen mondō.* Vol. 11, *Akizuki Ryōmin chosakushū.* Tokyo: San'ichi shobō.

———, 1985. *Hakuin zenji.* Vol. 790, *Kōdansha gendai shinsho.* Tokyo: Kōdansha.

———, 1986. "Hakuin ka kōan Inzan Bizen ha: Shitsunai issantō." In *Zen no shugyō,* ed. R. Akizuki. Tokyo: Hirakawa shuppan.

———, 1987. *Kōan: Jissenteki zen nyūmon.* Vol. 600, *Chikuma bunko.* Tokyo: Chikuma shobō.

App, Urs, 1994. *Master Yunmen: From the Record of the Chan Master "Gate of Clouds."* New York: Kodansha.

Araki Kengo, 1969a. *Daiesho.* Vol. 17, *Zen no goroku.* Tokyo: Chikuma shobō.

———, 1969b. *Chikusō Zuihitsu, Chūgoku koten shinsho.* Tokyo: Meitoku shuppan.

———, 1985. *Unsei Shukō no kenkyū.* Tokyo: Daizō shuppan.

Bielefeldt, Carl, 1988. *Dōgen's Manuals of Zen Meditation.* Berkeley: University of California Press.

———, 1995. "A Discussion of Seated Zen." In *Buddhism in Practice,* ed. D. S. J. Lopez. Princeton N.J.: Princeton University Press.

Bunkachō, 1996. *Shūkyō nenkan: Heisei shichi nen ban.* Tokyo: Gyōsei.

Buswell, Robert E., Jr., 1987. "The 'Short-cut' Approach of K'an-hua Meditation: The Evolution of a Practical Subitism in Chinese Ch'an Buddhism." In *Sudden and Gradual: Approaches to Enlightenment in Chinese Thought,* ed. P. N. Gregory. Honolulu: University of Hawaii Press.

————, 1992. *The Zen Monastic Experience: Buddhist Practice in Contemporary Korea.* Princeton N.J.: Princeton University Press.

Cleary, Christopher, 1977. *Swampland Flowers: The Letters and Lectures of Zen Master Ta Hui.* New York: Grove Press.

Collcutt, Martin, 1981. *Five Mountains: The Rinzai Zen Monastic Institution in Medieval Japan.* Vol. 85, *Harvard East Asian Monograph.* Cambridge, Mass.: Harvard University Press.

Demiéville, Paul, 1972. *Entretiens de Lin-tsi, Documents spirituels.* Paris: Fayard.

Donner, Neal, and Daniel B. Stevenson, 1993. *The Great Calming and Contemplation: A Study and Annotated Translation of the First Chapter of Chih-i's Mo-ho chih-kuan, Kuroda Institute Classics in East Asian Buddhism.* Honolulu: University of Hawaii Press.

Edgerton, Franklin, 1953. *Buddhist Hybrid Sanskrit Grammar and Dictionary.* 2 vols. London: Yale University Press (reprint Kyoto: Rinsen Book, 1985).

Foulk, Griffith, 1987. "The 'Ch'an School' and Its Place in the Buddhist Monastic Tradition." Ph.D. Dissertation, Department of Asian Languages and Cultures, University of Michigan, Ann Arbor.

————, 1988. "The Zen Institution in Modern Japan." In *Zen: Tradition & Transition,* ed. K. Kraft. London: Rider.

————, 1993a. "Issues in the Field of East Asian Buddhist Studies: An Extended Review of 'Sudden and Gradual: Approaches to Enlightenment in Chinese Thought.' " *The Journal of the International Association of Buddhist Studies* 16:147–208.

————, 1993b. "Myth, Ritual, and Monastic Practice in Sung Ch'an Buddhism." In *Religion and Society in T'ang and Sung China,* ed. P. Buckley Ebrey and P. N. Gregory. Honolulu: University of Hawaii Press.

Furuta Shōkin, 1991. *Hakuin o yomu: sono shisō to kōdō.* Tokyo: Shunjūsha.

Gattegno, Caleb, 1973. *In the Beginning There Were No Words: The Universe of Babies.* New York: Educational Solutions.

————, 1985. "The Silent Way and Zen." *Educational Solutions Newsletter* 14 (5):3–10.

————, 1987. *The Science of Education Part 1: Theoretical Considerations.* New York: Educational Solutions.

Gomez, Luis O., 1995. "Unspoken Paradigms: Meanderings through the Metaphors of a Field." *The Journal of the International Association of Buddhist Studies* 18/2:183–230.

Haskel, Peter, 1988. "Bankei and His World." Ph.D. Dissertation, Graduate School of Arts and Sciences, Columbia University, New York.

Hirano Sōjō, 1970. *Tongo yōmon.* Vol. 6, *Zen no goroku.* Tokyo: Chikuma shobō.

Hori, G. Victor Sōgen, 1994. "Teaching and Learning in the Rinzai Zen Monastery." *The Journal of Japanese Studies* 20/1:5–35.

————, 1996. "The Study of Buddhist Monastic Practice: Reflections on Robert Buswell's *The Zen Monastic Experience.*" *The Eastern Buddhist (New Series)* 29/2:239–261).

Hubbard, Jamie, and Paul L. Swanson, eds., 1997. *Pruning the Bodhi Tree: The Storm over Critical Buddhism, Nanzan Library of Asian Religion and Culture.* Honolulu: University of Hawaii Press.

Hucker, Charles O., 1995. *A Dictionary of Official Titles in Imperial China.* Taipei: SMC Publishing (Dept. of Stanford University Press edition).

Iida Tōin, 1943. *Zen'yū ni ataeru no sho.* Tokyo: Daitō shuppan.

————, 1954. *Kaiankokugo teishōroku.* Kyoto: Kichūdō (first published in five volumes, from 1920 to 1928).

Iriya Yoshitaka, 1973. *Hō koji goroku.* Vol. 7, *Zen no goroku.* Tokyo: Chikuma shobō.
———, 1985. Daiō kokushi no ge. *Dōhō* 80:1.
———, 1986. *Jiko to chōetsu.* Tokyo: Iwanami shoten.
Ishii Shūdō, 1987. *Sōdai zenshūshi no kenkyū: Chūgoku Sōtōshū to Dōgen zen, Gakujutsu sōsho: Zen bukkyō.* Tokyo: Daitō shuppan.
Izuyama Kakudo, 1983. *Hakuin zenji: Yasenkanna.* Tokyo: Shunjūsha.
———, 1985. *Oretegama.* Tokyo: Shunjūsha.
Jen Ying-ch'iu, ed., 1986. *Huang-ti nei-ching su-wēn chang-chü so-yin.* Peking 1986: Jenmin wei-sheng ch'u-pan-she.
Kagamishima Genryū, Satō Tatsugen, and Kosaka Kiyū, eds., 1972. *Yakuchū Zen'en shingi.* Tokyo: Sōtōshū shūmuchō.
Kajitani Sōnin, 1968. "Kōan no soshiki." In *Zen no koten: Nihon,* ed. K. Nishitani. Vol. 7, *Kōza Zen.* Tokyo: Chikuma shobō, pp. 263–270.
Kamata Shigeo, 1996. *Ki no dentō: Chōsokuhō o chūshin to shite.* Kyoto: Jinbun shoin.
Kasulis, Thomas P., Roger T. Ames, and Wimal Dissanayake, eds., 1993. *Self as Body in Asian Theory and Practice.*, ed. H. Eilberg-Schwartz, *SUNY Series, The Body in Culture, History, and Religion.* New York: State University of New York Press.
Katō Shōshun, 1969. "Shikyō Eryō to gōko dōjō no kaisō ni tsuite." *Zengaku kenkyū* 57:253–267.
———, 1985. *Hakuin oshō nenpu.* Vol. 7, *Kinsei zensō den.* Kyoto: Shibunkaku.
———, 1995. "Nippō Sōshun o meguru ni san no mondai." *Zengaku kenkyū* 73:101–130.
Kirchner, Thomas, 1996. "Modernity and Rinzai Zen: Doctrinal Change or Continuity?" *Zen Buddhism Today: Annual Report of the Kyoto Zen Symposium* 13:39–54.
Koga Hidehiko, 1991. *Zengo jiten,* ed. Iriya Yoshitaka. Kyoto: Shibunkaku.
Longman Group, 1991. *Longman Dictionary of the English Language,* 2nd ed. Hong Kong: Longman.
Mineo Daikyū, 1977. *Hakuin-zenji: Sokkōroku kaien fusetsu kōwa.* Tokyo: Shigensha (First edition in 1934).
Miura Isshū, and Ruth Fuller Sasaki, 1965. *The Zen Kōan: Its History and Use in Rinzai Zen.* New York: Harcourt Brace Jovanovich.
———, 1966. *Zen Dust: The History of the Kōan and Kōan Study in Rinzai (Lin-chi) Zen.* Kyoto: The First Zen Institute of America in Japan.
Mohr, Michel, 1993. "Experience in the Light of Zen Buddhism." *Zen Buddhism Today* 10:12–31.
———, 1994a. "Zen Buddhism during the Tokugawa Period: The Challenge to Go Beyond Sectarian Consciousness." *Japanese Journal of Religious Studies* 21/4:341–372.
———, 1994b. "Vers la redécouverte de Tōrei:" *Les Cahiers d'Extrême-Asie* 7:319–352.
———, 1997. *Traité sur l'Inépuisable Lampe du Zen: Tōrei (1721–1792) et sa vision de l'éveil.* 2 vols. Vol. XXVIII, *Mélanges chinois et bouddhiques.* Brussels (Bruxelles): Institut Belge des Hautes Études Chinoises.
Morohashi Tetsuii, ed., 1966–1968. *Daikanwa jiten.* 13 vols. Tokyo: Taishukan.
Mōru Missheru, 1995. "Konton no jikaku kara hyōgen e: Zen Bukkyō ni okeru kotoba no toraekata no ichisokumen." In *Keiken to kotoba,* ed. T. Kajiya, K. Fukui, and T. Mori. Tokyo: Taimeidō.
Mujaku Dōchū, 1979a. *Zenrin shōkisen.* Ed. S. Yanagida. Vol. 9a, *Zengaku sōsho.* Kyoto: Chūbun shuppan.
———, 1979b. *Kattōgosen, Zenrinkushū benmyō,* ed. S. Yanagida. Vol. 9b, *Zengaku sōsho.* Kyoto: Chūbun shuppan.

Muraki Hiromasa, 1979. *Shakuson no kokyūhō: Daianpanshuikyō ni manabu.* Tokyo: Hakujusha.

————, 1985. *Isō Hakuin no kokyūhō: "Yasenkanna" no kenkōhō ni manabu.* Tokyo: Hakujusha.

————, 1988. *Hakuin zenji "Yasenkanna" ni manabu tanden kokyūhō.* Tokyo: Mikasa shobō.

Murase Genmyō, 1982. Rinzai no shōshū bakumon ni okoru. *Zen bunka* 104:72–77.

Nagao Gadjin, 1991. *Mādhyamika and Yogācāra,* trans. Leslie S. Kawamura, ed. K. K. Inada. *SUNY Series in Buddhist Studies.* Albany: State University of New York Press.

Nakamura Hajime, 1981. *Bukkyōgo daijiten (shukusatsuban).* Tokyo: Tokyo shoseki.

Nakamura Sōichi, 1987. *Ryōkan no hokketen, Hokkesan no ge.* Tokyo: Seishin shobō.

Nishimura Eshin, 1982. *Tōrei oshō nenpu.* Vol. 8, *Kinsei zensōden.* Kyoto: Shibunkaku.

Obata Buntei, 1938. *Zoku Kinsei zenrin sōbōden.* Included in *Kinsei zenrin sōbōden,* 3 vols., Kyoto: Shibunkaku. Facsimile edition 1973.

Ogiso Jundō, 1958. *Bankei to Sonojidai. Zen Bunka* 10–11:28–37.

Ōishi Manabu, 1995. *Yoshimune to kyōhō no kaikaku.* Tokyo: Tōkyōdō shuppan.

Ōmori Sōgen, 1972. *Sanzen nyūmon.* Tokyo: Shunjūsha.

Ono Kazuko, 1987. "Dōran no jidai o ikita Ingen zenji." *Zen bunka* 124:83–92.

Osaka Kōryū, 1969. *Zaikezen nyūmon.* Vol. 4, *Daizō sensho.* Tokyo: Daizō shuppan.

Ōtsuki Mikio, Katō Shōshun, and Hayashi Yukimitsu, eds., 1988. *Ōbaku bunka jinmei jiten.* Kyoto: Shibunkaku.

Rikugawa Taiun, 1963. *Kōshō Hakuin oshō shōden.* Tokyo: Sankibō busshorin.

————, 1966. "Ōkami Genrō to Hakuin oshō." *Zen bunka* 40:51–53.

————, 1968. *Shinzenron.* Tokyo: Ryūginsha.

Rinoie Masafumi, 1981. *Ōbaku san ketsu: Egoku Dōmyō zenji den.* Tokyo: Daizō shuppan.

Ruegg, Seyfort D., 1995. "Some Reflections on the Place of Philosophy in the Study of Buddhism." *The Journal of the International Association of Buddhist Studies* 18/2:145–181.

Sasaki, Ruth Fuller, 1975. *The Recorded Sayings of Ch'an Master Lin-chi Hui-chao of Chen Prefecture.* Kyoto: The Institute for Zen Studies.

Sasaki, Ruth Fuller, Yoshitaka Iriya, and Dana R. Fraser, 1971. *A Man of Zen: The Recorded Sayings of Layman P'ang, A Ninth-Century Zen Classic.* New York: Tokyo: Weatherhill.

Scwaller, Dieter, 1989. *Der Japanische Ōbaku. Moench Tetsugen Dōkō: Leben, Denken, Schriften,* Scheizer Asiatische Studien/Études Asiatiques Suisses Monographie 9. Bern: Peter Lang.

Senzaki Nyogen and Ruth Strout McCandless, trans. and eds., 1964. *The Iron Flute: 1100 Kōan with Commentary by Genrō, Fūgai, and Nyōgen.* Rutland, Vermont: Charles E. Tuttle, 1985.

Shibayama Zenkei, 1943. "Hakuin kei kanna no ichikanken." *Zengaku kenkyū* 38:1–30.

Shimano Eidō T., 1988. "Zen Kōans." In *Zen: Tradition & Transition,* ed. K. Kraft. London: Rider; New York: Grove Press, pp. 70–87.

Shōgaku tosho jisho henshūbu, ed., 1981 *Kokugo daijiten.* Tokyo: Shōgakukan.

Sōtō-shū zensho, 18 vols., ed. 1970–1973 (orig. 1929–1935). Tokyo: Sōtōshū Shūmuchō.

Takayanagi Mitsunaga, and Takeuchi Rizō, ed., 1974. *Kadokawa nihonshi jiten.* 2nd ed. Tokyo: Kadokawa shoten.

Takenuki Genshō, 1989. *Nihon zenshūshi.* Tokyo: Daizō shuppan.

————, 1993. *Nihon zenshūshi kenkyū.* Tokyo: Yūzankaku.
Teeuwen, Mark, 1996. *Watarai Shintō: An Intellectual history of the Outer Shrine of Ise.* Vol. 52, *CNWS Publications.* Leiden: Research School CNWS, Leiden University.
Tokiwa Gishin, 1988. *Hakuin.* Vol. 27, *Daijōbutten.* Tokyo: Chūōkōron.
Tsuji Zennosuke, 1944–1955 (1969–1970). *Nihon bukkyōshi.* 10 vols. Tokyo: Iwanami shoten.
Ueda Shizuteru, 1983. "Ascent and Descent: Zen Buddhism in Comparison with Meister Eckhart." *The Eastern Buddhist: New Series* 16/1–2:52–73, 72–91.
————, 1993. *Zen bukkyō: Kongenteki ningen.* Vol. 142, *Dōjidai raiburarī.* Tokyo: Iwanami shoten.
Ueda Shizuteru, ed., 1996. *Nishida Kitarō zuihitsushū.* Vol. 124–7, *Iwanami bunko.* Tokyo: Iwanami shoten.
Veith, Ilza, 1966. *Huang Ti Nei Ching Su Wēn: The Yellow Emperor's Classic of Internal Medicine.* Berkeley: University of California Press.
Waddell, Norman, 1982. "Wild Ivy: The Spiritual Autobiography of Hakuin Ekaku (Part 1)." *The Eastern Buddhist (New Series)* 15/2:71–109.
————, 1983. "Wild Ivy: The Spiritual Autobiography of Hakuin Ekaku (Part 2)." *The Eastern Buddhist (New Series)* 16/1:107–139.
————, 1994a. "A Chronological Biography of Zen Priest Hakuin." *The Eastern Buddhist (New Series)* 27/1:96–155.
————, 1994b. "A Chronological Biography of Zen Priest Hakuin." *The Eastern Buddhist (New Series)* 27/2:81–129.
————, 1994c. *The Essential Teachings of Zen Master Hakuin: A Translation of the Sokkô-roku Kaien-fusetsu.* Boston: Shambhala. (Orig. published in *Eastern Buddhist* between 1985 and 1991).
Watson, Burton, 1993a. *The Lotus Sutra,* ed. W. T. de Bary, *Translations from the Asian Classics.* New York: Columbia University Press.
————, 1993b. *The Zen Teachings of Master Lin-chi.* Boston: Shambhala.
Yamada Mumon, 1974. *Endonshō kōwa.* Tokyo: Bukkyō bunka kōryūsentā.
Yampolsky, Philip B., 1971. *The Zen Master Hakuin: Selected Writings,* ed. W. T. de Bary. Vol. LXXXVI, *Translations from the Oriental Classics, Records or Civilization: Sources and Studies.* New York: Columbia University Press.
Yanagida Seizan, 1959. "Kidō to Daiō tono sōkai." *Zengaku kenkyū* 49:40–56.
————, 1976. "Zenseki kaidai." In *Zenke goroku,* ed. S. Yanagida and Nishitani Keiji. Tokyo: Chikuma shobō.
————, 1985. "Goroku no rekishi: Zenbunken no seiritsu shiteki kenkyū." *Tōhō gakuhō* 57 (March):211–663.
————, 1989. *Shamon Ryōkan: Jihitsubon "Sōdō shishū" o yomu.* Kyoto: Jinbun shoin.
Yü, Chün-fang, 1974. "Yün-ch'i Chu-hung: The Career of a Ming Buddhist Monk." Ph.D. Dissertation, Columbia University.
————, 1981. *The Renewal of Buddhism in China: Chu-hung and the Late Ming Synthesis.* New York: Columbia University Press.
Yuasa Yasuo, 1987. *The Body: Toward an Eastern Mind-Body Theory,* trans. Shigenori Nagatomo and T. P. Kasulis. Albany, New York: State University of New York Press.
Zen bunka henshūbu, ed., 1981. *Meiji no Zenshō.* Kyoto: Zen Bunka Kenkyūsho.
Zengaku daijiten hensansho, ed., 1978. *Zengaku daijiten.* Tokyo: Taishūkan (1985).

11

Kōan and Kenshō in the Rinzai Zen Curriculum

G. VICTOR SŌGEN HORI

Aᴄᴄᴏʀᴅɪɴɢ to a widely accepted model, a kōan is a clever psychological device designed to induce satori or *kenshō*. The kōan is said to pose to the Zen practitioner a paradox unsolvable by the rational, intellectualizing mind. Driven into an ever more desperate corner by his repeated futile attempts to solve what cannot be rationally solved, the practitioner finally breaks through the barrier of rational intellection to the realm of preconceptual and prelinguistic consciousness variously called pure consciousness, no-mind, without-thinking, or emptiness. This breakthrough is called satori or *kenshō*. The cleverness of the kōan consists in the fact that rather than attacking reason and logic from outside, the kōan uses reason to drive itself into a self-contradiction and cause its own destruction. In this picture, the kōan is fundamentally an instrument and has no use except as a means for psychologically inducing *kenshō*. These two notions—the kōan as nonrational, psychological instrument, and *kenshō* as the breakthrough to nonrational, noncognitive, pure consciousness—nicely support each other.[1]

However, these conceptions of kōan and *kenshō* were criticized long ago. Dōgen, in the "Sansuikyō" ("Mountains and Waters Sūtra") fascicle of the *Shōbōgenzō*, writes:

> In great Sung China today there are a group of scatterbrained people, whose number is so large that they cannot possibly be scared off by the faithful few. They argue, saying: "Talks such as 'The east mountain walks over the water,' Nan-ch'üan's sickle, and the like are incomprehensible utterances. The idea is that any talk concerned with discriminating thought is not the Ch'an talk of buddha-ancestors; only incomprehensible utterances are the talk of buddha-ancestors. Therefore, Huang-po's stick and Lin-chi's shout exceed comprehension and are never concerned with discriminating thought. This is known as the great enlightenment prior to the emergence of any incipient sign. The past mentors often employed as skillful means those phrases which cut off tangling vines,

but [such phrases] were beyond comprehension." (Translation by Hee-jin Kim [Kim 1985a: 297])

Dōgen attributes to the "scatterbrained" the same two views of kōan and *kenshō*—that "incomprehensible utterances" are merely skillful means to cut off the tangling vines of discriminating thought in order to bring one to the great enlightenment, and that great enlightenment itself is noncognitive, something "prior to the emergence of any incipient sign." Dōgen heaps scorn on this view. "People who utter such nonsense have not yet met a true mentor; hence they lack the eye of proper study. They are fools not worthy of mention. . . . What these pseudo-Buddhists regard as 'incomprehensible utterances' are incomprehensible only to them, not to buddha-ancestors" (Kim 1985a: 297). For Dōgen, these "pseudo-Buddhists" are merely rationalizing their ignorance. Not wishing to admit they have failed to comprehend enlightenment, they claim that enlightenment itself cannot be comprehended.

Because Dōgen was convinced of the fundamental "reason" or "rationality" (*dōri*) of the Buddha dharma, he took the view that kōan practice is a moment-by-moment total exertion that realizes—makes real (*genjō*)—the fundamental rationality of enlightenment.[2] Hee-jin Kim has offered the convenient labels "instrumentalist" to denote the concept of the kōan as merely a means to a breakthrough to nonrational consciousness, and "realizational" to refer to Dōgen's notion of the kōan as moment-by-moment actualization of the rationality of enlightenment (Kim 1985b, 1985c). Even though this chapter is concerned with Rinzai monastic practice, I adopt Dōgen's term "realization" (*genjō*) because it offers a clear alternative to the instrumental model of the kōan. No doubt there are differences in detail between what Dōgen and what any particular Rinzai monk may have said about enlightenment. These differences are, in my judgment, minor in contrast to what either would have said compared to the instrumentalist idea that a kōan is merely a nonrational instrument for a breakthrough to a noncognitive pure consciousness.

The first section of this chapter, "The Kōan as Irrational Instrument," discusses some examples of how kōan and *kenshō* have been depicted in Western literature, and it tries to show some of the internal conceptual difficulties inherent in the instrumental model. The second and third sections, "*Kenshō* and *Kyōgai*" and "Kōan and *Hōri* ('Reason')," examine how kōan and *kenshō* are understood in the context of Rinzai monastic practice, revealing that although the instrumental model may fit the beginning parts of kōan practice, the realization model gives a more accurate characterization of the total practice. The fourth section, "Realization: Kōan as Performance of *Kenshō*," argues for a realizational model of the kōan using the notion of performance. All of these questions are far more complex than as represented here; I regret there is not enough space to deal with all these issues fully.

The Kōan as Irrational Instrument

The Idea of a Pure Consciousness

In recent scholarly discussions of mystical experience in general and of Zen in particular, the acceptance of a distinction between two kinds of consciousness is extremely widespread and appears under a great many labels: pure (unmediated) versus mediated, noncognitive versus cognitive, experiential versus intellectual, intuitive versus intellectual, nonrational versus rational, nondiscursive versus discursive, nonpropositional versus propositional, and so on. The notion of a pure consciousness which is attained in religious or mystical experience has been undergoing sharp criticism in recent years.[3] Steven Katz has claimed, "There are no pure (unmediated) experiences" (Katz 1978b: 25; 1983b: 4) and has argued that all experience, including the Buddhist experience of *śūnyatā,* is mediated by intellectual and conceptual activity. Although Katz has made the most public attack on the idea of pure consciousness or pure experience, his argument is not the most persuasive. He does not make clear the logical status of what he is asserting and denying. Is his claim factual or conceptual? Is he saying merely, "No pure experiences have to date been found" (a factual statement), or is he saying, "There cannot be such a thing as a pure experience" (a conceptual claim)? He himself maintains, "I adopted as a working hypothesis the epistemic thesis that there are *no* pure (unmediated) experiences," as if the statement were a scientific or factual hypothesis that later facts would prove true or false (Katz 1983b: 4). Yet elsewhere he writes, "The notion of unmediated experience seems, if not self-contradictory, at best empty" (1978b: 25), as if the idea of a pure experience, like that of a square triangle, were conceptually impossible. Since this question remains unclarified, one is left suspecting that although Katz claims to be offering a "working hypothesis," he is actually legislating a particular concept of experience which, by definition, excludes mystical experience.

Also to support his claim that all cases of mystical experiences are contextually constructed (and are not therefore cases of pure or immediate experience), he takes as examples only those convenient cases of reported mystical experience that have much intellectual content; he systematically ignores those less tractable cases of mystical experience on the other end of the spectrum which, it is claimed, are devoid not only of intellectual content but also of all sensation, all sense of space and time, and all sense of self.[4]

While I too am critical of Zen enlightenment depicted as a breakthrough to a pure consciousness, I do not support Katz's position. The basic difference is that Katz and his opponents both agree in dividing the spectrum of consciousnesses into those with cognitive content and those without, into those that are mediated (not pure) and those that are unmediated (pure). They both assume that these categories are mutually exclusive and jointly exhaustive of all possibilities. They disagree only on whether there is or is not experience of pure consciousness. These assumptions lie behind Katz's claim that mystical experience is "reconditioning not deconditioning."[5] He does not consider the possibility that it could be both. Zen practice, on the other hand, seeks initially to destroy the habit of thinking in terms of mutually exclusive dichotomies like pure and impure in the first place (although later it seeks to reconstitute duality again). I will return to this topic at the end of the chapter.

In scholarly discussions of Zen, again a common view is that first there was an original pure experience and that afterwards thought and language entered and sullied its original purity. Thomas Kasulis in his textbook on Zen says, "Our common understanding of experience is therefore a *reconstruction* in that it imposes categories that were not present in that experience when it originally occurred" (Kasulis 1981, 60). This imposition of distinctions, categories, and conceptual characterizations is not a good thing, it seems. "We accept various distinctions and conceptual characterizations of reality, allowing them to interfere with our ability to be spontaneous and grounded in the present" (ibid. 58). Zen practice aims to free us by returning us to without-thinking, "a nonconceptual or prereflective mode of consciousness" (ibid. 75), "a primordial state of consciousness" (ibid. 59). To avoid falling into the nihilism to which this account seems to lead, Kasulis also offers a relational account of without-thinking which goes some way toward de-reifying the concept (ibid. 128–133). He also emphasizes that the Zen Master is embedded in a historical and cultural context which conditions (but does not determine) his responses (ibid. 134–139). Nevertheless the reader cannot help but come away with the impression that without-thinking is a special state of consciousness identifiable as separate and distinct in space and time from the usual states of consciousness. There is never a recognition that the thinking and not-thinking themselves instantiate without-thinking. To use an apt word which Kasulis has coined, there is no recognition that thinking and not-thinking themselves "presence" without-thinking (ibid. 83).

Is it really possible that there could be a realm of consciousness without cognitive content or intellectual activity?[6] At least one branch of Western epistemology insists that there cannot be knowledge without concepts to organize sensation into meaningful perception.[7] This view holds that ordinary perception is saturated with conceptual activity which gives meaning to sensation. For example, I see these flesh-like things as my hands; I see this flat brown surface as my desk; I hear this shrill sound as the ring of the telephone. Each such unsophisticated instance of seeing or hearing is really a "seeing as" or "hearing as" in which sensation is organized according to some concept like "hand" or "desk" or "ring of telephone." Off to the left of my visual field, I see the flash of an object flying past my window and then realize it was just light glinting on my glasses. I hear a sound of someone snoring and then realize that it is the sound of an old bicycle wheel creakily passing by outside. In these examples we see concepts—"something flying by," "glint on my glasses," "someone snoring," "creaky bicycle wheel"—competing to organize our sensory field into something meaningful. But a pure consciousness without concepts, if there could be such a thing, would be a booming, buzzing confusion, a sensory field of flashes of light, unidentifiable sounds, ambiguous shapes, color patches without significance. This is not the consciousness of the enlightened Zen master. Even he looks at lines on the wall and sees them as a door, hears a shrilling as the ring of a telephone, sniffs an odor and recognizes alcohol on your breath. A pure consciousness without concepts would not have "door," "telephone," "alcohol."

After the breakthrough in *kenshō,* one finally "sees things as they are," and it is tempting to think that "as they are" means "without conceptualization." (It could also mean, e.g., "without attachment" or "without value judgment," but these different nuances are not sorted out.) It is tempting to say, "You mistook a branch for a snake because conceptualization got in the way," as if conceptualization functioned only to distort veridical perception. Not so. Correctly seeing a brown shape as a branch presupposes as much conceptual activity as mistakenly seeing a brown shape as a snake. Sensational perception has meaning or significance only because a concept has first organized and given meaning to it. It is a secondary question whether that concept was applied correctly or incorrectly. Even the veridical "seeing things as they are" comes after conceptualization, not before. This means that "seeing things as they are" is one variation of, not the alternative to, seeing things as thought and language have conditioned us to see them. To state the point in rather radical terms, if conceptual activity were subtracted from experience, whatever remained would not be meaningful; it might not even qualify for the label "experience."

Dale Wright in his criticism of the notion of transcendence of language in Zen has constructed a *reductio ad absurdum* (Wright 1992). The enlightened Zen master is said to be free in the sense that in addition to being able to see and respond according to the socially determined dualistic categories of conventional thought and language nondualistically (unenlightened consciousness), the master also nondualistically sees things as they are in themselves (enlightened consciousness). But this account ironically entails that the enlightened Zen master's experience is dualistic while the unenlightened person's experience is nondual. With every act, the enlightened Zen master must make a dualistic choice whether to respond in a direct, "Zen," way or in a socially determined conventional way. Unenlightened persons see no distinction between a thing in itself and its socially determined meaning and merely respond without thinking (one is tempted to put a hyphen between "without" and "thinking").

Let me make two comments on this *reductio.* First, Wright is able to reduce Kasulis's distinction between dualistic ordinary experience and nondual primordial experience to absurdity just because the distinction between dual and nondual experience is itself dualistic. Every such attempt to depict a nondual realm that transcends the ordinary realm of dualistic experience itself reinstates duality, because transcendence itself is a dualistic concept. Second, in defense of Kasulis (although it is not obvious that Kasulis would make this defense himself), one can argue that the freedom of the enlightened Zen master does indeed consist in the fact that he has more dualistic choices to make. For the nonduality of *kenshō* never appears as the nonduality of *kenshō;* if it did, that would reinstate the duality that nonduality is supposed to transcend. The nonduality of *kenshō* is always instantiated in or makes a phenomenal appearance as ("presences" itself as), conventional duality. These matters are discussed in more detail below.

To make explicit the instrumental function of the kōan, Henry Rosemont, Jr., has offered a performative analysis. Wittgenstein taught that the meaning of a word is not always the object that the word labels, denotes, or refers to; in many cases the meaning of the word is its use.[8] J. L. Austin went further and said that many utterances in our language cannot be construed as descriptions of objects, states of affairs, or states of mind; they are instead performances of some act (Austin 1962). A sentence like "I do," uttered at the appropriate moment in a wedding ceremony, does not describe or denote an action, object, or state of affairs; given the appropriate social, legal, and ritual context, the utterance itself performs an act, an action with real consequences, just as surely as does any physical act. Such utterances do not report information and hence do not have truth-value. Rather they are meaningful as performance; while they cannot be said to be either true or false, they can be said in particular contexts to be either successful or unsuccessful. In similar fashion, Rosemont argued that the kōan is not descriptive but performative.

> Questions like "What is the sound of one hand clapping?" or "What was your face like before you were born?" have no cognitive answer whatever, so *a fortiori* they have no answer that might express some principle of Zen Buddhism, transcendent or otherwise.
> ... *Mondō* and *kōan* sentences have no truth value, nor, except incidentally, do they literary value; they can have, for the Zen apprentices, great shock value. (Rosemont 1970: 118)

The kōan gives the appearance of having rational or cognitive content described in a factual or a metaphorical way deliberately to deceive us in order to perform its true task: to make us "stop intellectualizing" (Rosemont 1970: 118). The performative analysis thus accounts for the seeming madness and the hidden method of the kōan.

To the extent that this performative analysis presupposes that enlightenment is a breakthrough to a noncognitive realm of pure experience, it is open to the same kinds of criticism as raised above. Nevertheless there is something correct about the performative account, for clearly in many kōan the proponents engage in shouting, bowing, slapping, going out the door, cutting cats in two, putting sandals on one's head, and so on—all performances. If they are not skillful means to attaining a breakthrough to pure consciousness, what are they?

Successive generations of scholars and monks in China, Japan, and now in the West have dissected kōan line by line and added their own commentary. In addition, in the Rinzai monastic training curriculum, the many kōan are categorized and ranked; the monks progressively learn more and more sophisticated ways of seeing them; they learn how to write their own commentary to the kōan. Working full time, a monk can expect to complete the entire Rinzai kōan curriculum in about fifteen years. If it were true that the kōan is nonrational, neither a kōan text tradition nor a monastic kōan curriculum would be possible. There must be a model of the kōan other than as a nonrational means to induce a breakthrough to pure consciousness. For an understanding of that different model, we now move to a more detailed examination of Rinzai kōan practice.

Kenshō *and* Kyōgai

I use here an old technique, an examination of the uses of certain key words or terms in Rinzai monastic vocabulary. This approach, associated with the philosophical movement called linguistic analysis, deliberately attempts to uncover the philosophical assumptions governing the ordinary use of words in their everyday settings. This approach also happily introduces an ethnographic element, because it examines actual Rinzai monastic use and practice. The headings for the two major divisions in this chapter contain the two terms *kyōgai* and *hōri,* not well known in Western scholarship on Zen but extremely important for kōan practice.

I once heard a Zen *rōshi* say that in kōan training, "Everything is *kyōgai*" (*subete wa kyōgai*).[9] Many years later I heard another *rōshi* state that one must also learn to grasp a kōan from the standpoint of *hōri.*[10] *Kyōgai* may be tentatively translated "consciousness," but the word *kyōgai* in Japanese behaves differently from "consciousness" in English, so much so that in some contexts it can be translated as "behavior." Similarly, although *hōri* can be translated "dharma reason," "dharma rationality," it is not the same concept as "rationality" in English. In English the presence of contradiction is a sign of irrationality, whereas the use of contradiction is part of the training in *hōri. Kyōgai* and *hōri* denote the two ways of approaching kōan training. The first half of kōan training puts major emphasis on *kyōgai* and a lesser emphasis on *hōri,* whereas the second half reverses these emphases.

What happens in the first half of kōan training? First, monks get *kenshō.*

The Uses of "Kenshō"

The term *kenshō* is now so well known to Western students of Zen that it is commonly used without translation. It is worth noting that though Western students of Zen are fascinated by the notion of *kenshō,* monks in a Japanese Rinzai monastery hardly ever use the word, and when they do, it is often in jest ("The cook finally turned out a good meal. He must have had *kenshō*"). Perhaps their silence about *kenshō* should be taken as a sign of its overwhelming importance to them, as if it were a taboo word; perhaps it merely indicates their lack of interest in Zen practice.

In any case, the term consists of two characters: *ken,* which means "see" or "seeing," and *shō,* which means "nature," "character," "quality." To "see one's nature" is the usual translation for *kenshō* (and will be used in this chapter) but the insertion of "one's" is already an interpretation. There is also the rendering, "It lets one see into nature and thus attain Buddhahood" (Radcliffe 1993: 101), which seems to render the phrase *kenshō jōbutsu,* and I have heard people recommend the translation "to see Buddha nature"—both of which are also interpretations. None of these translations accurately reflects Rinzai monastic usage.

In English, *kenshō* is used exclusively as a noun or an adjective. Here are some representative uses in English.

> Kōans can often trigger a *kenshō* experience . . .
> Is *kenshō* at all common? Can it happen before one is working on a kōan, in the practice of breath counting, let's say?
> You were talking earlier about how some people had a *kenshō* experience when a plum blossom fell, or when a bamboo was struck by a pebble.[11]

In English usage, people have *kenshō;* they do not do *kenshō.* In the Rinzai monastery, the word *kenshō* is used as a noun in this way, but in addition it is used as a verb, *kenshō suru.* As a verb, it has two usages: intransitive, where it is equivalent to "to become awakened," and transitive, where it takes an object. As an example of intransitive use, a *rōshi* may encourage his monks, "If you don't *kenshō* once, you can't be called a real monk" (*Ippen kenshō shite kon' to, honmono no unsui to wa ien*). Of course, instead of the verb construction "If you don't *kenshō,*" one could translate *kenshō shite kon'to* using a noun construction: "If you do not have *kenshō* . . ." but such a translation is unfaithful to the grammar of the original and does not capture the important nuance that *kenshō* has a volitional element; "If you do not have *kenshō*" may be a matter of chance, but "If you don't *kenshō*" is a matter of will.

Kenshō suru is also a transitive verb taking an object. A *rōshi* may very well present a kōan by challenging his monk with "How did you *kenshō* this?" (*Kore dō kenshō shita no ka?*). This question is grammatically similar to, for example, "How did you understand this?" "How did you interpret this?" "How do you explain this?" If understanding, explanation, and interpretation are intellectual acts with cognitive content, *kenshō* should also be an intellectual act with cognitive content.

What actual practices support these uses of the term?

Narikiru *"Become One With"*

In most Rinzai monasteries in Japan, as soon as monks enter, they receive their first kōan, usually the "Sound of One Hand" or "Jōshū's (Chao-chou's) Mu." Although there are differences in pace, they usually pass the first kōan within a year. They all receive the usual advice that the kōan is not a question to be answered by intellectual thought. Instead they are told to answer the kōan by "becoming one" with it. "Become one with . . ." (*narikiru*) is an important concept with several variant expressions in language: "to become one piece with) . . ." (*ichi mai to naru*); "to become the thing itself" (*sono mono to naru*); "to wrestle and fuse with . . ." (*torikunde gappei suru*) and so on. The monk penetrates the kōan not through understanding it but through the constant repeated effort to become one with it.[12] He constantly repeats and poses to himself the question of the kōan: "What is the sound of one hand?" At first the monk expects that the answer to the kōan will one day appear before him like the solution to a riddle. That is to say, he thinks it would be an object of consciousness, an object of seeing. This is what would be expected if he were trying to understand it intellectually. But constant repetition of the kōan imprints the kōan into his consciousness so that the kōan no longer is merely an object of seeing, but colors his very seeing. Eventually, without conscious effort the kōan "Sound of One Hand" always rises to consciousness, repeating itself over and over again, whenever attention is not fixed on anything else. This is a recognizable early stage in *narikiru,* in becoming one with the kōan. "Sound of One Hand" has so invaded his consciousness that it is no longer the object of attention in consciousness, but forms the background for whatever else is the object of attention.

Finally there comes a moment when the monk realizes that his very seeking the answer to the kōan, and the way he himself is reacting to his inability to penetrate the kōan, are themselves the activity of the kōan working within him. This is the difficult point to explain. The kōan is not merely a static entity, some thing with a fixed self-nature to be apprehended. If anything, it is an activity, the activity of seeking to understand the kōan which uses the monk and his mind as its arena. The kōan is both an object of consciousness and the subjective activity of consciousness seeking to understand the kōan. The monk himself in his seeking is the kōan. Realization of this is the insight, the response to the kōan. At first there was a subject of consciousness trying to penetrate a kōan which was treated merely as an object of consciousness. Subject and object—this is two hands clapping. When the monk realizes that the kōan is not merely an object of consciousness but is also he himself as the activity of seeking an answer to the kōan, then subject and object are no longer separate and distinct. He has become one with kōan, or perhaps it is more accurate to say, the kōan has become one with him. This is one hand clapping—*narikiru,* "becoming one." He "realizes" the kōan in both senses of the word "realize." On the one hand, it is a cognitive recognition, but on the other, it also "makes real," since the cognitive recognition could not have occurred unless he himself instantiated the unity of subject and object.[13]

Nonduality of Subject and Object

The "identification of opposites" is one of the great themes of Asian thought. But there is more than one kind of nonduality, of identity of opposites. As A. C. Graham has pointed out, some binary distinctions imply a third term, which is the maker of the distinction in the center, such as left/right, before/after, above/below (Graham 1992: 211). By moving the point of reference of the maker of the distinction (e. g., from the top of a hill to the bottom of the hill), the opposites are identified (every downhill is an uphill, or, canceling out the common factors, down is up). Thus is it possible to intellectually conceive the identity of opposites. But some binary distinctions are truly binary and do not have a hidden third term, such as I/you, I/it. For these cases, there is no possibility of moving the point of reference of the hidden maker of the distinction in the center, because the maker of the distinction is part of the distinction. For this reason, it is much harder to conceive the possibility of the identity of I/it, of subject/object. "I" am the center of my awareness and consciousness; the experienced universe spreads out in all directions and in time away from "I"; only "I," and no one else, is the subject of my experience; everyone else and all things are objects upon which "I" look. What could it possibly mean to say that I and it are one? While the identity of uphills and downhills can be understood intellectually, there is much more warrant for saying that the nonduality of I/it, of subject/object, cannot be understood intellectually but must be experienced.

In the early stages of kōan practice, a monk does not understand the nature of what he has experienced in seeing a kōan. Nevertheless in the regular lectures which monks receive from their *rōshi,* they hear constantly phrases that refer to the nonduality of subject and object: "The well looks at the ass; the ass looks at the well" (*I ro o mi, ro i o miru*); "Look at the flower and the flower also looks" (*Hana o mite, hana mo miru*); "Guest and host interchange" (*Hinju gokan*); and many others. More important, kōan after kōan explores the theme of nonduality. Hakuin's well-known kōan, "Two hands clap and there is a sound, what is the sound of one hand?" is clearly about two and one. The kōan asks, you know what duality is, now what is nonduality? In "What is your original face before your father and mother were born?" the phrase "father and mother" alludes to duality. This is obvious to someone versed in the Chinese tradition, where so much philosophical thought is presented in the imagery of paired opposites. The phrase "your original face" alludes to the original nonduality. The famous *Mu* (*Wu*) kōan is similarly phrased in dualistic terms, although English translations sometimes fail to capture that important point. The original question in Chinese, "Does a dog have Buddha-nature, or does it not?" clearly contrasts "have" (C. *yu,* J. *u*) and "have not" (C. *wu,* J., *mu*) and presents a dichotomized choice.[14]

"How Did You Kenshō This?"

The term *kenshō* refers to the realization of nonduality of subject and object in general, but some uses of the term apply *kenshō* to a particular context. In the challenge, "How did you *kenshō* this?" (*Kore dō kenshō shita no ka?*), the term *kenshō* is being used as a transitive verb taking an object. One does *kenshō* and one does it with a particular object, event, or situation. To some people, the very idea of *kenshō* applied to a particular context will seem a self-contradiction, but it does so only because *kenshō* is presumed to be a totally blank state of mind without cognitive content. This is not what *kenshō* means in Rinzai practice. Consistent with the notion that *kenshō* is the breakdown of the dichotomy of subject and object, *kenshō* used as a transitive verb denotes a total pouring of oneself into some particular object, event, or situation. This "becoming one" in particular contexts has two aspects: formal kōan training, and the daily activities of monastic life.

In formal kōan practice, a single kōan usually breaks into parts, the initial "main case" (*honsoku*) and numerous "checking questions" (*sassho*). In the response to the main case, the monk is usually required to demonstrate "Sound of One Hand" itself or "*Mu*" itself or "Original Face" itself. Then in the checking questions, he is asked to demonstrate "One Hand" or "*Mu*" or "Original Face" in many particular situations. Akizuki Ryūmin has published the kōan curriculum used by *Kazan* Genku Rōshi (1837–1917), a *rōshi* in the Myōshinji line who recorded the following *honsoku* and *sassho* for "*Mu*" (Akizuki 1987: 259–264).

1. Jōshū's *Mu* (*Mumonkan* case 1; *Kattō-shū* case 49): A monk asked Jōshū Oshō, "Does a dog have Buddha-nature or not?" Jōshū answered, "No!" ["*Mu!*"].
2. After seeing *Mu,* what is your proof?
3. The Patriarch Daruma Daishi said, "Point directly at one's mind, see one's nature [*kenshō*], and become Buddha." After seeing *Mu,* how do you *kenshō* this?
4. It is said that one sees *Mu* order to free yourself from life-and-death. Seeing *Mu,* how did you free yourself from life-and-death?

5. Seeing *Mu,* how did you quiet your heart and set your life on a firm basis?

6. How do you answer when asked, "What is *Mu* when you have died, been burned and turned into a pile of ash?"

7. Jōshū at one time said "*U*" ["Yes!"]. What about this?
   Or: A monk asked, "Does a dog have Buddha-nature?" Jōshū said "*U!*" ["Yes!"].

8. What is "It is because it has karmic consciousness [*gosshikishō*]."
   Or: A monk asked, "All sentient being has Buddha-nature. Why is it that a dog has not?" Jōshū said, "It is because it has karmic consciousness [*gosshikishō*]."

9. What is "To know but still offend?"
   A monk asked, "Already there, why jump into that bag of skin?" Jōshū said, "He knows but still offends."

10. That thing called "*Mu,*" what is it? Or: Why call it "*Mu*"?

11. Stop the sound of the bell. (Right here try to stop the sound of the bell which comes ringing from the faraway mountain temple.)

12. Stop the four sounds. (When the four sounds come at once, how about that?)

13. There is a tree which does not move when a typhoon blows. Go see it.

14. Stop the sailboat. (Right here try to stop the sailboat running on the far open seas.)

15. Stop the rowboat.

16. Place your four limbs on *tōfu.*

17. Coming from over there, is that older sister or younger sister?

18. When he constructed the Raimon Gate at Asakusa, where did the carpenter start in with his handaxe?

19. Try hiding inside a pillar.

20. With an empty hand, get the old monastic to stand up.
    (Reference: There was a layman called Ryōtetsu Koji. The nun Eshō asked him, "The nun is so old she cannot stand up by herself. I ask you, without putting forth your hand, get her to stand up.")

21. Stop the fight on the other side of the river.

22. Emancipate the ghost.

All these *sassho* ask the monk to explore *kenshō* as manifested in some particular circumstance. Unfortunately, we do not have the space in this chapter to discuss the structure of *sassho* questions and other related matters, such as the different *sassho* lineages. A monk in practice is told to become one not only with the kōan in meditation but also with all daily acts. The proper way to chant sûtras, to chop vegetables, to sit in meditation is to become the sûtra-chanting itself, to become totally the act of chopping, to just sit. Again, "become one with" does not imply that one first gets into some state of blank consciousness without cognitive content and then try to chop vegetables. It means to perform one's work without indulging in subject–object duality. More concretely, it means to work with genuineness, without hesitation, with authority, without reifying self on one side and the work on the other side. Not surprisingly, in the Rinzai monastery daily work (*samu*) is highly valued as a locus of practice. Robert Buswell has implied that the emphasis on work in a Zen monastery is a misleading stereotype. He has described the Korean Sŏn monastery, in which most of the daily work is done by outside help, often paid, while the Korean monks themselves engage in very little work and do not consider it part of their practice (Buswell 1992: 220). This may be so in a Korean monastery, but in a Japanese Rinzai monastery *samu* is an integral part of practice in which every monk participates. Although monks do not engage in precious kōan dialogue while working the fields, as depicted in old kōan cases, nevertheless if a monk is daydreaming and inattentive, it is quite common for an older monk to bark, "Wake up!" (*Bokeru na!* literally "Don't lose focus!"). If one thinks that *kenshō* is a blank state of mind, one should not participate in *samu*.

Although the initial struggle that the monk has with the kōan looks like the process described in the instrumentalist model of the kōan, when one looks at how the term *kenshō* is actually used, one can see that it marks not a breakthrough to a pure consciousness without cognitive content but instead a breakdown of subject and object within the cognitive complexity of ordinary experience. This means that the usual translation for *kenshō* as "see one's nature" (or "see nature" or "see Buddha-nature") is misleading, for "see one's nature" implies both a subject and an object of seeing. It fails to convey just what is unique about this moment, the fact that the seeing subject "realizes" (both comprehends and instantiates the fact) that it is not separate and distinct from the object it is seeing.[15]

Kyōgai ("Consciousness" or "Behavior")

How does a *rōshi* judge whether a monk has seen a kōan? He judges by the monk's *kyōgai*. An investigation of this term will show, by contrast, some of the philosophical assumptions that proponents of pure consciousness bring to the examination of Zen.

Kyōgai originally translated the Sanskrit term, *visaya,* meaning "world" or "place," the object of the senses and the consciousnesses (Mochizuki vol. 1 1958: 566) but in the Rinzai monastery it now has quite different meanings. In some cases one can translate *kyōgai* as "consciousness" or "experience," for in these cases the concept *kyōgai* does share some of the logical features of the concepts of "experience" or "consciousness" in English. One of those logical features is privacy. Just as consciousness or experience is often said to be private in the sense that one person cannot "really" understand another's person's consciousness or experience, so also *kyōgai* is described in much the same way.

> This thing called *kyōgai* is an individual thing. Only a sparrow can understand the *kyōgai* of a sparrow. Only a hen can understand the *kyōgai* of a hen and only another fish can understand the *kyōgai* of a fish. In this cold weather, perhaps you are feeling sorry for the fish, poor thing, for it has to live in the freezing water. But don't make the mistake of thinking it would be better off if you put it in warm water; that would kill it. You are a human and there is no way you can understand the *kyōgai* of a fish. (Yamada 1985: 56)

That experience is private is clearly presupposed by other ideas characteristic of Zen. For example, the idea of "mind-to-mind transmission" of Zen experience is so striking just because it shatters the ordinary notion of privacy.

However, *kyōgai* has other features which make it clear that it cannot be equated with a noncognitive pure consciousness. First of all, *kyōgai* can be said to be good or bad, ripe or unripe, interesting or uninteresting. In a fire drill most monks will go through the motions in the pro forma manner characteristic of people merely practicing a drill. But if a monk acts with great energy and seriousness as if he were really in a fire, an observer might comment, *kyōgai ga ii* ("His *kyōgai* is good"). What is meant by that compliment is that the monk acts without self-consciousness, totally pouring himself into the activity and leaving no remainder of self-consciousness behind. By contrast, anyone who hesitates or is self-conscious or self-reflective or in any way not totally one with the task at hand ("It's just a fire drill. Why bother?") may be criticized as *kyōgai ga warui* ("His *kyōgai* is not good"). Furthermore, *kyōgai* can be said to change and develop, for it is a product of human effort. Thus one can say "His *kyōgai* is still unripe" (*Mada kyōgai ga mijuku*) or "His *kyōgai* is still shallow" (*Mada kyōgai ga asai*), implying that even though the monk has been working at overcoming his indecision, or fear, or pride, he still shows traces of self-consciousness. Finally, *kyōgai* bears the quite personal imprint of the particular individual. One person's way of acting in a fire drill, cooking in the kitchen, carrying on the tasks of daily life may be energetic and impassioned; another may do the same tasks coolly and methodically. Yet each may in his own fashion be *narikitta* in the way he acts. Thus one can say of monk Daijō's way of performing some task, "That is typically Daijō *kyōgai*."[16] Because these uses of the term *kyōgai* emphasize action and behavior, the simple word "consciousness" (much less the more contrived "pure consciousness") would not be an accurate translation. Here, "way of acting" or "style" and even "behavior" are better translations, because they reflect the behavioral component of *kyōgai*.

When a *rōshi* says about kōan training, "All is *kyōgai*," he is denying that a monk can pass a kōan by "intellectualizing," by *rikutsu*, a term that implies that the intellectual explanation is tedious and misses the point. He may scold the monk, saying that Zen is *kyōge betsuden, furyū monji,* "A separate transmission outside scripture, Not founded on words and letters." By this, he is not emphasizing that Zen is a realm of blank noncognitive consciousness; although there is certainly a lot of language dealing with emptiness, no-mind, and the like, which gives that impression. Rather by this he means that Zen concerns itself not with labels but with facts, not with description but with the thing described, not with intellectual explanation but with performance. He is not making a move on the spectrum of states of mind from the intellectual, cognitive end to the nonintellectual, noncognitive end, or from mediated consciousness to pure consciousness. Rather he is jumping from the entire spectrum of states of mind to another spectrum altogether of act and behavior. In the context of kōan training, the opposite of intellectual explanation is not noncognitive awareness or pure consciousness; the opposite of intellectual explanation here is the thing itself, the act itself. When the monk demonstrates through performance his oneness in some particular act, there the *rōshi* can judge the authenticity, the genuineness, the flair with which he acts—his *kyōgai.*

Here it is appropriate to say something about so-called "cheating" in kōan practice. Because the responses for kōan have now become standardized, it is possible for a monk who learns the standard answer to play-act his way through a session with the *rōshi* without having had any real insight into the kōan assigned. The kōan curriculum, however, is long. There is always the next kōan and the next kōan, and one cannot fake one's way through the entire curriculum. It is also worth remembering that the very activity of play-acting is a training in overcoming subject and object duality, of *narikiru.* And a *rōshi* will often demand that a monk repeat and repeat his response to a kōan until he is able to perform it with genuineness, real conviction and personal flair. A *rōshi* can usually spot play-acting, but if play-acting is fakery, then let it be genuine fakery.[17]

To many readers this discussion of *kyōgai*—sometimes "consciousness," sometimes "behavior"—will seem puzzling. I suggest that a sense of being puzzled arises from the fact that *kyōgai* violates the Cartesian assumption that mind and body are separate and distinct. *Kyōgai* is like mind in being private but like body in being instantiated in action and behavior. If one thinks that enlightenment is a private state of pure consciousness, which has no connection with outward behavior, then all the skeptical doubts that gave rise to the private language argument and to the issue of "other minds" will arise again in the context of Zen.[18] One can always doubt, so the skeptic claims, that any outward behavior is absolute proof of an enlightened mind. And if one insists that the *rōshi* has an unerring ability to judge enlightenment, this ability to judge will seem to be a kind of mind reading. These are the conundrums that arise if one attempts to see *kenshō* and kōan training through the lens of "pure consciousness" and its Cartesian assumptions. It is not possible here to discuss fully the inappropriateness of trying to discuss Zen in a Cartesian framework, but it is worth noting that even the phrase "*kenshō* experience" in Japanese is *kenshō taiken* where *tai* means "body." Similarly a synonym for *kenshō* in the monastery is the term *taitoku*, literally "body-attainment."[19] Here we have prima facie evidence that "experience" is not a matter of mere consciousness but is embodied activity. Unfortunately the English word "experience" is more and more being associated with private states of mind, emphasizing exactly the wrong nuance.[20] The fundamental point of misapplication is this: in Cartesianism, mind is dualistically separate and distinct from body, and if one interprets *kenshō* according to Cartesian assumptions, then it becomes a state of pure consciousness separate and distinct from body and behavior. But if one takes *kenshō* to be nonduality in subject and object, then *kenshō* must be realized in some bodily form (this is discussed below) and then a concept like *kyōgai*, which is neither totally mind nor totally body, will be not only possible but necessary.

Kenshō as it is understood in Rinzai practice is at once more prosaic and more mysterious than enlightenment depicted as a featureless state of pure consciousness. On the one hand, it is more prosaic and quotidian, for in *kenshō* in particular contexts, there are mountaintops, older sister and younger sister, travelers met on the road, blinds to be rolled up, old women who serve tea. On the other hand, it is much more mysterious, for *kenshō* is the realization of the nonduality of subject and object. The entire kōan curriculum of the Rinzai monastery is designed to take the monk's original insight into nonduality and generalize it into every facet of life. This training program might justly be called reconditioning, since it proceeds not by intellectual understanding but by the ritualistic repetition of the kōan. But it might also justly be called deconditioning, since it leads to the insight that our daily dualistic distinctions hitherto thought to be absolute are not. The kōan training makes a monk see that indeed all experience is conditional and all experience has a nondual aspect. Even when there is subject and object in ordinary experience, there is also the nonduality of subject and object. Traditional Zen slogans such as *bonnō soku bodai* ("Delusive passions are themselves enlightenment") describe this goal. The notion of a pure consciousness is at least conceivable, although we may disagree on whether such a thing exists. But the very idea of the nonduality of subject and object seems inconceivable, conceptually incomprehensible. This is far more mysterious than enlightenment depicted as a state of pure consciousness.

Kōan *and* Hōri *("Reason")*

The focus on the *kenshō* experience has obscured the fact that traditional Rinzai monastic kōan practice includes many years of literary and intellectual study. This section will give a rough sketch of the "reason," the logic behind the kōan curriculum. (In another paper I will describe the second half of kōan practice, the literary study, which includes the appending of capping verses to kōan, the writing of lectures, the composition of Chinese verse, the memorization of large amounts of text, the practice of good calligraphy. This traditional form of scholarship is such an important part of kōan practice that it is fair to say that the true modern descendant of the Confucian literary scholar is the Japanese Zen *rōshi.*)

Hōri means "dharma reason," "dharma principle," "dharma rationale." Some modern dictionaries explain that the word *hōri* is an abbreviation of *buppō no rihō* (Nakamura 1981: 1238), meaning "principles of Buddhist teaching," or *buppō no shinri,* "true principles of Buddhist teaching" (Morohashi 1984: 6: 1053, Character 17290.335) In kōan collections, such as the *Hekiganroku* (C. *Pi-yen lu*) or the *Mumonkan* (C. *Wu-men kuan*), each kōan case is followed by a commentary or lecture which expounds the *hōri* of the kōan, the reason or principle or rationale expressed by the kōan.

Kyōge Betsuden *("A Separate Transmission outside of Scripture")*

An introduction to Zen, both in Japan and in the West, will often start with the verse attributed to Bodhidharma.

Kyōge betsuden	A separate transmission outside of scripture
Furyū monji[21]	Not founded on words or letters
Jikishi jinshin	Point directly to one's mind
Kenshō jōbutsu	See one's nature and become Buddha

These lines "A separate transmission outside of scripture, Not founded on words and letters" are often taken to imply that Zen practice does not include intellectual or literary study, sometimes even taken to imply that intellectual and literary study hinders Zen practice. Rinzai Zen teachers in Japan give the standard lesson that the intellectual understanding of Zen is not Zen itself, that one must have the experience of *kenshō* (*kenshō taiken*). Shibayama Zenkei makes a typical statement: "From earliest times Zen has insisted on 'not relying on letters,' stressing that 'it' has to be attained by oneself personally, has to be experienced as one's own actual fact" (Shibayama 1974: 4). But quite contrary to expectations, Rinzai Zen teachers do *not* teach that intellectual understanding has nothing to do with Zen; instead they teach the quite opposite lesson that Zen requires intellectual understanding and literary study. In a typical lecture given to monks, Yamada Mumon *Rōshi* urged his charges:

First, we must study the sūtras and read reverently the records left by the teachers of the past in order to determine where our own nature is. Sometimes you hear it said that Zen monks do not have to read books or to study. When did this misleading idea get started? It's ridiculous to think that this could possibly be true. We say Zen is "a separate transmission outside the teachings," but it is only because there are teachings that there is something transmitted separate from it. If there were no teaching necessary in the first place, you could not speak of a transmission separate from it. If we do not first study the sūtras and ponder the records of the ancients, we will end up going off in the wrong direction altogether.

The ancient teachers engaged in all branches of scholarship and studied all there was to study; but just through scholarship alone, they were not able to settle what was bothering them. It was then that they turned to Zen. That is why their Zen has real power and dynamism. If you have no understanding of Buddhism, no knowledge of the words of the Dharma, it does not matter how many years you sit, your *zazen* will all be futile. (Yamada 1985: 51)

In Western presentations of Zen, the intellectual understanding of Zen and the experience itself are presented as mutually exclusive either/or alternative, but in the Rinzai monastery the intellectual understanding of Zen and the experience itself are presented as standing in a complementary, both/and relationship. The full product of Rinzai monastic training is "The Master of Zen who uses the two swords of the teaching and the power of the way" (*Kyōsō to dōriki no ryōtōzukai no shūshō*) (Akizuki 1987: 14). That is to say, both intellectual training (*kyōsō*, teaching) and experience (*dōriki*, power of the way) are equally necessary. In Rinzai parlance, one who has only intellectual understanding without experience is said to practice *yako-zen*, "wild fox Zen"; one who has only experience without intellectual understanding is a *zen temma*, "Zen devil."

Speech and Silence: The Logical Problem of the Kōan

The kōan is unlike an essay or sūtra commentary or other discursive literature. It deals with the particular problem of how to express what is said to be inexpressible. In the *Vimalakīrti Nirdeśa Sūtra,* the great bodhisattva Mañjuśrī leads a host of lesser bodhisattvas to visit the sick bodhisattva Vimalakīrti, who is residing in the town of Vaisali in the guise of a layman. The dramatic climax of the sūtra comes in chapter 9, in which Vimalakīrti asks the attending bodhisattvas to explain how to enter the Dharma-door of nonduality, the door to the inconceivable liberation. Several of the bodhisattvas, 33 in all, take turns stating that such and such a dualism is fundamentally false and that on realization of this fact, one enters the Dharma-door of nonduality. Mañjuśrī criticizes all the previous replies thus: "Good sirs, you have all spoken well. Nevertheless, all your explanations are themselves dualistic. To know no one teaching, to express nothing, to say nothing, to explain nothing, to announce nothing, to indicate nothing, and to designate nothing—that is the entrance into non-duality" (Thurman 1976: 77). Mañjuśrī then asks Vimalakīrti to respond. Vimalakīrti responds by sitting in silence. Mañjuśrī applauds, saying, "Excellent! Excellent, noble sir. This is indeed the entrance into the nonduality of the bodhisattvas. Here there is no use for syllables, sounds, and ideas." This is Vimalakīrti's "thunderous silence" (Thurman 1976: 77).

This incident, which is cited as an early example of a Zen kōan dialogue,[22] presents the logical problem of the kōan. In a kōan dialogue one of the speakers asks about that which is beyond speech and thought; this is referred to in a variety of locutions—"the inconceivable liberation," "enlightenment," "the Great Matter," "the First Ancestor's Purpose in Coming from the West," "Buddha," "the First Principle," "the Sound of One Hand," and others. The logical character of the inconceivable liberation, or of enlightenment, or of the Sound of One Hand, and so on, is that it is nondual. The difficulty is that speech and thought represent whatever they describe as dualistic. Whenever we speak in language, we ascribe predicates. Any predicate P defines a logical space which is divided into two, one labeled P and the other labeled not-P, and any entity we are considering must fall into one or the other half but not into both (the law of the excluded middle). Thus the very use of simple ordinary descriptive language seems to involve us in making dichotomies. Now, if it is possible to speak of the inconceivable liberation in language in which we ascribe predicates to it, this very fact would seem to imply that the inconceivable liberation is dualistic in nature. But the inconceivable liberation, says Vimalakīrti, is nondual. How then can one even talk of the nondual inconceivable liberation if the very act of talking about it implies that it is dualistic in nature? It seems then that the only possible response one can make is to remain silent.

But if one takes the logic of nonduality to its inexorable conclusion, one can argue that Vimalakīrti did not really solve the problem of duality by sitting in silence. After all, although Vimalakīrti avoided any dualism within speech, nevertheless speech itself when contrasted with silence presents another duality, though at a higher level. By opting for silence, Vimalakīrti has hung himself on one of the horns of dualism again. In fact, just such a criticism of Vimalakīrti is offered by the *Vimalakīrti Sūtra* itself. In chapter 7 the disciple Śāriputra engages in a conversation with a figure called the "goddess" (in Robert Thurman's translation). In this conversation, the hapless Śāriputra is reduced to silence by the aggressive questions of the goddess. He gives the excuse, "Since liberation is inexpressible, goddess, I do not know what to say." The goddess scolds Śāriputra for his silence, but her reprimand can also apply to Vimalakīrti:

All the syllables pronounced by the elder have the nature of liberation. Why? Liberation is neither internal nor external, nor can it be apprehended apart from them. Likewise, syllables are neither internal nor external, nor can they be apprehended anywhere else. Therefore, reverend Śāriputra, do not point to liberation by abandoning speech! Why? The holy liberation is the equality of all things. (Thurman 1976: 59)

Since "the holy liberation is the equality of all things," then not only do speech and silence both partake of the nature of liberation equally, but also liberation cannot be apprehended apart from syllables and speech. Thus she says, "Do not point to liberation by abandoning speech"—a criticism of both Śāriputra and Vimalakīrti.

The Nonduality of Duality and Nonduality

The *Vimalakīrti Sūtra* presents us with a quite different logical system. In the conventional realm in which we normally reside, we usually abide by the rules of Either/Or logic, the logic of duality. Here a thing is a thing and not another thing. Here if we make a statement, implying that it is true, we are also implying that its negation is false. But in the inconceivable liberation, this dualistic logic does not work. In this realm it is possible to make contradictory statements. The bodhisattvas Vimalakīrti and Mañjuśrī, both of whom reside in the inconceivable liberation, converse in such contradictions.

"Welcome, Mañjuśrī! You are very welcome. There you are, without any coming. You appear, without any seeing. You are heard, without any hearing."
Mañjuśrī declared, "Householder, it is as you say. Who comes, finally comes not. Who goes, finally goes not. Why? Who comes is not known to come. Who goes is not known to go. Who appears is finally not to be seen. (Thurman 1976: 43)

In this realm, what we normally take to be opposites are made identical: form is emptiness and emptiness is form; the delusive passions are at once enlightenment; saṃsāra is nirvāṇa. These statements appear to conventional understanding as examples of a different kind of logic, the logic of Both/And. *Both* a statement *and* its opposite are true. Also in this realm, we are not forced to categorize anything into either coming or going, seeing or not seeing, good or bad, up or down, left or right. The inconceivable liberation is neither coming nor going, neither seen nor not seen. *Neither* a statement *nor* its opposite need be affirmed. To conventional understanding, this too appears as a different kind of logic, the logic of Neither/Nor. (These categories—Either/Or, Neither/Nor, Both/And—which attempt to characterize nondual logic, are of course themselves taken from dualistic logic. The problem of self-reference here is similar to that in mathematics, where attempts to construct a model of a three-value logic can be done only in two-value logic.)

The logic of nonduality, however, when applied consistently, destroys the very notion of a separate and distinct realm of nonduality. That is, from the

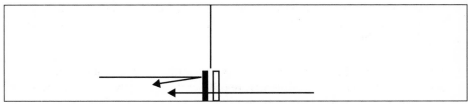

Conventional	Ultimate
Conceptual duality	Inconceivable nonduality
Logic of Either/Or	Logic of Both/And ("Form is emptiness")
	Logic of Neither/Nor ("Not this, not that")
Duality between dual and nondual	No duality between dual and nondual
Reflection	See-through

FIGURE 11.1. *The line between the conventional and inconceivable liberation*

side of conventional understanding where one sees in dualistic terms, there is a distinction between the dual and the nondual, between the conventional realm and the inconceivable liberation. But from the side of inconceivable liberation in the nondual dharma, even the dualism between the dual and the nondual is merely apparent and not real. The line between the conventional and the inconceivable liberation is a very strange line. From the conventional side, there is a distinction between this side and that side; from the side of inconceivable liberation, there is no distinction between this side and that side. The conventional realm and inconceivable liberation are like the two sides of a one-way mirror. From the side of the conventional, one is convinced that there is a duality between the conventional and inconceivable liberation, but unfortunately one can see only one side of the duality; when one tries to conceive of the other side, one imagines the inconceivable liberation according to the dualistic concepts of the conventional. This is like being on the mirror side of a one-way mirror: one is sure there is something on the other side of the glass but one cannot see it. When one looks, one sees only images of oneself. But from the side of inconceivable liberation, one can see that the distinction between duality and nonduality is itself nondual, that there is no fundamental difference between the conventional and inconceivable liberation. This is like being on the see-through side of the mirror. One can see both sides of the glass and the two sides are really the same. Figure 11.1 represents this asymmetry. I have used the terms Conventional and Ultimate because later I link this schema to the notion of twofold truth in Buddhism. (Yes, I know, the chart itself belongs to the Conventional.)

When the concept of nonduality is applied to itself, it becomes clear that any judgment "That's dualistic!" is itself a dualistic act, and that the nonduality of duality and nonduality reaffirms duality rather than obliterates it. In simple first-order nonduality, one cannot affirm that such and such is true or good and its opposite false or bad, but in second-order nonduality (the nonduality of duality and nonduality), one can affirm that such and such is true or good and its opposite is false or bad (although one can deny it as well).

As Hee-Jin Kim points out, "nondualism does not signify primarily the transcendence of dualism so much as the realization of dualism" (Kim 1975/1987:100). A traditional Zen verse runs, "At first the mountains are mountains and the rivers are rivers. Then the mountains are not mountains and the rivers are not rivers. Then finally the mountains are mountains and the rivers are rivers." The first negation of the standpoint of duality (the first "the mountains are mountains and the rivers are rivers") is simple nonduality ("the mountains are not mountains and the rivers are not rivers"). But plain and simple nonduality is itself part of the dualism of dual and nondual. If one takes nonduality to its logical conclusion, one must negate even the standpoint of nonduality and move to a second-order nonduality, the nonduality of duality and nonduality (the second "the mountains are mountains and the rivers are rivers"). When one does this, then the distinctions and differentiations of the ordinary dualistic, conventional standpoint are resurrected. The second appearance of the dualistic conventional standpoint is different from its first appearance. The first appearance of the dualistic conventional standpoint is differentiated from the nondual ultimate standpoint, whereas the second appearance of the dualistic conventional standpoint is identical with the nondual ultimate standpoint. As Kim says about Dōgen's views on the absolute freedom of the *samādhi* of self-fulfilling activity: "It refers to an absolute freedom of self-realization absent [of] any dualism of antitheses. . . . The absolute freedom in question here is that freedom which realizes itself in duality, not apart from it" (Kim 1975, 52–53).

A corollary of this logic is that nonduality never appears as nonduality; it always appears as duality. For if nonduality appeared as nonduality, it would be dualistically opposed to duality. (For similar reasons, emptiness never appears as emptiness; it always appears as form.) That is why *kenshō* is not to be identified with a noncognitive pure experience dualistically contrasted with conventional experience, and why Dōgen and the *Vimalakīrti Sūtra* say thought and language, rather than hindering enlightenment, liberate it. The logic of nonduality introduces a systematic ambiguity into the characterization of all experience, revealing it to be in one sense dual and in one sense nondual. We now proceed to discuss this systematic ambiguity in the context of language.

Twofold Truth and Puns

The idea of higher and lower truths, or sacred and mundane truths, is an ancient idea in many religious traditions. The Buddhist version was the idea of twofold truth, Conventional Truth (S. *saṃvṛti-satya*) and Ultimate Truth (*paramārtha-satya*). The idea that there were two kinds of truth was given several rebirths as Buddhism traveled from early India to China, Tibet, and Japan.[23] In this chapter I will point to only one set of significant changes in the idea of twofold truth as it applies to present Rinzai kōan practice. Outside of Zen, the distinction between Conventional and Ultimate Truth often amounts to a distinction between two kinds of language with different vocabularies; in the Rinzai monastery, however, the distinction amounts to two different standpoints which use the same language and vocabulary but with different meaning.

In the early Theravada Buddhist tradition, according to Steven Collins's account, Conventional truth was that language whose vocabulary contained words that labeled selves, persons, spirits, gods, and so on. This is the language of ordinary people, the language that presupposes that both the objects of the world and the self have an enduring self-existence (*svabhāva*) in some strong sense. Ultimate language, on the other hand, avoids the use of words that refer to self and objects by using instead a technical vocabulary which refers only to the *skandha*-elements out of which these putative existent entities are compounded. Thus Ultimate truth speaks only in terms of the analytical categories of Buddhist doctrine (Collins 1982: 153–156, 179–182).[24] The difference between Conventional and Ultimate languages here is similar to that of the two languages used for talking about computers. Ordinary people often speak as if the computer were a person. We say, "It is thinking" or "It is being uncooperative today," as if the computer possessed a *svabhāva*-like self and engaged in human acts like "thinking" and "being uncooperative." However, the computer engineer's language to describe what is actually going on in the computer merely describes the plus–minus state of the switches on its chips and control board and does not attribute personality or selfhood to the computer.[25]

In Rinzai Zen kōan practice, the distinction between Conventional and Ultimate truth appears as the distinction between *hen'i* and *shōi*. Here *hen* originally means "crooked," "bent," "inclined" or "partial"; *hen'i* indicates the realm of duality, of *svabhāva*. On the other side, *shō* means "straight," "correct," "true"; *shōi* indicates the realm of nonduality, of absence of *svabhāva*. Miura and Sasaki have translated *hen'i* and *shōi* as "Apparent" and "Real" (Miura and Sasaki 1966: 67ff, 315ff).[26]

In the Zen context, however, *hen'i* and *shōi* do not distinguish two separate languages with different vocabularies; they distinguish two standpoints which use the same language and the same vocabulary but with different meaning. When the language is being used to indicate some aspect of the differentiated, the manifest, the conditioned, the realm of dualism, then it is expressing the standpoint of *hen'i*. The very same language, the very same sentence, can also be used to express some aspect of the undifferentiated, the unmanifest, the unconditioned, the realm of the nondual. When it does so, it is expressing the standpoint of *shōi*. This means that Zen kōan and Zen language in general are full of puns in a special sense—words and phrases that are used with both Conventional and Ultimate meaning. To understand the Zen kōan requires one to be sensitive to the pun, to the constant ambiguity between *hen'i* and *shōi* in the usage of words. The punning expression of one meaning inside another is an essential part of the kōan. And accurate translations of Zen language into English should preserve, not eliminate, that ambiguity.

One should not, however, think that one has "solved" the kōan if one can find a nonconventional interpretation of a statement in Zen. D. T. Suzuki remarked that the "utterances of *satori*" are marked by "uncouthness and incomprehensibility" (Suzuki 1953: 110–111). "One doesn't know the smell of one's own shit" (*Jishi kusaki o oboezu*) is a typically uncouth Zen phrase. When pressed to explain what it means, beside giving the literal meaning, most people would probably interpret it to mean, "One is unaware of one's own self-centeredness" or some such. This would be a *hen'i* reading, a Conventional interpretation. But in Zen this statement also expresses: "Sentient being does not realize its own awakening" or "One is unaware of one's own Buddha-nature," taking "one's own shit" as a metaphor for awakening or Buddha-nature. Here it is necessary to be careful. It is not correct to say that "One is unaware of one's own Buddha-nature" is the Ultimate interpretation as if the difference between Conventional and Ultimate were merely one of different levels of interpretation. One cannot "solve" a kōan just by coming up with an interpretation more profound than the obvious Conventional one. Even "One is unaware of one's own Buddha-nature" is a statement in the Conventional interpretation whose meaning and truth are taken dualistically. The element of nonduality is the metaphor itself in which the unclean and impure "one's own shit" indicates the immaculately clean and pure Buddha-nature.[27] And even the nonduality of this metaphor can be reduced to the Conventional. One can take the Zen phrase as merely expounding the nonduality of clean and dirty, a nonduality that implies a hidden self in the center making the judgments "clean" or "dirty." Doing this reduces the nonduality to a mere intellectual nonduality, a variant of "All uphills are downhills." The mistake here is that every attempt to understand *shō'i* as an interpretation reduces it to *hen'i*. Every attempt to understand nonduality as an interpretation reduces it to duality, since interpretations divide into dualistic categories like true/false. It is at this point that the notion of a performative utterance is useful, for a kōan utterance is better seen as a pun encompassing not two interpretations but two functions, one descriptive and one performative. And in the same vein it helps to remember that Zen monks are often depicted as expressing their *kyōgai* not by making a statement but by performing an action like raising a finger, putting their shoes on their head, or performing a bow.

It is now time to consider a realizational model of the kōan using a revised notion of performance.

Realization: Kōan as Performance of *Kenshō*

Earlier we noted that although Rosemont's performative account of the kōan was open to the same criticisms as other instrumentalist accounts of the kōan, nevertheless he had a useful insight: a kōan is not a description but a performance. Before his account can be used to clarify how language works in a kōan, some modifications have to be made to his formulation. First, we need to distinguish between utterances that cause a performance of an act from utterances that are themselves the performance of an act. Second, we need to recognize that utterances can pun in a special sense; they can be both performative and descriptive at the same time. These modifications transform Rosemont's instrumentalist model of the kōan into a realizational model.

When John Austin first coined the term "performative," he focused on first-person present-tense utterances such as "I apologize," "I promise," "I name," "I guarantee," which typically did not describe, but performed, the actual act of apologizing, promising, and so on. Austin soon saw the necessity for distinguishing numerous kinds of performatives; locutionary, illocutionary and perlocutionary utterances were recognized with many subspecies. Of all these distinctions, only one kind concerns us here. Different from the original class of "I apologize" kind of performatives were utterances like "Shoot her!" This involves causation; my saying "Shoot her!" causes a gunman to fire a gun whose bullet kills her (Austin 1962: esp. 94–131). The utterance of "I apologize" is itself the performance of the act of apologizing, but the utterance of "Shoot her" is not itself the performance of the act of killing her but rather its cause. Now Rosemont's performative analysis of the kōan assumes that kōan utterances are like "Shoot her!" that is, they are thought to be the causal means to enlightenment. He does not consider the possibility that kōan utterances may be like "I apologize" where the utterance of "I apologize" itself performs the act of apology.

In addition, Rosemont seems to think that an utterance is either descriptive or performative but not both. However, there is no reason why the same language cannot be both descriptive and performative. The difference between descriptive and performative is a matter not of the words that compose the utterance—the content, so to speak—but of the context of their utterance on a particular occasion. Father and son, sorting out their laundry, pass socks and underwear to each other saying, "This is yours, this is mine." Here "This is yours" is a descriptive utterance because in this context it merely classifies objects under descriptions. But when father hands over a deed of property or a family heirloom passed down through several generations to his son and says, "This is yours," the utterance "This is yours" is a performative, for by so saying he transfers the right of possession for that property or heirloom from himself to his son. "This is yours" as descriptive merely classifies which objects are yours and which are mine; but "This is yours" as performative *makes* these objects yours.

How is it possible for an utterance to be both descriptive and performative at the same? To show how these possibilities work in more easily recognizable contexts, look at these examples.

1. A: "What is the difference between ignorance and apathy?"

   B: "I don't know and I don't care."

2. A: "People today don't listen to what other people have to say."

   B: "Were you saying something?"

   A: "What?"

3. LINGUISTICS PROFESSOR: "In the English language, you can combine an affirmative with a negative to express a negative, a negative and a negative to express a negative, an affirmative with an affirmative to express an affirmative, but you can never combine an affirmative with an affirmative to express a negative."

   VOICE FROM THE BACK OF THE HALL: "Yes! Yes!"

These are puns but not in the ordinary sense in which one statement has two descriptive meanings. They are puns in the sense that each statement can be taken both descriptively and performatively. In example (1) above, "I don't know and I don't care" is not only descriptive of the speaker's state of mind but also an expression of, a performance of, the speaker's own ignorance and apathy. Just as "I apologize" is a performance of apologizing, so also "I don't know and I don't care" is a performance of ignorance and apathy, though perhaps inadvertent. "I don't know and I don't care" as descriptive refuses to answer the question but as performative gives a very good answer to the question by providing a real example of ignorance and apathy itself.

Kōan dialogues do not all fit into one pattern. Nevertheless it is always useful to look for the performative dimension. In *Hekiganroku* case 1, Bodhidharma's answer "Not know!" to the emperor's question, "Who is it that stands before me?" is to be understood as both a description and a performance. As a descriptive, "Not know" refuses to answer the question. As performance, Bodhidharma presents nonduality itself. In *Mumonkan* case 7, a monk asked Jōshū, "I have just entered the monastery. Please teach me." Jōshū asked, "Have you finished eating your rice gruel?" The monk said, "I have finished." Jōshū said, "Go wash your bowl." This answer, "Go wash your bowl," is not a description but a performance. But it can be taken as performance at more than one level. If one thinks that the new monk is merely asking for instruction in monastery regulations, then "Go wash your bowl" is a concrete performance of one such regulation. But if we take the monk's question as a direct request to Jōshū, "Show me your nonduality" in the guise of the question "Please teach me," then Jōshū's "Go wash your bowl" is a performance of nonduality dressed up as a performance of monastery regulation and a fitting answer to the monk's question.

Zen students early catch on to the fact that they must perform in front of the *rōshi,* and at first they assume that any kind of physical movement will do. After a few rounds with the *rōshi,* they learn that nonsense action is just as wide of the mark as purely intellectual explanation. Their response must be a performance but one that is appropriate to the context of the kōan. This two-sided response reflects the double sense of "realize." One realizes, in two senses of "realize," the nonduality of subject and object. It is important to understand the sequence of the two kinds of "realize." One does not first decipher the allusive language into ordinary language and then treat the decoded language as a script for some performance. As is described above, one understands a kōan not intellectually but through the process of constantly repeating it to oneself, constantly asking what it means, until eventually one realizes that one's own seeking to answer the kōan is itself the activity of the kōan. This realization takes place within the particular context of the kōan. The monk's nondual realization of the kōan is at first expressed in terms of hands if one is asked about the sound of one hand, in terms of a young woman if one is asked about "Senjo and Her Soul" (*Mumonkan* case 35), in terms of causality and karma if one is asked about "Hyakujō (C. Pai-chang) and the Fox" (*Mumonkan* case 2), in terms of a bath if one is asked about "Bodhisattvas Take a Bath" (*Hekiganroku* case 78), in terms of flowers if one is asked about "Nansen (C. Nan-ch'uan) and the Flower" (*Hekiganroku* case 40). When one has experienced the nonduality of subject and object in each particular context, then one starts to understand what kōan language alludes to. After a while one starts to see common patterns, but in the beginning, cognitive realization, the analytical understanding and interpretation of kōan language, originally follows and does not precede experiential realization.

To an outside observer, nothing much seems to be taking place. Even granted that a kōan dialogue involves a performance of nonduality, what more is going beyond the utterance "Not know" or "Go wash your bowl"? What is merely descriptive to one person may be performative to another. Consider an earlier example: "One does not know the smell of one's own shit." We have already discussed different descriptive interpretations ("One is unaware of one's self-centeredness," "One is unaware of one's own Buddha-nature"), but how is it performative? All practitioners at first seek to penetrate the kōan thinking that it is some object, that it is some thing. Finally they come to realize that their own seeking after the kōan is the kōan itself at work within them, and also that this seeking both hindered their realization and yet made it possible at the same time. For them indeed the seeking that hindered their realization (their "shit") is identical with their Buddha-nature (the identity of subject seeking for the kōan and the object as kōan). "It hurts" for a person without pain is a description, but for a person wincing in pain, "It hurts!" is an expression of, a performance of, pain and does not describe it. For one without experience of nonduality "One does not know the smell of one's shit" is only a metaphorical or allusive description, but for one who experiences the nonduality of subject and object, of shit and Buddha-nature, the utterance "One does not know the smell of one's shit" is an expression of, a performance of, nonduality.

In a realizational model, *kenshō* and kōan are depicted quite differently from they way they are depicted in the instrumental model. *Kenshō* is not a state of noncognitive consciousness awaiting the monk on the other side of the limits of rationality. In the context of the Rinzai kōan curriculum, *kenshō* is the realization of nonduality within ordinary conventional experience. If *kenshō* is to be described as a breakthrough, then it is a breakthrough not out of, but into, conventional consciousness. This is in the nature of the case, in the nature of the logic, or *hōri,* of nonduality itself. If *kenshō* is the realization of nonduality, then it itself cannot be separate and distinct from ordinary dualistic experience. Thus the original nonduality of subject and object at first obliterates duality and then resurrects it. Furthermore, a kōan is not merely a blunt psychological instrument, an irrational puzzle designed to push the monk beyond the limits of rationality. A kōan is a test case, one part of a long sophisticated curriculum of kōan cases built upon the *hōri,* the logic of, nonduality. The early part of the kōan curriculum ritually trains the monk at performance of nonduality until his *kyōgai* matures. The latter part of the kōan curriculum leads the monk through the *hōri,* of *hen'i* and *shōi,* of the Five Ranks, and so on. The final product of the kōan curriculum is a monk trained, on the one hand, to realize the many expressions of nonduality depicted in kōan and, on the other hand, to expound the "reason" (*dōri, hōri*) of Zen as expressed in the language and philosophy of kōan.

Reflections

The idea of a pure consciousness functions in the study of religion very much like the idea of a state of nature functions in political philosophy. Both model philosophical assumptions but they do not depict an actual state of affairs. Just as the state of nature is said to exist prior to the development of society and state, so also the state of pure consciousness is said to exist prior to the development of thought and language. In Rousseau's romantic version of the original state of nature, primitive individuals lived freely and happily without the artificiality, class inequalities, and vanity of social life. In Hobbes's version, equally romantic, the state of nature was a realm of savage incivility which eventually forced individuals to create society because only some authority stronger than the individual could guarantee security. Accounts of such states of nature contain bad logic, for the individuals residing in the state of nature before the development of society behave in ways possible only after the development of society. For example, state-of-nature individuals get together in political meetings and draw up social contracts, but strictly speaking, political meetings and drawing up social contracts are activities possible only after society has gotten started. Descriptions of a state of nature can be instructive even if they contain faulty logic because they model an author's fundamental beliefs about human nature, but it is a serious confusion to take such a model as factual description. It is reassuring to know that neither Rousseau nor Hobbes thought of the state of nature as an actual stage in the historical development of human societies.

What the state of nature is to political philosophy, pure consciousness is to the study of Zen. Theories that describe *kenshō* as the breakthrough of thought and language to pure consciousness contain the same sort of bad logic. For example, in pure consciousness without conceptual activity, we "see things as they are" but "seeing things as they are" is possible only after conceptual activity gets started; it arises epistemologically at the same level as "seeing things as they are not." Just as we distinguish between model and fact when talking about the state of nature in political philosophy, we should do the same in the study of Zen. The belief in a pure consciousness models the believer's views of human nature and society but we should leave open the question of whether that description of pure experience describes an actual state.

In Buddhism, however, there is the state of meditation, called *samādhi,* which does indeed seem to be a state of pure consciousness, a state without self-consciousness, awareness of space or time, or even sensory input. But *samādhi* is not pure consciousness because pure consciousness is really a political concept.

What fundamental beliefs about human nature and society are reflected in the idea that *kenshō* is a breakthrough to a pure consciousness? Why do people want to believe in enlightenment as a breakthrough to pure consciousness? The belief in pure consciousness is often an expression of a vision of human freedom. Society has conditioned us, so it is said, so that the very concepts and vocabulary we use encapsulate society's stereotypes and prejudices. Ultimately we learn to see even ourselves in terms of society's concepts and norms, thus becoming alienated from ourselves. Society is thus depicted as the source of suffering to the individual. To the extent that this is so, the breakthrough to pure consciousness labeled *kenshō* is the psychological version of a return to the innocence of the state of nature before dehumanizing society got started.[28] Not only is this account of the origin of human problems proffered by modern Western apologists for Buddhism, it is also the standard diagnosis offered by most students in the university classroom. This account seems self-evident because it is given within a society much dominated by modern notions of individualism, but it is not Buddhism. In Buddhism, the source of suffering is not society; in Buddhism, the source of human suffering is one's own ignorance and attachments. That ignorance and those attachments have long karmic roots for which one is also responsible. *Samādhi* gets its meaning from being imbedded inside that picture of the human condition. Pure consciousness, by contrast, is a political concept which wants to affirm the original purity of the individual against the demeaning influence of society.

At one time, humans imagined that if they could free themselves of gravity, they would be free, able to fly like the birds. Now that we have rockets that can actually put us in space beyond the reach of gravity, we find that humans free-floating beyond gravity are not free at all. Instead they float helpless and out of control. Gravity, we find, does not deprive us of freedom, but on the contrary gravity is what gives human beings control over their movements and thus freedom. The lesson here is that one should put aside dreams of escaping gravity and learn instead the discipline of how to handle the body in gravity. Just as there is no free flying above the reach of gravity, there is no Zen enlightenment beyond thought and language in a realm of pure consciousness. Instead of blaming thought and language for defiling a primordial consciousness, one should recognize that only in thought and language can enlightenment be realized.

NOTES

1. Some samples:

The essence of the kōan is to be rationally unresolvable and thus point to what is arational. The kōan urges us to abandon our rational thought structures and step beyond our usual state of consciousness in order to press into new and unknown dimensions. (Dumoulin 1988: vol. 1, 246)

The kōan is thus like the demand for a description of a four-sided triangle. The explicit purpose is to confuse and frustrate until, in desperation, one is forced to abandon all conceptual thinking. When finally taken to such a point, one has "solved" the kōan by learning to let go of the artificial and restraining framework of conventional thought. (Radcliffe 1993: 7)

These two notions—*kenshō* as the breakthrough to pure consciousness and the kōan as nonrational, psychological instrument—nicely support each other, but they are not conceptually tied together. It is possible to conceive of the kōan as instrument to another form of consciousness and assume that the other form of consciousness is still a form of conventional consciousness. This is, in fact, Steven Katz's position in Katz 1992b: 6–7.

2. I follow Hee-Jin Kim in translating *dōri* as "reason" (Kim 1987: 104) or "rationality" (Kim 1985b, 2) and *genjō* as "realization" (Kim 1985b: 4; Kim 1987: 61, 76ff). As an indication of the importance of the notion of rationality for Dōgen, Kim cites Katō Shūkō's finding that the term *dōri* appears 272 times in the *Shōbōgenzō* and the

term *kotowari* (which also means reason) 12 times for a total of 284 occurrences. See Katō Shūkō, *Shōbōgenzō yōgo-sakuin,* 2 vols. (Tokyo: Risōsha, 1962–63) cited in Kim 1987: 271 n7.

3. For this debate, see the several books edited by Steven T. Katz (Katz 1978a, 1983a, 1992a) and the criticism by Robert K. C. Forman (Forman 1986, 1990, 1993). See also Proudfoot 1985.

4. Forman takes the opposite tack of never discussing reported cases of mystical experience that have much cognitive content and detail.

5. "Properly understood, yoga, for example, is *not* an *un*conditioning or *de*conditioning of consciousness, but rather it is a *re*conditioning of consciousness, i.e., a substituting of one form of conditioned and/or contextual consciousness for another, albeit a new, unusual, and perhaps altogether more interesting form of conditioned-contextual consciousness." (Katz 1978b: 57)

6. In this paragraph, I adapt an argument taken from Wright 1992.

7. "Thoughts without content are empty, intuitions without concepts are blind." "The understanding can intuit nothing, the senses can think nothing. Only through their union can knowledge arise." Kant 1963: A 51; B 75.

8. "For a *large* class of cases—though not for all—in which we employ the word 'meaning' it can be defined thus: the meaning of a word is its use in the language." (Wittgenstein 1963: ¶ 43)

9. Nakamura Kan'un Shitsu, former Rōshi of the Daitokuji Sōdō, Kyoto. Conversation April 1981.

10. Asai Gisen, Rōshi of the Nagaoka Zenjuku, Nagaoka. Lectures 1987.

11. These examples are all extracts from recorded conversations in Loori 1994: "kōans can often trigger a *kenshō* . . ." 309; "Is *kenshō* at all common?" 314; "You were talking . . ." 330.

12. I have described the relationship between ritual formalism and insight in Rinzai monastic life in "Teaching and Learning in the Rinzai Zen Monastery" (Hori 1994).

13. Nishitani Keiji uses the English word "realize" precisely because it has these two uses. See his discussion in Nishitani 1982: 5–6.

14. A quick look through the standard kōan collections shows quite a large number of kōan built around some problem of duality or nonduality, although the words "duality" and "nonduality" are never used. In the *Mumonkan* (C. *Wumen-kuan*), the following cases all deal with the theme of one and two: case 5, "Kyōgen (C. Hsiang-yen) Up a Tree"; case 11, "Jōshū (C. Chao-chou) and the Hermits"; case 14, "Nansen (C. Nan-ch'üan) Cuts a Cat"; case 23, "Think Neither Good Nor Evil"; case 24, "Separate from Words and Language"; case 26, "Two Monks Roll Up Blinds"; case 35, "Senjo (C. Ch'ien-nü) Separated from Her Soul"; case 36, "On the Road Meet an Adept of the Way"; case 43, "Shuzan's (C. Shou-shan's) Bamboo Rod"; case 44, "Basho's (C. Pa-chiao's) Staff."

15. D. T. Suzuki pointed out that "seeing one's nature" was a misleading translation for *kenshō* because it presupposed a nature to be seen. Rather, "in the satori seeing there is neither subject nor object; it is at once seeing and not seeing; that which is seen is that which sees, and vice versa. This idea has led many superficially minded people to imagine that Zen's seeing is seeing into the Void, being absorbed in contemplation, and not productive of anything useful for our practical life." (Suzuki 1950; 72; see also Suzuki 1956: 160ff and a discussion in Hsueh-Li Cheng 1986b)

16. Furuta Shōkin has a short discussion of "individual character" (*kobessei*) in satori (Furuta 1983: 28).

17. Cheating is not a serious problem but *sudōri* is—the tendency of some *rōshi* to pass a student on to the next kōan even though the student has not seen the kōan for himself.

18. See the entries for "Other Minds" (Vol. VI, 7–13) and "Private Language Argument" (Vol. VI, 458–464) in *The Encyclopedia of Philosophy,* Edwards 1967. Wittgenstein attacked the assumptions upon which the skeptic's argument was based, but unfortunately Wittgenstein's own remarks are so cryptic that there is disagreement about what he said. More relevant for our purposes is the work of Maurice Merleau-Ponty, who, in *The Phenomenology of Perception,* systematically attacked the Cartesian assumptions behind contemporary psychological theory and attempted to construct an alternate phenomenology. He was one of the first to use the notion of the body as a subject of consciousness not present to ordinary awareness, and many of his comments about perception and judgment can be applied without difficulty to the notion of *kyōgai.* See Merleau-Ponty 1962.

19. Sasaki Jōshū Rōshi has said that before World War II, the common word for enlightenment in the monastery was *taitoku,* but after the war, because of the writings of D. T. Suzuki and Nishida Kitarō, the younger generation of Zen *rōshi* now sometimes use the terminology of *junsui keiken* "pure experience." (Sasaki Jōshū, personal communication, Dec. 23, 1993)

20. Wayne Proudfoot's book *Religious Experience* (Proudfoot 1985) analyzes the way "experience" has been used in ideological defense of religious positions. See the discussion of this issue in Sharf 1995.

21. Also read *furu moji.*

22. D. T. Suzuki makes it the frontispiece of his *Manual of Zen Buddhism.* The incident appears as case 84 of the *Hekiganroku.*

23. Nagao 1989, Swanson 1989.

24. Robert Gimello gives an example of translating from one to the other. The Conventional language, "I hear beautiful music," is misleading for it seems to imply the existence of *svabhava* like "I," "hear," "beautiful," and "music." Ultimate language would replace such misleading words and substitute technical language, which implied no *svabhava.* Thus "I hear beautiful music" in Ultimate language would be something like this.

> These arises as aural perception (*saṃjña*), an impulse of auditory consciousness (*vijñāna*) which is produced in dependence upon contact (*sparśa*) between the auditory faculty (*indriya*) and certain palpable vibrations emanating from a material (*rūpa*) instrument; this impulse of consciousness, in concert with certain morally conditioned mental predispositions (*samskāra*), occasions a feeling or hedonic tone (*vedanā*) of pleasure which in turn can produce attachment (*upādāna*), and so on. (Gimello 1983, 74–5)

25. I am indebted to Bhante Vimala of Toronto for this useful analogy.

26. The terms *hen'i* and *shōi* are taken from Tung-shan's (J. Tōzan) Five Ranks and are used in Rinzai Zen as analytical categories for organizing the many kōan into an integrated system. The Five Ranks constitute one of the last categories of kōan in the kōan curriculum (see Akizuki 1987, Asahina 1941, Ito 1970, Itō and Hayashiya 1952).

Tōzan's Five Ranks are presented in a work authored by Hakuin called *Tōjō goi henshō kuketsu* (The Five Ranks of the Apparent and the Real: The Orally Transmitted Secret Teachings of the [Monk] Who Lived on Mount Tō). This has been translated in Miura and Sasaki 1966, 63–72. The original character text can be found in the Zen monk's handbook called *Zudokko* (*The Poison-Painted Drum*, Fujita Genro 1922). The Five Ranks are:

Shōchūhen	The Apparent within the Real
Henchūshō	The Real within the Apparent
Shōchūrai	The Coming from within the Real
Kenchūshi	The Arrival at Mutual Integration
Kenchūtō	Unity Attained

So far as I know, there is no complete study of the Five Ranks, but there are several brief explanations including Miura and Sasaki 1966, 309–312, 379–381; Dumoulin 1988, Vol. 1 222–230; "Interfusion of University and Particularity" in Chang 1969; Lai 1983; Powell 1986, and the entry under *"Goi"* in the *Zengaku daijiten* (Komazawa 1977). Tokiwa Gishin has a short discussion of the Five Ranks in connection with Hakuin's Sound of One Hand (Tokiwa 1991).

27. Scatological reference in general is often used this way. There are many other examples. The best-known is probably *Mumonkan* case 21, where in reply to a monk's question, "What is Buddha?" Ummon replies "A dried up turd of shit." I follow the ZGJT (Iriya 1991:66) reading here: the usual reading of *kanshiketsu* as "A stick for wiping shit" is mistaken; Buddha is the turd of shit itself. For more on scatological references in Zen, see my paper on Ritual Vulgarity, Hori 1995.

28. Wright discusses this point in greater deal in his examination of Erich Fromm's critique of society in Wright 1992.

REFERENCES

Akizuki, Ryūmin. 1987. *Kōan*. Tokyo: Chikuma Shobō.

Asahina Sōgen. 1941. *Zen no Kōan* (*The Zen Kōan*). Tokyo: Yūzankaku.

Austin, J. L. 1962. *How to Do Things with Words*. Oxford: Clarendon Press.

Buswell, Robert E., Jr. 1992. *The Zen Monastic Experience: Buddhist Practice in Contemporary Korea*. Princeton, N.J.: Princeton University Press.

Chang Chung-yuan. 1969. "Interfusion of University and Particularity," in *Original Teachings of Original Teachings of Ch'an Buddhism: Selected from The Transmission of the Lamp*. New York: Random House, pp. 41–57.

Cheng Hsueh-li. 1984. *Empty Logic: Mādhyamika Buddhism from Chinese Sources*. New York: Philosophical Library.

———. 1986a, June. "Negation, Affirmation and Zen Logic." *International Philosophical Quarterly*, no. 26:241–251.

———. 1986b. "Psychology, Ontology and Zen Soteriology." *Religious Studies*, no. 22:459–472.

Collins, Steven. 1982. *Selfless Persons: Imagery and Thought in Theravada Buddhism*. Cambridge: Cambridge University Press.

Dumoulin, Heinrich. 1988–90. *Zen Buddhism: A History, vol. 1: India and China; vol. 2: Japan*, trans. James W. Heisig and Paul Knitter. New York: Macmillan.

Edwards, Paul (editor in chief). 1967. *The Encyclopedia of Philosophy*. 8 vols. New York: MacMillan.

Eido, Shimano. 1988. "Zen Koans," in *Zen: Tradition and Transition*, ed. Kenneth Kraft. New York: Grove Press, pp. 70–87.

Forman, Robert K. C. 1986. "Mysticism and Pure Consciousness Events." *Sophia*, no. 25:49–58.

————, ed. 1990. *The Problem of Pure Consciousness: Mysticism and Philosophy.* New York: Oxford University Press.

————, 1993, December. "Mystical Knowledge: Knowledge by Identity." *Journal of the American Academy of Religion,* no. 61:705–738.

Fujita Genro, compiler. 1922. *Zudokko (Poison-Painted Drum),* 2 vols. Kyoto: Kenninji Sōdō.

Furuta Shōkin, 1983. *Sengai.* Tokyo: Idemitsu Bijutsukan.

Gimello, Robert M. 1983. "Mysticism in Its Contexts," in Katz 1983a, pp. 61–88.

Graham, A. C. 1992. "Poetic and Mythic Varieties of Correlative Thinking," in *Unreason Within Reason: Essays on the Outskirts of Rationality.* LaSalle, Ill.: Open Court, pp. 207–223.

Hakuin Ekaku, "The Five Ranks of the Crooked and the Straight: The Orally Transmitted Secret Teachings of the [Monk] Who Lived on Mount Tō," in Fujita, *Zudokko,* vol. 1.

Heine, Steven. 1990, September. "Does the Kōan Have Buddha-Nature?" *Journal of the American Academy of Religion,* no. 58:357–387.

Hori, G. Victor Sōgen. 1994. "Teaching and Learning in the Rinzai Zen Monastery." *Journal of Japanese Studies,* no. 20:5–35.

————. 1995. "Ritual Vulgarity in Zen" Unpublished paper presented at the Tri-Regional Conference of the AAR, Boston, Mass.

Iida Rigyō. 1994. *Shinshaku Zenrin Yōgo Jiten (New Zen Forest Terminology Dictionary).* Tokyo: Haku Bijutsu Shuppan.

Imai Fukúzan, compiler. 1935. *Zengo Jii,* ed. Nakagawa Jūan. Tokyo: Hakurinsha.

Iriya Yoshitaka, general editor. 1991. *Zengo Jiten (Zen Word Dictionary),* ed. Koga Hidehiko. Kyoto: Shibunkaku.

Iriya Yoshitaka, Kajitani Sōnin, and Yanagida Seizan. 1981. *Zen no Goroku 15: Sechō Juko (Zen Records 15: Setchō's Old Cases).* Tokyo: Chikuma Shobo.

Itō Kokan. 1970. *Zen to Kōan (Zen and the Kōan).* Tokyo: Shunjūsha.

Itō Kokan and Hayashiya Yūjiro. 1952. *Zen no Kōan to Mondō (Zen Kōan and Dialogue).* Tokyo: Shunyōdō.

James, William. 1967. "A World of Pure Experience," in *The Writings of William James,* ed. John J. McDermott, pp. 194–214. Chicago: University of Chicago Press.

Jung, Carl. 1934/1967. "Foreword" to D. T. Suzuki's *An Introduction to Zen Buddhism.* New York: Grove Weidenfeld, pp. 9–29.

Kant, Immanuel. 1963. *Critique of Pure Reason,* trans. Norman Kemp Smith. London: Macmillan.

Kasulis, T. P. 1981. *Zen Action, Zen Person.* Honolulu: University of Hawaii Press.

Katz, Steven T., ed. 1978a. *Mysticism and Philosophical Analysis.* New York: Oxford University Press.

————. 1978b. "Language, Epistemology and Mysticism," in Katz 1978a, pp. 22–74.

————, ed. 1983a. *Mysticism and Religious Traditions.* New York: Oxford University Press.

————. 1983b. "The 'Conservative' Character of Mystical Experience," in Katz 1983a, pp. 3–60.

————. 1992a. *Mysticism and Language.* New York: Oxford University Press.

————. 1992b. "Mystical Speech and Mystical Meaning," in Katz 1992a, pp. 3–41.

Kim, Hee-Jin. 1975. *Dōgen Kigen-Mystical Realist.* Tuscon, Ariz: University of Arizona Press.

————, trans. 1985a. *Flowers of Emptiness: Selections from Dogen's Shōbōgenzō.* Lewiston/Queenston: Edwin Mellen Press.

————. 1985b. "Introductory Essay: Language in Dōgen's Zen," in Kim 1985a, pp. 1–47.

————. 1985c. "The Reason of Words and Letters: Dōgen and *Kōan* Language," in William R. LaFleur, ed., *Dōgen Studies.* Honolulu: University of Hawaii Press, pp. 54–82.

————. 1987. *Dogen Kigen: Mystical Realist.* Tucson: University of Arizona Press.

Komazawa Daigaku Zengaku Daijiten Hensansho (Komazawa University Great Dictionary of Zen Studies Editorial Board). 1977. *Zengaku daijiten (Great Dictionary of Zen Studies).* Tokyo: Daishūkan.

Lai, Whalen. 1980. "Further Developments of the Two Truths Theory in China." *Philosophy East and West,* no. 30:139–162.

————, 1983. "Sinitic Mandalas: The Wu-wei-t'u of Ts'ao-shan," in *Early Ch'an in China and Tibet,* ed. Whalen Lai and Lewis R. Lancaster. Berkeley, Cal.: Asian Humanities Press, pp. 229–257.

Loori, John Daido 1994: *Two Arrows Meeting in Mid-Air: The Zen Kōan.* Boston: Tuttle.

Loy, David. 1988. *Nonduality: A Study in Comparative Philosophy.* New Haven, Conn.: Yale University Press.

Luk (Lu K'uan Yü), Charles, trans. 1972. *The Vimalakīrti Nirdesa Sūtra.* Boston: Shambhala.

Merleau-Ponty, Maurice. 1962. *The Phenomenology of Perception,* trans. Colin Smith. London: Routledge and Kegan Paul.

Miura, Isshu, and Ruth Fuller Sasaki. 1966. *Zen Dust: The History of the Koan and Koan Study in Rinzai (Lin-chi) Zen.* Kyoto: The First Zen Institute of America.

Mochizuki, Shinkyō, compiler. *Zōteiban Mochizuki Bukkyō Daijiten* (Expanded and Amended Edition of the Mochizuki Great Dictionary of Buddhism). Kyoto: Sekai Seiten Kankō Kyōkai, 1958.

Morohashi, Tetsuji, compiler. *Shūtei Dai Kanwa Jiten* (Great Chinese-Japanese Dictionary, rev. ed.). Tokyo: Daishūkan Shoten, 1984.

Nagao, Gadjin M. 1989. *The Foundational Standpoint of Madhyamika Philosophy,* trans. John P. Keenan. Albany, N.Y.: SUNY Press.

Nakamura, Hajime, compiler. 1981. *Bukkyōgo daijiten* (The Great Dictionary of Buddhist Terms). Tokyo: Tokyo shoseki K. K.

Nishitani Keiji. 1982. *Religion and Nothingness,* trans. with introduction by Jan Van Bragt. Berkeley: University of California Press.

————. 1987. *Nishitani Keiji Chosakushū* 10: *Shūkyō to wa Nanika.* Tokyo: Sōbunsha.

Powell, William F., trans. 1986. "The Gatha of the Five Ranks, the Lords and Vassels," in *The Record of Tung-shan.* Honolulu: University of Hawaii Press, pp. 61ff.

Proudfoot, Wayne. 1985. *Religious Experience.* Berkeley: University of California Press.

Radcliffe, Benjamin, and Amy Radliffe. 1993. *Understanding Zen.* Boston: Tuttle.

Rosemont, Henry, Jr. 1970. "The Meaning Is the Use: Koan and Mondo as Linguistic Tools of the Zen Masters." *Philosophy East and West,* no. 20:109–119.

Sasaki, Ruth Fuller, trans. 1975. *The Record of Lin-chi: The Recorded Sayings of Ch'an Master Lin-chi Hui-chao of Chen Prefecture.* Kyoto, Japan: The Institute for Zen Studies.

Sharf, Robert H. 1995. "Buddhist Modernism and the Rhetoric of Meditative Experience." *Numen,* no. 42:228–283.

Shibayama, Zenkei. 1974. *Zen Comments on the Mumonkan,* trans. Sumiko Kudo. New York: Mentor/New American Library.

Sprung, Mervyn, ed. 1973. *The Problem of Two Truths in Buddhism and Vedanta.* Dordrecht: Reidel.

Suzuki, D. T. 1935/reprinted 1960. *Manual of Zen Buddhism.* New York: Grove Press.

———. 1949. "Zen as the Chinese Interpretation of the Doctrine of Enlightenment," in *Essays in Zen Buddhism (First Series).* London: Rider, pp. 39–117.

———. 1950. *Living by Zen.* London: Rider, Reprint 1972.

———. 1953. "The Koan Exercise," in *Essays in Zen Buddhism (Second Series).* London: Rider, pp. 18–226.

———. 1956. *Zen Buddhism.* Garden City, N.Y.: Doubleday.

Swanson, Paul L. 1989. *Foundations of T'ien-t'ai Philosophy: The Flowering of the Two Truths Theory in Chinese Buddhism.* Berkeley, Cal.: Asian Humanities Press.

Thurman, Robert A. F., trans. 1976. *The Holy Teaching of Vimalakirti: A Mahayana Scripture.* University Park: Pennsylvania State University Press.

Tokiwa, G. 1991, March. "Hakuin Ekaku's Insight into 'The Deep Secret of *Hen (Pian)-sho (Zheng)* Reciprocity' and His Koan 'The Sound of a Single Hand.' " *Journal of Indian and Buddhist Studies,* no. 39 (2):989–983.

Wittgenstein, Ludwig. 1963. *Philosophical Investigations,* trans. G. E. M. Anscombe. Oxford: Basil Blackwell.

Wright, Dale S. 1992. "Rethinking Transcendence: The Role of Language in Zen Experience." *Philosophy East and West,* no. 42:113–138.

Yamada Mumon. 1985. *Jūgyūzu (Ten Ox-Herding Pictures).* Kyoto: Zen Bunka Kenkyūjō.

ZGJT. See listing under Iriya Yoshitaka.

Index